KNIGHTS and WARHORSES

Military Service
and the
English Aristocracy under
Edward III

KNIGHTS and WARHORSES

Military Service
and the
English Aristocracy under
Edward III

Andrew Ayton

THE BOYDELL PRESS

First published 1994
The Boydell Press, Woodbridge
Reprinted in paperback 1999

Transferred to digital printing

ISBN 978-0-85115-568-5 hardback
ISBN 978-0-85115-739-9 papeback

The Boydell Press is an imprint of Boydell & Brewer Ltd
PO Box 9, Woodbridge, Suffolk IP12 3DF, UK
and of Boydell & Brewer Inc.
668 Mt Hope Avenue, Rochester, NY 14620, USA
website: www.boydellandbrewer.com

A catalogue record for this book is available
from the British Library

This publication is printed on acid-free paper

Contents

Tables

Abbreviations

Anonimalle	*The Anonimalle Chronicle*, 1333–81, ed. V.H. Galbraith (Manchester, 1927)
Avesbury	Robert de Avesbury, *De Gestis Mirabilibus Regis Edwardi Tertii*, ed. E.M. Thompson, Rolls Ser. (London, 1889)
Bain	*Calendar of documents relating to Scotland*, ed. J. Bain, 4 vols (London, 1881–88)
	Calendar of documents relating to Scotland, v, ed. G.G. Simpson and J.D. Galbraith (Edinburgh, 1986)
BIHR	*Bulletin of the Institute of Historical Research*
BL	British Library
BPReg	*Register of Edward the Black Prince*, ed. M. Dawes, 4 vols (London, 1930–33)
Canterbury Tales	*The Canterbury Tales. The complete works of Geoffrey Chaucer*, ed. F.N. Robinson, 2nd edn (London, 1957)
CCR	*Calendar of Close Rolls*
CFR	*Calendar of Fine Rolls*
CIPM	*Calendar of Inquisitions Post Mortem*
CLR	*Calendar of Liberate Rolls*
CPR	*Calendar of Patent Rolls*
Crecy and Calais	*Crecy and Calais*, ed. G. Wrottesley (London, 1898)
EcHR	*Economic History Review*
EHD	*English Historical Documents*
EHR	*English Historical Review*
Froissart, ed. Johnes	*Chronicles of England, France and Spain . . . by Sir John Froissart*, ed. and trans. T. Johnes, 2 vols (London, 1848)
Froissart, ed. Lettenhove	*Oeuvres de Froissart*, ed. K. de Lettenhove, 28 vols (Brussells, 1867–77)

GEC	*The complete peerage*, ed. G.E. Cokayne, revised edn, 12 vols in 13 (London, 1910–57)
Gough	*Scotland in 1298: documents relating to the campaign of Edward I in that year*, ed. H. Gough (London, 1888)
Jean le Bel	*Chronique de Jean le Bel*, ed. J. Viard and E. Déprez, 2 vols (Paris, 1904–5)
JGIndRet	'Indentures of retinue with John of Gaunt, duke of Lancaster, enrolled in Chancery, 1367–1399', ed. N.B. Lewis, *Camden Miscellany, xxii*, Camden Soc., 4th ser., i (1964), pp. 77–122
JGReg	*John of Gaunt's Register, 1371–75*, ed. S. Armitage-Smith, 2 vols, Camden Soc., 3rd ser., xx–xxi (1911)
	John of Gaunt's Register, 1379–83, ed. E.C. Lodge and R. Somerville, 2 vols, Camden Soc., 3rd ser., lvi–lvii (1937)
Knighton	*Chronicon Henrici Knighton*, ed. J.R. Lumby, 2 vols, Rolls Ser. (London, 1889–95)
Le Baker	*Chronicon Galfridi le Baker de Swynebroke (1303–56)*, ed. E.M. Thompson (Oxford, 1889)
Melsa	*Chronicon Monasterii de Melsa*, ed. E.A. Bond, 3 vols, Rolls Ser. (London, 1866–68)
Murimuth	Adam Murimuth, *Continuatio Chronicarum*, ed. E.M. Thompson, Rolls Ser. (London, 1889)
Norwell	*The Wardrobe Book of William de Norwell*, 12 July 1338 to 27 May 1340, ed. M. Lyon, B. Lyon, H.S. Lucas and J. de Sturler (Brussells, 1983)
Parl. Writs	*Parliamentary writs and writs of military summons*, ed. F. Palgrave, 2 vols in 4 (London, 1827–34)
PRO	Public Record Office
Rot. Parl.	*Rotuli Parliamentorum*, ed. J. Strachey et al., 6 vols (London, 1767–83)
Rot. Scot.	*Rotuli Scotiae*, ed. D. Macpherson et al., 2 vols (Record Comm., 1814)
Rymer	*Foedera*, ed. T. Rymer, revised edn, 4 vols in 7 parts (Record Comm., 1816–69)
Scalacronica	*Scalacronica. The reigns of Edward I, Edward II and Edward III as recorded by Sir Thomas Gray*, ed. and trans. H. Maxwell (Glasgow, 1907)
Scrope-Grosvenor	*The Scrope and Grosvenor controversy*, ed. N.H. Nicolas, 2 vols (London, 1832)
Topham	*Liber Quotidianus Contrarotulatoris Garderobiae, 1299–1300*, ed. J. Topham et al. (London, 1787)
Tout, *Chapters*	T.F. Tout, *Chapters in the administrative history of medieval England*, 6 vols (Manchester, 1920–33)
TRHS	*Transactions of the Royal Historical Society*
Westminster	*The Westminster Chronicle, 1381–1394*, ed. and trans. L.C. Hector and B.F. Harvey (Oxford, 1982)

Documents cited in the footnotes by class number alone are to be found in the Public Record Office, London.

Preface to the Paperback Edition

The arrival of a paperback edition of this book offers an opportunity to take account of relevant works which have appeared since early 1994. It also allows me to re-examine the research agenda outlined in the Introduction and to review progress on what may well turn out to be a career-long project. *Knights and Warhorses* was written with the intention of providing a solid foundation for the study of the Edwardian military community. It is not primarily a book about horses, although one of its aims is to determine what warhorses can tell us about their masters; or, to put it more precisely, what the descriptions and valuations recorded in the horse inventories can be made to reveal about the status and attitudes of the knights and esquires in Edwardian armies. Of course, analysis of the inventories, together with other royal administrative records, yields a great deal of quantitative information about the horses themselves. Indeed, it is argued in this book that such analysis reveals general fluctuations in the quality of horseflesh used by English men-at-arms during the course of the Edwardian period.[1] But given that the inventories tell us nothing about the size, age or provenance of the horses listed, or about the equipment borne by them, it is difficult from these sources alone to conjure up a clear image of a destrier, a courser or a rouncy. The warhorse of the inventories remains something of a clerical abstraction.

It is, therefore, a real pleasure to note that the medieval warhorse has now received attention befitting his historical importance. Since the publication of *Knights and Warhorses*, the ground-breaking surveys of Miklós Jankovich and R.H.C. Davis have been substantially built upon by Ann Hyland and Charles Gladitz.[2] Both authors adopt impressive, indeed breathtaking, chronological and geographical frames of reference. Taken together, their books combine the evidence of documentary sources and archeological finds with practical field experimentation and a profound knowledge of horsemanship and equine behaviour. The essential elements of a lost equestrian world, including breeding and horse management practices, have been brought back to life and (of particular relevance to the present book) our understanding of the emergence and heyday of the western European warhorse has been greatly advanced. It can now be argued with greater confidence that the *magnus equus* of the fourteenth century stood to a height of no more than 15 to 16 hands at its withers;[3] and yet, the destrier, the true 'great horse', was the Rolls Royce of warhorses.[4] That he was anything but typical is shown with great clarity by the horse inventories, for there we find much variety – in

---

[1] Cf. M. Prestwich, '*Miles in armis strenuus*: the knight at war', *TRHS*, 6th ser., v (1995), pp. 201–220, at 210–12.

[2] A. Hyland, *The medieval warhorse from Byzantium to the Crusades* (Stroud, 1994); idem, *The warhorse, 1250–1600* (Stroud, 1998). C. Gladitz, *Horse breeding in the medieval world* (Dublin, 1997). For a lively survey of recent work, see M. Bennett, 'The medieval warhorse reconsidered', *Medieval knighthood V*, ed. S. Church and R. Harvey (Woodbridge, 1995), pp. 19–40. Note also, J. Clark, ed., *The medieval horse and its equipment, c. 1150–c. 1450* (London, 1995), a volume in the *Medieval finds from excavations in London* series.

[3] Whether we should be visualising a heavily-built hunter, or perhaps a cob, remains open to discussion: Bennett, 'The medieval warhorse reconsidered', pp. 22–26.

[4] Such epithets may not be appropriate: the fourteenth-century Arab poet Abou Bekr ibn Bedr regarded the western-style warhorse as the 'softest and worst' of breeds!

terms of type and quality – of horses. Diversity of colours and markings is a further feature of the warhorses listed. Although this information receives only cursory attention in the present study, that it is actually of much more than passing interest is suggested by Charles Gladitz's careful analysis of a selection of horse inventories from Edward I's reign.[5] His exploration of the relationship between colouration, type of horse and breeding policy could profitably be extended to a larger corpus of records. It would seem, then, that the inventories may yet have more to reveal about both the knights and esquires listed in them and the relationship between warhorse and master.[6]

One of the underlying themes of this book is the transformation of the English fighting machine during the reign of Edward III and the consequent emergence of England as a front-rank military power. Given the scale of the changes that occurred – in the structure and composition of armies, in the methods by which they were recruited, and in the ways in which they were employed, both strategically and tactically; given the degree to which military performance was improved and the reputation of English arms enhanced; and given that all this occurred in so short a period of time, is it not reasonable to suggest that a 'military revolution' had taken place in England during the second and third quarters of the fourteenth century? Some historians would question the appropriateness of such terms as 'military revolution', arguing that they may serve to 'exaggerate the extent and character of change at the expense of continuity'.[7] Others have identified somewhat differently constituted 'military revolutions' in the fourteenth century. Suggesting that the 'most plausible arguments are those based on the total experience of war', Michael Prestwich has explored the ways in which the conduct and organisation of war (including finance and logistics) were transformed in England during the period from the late thirteenth century to the 1340s. But he concludes that the important changes were not sustained; indeed, the late fourteenth and fifteenth centuries were marked by 'the weakening of central control' and a 'striking failure to innovate'.[8] For Clifford Rogers, the emergence of English military effectiveness under Edward III rested squarely on the skilful exploitation of the longbow in a defensive tactical system involving dismounted men-at-arms and archers. This was at once the key to the English offensive strategy of battle-seeking *chevauchées* and an important thread in a more general 'infantry revolution' in fourteenth century Europe, the latter having important consequences for the conduct and character of war and bringing greater political influence for the non-aristocratic population.[9]

---

5 Gladitz, *Horse breeding in the medieval world*, pp. 157–65, 203; Appendices B–H.

6 On the role of the warhorse as symbol of aristocratic power and status, a subject discussed in Chapter 2, see R. Marks, 'Sir Geoffrey Luttrell and some companions: images of chivalry, c. 1320–50', *Wiener Jahrbuch für Kunstgeschichte*, xlvi/xlvii (1993–94), pp. 343–55, 463–66.

7 M. Vale, *The origins of the Hundred Years War: the Angevin legacy, 1250–1340* (Oxford, 1996), pp. viii–ix, where the importance to English success of Edward III's abandonment of 'large, mixed armies composed of foreign allies and mercenaries, as well as his own subjects' in favour of 'smaller, more disciplined and united Anglo-Gascon forces' is also emphasised.

8 M. Prestwich, 'Was there a military revolution in medieval England?', *Recognitions: essays presented to Edmund Fryde*, ed. C. Richmond and I. Harvey (Aberystwyth, 1996), pp. 19–38; idem, *Armies and warfare in the middle ages: the English experience* (New Haven and London, 1996), ch. 14.

9 C.J. Rogers, 'The military revolutions of the Hundred Years War', *The military revolution debate*, ed. C.J. Rogers (Boulder, 1995), pp. 55–93; idem, 'Edward III and the dialectics of strategy, 1327–1360', *TRHS*, 6th ser., iv (1994), pp. 83–102; idem, 'The offensive/defensive in medieval strategy', *Von*

Whilst these three characterisations of the Edwardian military revolution have a certain amount in common, there are also significant differences of emphasis. This book argues that profound changes occurred in the structure and composition of English armies, the most fundamental of which being the emergence of 'mixed retinues' composed of mounted archers and men-at-arms, which were recruited by captains who had contracted with the crown to supply a contingent for the army. These developments appear to have given rise to changes in the social composition of armies, whilst enabling the full potential of the distinctive battlefield tactics, and the strategic possibilities associated with them, to be realised. A somewhat different emphasis is placed by Michael Prestwich on the rise of the mounted archer. Having drawn attention to the large armies which were such a notable feature of earlier Edwardian campaigns, he sees 'the introduction of the mounted archer in the 1330s [as] one of the factors that contributed to a decline in the size of armies, for such men could not be recruited in the numbers that ordinary footsoldiers might be'.[10] Clifford Rogers's discussion of the English dimension of the fourteenth-century infantry revolution is little concerned with the structure and composition of armies, beyond an insistence on the sharp social and economic divide between the knightly men-at-arms and the 'common infantry'. The emergence of the mounted archer is not regarded as significant.[11]

To understand the military renascence of Edward III's reign it is necessary to understand the workings and composition of that king's armies: their organisational structures and the men who served in them. The structures are gradually becoming clearer, as further studies of individual armies,[12] or aspects of army organisation,[13] build on existing knowledge. However, where the personnel of English armies are concerned, a great deal of research remains to be done. For example, the extent to which Edward III's armies in France were packed with veterans from the Scottish wars is, as yet, uncertain.[14] We are equally ill-informed about the composition of retinues:

Crécy bis Mohács: Kriegswesen im späten Mittelalter (1346–1526) (Vienna, 1997), pp. 158–171; idem, 'The efficacy of the English longbow: a reply to Kelly DeVries', *War in History*, v (1998), pp. 233–42; idem, 'An unknown news bulletin from the siege of Tournai in 1340', *War in History*, v (1998), pp. 358–66.

10 Recruitment by indenture of war contributed to the same process: Prestwich, *Armies and warfare*, pp. 342–3. The constraints imposed by the necessity of sea transportation might also be mentioned in this connection.

11 Rogers, 'The military revolutions of the Hundred Years War', pp. 57–58 and nn. 21–22; 60 and n. 42.

12 For the forces employed in the defence of northern England, 1311–22, see C. McNamee, *The wars of the Bruces: Scotland, England and Ireland, 1306–1328* (East Linton, 1997), ch. 4. This is particularly important for its discussion of the *chevetaignes* (superior captains), Sir Andrew de Harcla and the role played by hobelars and *schavaldores* (mounted brigands). On the armies involved in the three major continental expeditions from 1338 to 1343, see A. Ayton, 'Edward III and the English aristocracy at the beginning of the Hundred Years War', *Armies, chivalry and warfare in medieval Britain and France*, ed. M. Strickland (Stamford, 1998), pp. 173–206. For overviews summarising current knowledge, see A. Ayton, 'English armies in the fourteenth century', *Arms, armies and fortifications in the Hundred Years War*, ed. A. Curry and M. Hughes (Woodbridge, 1994), pp. 21–38; and M. Prestwich, *Armies and warfare*.

13 M. Keen, 'Richard II's ordinances of war of 1385', *Rulers and ruled in late medieval England: essays presented to Gerald Harriss*, ed. R.E. Archer and S. Walker (London and Rio Grande, 1995), pp. 33–48: a valuable study of 'the only standing orders for an English royal army that have survived from the fourteenth century'.

14 It is generally assumed that they were: e.g. Rogers, 'Edward III and the dialectics of strategy, 1327–1360', p. 93.

did the 'strikingly rapid turnover of membership',[15] so characteristic of the late thirteenth and early fourteenth centuries, remain a feature of retinues during the French war? The Edwardian military community is still a decidedly shadowy subset of the population at large; patterns of service among both men-at-arms and archers remain obscure, the social, political and administrative consequences of such service insufficiently understood.

This book should be regarded as the first of a projected series of studies arising from a research project the ultimate goal of which is the comprehensive investigation of the Edwardian military community. For the reasons outlined in the Introduction, it is the military service of the Edwardian nobility and gentry which occupies centre stage in this volume. As is appropriate with a foundation study, it contains a detailed, critical assessment of the primary sources. For those reviewers who found the 'source criticism' wearisome, I can only restate that, given the richness and variety of the documentary materials and the absence of a methodological tradition for the study of them, there appeared to be no alternative to the approach adopted. At least it will not need to be repeated. This is not to suggest that amendments and additions will not be forthcoming; indeed, some have already appeared. An edition of private indentures for life service in peace and war has cast further light on the development of the terms of service offered by captains to their retainers,[16] thereby providing additional detail for the treatment of this topic in Chapter 4, whilst also illuminating several of the military relationships discussed elsewhere in this book.[17] A recent study of the Lovel v. Morley armorial dispute similarly supplements the discussion of the Court of Chivalry records in Chapter 5 (pp. 187–90).[18]

Whilst it is hoped that *Knights and Warhorses* offers something more substantial than source criticism, in some respects it cannot claim to do more than propose directions for future research. How could it be otherwise, given that prosopographical research into the military service of the Edwardian chivalrous community is still in its infancy? In recent years, valuable contributions to our understanding of the fourteenth-century gentry and Edward III's 'new nobility' have been made, respectively, by Peter Coss and James Bothwell;[19] but research directly focused on the military role of the noblemen, knights and esquires of Edwardian England has progressed only slowly.

---

[15] Prestwich, *Armies and warfare*, pp. 44–45.

[16] 'Private indentures for life service in peace and war, 1278–1476', ed. M. Jones and S. Walker, *Camden Miscellany*, xxxii (London, 1994), pp. 1–190.

[17] E.g. 'Private indentures', nos 34 (Sir Henry de Percy and Sir Ralph de Neville; *infra*, p. 171); 37 (Earl of Warwick and Sir Robert Herle; *infra*, p. 244 n. 219).

[18] A. Ayton, 'Knights, esquires and military service: the evidence of the armorial cases before the Court of Chivalry', in A. Ayton and J.L. Price, *The medieval military revolution* (London and New York, 1995, repr. 1998), pp. 81–104.

[19] P.R. Coss, 'The formation of the English gentry', *Past and Present*, no. 147 (May 1995), pp. 38–64; idem, 'Knights, esquires and the origins of social gradation in England', *TRHS*, 6th ser., v (1995), pp. 155–78. J. Bothwell, ' "Until he receive the equivalent in land and rent": the use of annuities as endowment patronage in the reign of Edward III', *Historical Research*, lxx (1997), pp. 146–69; idem, 'Edward III and the "new nobility": largesse and limitation in fourteenth-century England', *EHR*, cxii (1997), pp. 1111–40. For a methodological discussion, based on a prosopographical study of fourteenth-century shire administrators, see R. Gorski, 'A methodological holy grail: nominal record linkage in a medieval context', *Medieval Prosopography*, xvii (1996), pp. 145–79. See P. Morgan, 'Making the English gentry', *Thirteenth century England V*, ed. P.R. Coss and S.D. Lloyd (Woodbridge, 1995), pp. 21–28, for a thought-provoking view of the thirteenth century.

Admittedly, the martial activities of such men in the mercenary and crusading spheres have been carefully pieced together in recently published articles by Kenneth Fowler and Anthony Luttrell.[20] Individual Englishmen are to be glimpsed in studies concerned with war and military elites in other regions of Europe.[21] But what of the English king's wars? An article focusing on the early campaigns of Edward III's French enterprise has shown that the comital community, the peerage and the gentry were all heavily involved in the war effort.[22] The creation of six new earls in March 1337 appears to have been partly motivated by recruitment considerations: by the recognition that in order to gain access to the military potential of the gentry it was necessary to utilise the recruitment networks of great men. The gentry itself provided at least 1,500 men for each of the first three major expeditions of the French war, these men being drawn from a 'pool' which, according to the most generous estimate, may have consisted of 9,000 to 10,000 families. The significance of these figures is thrown into sharper relief when it is realised that in July 1338, as the army was embarking for the Low Countries, only a little over 300 knights and esquires were engaged in shire administration and related activities in England. When it is recalled that there may have been as many as 4,000 English men-at-arms at the siege of Calais and that well over 3,000 were involved in the Reims campaign (1359–60), who could doubt that 'of the forms of public service open to men of gentle blood, that which was performed by the largest number, if only occasionally, was campaigning in the king's armies'?

However rough-and-ready such an attempt at quantification may appear to be, the essential validity of the message conveyed by it is surely incontestable: that we need to take the military service of the whole aristocracy – from earls to esquires – much more seriously than has been usual in the past. As Michael Prestwich has observed, 'war was more important to medieval knights than to many of their historians'.[23] Is it not time that scholars concerned themselves with the mental world and predominant activities of the fourteenth-century aristocracy, and abandoned an interpretation of that period coloured by the preoccupations of the late twentieth century or, still worse, by those of Bishop Stubbs and his followers?

A.C.A.
Cottingham, East Yorkshire
December 1998

---

[20] K. Fowler, 'Sir John Hawkwood and the English condottieri in trecento Italy', *Renaissance Studies*, xii (1998), pp. 131–48. A. Luttrell, 'English levantine crusaders, 1363–67', *Renaissance Studies*, ii (1988), pp. 143–53; idem, 'Chaucer's Knight and the Mediterranean', *Mediterranean History*, i (1994), pp. 127–60.

[21] In 1366, Norman Swinford, esquire, entered the service of Charles, king of Navarre, and became 'his man', in return for an annual fee of 200 *livres tournois*: J.A. Fernández de Larrea Rojas, *Guerra y sociedad en Navarra durante la Edad Media* (Bilbao, 1992), apenice XX, no. 16 (pp. 144–5); cf. no. 2 (p. 139), concerning an archer, Robert l'Inglés.

[22] Ayton, 'Edward III and the English aristocracy at the beginning of the Hundred Years War'.

[23] Prestwich, '*Miles in armis strenuus*: the knight at war', p. 201.

Preface

Like so many works of medieval history, this book was conceived in the Round Room of the Public Record Office at Chancery Lane. It was there that I encountered and transcribed many of the documents which form the backbone of this study; and it was there that I came to realise how important the horse inventories would be to an investigation of English armies and military service during the Edwardian period. The warhorse appraisal records provide the names of thousands of serving men-at-arms and reveal much about the structure and day to day activities of armies in the field. Indeed, these records can tell us a good deal more about individual members of the chivalrous community than simply that they had served in a particular royal army with a certain captain. In their association of appraised warhorse and man-at-arms, the inventories offer a measure of status and a guide to the attitudes of many knights and esquires as they prepared for service in a variety of theatres of war. Yet this volume is intended to be rather more than a study of 'warhorses and their masters'. The horse inventories have been used as a point of entry into an important but comparatively neglected area of research, namely the military community of fourteenth-century England. If this book has served to highlight the importance of military service and the role of the militarily active in Edwardian England, and if it has opened up a variety of topics for discussion (not least the strengths and weaknesses of fourteenth-century military records), then it will have fulfilled its main purpose.

During the course of researching and writing this book I have received advice, support and information from many people. I hope that those whose help has not been specifically acknowledged will forgive the omission. I would like, in particular, to thank Professor Anthony Goodman and Professor Michael Jones, the external examiners of the doctoral thesis upon which this book is based, for their suggestions, encouragement and a number of documentary references; Mr Matthew Bennett for his helpful comments on an earlier draft; Dr Nigel Saul and Dr Philip Morgan for providing transcripts of several useful documents (the debt I owe to their published monographs will be apparent in the footnotes); and Dr Anne Curry for inviting me to contribute papers to two conferences, thereby obliging me to think again about records and problems relevant to the present study. I would also like to extend my thanks to Miss Anne Pitman, whose hospitality made lengthy periods of archival research in London possible; and to Dr Virginia Davis, with whom I shared an office at a time when many of the ideas in this book were forming and who put up with 'warhorses and their masters' in a good humoured way. I owe a great deal to my colleagues at the University of Hull, where the Department of History has provided a most congenial and stimulating academic home throughout my career. Especially important has been the friendship, support and forbearance of my former tutor and supervisor, and present colleague, Dr John Palmer. He did much to stimulate my interest in the Middle Ages, guided my research and has patiently tolerated the incessant borrowing of his books. This monograph is somewhat different from the one originally planned, but I hope that he is not too disappointed.

Lastly, I should like to thank my parents whose interest in what must have seemed an interminable project has endured throughout the years. They encouraged my love of history and it is to them that this book is dedicated with gratitude and affection.

A.C.A.
Cottingham, East Yorkshire
April 1994

FOR MY MOTHER AND FATHER

Introduction

There are few aspects of medieval English history as worthy of investigation, yet as neglected, as military service. This is not to suggest that the study of *war* has been eschewed by scholars of the Middle Ages, for this is very far from being the case. Much attention has been devoted to such diverse matters as military obligation and the *mentalité* of the chivalrous class; to the size, structure and financing of armies and the mechanisms of their recruitment; and to the martial aspects of knightly culture, such as the tournament and crusading. On a more general level, there has been intense debate over the effects of war on society, the economy and the institutions of the state. It is not so much war, then, that has been neglected, as the 'military community':[1] the many thousands of men who served in English royal armies and garrisons during the Middle Ages. These men – their careers in arms, their backgrounds, their peacetime lives – remain, if not wholly in shadow, then very much in the penumbra of history. So far, indeed, are we from a comprehensive study of those who engaged in military activity in later medieval England that we lack a full prosopographical study for even a single major royal army.[2] The contrast with, for example, the history of parliamentary representation is indeed striking. Whilst a good deal is now known about the men who 'were prepared to be at the pains of repeatedly riding across England to serve as representatives in parliament',[3] we are far less well informed about those who took up arms to ride across France and Scotland; yet we surely need to

---

1   This expression would seem apposite; see P. Morgan, *War and society in medieval Cheshire, 1277–1403* (Manchester, 1987), especially chapter 4. But for critical comment on the proliferation of 'communities' in recent historical writing, see M. Rubin, 'Small groups: identity and solidarity in the late Middle Ages', *Enterprise and individuals in fifteenth-century England*, ed. J. Kermode (Gloucester, 1991), pp. 132–35.

2   H.J. Hewitt, *The Black Prince's expedition of 1355–1357* (Manchester, 1958), discusses the composition of the prince of Wales' army (chapter 2), but provides the materials for a much fuller treatment (appendix C: 'A nominal roll of men who served in the expedition'). Much the same applies to G. Wrottesley, *Crecy and Calais* (London, 1898) and N.H. Nicolas, *History of the battle of Agincourt*, 3rd edn (London, 1833). For serious attempts at the prosopographical approach to medieval armies, see J.M. Powell, *The anatomy of a crusade, 1213–1221* (Philadelphia, 1986) and S. Lloyd, *English society and the crusade, 1216–1307* (Oxford, 1988), chapter 4 ('The crusade of 1270–72: a case study') and appendix 4.

3   J.G. Edwards' words, quoted in J.S. Roskell, *The Commons in the Parliament of 1422* (Manchester, 1954), p. v. J.S. Roskell, L. Clark and C. Rawcliffe, eds, *The history of Parliament: the House of Commons, 1386–1421*, 4 vols (Stroud, 1993) offers exhaustively researched biographies of well over three thousand individuals who were elected to the Commons during this period.

understand the social composition of the king's armies quite as much as the origins and affiliations of the membership of the king's parliaments.

The neglect of the men who engaged in military service, and in particular the ordinary men-at-arms and archers who formed the backbone of Edwardian expeditionary forces and garrisons, has significantly weakened our understanding of the performance of English armies; but the implications of this neglect extend far beyond the province of 'military history' into the study of many aspects of late medieval English society. How, for example, are we to assess the likely extent, distribution and effects of campaigning profits (and, indeed, costs) within society – or the impact of military service on the workings of shire administration, or the influence of war on the retaining practices of the nobility and gentry – without first establishing the identities of the men who served in the king's armies during this period? There can be few major research undertakings in the field of late medieval English history that would offer such wide-ranging benefits as a full-scale reconstruction of the military community.

The great majority of ordinary fighting men, the infantry and horse archers, will probably prove to be unidentifiable. We may often be able to ascertain their numbers, but rarely more than a small proportion of their names. An altogether more promising subject for study is the military service of the nobility and gentry, the 'upper ranks of society', which might conveniently be termed the 'aristocracy'.[4] It is a broad social group which can include both super-magnates, like the dukes of Lancaster, and members of the lesser, or 'parish', gentry;[5] but wealth *per se* was not the essential unifying characteristic of the aristocracy, rather that the bulk of their income, their privileges and their military and administrative responsibilities rested upon the lordship of land: 'judged by their economic role as lords, and their consciousness of their social position, the aristocracy can be regarded as a social class'.[6] The characteristics which define the aristocracy have also assured them a predominant place in the surviving military records. Yet the service of the nobility and gentry in the king's armies has received considerably less scholarly attention than, for example, their landed estates. The relative neglect of aristocratic military service is actually rather surprising. Although not free of interpretative problems, the records casting light on their war service are generally quite plentiful and, on occasion, voluminous and detailed. Moreover, the apparent conflict between, on the one hand, the centrality of martial values to the aristocratic ethos – the image of the nobleman as warrior – and, on the other, the diversification of the secular landowning community's responsibilities, would seem to offer a research field pregnant with possibilities. Does the fourteenth century witness a steady demilitarisation of the

---

4 C. Dyer, *Standards of living in the later Middle Ages* (Cambridge, 1989), p. 18.

5 On the 'parish gentry', see C. Given-Wilson, *The English nobility in the late Middle Ages* (London, 1987), pp. 71–73.

6 Dyer, *Standards of living in the later Middle Ages*, p. 19.

aristocracy or do the nobility and gentry function, in effect, as a military class during this period of heavy, if intermittent, recruiting demands? Historians have, of course, offered opinions on these matters. Some have emphasised the effects of increasing administrative commitments;[7] others argue for an enduring, even burgeoning, involvement in war.[8] According to Peter Coss, 'the extent to which the gentry was involved in the wars was remarkable . . . the knights of fourteenth-century England were a military class, and military experience confirmed, if it did not confer, status'.[9] Whilst certainly stimulating, this debate has yet to be firmly rooted in weighty, quantitative research: work which would involve correlation of military service records with the 9,000 to 10,000 noble and gentry families in fourteenth-century England.[10] Only when such research is undertaken will it be possible to escape from impressionistic generalisations about a subject of central importance to late medieval English history.

The main impediment to systematic study of the military community, even if restricted to the aristocracy, is the immensity of the research task involved. Reconstructing the careers of those who are known to have served in the king's armies in the later Middle Ages represents a most daunting undertaking, for the number of individuals involved is very great and the source materials are varied, bulky, sometimes enigmatic and, in the main, not available in printed form. A major assault on the records has yet to be made,[11] though there have been a number of small-scale attacks, with varying degrees of success. Most of these have been undertaken as part of broader-based studies, focusing on either an individual magnate and his retinue, or on

---

7 'Many knights and esquires were [by the later fourteenth century] as much administrators (either at county level or in the service of magnates) as they were soldiers': C. Given-Wilson, 'The king and the gentry in fourteenth-century England', *TRHS*, 5th ser., xxxvii (1987), p. 89. 'It would be going too far to say that there was a demilitarisation of the knightly class in the course of the fourteenth century, but the prospect of active service does not seem to have exercised an appeal that was any more than intermittent': N. Saul, *Knights and esquires: the Gloucestershire gentry in the fourteenth century* (Oxford, 1981), pp. 52–53.

8 M. Ormrod, *The reign of Edward III* (New Haven and London, 1990), p. 149: 'it is quite wrong to suppose that the knights simply renounced their traditional function and allowed royal armies to pass under the control of professional mercenaries . . . a high proportion of the gentry eagerly took up their place on the battlefields of Europe'.

9 P. Coss, *The knight in medieval England, 1000–1400* (Stroud, 1993), pp. 104, 108. For a similar view, see A. Ayton, 'War and the English gentry under Edward III', *History Today*, xlii, 3 (March 1992), pp. 34–40; and idem, 'English armies in the fourteenth century', *Arms, armies and fortifications in the Hundred Years War*, ed. A. Curry and M. Hughes (Woodbridge, 1994).

10 Size of aristocracy: Given-Wilson, *The English nobility in the late Middle Ages*, pp. 69–83.

11 Dr Anne Curry is, however, currently engaged in a major prosopographical study of field army and garrison personnel in Lancastrian Normandy, thereby building on her 'Military organisation in Lancastrian Normandy, 1422–50', Ph.D. thesis, Council for National Academic Awards, 1985.

county communities.[12] The most valuable published work so far has been Philip Morgan's recent study of the military community of fourteenth-century Cheshire.[13] Although Cheshire's military traditions and patterns of lordship make it something of a special case, the themes explored in Morgan's pioneering book are of relevance to the wider community of militarily active Englishmen. This monograph, however, stands very much on its own. The military community of late medieval England has yet to receive treatment comparable with Philippe Contamine's magisterial study of 'guerre, état et société' in later medieval France.[14]

Fundamental to the foundations upon which systematic study of the military community should be built is a proper appreciation of the possibilities and limitations of the source materials. Although self-evident, this must be firmly stated since such appreciation has not always been displayed in the past. Indeed, there has been very little discussion of how the military records should be used. There is, for example, no methodological tradition for the study of the *vadia guerre* accounts (or pay-rolls), those detailed, retinue-by-retinue summaries of personnel numbers and periods of service, which are potentially so valuable to the historian of fourteenth-century English armies. This has led to a degree of naivety in analysis, a tendency to take the pay-rolls at face value: an approach, in other words, which would hardly be taken seriously if the sources under investigation were manorial records, where modern research methodologies rest upon several generations of meticulous, thoughtful scholarship. Much the same can be said of the nominal records for royal armies (e.g. enrolled letters of protection), for these too have often been used without sufficient consideration for their shortcomings, with the result that impressive-looking castles have been built upon very insecure foundations. Prompted by the need for a thorough investigation of the documentary sources for military service, one of the underlying aims of this book is to explore the strengths and weaknesses of the full-range of relevant records for the fourteenth century. This period witnessed great changes in military

---

[12] For example: K. Fowler, *The king's lieutenant: Henry of Grosmont, first duke of Lancaster, 1310–1361* (London, 1969), pp. 181–86 and appendix 3; A.J. Pollard, *John Talbot and the war in France, 1427–1453* (London, 1983), chapter 5; S. Walker, *The Lancastrian affinity, 1361–1399* (Oxford, 1990), chapter 3 and appendix 1; N. Saul, *Knights and esquires: the Gloucestershire gentry in the fourteenth century* (Oxford, 1981), chapter 2; M.J. Bennett, *Community, class and careerism: Cheshire and Lancashire society in the age of Sir Gawain and the Green Knight* (Cambridge, 1983), chapter 9. There have been a few studies of the leaders of the military community, the 'captains'. For example: M.R. Powicke, 'Lancastrian captains', *Essays in medieval history presented to B. Wilkinson*, ed. T.A. Sandquist and M.R. Powicke (Toronto, 1969), pp. 371–82; M. Jones, 'Edward III's captains in Brittany', *England in the fourteenth century*, ed. W.M. Ormrod (Woodbridge, 1986), pp. 99–118.

[13] P. Morgan, *War and society in medieval Cheshire, 1277–1403* (Manchester, 1987).

[14] P. Contamine, *Guerre, état et société à la fin du Moyen Age. Etudes sur les armées des rois de France, 1337–1494* (Paris, 1972).

organisation, including the demise of feudal service, the emergence of wholly paid armies and ultimately the 'indenture system', and it consequently offers a rich, varied and at times perplexing corpus of documentation. An investigation of these records will involve several key questions. How complete and reliable a picture of military service do they provide? What proportion of those engaged in military activity can actually be known by name? What is the nature of the distortions introduced by incomplete or imperfect evidence?

Of the various categories of source material available to the historian of Edwardian military service, the horse inventories stand out as perhaps the most distinctive and illuminating separate collection of records. On one level, they reveal the names of a great many serving men-at-arms, together with information on where, when and with whom the service was performed; and there is rarely any reason to doubt the reliability of the evidence. Admittedly, the coverage may not be complete. The unevenness of documentary production and survival means that the inventories usually offer no more than a sample of an army's heavy cavalry; but it is likely to be a sample composed of either a random selection of personnel (as, for example, with lists of lost warhorses, the *restauro equorum* accounts) or a slice through the military community with representatives from each of its layers, as we find with the many surviving retinue-level inventories. Most military records, whether of a conventional kind, like enrolled letters of protection, or rather more unusual, like rolls of arms, tend to reveal only the more prominent members of the military community, the *milites strenui*. Muster rolls are, of course, an exception to this, but comparatively few have survived from the earlier fourteenth century. The greatest yield of detailed nominal data on the 'ordinary' men-at-arms in Edwardian armies is to be had from the horse inventories, where the modestly-priced mounts of these men are listed alongside the destriers and coursers of their wealthier or more celebrated comrades-in-arms.

Most types of record offer no more than fleeting glimpses of the ordinary *homini ad arma*, which is a serious weakness given the importance of such men to the functioning of the Edwardian fighting machine. Typically, over 75% of an army's men-at-arms were of sub-knightly status. As far as we can tell, many were regular soldiers, forming a reliable, experienced backbone to a royal army or garrison. They are also a most interesting, heterogeneous group, consisting of men awaiting inheritances, younger sons who were never likely to inherit, members of modestly endowed families 'hovering perilously close to the level of the richer peasantry'[15] and 'professional' soldiers, men from the yeomanry or below, whose status had been enhanced by a career in arms. There has been a tendency to underestimate the contribution made by these unknighted *homini ad arma* to the Edwardian war effort. The argument that 'it was the substantial, knightly families that had on the whole the most

[15] C. Carpenter, *Locality and polity. A study of Warwickshire landed society, 1401–1499* (Cambridge, 1992), p. 38.

strenuous [military] records' – that 'the higher one looks in the scales of the estate of gentility, the sharper the mark of its martial tradition'[16] – might reflect accurately the relative percentage involvement in war of county and 'parish' gentry families: that a larger *percentage* of the former played a sig-nificant role in the king's wars. This may well be true (though such a conclu-sion is not yet based on systematic research); but by the last quarter of the fourteenth century, the numbers of county knights serving in the king's ar-mies *had* fallen sharply – perhaps more sharply than the general decline in the numbers of knights in society. In most of the armies raised during the later decades of the century, fewer than 10% of serving men-at-arms were knights.[17] As yet, we cannot be sure what proportion of the numerically predominant *homini ad arma* were drawn from sub-knightly, 'parish' gentry families; but there can be no doubt about the enhanced military status of the esquire during the late fourteenth and early fifteenth centuries. Newly armige-rous and socially respected, their status in the warrior caste nicely illustrated by their prominence as deponents in the Court of Chivalry armorial cases of the 1380s, the military role of esquires grew steadily. From being rank and file men-at-arms, sometimes subcontractors, in the retinues of knights in the 1370s and '80s, esquires have themselves become captains of retinues under Henry V.[18] The horse inventories have disappeared before the end of the Edwardian period; but earlier in the century these records show the emerging sub-knightly group in considerable detail, and more generally take us to the heart of the chivalrous community, revealing it as a diverse, dynamic collec-tion of men.

Unlike conventional muster rolls, the horse inventories offer more than merely lists of names; they supply abundant, if hitherto surprisingly under-utilised, information about the Edwardian warhorse.[19] Such data could pro-vide a major documentary thread in a monograph on the medieval warhorse in England;[20] but the present study, rather than focusing primarily on the

16 M. Keen, *English society in the later Middle Ages, 1348–1500* (Harmondsworth, 1990), pp. 135–36; for a similar view, see M. Powicke, *Military obligation in medieval England* (Oxford, 1962), p. 171.

17 J. Sherborne, 'Indentured retinues and English expeditions to France, 1369–1380', *EHR*, lxxix (1964), pp. 718–46.

18 A. Goodman, 'The military subcontracts of Sir Hugh Hastings, 1380', *EHR*, xcv (1980), pp. 116–17; C. Allmand, *Henry V* (London, 1992), p. 206.

19 For the purposes of this study, a man-at-arms' horse, appraised at the start of a period of paid military service and listed in an inventory, is taken to be a 'warhorse'. I do not, therefore, confine the use of this term to 'great horses' (or destriers), but apply it to all horses listed in inventories, from the moderately valued (but, nevertheless, barded) roun-cies of Edward I's reign – the mounts of the rank and file men-at-arms – to the highly priced steeds, coursers and destriers, of the nobility.

20 Such a monograph, drawing on the full range of available documentary evidence, includ-ing royal stud accounts and the fragmentary equestrian records of the aristocracy, has yet to be written. For the moment, the present study, which focuses primarily on the evidence offered by the horse inventories, might be set alongside R.H.C. Davis, *The medieval*

warhorses themselves, seeks to exploit the unique feature of the horse inventories, namely the association of warhorse and named man-at-arms, in order to determine what the equestrian descriptions and valuations can tell us about their aristocratic owners.[21] Here, indeed, we have an opportunity (as Lucien Febvre put it) to 'make mute things talk',[22] for the warhorse data can be made to reveal a good deal about social and military status, and about attitudes to campaigning. Viewing the information in bulk allows patterns to emerge for the chivalrous class as a whole; and because the inventories are available for the greater part of the Edwardian period, it is possible to trace changes in these patterns over a respectable length of time. Against the background trend in values can be uncovered the individuality – or conformity – of particular members of the chivalrous community, as revealed by the quality of their warhorses.

The primary aim of this book, therefore, is to determine what exactly can be learned about the chivalrous community of Edwardian England from an analysis of the horse inventories. By way of preparation, we must formulate answers to several important questions. What was the nature of the relationship between the warhorse and the aristocracy, the traditional 'military class', in the fourteenth century, and how far was this relationship altered in practice, and in popular perception, by the 'military revolution' of the Edwardian period? To what extent can the evidence of the inventories be supplemented by reference to sources of other kinds? Lastly, how and for precisely what purpose were the inventories compiled? An appreciation of the administrative mechanisms and other circumstances involved in the creation of these records is central to a proper assessment of the reliability, comprehensiveness and consistency of the information supplied by them.

The inventories are written records of the process of horse appraisal, the valuation of his warhorse being one element in a package of payments and benefits, the *terms of service*, offered to a man-at-arms serving for the king's pay.[23] The elements in the package were by no means constant during the

---

warhorse: origin, development and redevelopment (London, 1989). A further book on the medieval warhorse is expected soon from Ann Hyland, the author of *Equus: the horse in the Roman world* (London, 1990). Also worthy of note: J. Langdon, *Horses, oxen and technological innovation* (Cambridge, 1986); and J. Thirsk, *Horses in early modern England: for service, for pleasure, for power*, Stenton lecture, University of Reading, 1977 (Reading, 1978).

21 Cf. M. Vale, 'Warfare and the life of the French and Burgundian nobility in the late Middle Ages', *Adelige Sachkultur des Spätmittelalters. Internationaler Kongress, Krems an der Donau, 22 bis 25 September 1980* (Vienna, 1982), pp. 170–80 (and Tables 1 and 2), for a similar analysis, but focusing on the Gascon nobility. I am grateful to Professor Michael Jones for drawing my attention to this article.

22 P. Burke, ed., *A new kind of history: from the writings of Febvre* (London, 1973), p. 34.

23 These terms were in fact offered to the captain of the retinue in which the man-at-arms served. It is by no means clear whether the terms under which the ordinary man-at-arms served usually differed from those which the crown made available to captains. Studies of

Edwardian period. Horse appraisal was not available for all forms of military service, nor even for all major royal expeditions. The analysis of the package of terms of service as it evolved during the period, which forms the subject matter of Chapter 4, should certainly enhance our understanding of the horse inventories as records of military service (revealing, for example, whether the extent of documentary survival is broadly in line with the pattern of actual compilation); but it is also intended as a commentary on the predicament of the man-at-arms in the Edwardian military system. This predicament is by no means perfectly understood; a really convincing analysis of the benefits and costs of war as they affected the typical man-at-arms has yet to be written. As a modest contribution to an intriguing and hotly debated subject, this book is concerned not with the glamour of ransoms, the chance windfalls of war, but with the more mundane matters of day to day costs and remuneration.

The horse inventories which are at the heart of this book have survived in considerable numbers from the reign of Edward I and the early years of that of his son, but are less plentiful for the period following Edward II's deposition, and the last examples to have come down to us date from the mid-1360s. Why, then, choose to focus attention primarily on Edward III's reign, the decades during which these records are rapidly thinning out? The unevenness of the evidence is certainly regrettable, but the second and third quarters of the fourteenth century nevertheless stand out as a period likely to yield interesting results. It was, after all, a period which witnessed momentous changes in the organisation of the English fighting machine: changes in army structure and patterns of recruitment, in types of troops raised and in the social background of personnel; changes in military obligation and the terms of service, and in related administrative mechanisms; and changes in the practice of war, in campaigning methods and battlefield tactics. As documents produced during this period of change, and in some ways at the very heart of it, the horse inventories of the 1320s to '60s throw powerful illumination on the character and attitudes of the military community at a time when their traditional role and *raison d'être* were in the course of re-evaluation.

the small collections of surviving sub-contracts from this period suggest that captains were often able to recruit men of respectable quality and preserve a margin of profit for themselves.

1

The Military Revolution in Edwardian England

In my youth the Britons, who are called Angles or English, were taken to be the meekest of the barbarians. Today they are a fiercely bellicose nation. They have overturned the ancient military glory of the French by victories so numerous that they, who once were inferior to the wretched Scots, have reduced the entire kingdom of France by fire and sword to such a state that I, who had traversed it lately on business, had to force myself to believe that it was the same country I had seen before.

Francesco Petrarch, 1360[1]

England's emergence as a front-rank military power forms one of the primary themes of that kingdom's history during the second and third quarters of the fourteenth century. It has become customary, in explaining the extraordinarily improved performance and correspondingly enhanced reputation of English arms during this period, to focus on changes in military organisation, in the composition of armies and in the conduct of war. So significant were these changes, and their consequences, that it would not be going too far to suggest that England had experienced a 'military revolution'.[2]

The extent to which the English fighting machine was transformed during the reign of Edward III can be conveyed most effectively by contrasting the character and structure of the royal army which was routed by the Scots at

---

[1] From *Petrarcae epistolae familiares*, quoted in R. Boutruche, 'The devastation of rural areas during the Hundred Years War and the agricultural recovery of France', *The recovery of France in the fifteenth century*, ed. P.S. Lewis (London, 1971), p. 26.

[2] For example, Michael Prestwich, *The three Edwards. War and state in England, 1272–1377* (London, 1980), pp. 62, 213. Michael Powicke had earlier perceived 'a revolution in the English army' which 'laid the foundations for Crécy and Poitiers' in the reign of Edward I: *Military obligation in medieval England* (Oxford, 1962), p. 96; but Prestwich is surely right in seeing the principal developments as occurring *after* Bannockburn. For an extended discussion of the Edwardian military revolution, see A. Ayton, 'English armies in the fourteenth century', *Arms, armies and fortifications in the Hundred Years War*, ed. A. Curry and M. Hughes (Woodbridge, 1994). This chapter focuses primarily on changes in the structure and composition of Edwardian armies, together with the accompanying developments in fighting methods; the terms of service are discussed in Chapter 4. Other aspects of the late medieval military revolution, notably the fuelling of war by means of regular direct and indirect taxation, and the emergence of gunpowder weapons, fall outside the scope of this book.

Bannockburn in 1314 – the humiliating defeat to which Petrarch alludes – with the army which marched defiantly through France at about the time that the Italian poet had been writing. The years separating the débâcle of 1314 from the expedition of 1359-60 witnessed a major overhaul of the kingdom's military resources. The English army at Bannockburn probably consisted of about 2,500 men-at-arms, serving in companies of various sizes, and 15,000 foot soldiers (of whom a proportion would have been archers) raised in the shires by commissions of array.[3] The two parts of the army, the aristocratic retinues and shire levies, were numerically unbalanced, they were recruited separately and they fought separately. The contrast with the English army which set out on the march to Reims in 1359 is striking indeed. This consisted of nearly 10,000 men, of whom the most important elements were about 4,000 men-at-arms and over 5,000 mounted archers.[4] Given the practical difficulties of shipping large numbers of men and horses across the Channel, this was an army of exceptional size; but what really stands out, by comparison with the army of 1314, is the predominance of *mounted* troops, the roughly equal numbers of men-at-arms and mounted archers, and the fact that the great majority of these troops were serving in 'mixed' retinues. The earl of Northampton, for example, appears on the pay-roll with a retinue composed of 160 men-at-arms and 200 mounted archers; the earl of Warwick, with 120 men-at-arms and an equal number of horse archers.[5]

In emphasising the extent to which royal armies had been transformed by 1360, we should not overlook points of continuity. First, the aristocracy continued to perform a fundamentally important military role. Their function as war leaders was actually enhanced, since the great majority of troops were now recruited by aristocratic captains for service in their retinues (and this remained the case until the 1540s, when county-level musters replaced noble retinues as the basis of armies).[6] Moreover, the role of the gentry as rank and file knights and esquires also appears to have grown during the 1340s and '50s. The way for this 're-militarisation' of the aristocracy – and the major change in their attitude to overseas campaigning which accompanied it – was paved by the relatively attractive terms of service associated with the king's pay. But the final stimulus involved a combination of

---

3   These are informed estimates, in the absence of any surviving pay-rolls or horse inventories: see J.E. Morris, *Bannockburn* (Cambridge, 1914), p. 41.

4   *Vadia guerre* accounts for this army: E101/393/11, fos 79r-116v. The manpower total excludes non-combatants, as well as the contingents of continental men-at-arms, Welsh infantry and others who left the king's pay during the first few days of the campaign. The pay-roll suggests further shrinkage during the course of the campaign as various contingents, including the rest of the Welsh troops and the greater part of the shire levies, left the king's pay. The earl of Arundel's substantial retinue appears not to have left England (ibid., fo. 80r). Cf. A.E. Prince, 'The strength of English armies in the reign of Edward III', *EHR*, xlvi (1931), p. 368, which over-estimates the *effective* strength of this army.

5   E101/393/11, fo. 79v.

6   H. Miller, *Henry VIII and the English nobility* (Oxford, 1986), pp. 159–60.

royal pressure, through a short-lived military assessment based on landed income, and well-publicised campaigning successes in France. It soon became evident that this was a war offering not only the prospect of honourable service, but also the possibility of great profit. One of the important, if only temporary, side-effects of the military revolution, and of the successful war in France, was an environment in which the military potential of the aristocracy, the traditional warrior caste, could be harnessed more effectively.

A second point of continuity from the armies of Edward III's father, grandfather and indeed earlier was the presence of a major contingent of royal household troops in the expeditionary force of 1359–60. The retinues brought by household bannerets and knights contributed about a sixth of the heavy cavalry to the army which assembled in 1359. Although generally smaller than the corresponding contribution to Edward I's armies, the household division in Edward III's armies – and indeed in Richard II's in Ireland in 1394 and 1399[7] – represents a thread of continuity stretching back to the Norman kings.[8] The presence of the king at the head of an army meant that it was still in effect 'the household in arms'; and it explains why a central feature of the Edwardian military revolution, the indenture system, was not employed for the recruitment of this great army in 1359. Neither this, nor the other armies which Edward III led to the continent, were raised by indentures of war, apparently because such formal written contracts were not deemed necessary for armies under direct royal command and administered by the wardrobe, the royal household's financial department. But the climactic Reims campaign was to be the last expedition which the king led in person[9] and the indenture system was the mechanism which took over when the staff of the royal household were no longer holding the administrative reins.[10] Indentures

---

[7]　On the household division under Edward I, see M. Prestwich, *War, politics and finance under Edward I* (London, 1972), chapter 2; for Richard II, see C. Given-Wilson, *The royal household and the king's affinity: service, politics and finance, 1360–1413* (New Haven and London, 1986), pp. 63–66, chapter 4. The distinction in the *vadia guerre* accounts between household contingents and other retinues was 'becoming blurred by the end of Edward I's reign' and such differentiation is only occasionally found in Edward III's military records: M. Prestwich, 'English armies in the early stages of the Hundred Years War: a scheme of 1341', *BIHR*, lvi (1983), p. 109. For the winter Roxburgh campaign of 1334–35, the retinues of Edward III's household knights contributed about 30% of the men-at-arms in the army: R. Nicholson, *Edward III and the Scots. The formative years of a military career, 1327–1335* (Oxford, 1965), pp. 176–77, appendices 2 and 3.

[8]　J.O. Prestwich, 'The military household of the Norman kings', *EHR*, xcvi (1981), pp. 1–35.

[9]　Edward III had planned to lead the expeditionary force which landed in Calais in August 1369 and its composition was strongly influenced by his intended presence: it was the *retinencia regis*, the household in arms. J. Sherborne, 'John of Gaunt, Edward III's retinue and the French campaign of 1369', *Kings and nobles in the later Middle Ages*, ed. R.A. Griffiths and J. Sherborne (Gloucester, 1986), pp. 48–49.

[10]　Albert Prince's pioneering articles on the indenture system are still valuable: 'The indenture system under Edward III', *Historical essays in honour of James Tait*, ed. J.G.

of war had been employed to recruit garrisons during the Scottish wars. In the 1340s they had facilitated the mounting of a multi-front war involving the service of armies led by the king's lieutenants in secondary campaigning areas. Commanders like Henry of Grosmont and Sir Thomas Dagworth accounted for their periods of service directly at the Exchequer. After 1369, with an increasingly aging and inactive king, the indenture system became the invariable method of raising armies for the war in France.

If the army of 1359 was, in some respects, traditional in appearance, we cannot seriously doubt the extent to which the English fighting machine had already been radically transformed. As we have seen, the transformation involved two crucial developments: first, the emergence of the mounted (or 'horse') archer, emphatically described by J.E. Morris as 'the finest fighting man of the Middle Ages';[11] and second, the establishment of the retinue of mixed composition, consisting of men-at-arms and mounted archers, recruited by a re-invigorated class of aristocratic captains, and 'capable of assuming a variety of military roles'.[12] If, by the time of the Treaty of Brétigny, the English had become '[les] plus nobles et les plus frisques combastans qu'on sache',[13] thoroughly skilled in arms and accustomed to achieving victory in battle,[14] it is important to recognise that the dramatic transformation of the military machine since Bannockburn had only been gradually achieved. The battle of Boroughbridge (1322) may well have been a significant landmark in the development of English battlefield tactics, but the experiments in military organisation during Edward II's reign were largely unsuccessful.[15] It is only after Halidon Hill (1333) that really significant developments in the character and organisation of English royal armies can be detected. The mounted archer appears on the scene, a response, like the hobelar before him, to the need for mobility in the Scottish wars, but a superior breed of fighting man, because of his potent weapon.[16] The great army with which Edward III campaigned in Scotland during the summer of 1335 consisted of about 13,000–13,500 men, of whom in the region of 3,350

Edwards, V.H. Galbraith and E.F. Jacob (Manchester, 1933), pp. 283–97; 'The payment of army wages in Edward III's reign', *Speculum*, xix (1944), pp. 137–60.

11 J.E. Morris, 'Mounted infantry in medieval warfare', *TRHS*, 3rd ser., viii (1914), p. 78.

12 For an excellent summary of these developments, see Morgan, *War and society in medieval Cheshire*, pp. 37–49.

13 *Jean le Bel*, i, p. 156.

14 Ranulph Higden, *Polychronicon*, ed. C. Babington and J.R. Lumby, 9 vols, Rolls Ser., (London, 1865–86), ii, pp. 166–69.

15 Powicke, *Military obligation in medieval England*, chapter 8.

16 On the hobelar, see Morgan, *War and society in medieval Cheshire*, pp. 38–39, 43; J.F. Lydon, 'The hobelar: an Irish contribution to medieval warfare', *The Irish Sword*, II, v (1954), pp. 12–16. On the continued importance of hobelars in Ireland, see R. Frame, 'Military service in the lordship of Ireland, 1290–1360: institutions and society on the Anglo-Gaelic frontier', *Medieval frontier societies*, ed. R. Bartlett and A. MacKay (Oxford, 1989), pp. 114–15 and table 1.

were mounted archers. This is certainly an impressive number, given that horse archers had first been recorded in significant numbers (at least in the surviving records) only during the previous year; but of these 3,350 men, only 1,095 were serving with men-at-arms in mixed retinues, and the greater part of the king's army in the summer of 1335 was still being raised in the shires by commissions of array.[17]

The onset of the war with France increased the pace of change in English military organisation, adding further stimulus to the rise of the mixed retinue.[18] But arrayed troops were not to be displaced over-night; county and urban levies continued to contribute large numbers of men to English armies until at least the expedition of 1359–60.[19] The initial recruiting target for arrayed troops prior to the Normandy campaign of 1346 was about 13,000 men (of whom over half were to be Welshmen); and if only a proportion of this figure actually landed at Saint-Vaast La Hougue, it is likely that a considerably larger number of arrayed foot archers and spearmen *were* assembled for the subsequent siege of Calais.[20] The king's reliance on old-fashioned manpower reserves in 1346–47 arose from the specific requirements of this campaign: initially, the need for an army large enough to challenge Philip de

---

[17] Nicholson, *Edward III and the Scots*, pp. 198–200 and appendices 4–7; the personnel numbers are based on the *vadia guerre* accounts in Richard Ferriby's Wardrobe Book: BL Cotton MS, Nero C. VIII, fos 236r–38r, 255r–56r. About 2,500 men-at-arms served in the retinues of magnates. For the Roxburgh campaign during the winter of 1334–35, the ratio of men-at-arms to mounted archers in magnate retinues had been more evenly balanced: 838 to 771 (Nicholson, *Edward III and the Scots*, pp. 176–7; appendix 3; BL Cotton MS, Nero C. VIII, fos 233r–34r, 252v–53v). On the raising of shire levies, see A.E. Prince, 'The army and navy', *The English government at work, 1327–1336*, ed. J.F. Willard and W.A. Morris (Cambridge, Mass., 1940), i, pp. 355–64.

[18] An interesting side-light on the evolution of the mixed retinue is offered by a planning document dating from 1341 (C47/2/33), for which, see Prestwich, 'English armies in the early stages of the Hundred Years War: a scheme in 1341'. It envisages an army composed (with the exception of a Welsh contingent) entirely of magnate retinues, these consisting of varying proportions of men-at-arms, armed men and archers. By contrast, a document drawn up four years earlier lists the retinues of a projected army, but specifies numbers of men-at-arms without any mention of archers: E101/15/17, for which, see N.B. Lewis, 'The recruitment and organisation of a contract army, May to November 1337', *BIHR*, xxxvii (1964), pp. 1–19. The omission may not be significant, however; royal officials remained much given to equating magnate retinues with numbers of men-at-arms. For example, see C81/1750, no. 106, which is a list of twenty-five captains (beginning with the earl of Northampton), each of whom is assigned a number of *hommes darmes*. It dates from c.1341–42, but its purpose is unclear.

[19] Powicke, *Military obligation in medieval England*, p. 185. In 1359 the shire levies merely supplemented the far larger numbers of mounted archers serving in retinues. Although the initial recruitment target for the shires was 2,600 archers, this was later reduced to just under 1,000, which is close to the number allowed for in the pay-rolls: *Rymer*, III, i, 415–16 (12 January 1359); 440–41 (4 August 1359); E101/393/11, fos 115r–16v.

[20] A. Ayton, 'The English army and the Normandy campaign of 1346', *England and Normandy in the Middle Ages*, ed. D. Bates and A. Curry (London, 1994).

Valois in the field, without having to resort to expensive and unreliable continental mercenaries; later, the suitability of infantry for a protracted siege. The humble footsoldier had, then, played a part in the triumphs of 1346–47, but a strategy based on *chevauchées* would depend upon mounted troops. The future lay with the 'horse soldiers' and there are clear signs that the wind was blowing in this direction long before 1359. This is shown, for example, by the English expeditionary forces campaigning in Brittany in 1342–43.[21] The final set of *vadia guerre* accounts suggests that the main body of this army, which arrived in the duchy under the king's personal command in the autumn of 1342, included 1,700 foot soldiers. Upon closer inspection we can see that the great majority of these men either left the king's pay very quickly or never actually arrived in Brittany, with the result that the effective strength of Edward III's army was about 1,800 men-at-arms and 1,800 mounted archers. As in 1359, there was no significant role for arrayed foot soldiers; and the great majority of mounted archers served in mixed retinues alongside men-at-arms,[22] with most of the retinues consisting of balanced, often equal, numbers of each.

If the structure of the great army of 1359 had been anticipated in the smaller expedition of 1342–43, then the emergence of the indenture system as the usual method of raising armies in the later fourteenth century was probably decisive in ensuring that the structural reforms endured. Shire levies were to have no more than a limited role following the resumption of the French war in 1369,[23] and English expeditionary forces during the period 1369–80 were dominated by mixed retinues, consisting usually of equal numbers of men-at-arms and archers, though occasionally having a preponderance of archers.[24] A roll of the captains assembling under Sir Robert Knolles' command in 1370 records that the great majority of their retinues, both large and

---

[21] For a fuller discussion of these forces, see Appendix 2.

[22] There were only two significant exceptions: a company of eighty horse archers from Cheshire led by John Ward and twenty under the command of Guy de Brian (E36/204, fo. 109v). On John Ward, see Morgan, *War and society in medieval Cheshire*, pp. 43–49. There *were* a number of retinues consisting exclusively of men-at-arms, but only that of Sir Bartholomew de Burgherssh *senior* was numerically important (sixty-eight men-at-arms); his son's company was composed of only three men-at-arms: E36/204, fos 106v, 107r. R. Nicholson, in noting the existence of similarly unbalanced retinues in 1334–35, is sceptical about the completeness of the pay accounts: *Edward III and the Scots*, p. 177. The same may well be true of the pay-rolls for the Breton campaign.

[23] J. Sherborne, 'Indentured retinues and English expeditions to France, 1369–1380', *EHR*, lxxix (1964), pp. 741–42. Commissions of array were sometimes used to raise archers for the retinues of leading captains: see, for example, A. Goodman, *John of Gaunt. The exercise of princely power in fourteenth-century Europe* (Harlow, 1992), pp. 218–19.

[24] Sherborne, 'Indentured retinues and English expeditions to France, 1369–1380', especially Tables A–D. As early as the 1340s, a numerical superiority of horse archers was sometimes preferred. Sir Thomas Dagworth's retinue, raised for service in Brittany in 1346, consisted of eighty men-at-arms and 120 horse archers (as well as forty *bidouers*): E101/68/3, m. 62 (indenture); E101/25/17 (pay account).

small, consisted of men-at-arms and archers in equal numbers.[25] A document headed 'Pur le viage de Portugale', showing the contingents expected to comprise Edmund of Cambridge's expeditionary force in 1381, lists ten retinues (ranging in size from 1,000 men to 40), each with exact parity of *homes darmes* and *archers*.[26] If such parity represented the ideal tactical balance of complementary personnel, then it was an ideal which could not be sustained. As the fourteenth century progressed, underlying social trends, perhaps combined with financial considerations (the 'cost effectiveness' of the archer at 6d per day), ensured that a numerical predominance of archers became the norm in English armies. Archers outnumber men-at-arms (by up to three to one) in many of the retinues listed in the 'Order of Battle' for Richard II's Scottish campaign in 1385,[27] and at the start of the Lancastrian occupation of northern France the optimum archer to man-at-arms ratio was deemed to be three to one, though in practice during the later stages of the war the ratio was sometimes nearer to ten to one.[28]

The emergence of the mounted archer as associate of the man-at-arms in mixed retinues brought about a significant shift in the social composition of the military community. Changes in military organisation were, thus, paralleled by changes in the patterns of recruitment. The arrayed infantry of Edward I's day were ill-equipped and undisciplined;[29] and as the *Poem on the evil times of Edward II* reminds us, 'the richest buy themselves off for ten or twelve shillings, whilst the poor are conscripted'.[30] By contrast, the mounted archers of the mid-late fourteenth century were more expensively equipped (an archer hackney might cost 20s), and frequently drawn from a wealthier social group. Mounted archers were admittedly a heterogeneous body of men, perhaps increasingly so as their numbers expanded in the later

[25] E101/30/25.

[26] C47/2/49, no. 2.

[27] For what appears to be the 'most authoritative text' of this document, see S. Armitage-Smith, *John of Gaunt* (London, 1904), appendix 2, pp. 437–39. Cf. N.B. Lewis, 'The last medieval summons of the English feudal levy, 13 June 1385', *EHR*, lxxiii (1958), pp. 3ff on the 'Order of Battle' and appendix 2 (pp. 17–21) for details of the paid contingents in Richard II's army. In the expeditionary force taken by Henry IV to Scotland in 1400 (numbering in all over 13,000 men), archers outnumbered men-at-arms by more than six to one, though at the retinue-level the ratio was often more in the region of four or five to one: A.L. Brown, 'The English campaign in Scotland, 1400', *British government and administration. Studies presented to S.B. Chrimes*, ed. H. Hearder and H.R. Loyn (Cardiff, 1974), pp. 40–54.

[28] C. Allmand, *Henry V*, p. 213; C. Allmand, *Lancastrian Normandy, 1415–1450* (Oxford, 1983), p. 200; J.R. Lander, 'The Hundred Years War and Edward IV's 1475 campaign in France', *Crown and nobility, 1450–1509* (London, 1976), pp. 239, 321 (appendix E).

[29] See M. Prestwich, *War, politics and finance under Edward I* (London, 1972), chapter 4.

[30] J.R. Maddicott, 'Poems of social protest in early-fourteenth-century England', *England in the fourteenth century*, ed. W.M. Ormrod (Woodbridge, 1986), p. 143.

fourteenth and fifteenth centuries;[31] but many were men of yeoman stock, aptly described by Maurice Keen as 'minor landholders, not gentry, but a cut above the ordinary peasant husbandman'.[32] Given the growing prosperity of the yeoman farmer in the decades following the first plague visitation, mounted archers were often 'men of some standing in local society'.[33] With a diminishing role for massed infantry levies and the rise of the mounted archer, serving alongside men-at-arms in retinues led by aristocratic captains, military service in the king's armies was becoming the preserve of a more restricted section of the population; the military community had a narrower social base. Moreover, the gap between chivalrous and non-chivalrous combatants had also narrowed. Just as the heraldic separation of knights and esquires became blurred during the fourteenth century,[34] so the social and economic distinctions between archer and man-at-arms were also becoming less pronounced. Some gentry families adopted archery symbols for their seals.[35] By 1421 it was possible for Henry V to call for skilled archers 'de progenie generosa'.[36] This process is more noticeable in some parts of England than others. Philip Morgan has pointed out, for example, that there were many Cheshire archers 'whose standing, within the context of county society, was analogous to that of men-at-arms raised elsewhere in England'.[37] A single family might contribute both men-at-arms and archers to a royal army.[38] A man might serve in both capacities during the course of his career, perhaps as a consequence of changes in fortune.[39]

The emphasis on mounted troops and recruitment on the basis of individual retinues consisting of roughly equal numbers of men-at-arms and archers greatly enhanced the effectiveness of the English fighting machine under

---

31 See A. Ayton, 'Military service and the development of the Robin Hood legend in the fourteenth century', *Nottingham Medieval Studies*, xxxvi (1992), pp. 136ff.

32 M. Keen, *The outlaws of medieval legend*, revised paperback edn (London, 1987), p. xvii.

33 Morgan, *War and society in medieval Cheshire*, p. 41. According to a definition of the various levels of the military community, established by the crown as part of an experimental military levy in the mid 1340s (*CPR, 1343–45*, p. 495), a man with £5 a year in land should be equipped as a mounted archer, whilst £10 required him to be a hobelar (partially armoured horseman) and £25, a man-at-arms. In practice, hobelars were employed less and less frequently under Edward III, and so a typical royal army would probably include many archers and men-at-arms of roughly similar social status.

34 On this process, see Saul, *Knights and esquires*, pp. 20–25; D. Crouch, *The image of aristocracy in Britain, 1000–1300* (London and New York, 1992), pp. 235–36.

35 J. Bradbury, *The medieval archer* (Woodbridge, 1985), p. 173; Morgan, *War and society in medieval Cheshire*, p. 41 n. 69.

36 Allmand, *Henry V*, p. 206.

37 Morgan, *War and society in medieval Cheshire*, p. 109.

38 For example, among the citizens of Norwich in the mid fourteenth century: W. Hudson, 'Norwich militia in the fourteenth century', *Norfolk Archaeology*, xiv (1901), p. 290.

39 For men who began their careers as archers but rose into the chivalrous class, see Bennett, *Community, class and careerism*, pp. 182–83. For further examples from Normandy in the 1440s, see A.J. Pollard, *John Talbot and the war in France, 1427–1453* (London, 1983), p. 90; but Pollard observes that 'only a handful of the archers were ever promoted'.

Edward III. A wholly mounted force of men-at-arms and archers could conduct a fast-moving, destructive campaign (*chevauchée*) and if brought to battle would offer a most effective and flexible tactical response. The *chevauchée*, which was employed so often in the Hundred Years War, at times with spectacular success,[40] had been influenced by the experience of the protracted Scottish wars, in which both the English and the Scots recognised the importance of mobility. Mounted raids had been commonplace.[41] In 1336, on the eve of the French war, Edward III himself led a small-scale raid into the Scottish Highlands and gained first-hand experience of the effectiveness of a wholly mounted force of men-at-arms and archers.[42] The Breton campaign of 1342–43 revealed the system operating on a more expansive scale. After landing at Brest, Edward III's compact army swept through Brittany to lay siege to Vannes. Several detachments were sent on separate raids to secure other important towns in the duchy.[43] They managed to avoid serious confrontations, but earlier in the year, the earl of Northampton's small army had been attacked whilst besieging the town of Morlaix in northern Brittany. In the resulting hard-fought battle, Northampton's dismounted men-at-arms and archers, occupying defensive positions, repulsed the attacks of a numerically superior opponent.[44] Similar tactics were employed at Crécy (1346), Mauron (1352), Poitiers (1356) and numerous small-scale fights during the first phase of the French war. Whilst accepting the crucial part played by the longbow in these successes,[45] it is important to recognise that archers did not win the

---

[40] See, for example, H.J. Hewitt, *The Black Prince's expedition of 1355–1357* (Manchester, 1958).

[41] For example, in March 1333, Sir Anthony de Lucy and 800 men crossed into Scotland and 'chivaucherent la nuyte xx lieux': *The Anonimalle Chronicle, 1307–1334*, ed. W.R. Childs and J. Taylor. Yorkshire Archaeological Soc., Record Ser., cxlvii (1991 for 1987), pp. 156–59. Another influence on the development of the *chevauchée* was the *cavalcante*, a feature of private wars in thirteenth-century Gascony and employed during 'public' war in the 1290s: M. Vale, 'The Gascon nobility and the Anglo-French war, 1294–98', *War and government in the Middle Ages*, ed. J. Gillingham and J.C. Holt (Woodbridge, 1984), pp. 140–41; idem, *The Angevin legacy and the Hundred Years War, 1250–1340* (Oxford, 1990), pp. 210–11.

[42] Morgan, *War and society in medieval Cheshire*, pp. 41–42.

[43] For the movements of Edward III's lieutenants, see M. Jones, 'Edward III's captains in Brittany', *England in the fourteenth century*, ed. W.M. Ormrod (Woodbridge, 1986), p. 107, based in part upon Edward III's letter to his son, dated 5 December: *Avesbury*, pp. 340–44. See also a useful map in M. Jones, 'The Breton civil war', *Froissart: historian*, ed. J.J.N. Palmer (Woodbridge, 1981), p. 66. For a lively account of the whole campaign, see J. Sumption, *The Hundred Years War: trial by battle* (London, 1990), chapter 11.

[44] T.F. Tout, 'The tactics of the battles of Boroughbridge and Morlaix', *EHR*, xix (1904), pp. 711–15; cf. the ingenious reconstruction of the battle by A.H. Burne, *The Crecy war* (London, 1955), pp. 71–78.

[45] On the technology of the longbow, see G. Rees, 'The longbow's deadly secrets', *New Scientist*, 5 June 1993, pp. 24–25; C.J. Rogers, 'The military revolutions of the Hundred Years War', *The Journal of Military History*, lvii (1993), pp. 249–51. For discussions of the major battles, see Bradbury, *The medieval archer*, chapter 6.

battles on their own. The tactical system depended upon cooperation between the two main sections of the army. The massed hitting-power of the archers could prevent the effective deployment of bowmen by the enemy (as at Crécy) and would thin-out an attacking force at a distance, blunting their impetus, thereby giving the English men-at-arms, fighting shoulder to shoulder in disciplined formations, the edge in the hard-fought mêlées which these battles invariably involved. But archers were only effective for as long as their supply of arrows lasted; and they were not invincible in the field, as the collapse of Sir Walter Bentley's right flank at Mauron shows.[46]

Like the *chevauchée*, the distinctive English tactics of the Hundred Years War were shaped by the experience of the Anglo-Scottish wars earlier in the fourteenth century. Although large numbers of foot archers had been recruited in Edward I's reign, they were not well equipped, nor well disciplined; nor were they yet employed in a coordinated fashion. The real tactical turning point was not the battle of Falkirk (1298), but the battle of Bannockburn, where the flower of English chivalry, fighting in the traditional fashion on warhorses, were routed by a Scottish army consisting mainly of pikemen. It was this humiliating defeat which seems to have brought about a major shift in tactical thinking in England. A combination of dismounted men-at-arms, hobelars and archers in defensive formations reminiscent of Scottish schiltroms was the basis of Sir Andrew Harcla's success at Boroughbridge in 1322.[47] The tactical combination of dismounted men-at-arms and archers was apparently envisaged prior to mobilisation for the Weardale campaign in 1327[48] and was employed to devastating effect in the defensive battles against the Scots at Dupplin Moor in 1332 and Halidon Hill in 1333.[49] It was entirely natural that these tactics should also be used in France where numerical inferiority usually obliged the English to adopt a defensive posture.

Some historians have argued that both the *chevauchée* and the tactical combination of archers and dismounted men-at-arms had long been features of medieval warfare. Discussing the 'typical activities' of medieval armies during the eleventh, twelfth and thirteenth centuries, John Gillingham concludes, quite rightly, that 'ravaging, and foraging while ravaging, was the principal strategy of attack'.[50] 'In the Hundred Years War', notes Sean

---

[46] T.F. Tout, 'Some neglected fights between Crécy and Poitiers', *EHR*, xx (1905), pp. 726–30.

[47] Tout, 'The tactics of the battles of Boroughbridge and Morlaix', drawing on the *Chronicle of Lanercost*; cf. Bradbury, *The medieval archer*, p. 87.

[48] A.E. Prince, 'The importance of the campaign of 1327', *EHR*, l (1935), p. 301.

[49] Nicholson, *Edward III and the Scots*, pp. 86–90, 132–37; Bradbury, *The medieval archer*, pp. 88–90.

[50] J. Gillingham, 'William the Bastard at war', *Studies in medieval history presented to R. Allen Brown*, ed. C. Harper-Bill, C.J. Holdsworth and J.L. Nelson (Woodbridge, 1989), p. 149; see also the same author's classic article 'Richard I and the science of war in the Middle Ages', *War and government in the Middle Ages*, ed. J. Gillingham and J.C. Holt

McGlynn, 'ravaging is better known as the *chevauchée*'.[51] In the sphere of battlefield tactics, Jim Bradbury has shown that, in the first half of the twelfth century, 'the common method of fighting was to combine dismounted knights with archers, and with cavalry'. Was this not 'in essence exactly the combination that would win so many battles in the Hundred Years War?'[52] That neither these battlefield tactics nor the *chevauchée* was new in the fourteenth century is clear enough to modern historians, but contemporaries may well have seen it otherwise. Sir Thomas Gray, an active and well-informed fighting man, wrote of the English at Bannockburn that 'they were not accustomed to dismount to fight on foot; whereas the Scots had taken a lesson from the Flemings, who before that had at Courtrai defeated on foot the power of France'.[53] Whether or not English fighting men in the fourteenth century were aware of tactics employed in the twelfth century,[54] the distinctiveness of the *chevauchées* and battlefield tactics of the Hundred Years War arose from the fact that the reformed English military machine, particularly suited to these methods of fighting, was able to exploit their potential to the full. To find the mounted raid, archers and dismounted knights all employed in the twelfth century is not to diminish the importance of the Edwardian Scottish wars as a training ground for English armies. The formidable opposition presented by the Scots, the tough campaigning conditions, the rout at Bannockburn – all these forced a reappraisal of both military resources and campaigning methods, so that the experience of the protracted Scottish wars can indeed be seen to have stimulated the emergence of a combination of army structure and fighting techniques which complemented each other ideally. For those few men like Sir John de Hardreshull, whose careers stretched from Bannockburn to the battlefield triumphs of the 1340s, it must surely have seemed that a military revolution had indeed taken place.[55]

The tactical developments which bore such abundant fruit during the Hundred Years War may not represent the most significant dimension of the Edwardian military revolution,[56] but for the English aristocracy they heralded a major change to established fighting methods. In commenting on how the

(Woodbridge, 1984), pp. 78–91. Cf. C. Marshall, *Warfare in the Latin east, 1192–1291* (Cambridge, 1992), chapter 5.

[51] S. McGlynn, 'The myths of medieval warfare', *History Today*, xliv, 1 (January 1994), p. 32.

[52] Bradbury, *The medieval archer*, chapter 3 (at p. 55).

[53] *Scalacronica*, p. 55.

[54] Bradbury concedes that 'the tactics of the fourteenth century were certainly adopted anew; there is no clear line of continuity': *The medieval archer*, p. 57.

[55] Hardreshull appears to have been at both Bannockburn and Morlaix: C71/6, m. 3 (1314: in John de Hastings' retinue); C76/17, m. 37 (1342: with Robert d'Artois). Hardreshull's career is examined in detail in M. Jones, 'Edward III's captains in Brittany' and idem, 'Sir John de Hardreshull, king's lieutenant in Brittany, 1343–5', *Nottingham Medieval Studies*, xxxi (1987), pp. 76–97.

[56] Morgan, *War and society in medieval Cheshire*, p. 41.

English at Halidon Hill 'contra antiquatum morem suorum patrum, pedes pugnare', Geoffrey le Baker was doubtless expressing the thoughts of many of the knights and esquires in Edward III's army.[57] Some may even have felt a jolt to their sense of identity as members of society's warrior class. Yet the militarily active among the nobility and gentry seem quickly to have accepted the requirements of the tactical revolution and a clear distinction emerged between deeds of chivalry, which were most appropriately performed on horseback amongst their peers – on the tournament field and, on campaign, in individual combats and small-scale encounters – and the practical business of battlefield fighting which was most effectively done on foot in disciplined tactical formations, often in association with archers. Sir Thomas Gray illustrates this point well in the contrast which he draws between the impetuous behaviour of Sir Thomas Marmion, concerned to make his crested helmet famous in the most dangerous place in Britain, and that of his rescuers, the Norham garrison, advancing steadily on foot with levelled lances.[58]

In France, numerical inferiority usually forced the English to adopt a defensive posture. The sons and grandsons of men who had fought astride great warhorses at Falkirk and Bannockburn would rarely find themselves riding into battle during the reign of Edward III; they would more likely fight on foot, wielding the lance – the cavalry weapon par excellence – as a pike in bristling 'hedgehog' formations.[59] The king's letter after Crécy describes in a matter of fact way how the English 'drew up in battle array and waited on foot';[60] by 1346 this was routine procedure. Circumstances demanding a mounted charge were occasionally encountered, of course – as at the battle of Auberoche in 1345[61] and at the Blanchetaque ford shortly before Crécy, when mounted men-at-arms were well supported by archery. But the great majority of engagements, whether fought offensively (as at Roche Derrien in 1347)[62] or defensively (as at Mauron), saw the English men-at-arms operating on foot, accompanied by dismounted archers. To appreciate the completeness of the tactical revolution, the extent to which the English aristocracy had abandoned fighting on horseback, it is necessary to consider not just the few great battles of the period, but also those numerous medium- and small-scale encounters which fill the pages of the best-informed writers, soldier-authors like Sir Thomas Gray: skirmishes in which the English showed great

57 *Le Baker*, p. 51.
58 *Scalacronica*, p. 62. Gray attributes the English defeat at Presfen in the late 1330s to a breakdown of the usual disciplined approach to fighting (ibid., p. 105).
59 *Scalacronica*, pp. 136–37; M. Mallett, *Mercenaries and their masters. Warfare in Renaissance Italy* (London, 1974), p. 37.
60 *The life and campaigns of the Black Prince*, ed. R. Barber (Woodbridge, 1986), p. 22; cf. *Life of the Black Prince by the herald of Sir John Chandos*, ed. M.K. Pope and E.C. Lodge (Oxford, 1910), p. 10 (lines 321–22).
61 *Froissart*, ed. Lettenhove, iv, pp. 254–55, 263, 270. The English men-at-arms attacked the French camp on horseback to achieve surprise.
62 See Sir Thomas Dagworth's letter after the battle: *Avesbury*, pp. 388–90.

consistency in their tactical methods.[63] These methods were employed wherever in Europe they happened to be fighting. In the Scottish border country in the years after Bannockburn, the English dismounted to fight as a matter of course.[64] By the early 1360s Englishmen serving in the White Company had introduced their distinctive tactical methods into Italian warfare,[65] and by the 1380s, the 'English' style of fighting had also left its mark in Portugal.[66] Mercenaries from England were employed by King Louis the Great of Hungary for garrison duty at the border fortress of Törcsvár[67] and it may not be entirely fanciful to identify the influence of the English mounted archer on the *pharetrarium* which was the basis the *militia portalis* established by King Sigismund's decree of 1397.[68]

At the heart of English tactics from the early 1330s, therefore, was a much diminished role for the warhorse. Its battlefield function was usually confined to the closing stages of an engagement. A successful action fought on foot might very profitably be followed-up by a mounted pursuit, as was the case after Dupplin Moor and Halidon Hill.[69] Conversely, of course, it might be necessary to flee the field in some haste. In either case, grooms, who had been holding the horses in readiness behind the battle-line, would bring them forward for their masters to mount.[70] Away from the battlefield, good horses

---

63 See, for example, *Scalacronica*, pp. 136, 140, 143, 152–53, 156, 158; Tout, 'Some neglected fights between Crécy and Poitiers'.

64 See, for example, an anonymous newsletter of c.1340 which describes how the Roxburgh garrison encountered a Scottish raiding party and dismounted to fight with them: SC1/54, no. 30, calendared in *Bain*, v, no. 809.

65 For the English in Italy, see Mallett, *Mercenaries and their masters*, pp. 36–38.

66 On English influence on Portuguese military organisation and tactics: *Fernao Lopes: The English in Portugal, 1367–87*, ed. D.W. Lomax and R.J. Oakley (Warminster, 1988), pp. 179–80, 260–63; P.E. Russell, *The English intervention in Spain and Portugal in the time of Edward III and Richard II* (Oxford, 1955), pp. 379–80, 384–86.

67 János Thuróczy, *Chronica Hungarorum, i*, ed. Elisabeth Galántai and Gyula Kristó (Budapest, 1985), p. 182.

68 *Decreta regni Hungariae, 1301–1457*, ed. F. Döry, G. Bónis and V. Bácskai, Publicationes archivi nationalis Hungarici, fontes ii (Budapest, 1976), p. 162. Sigismund's decree of 8 March 1435 refers specifically to *pharetraria equestres*: see A. Borosy, 'The *militia portalis* in Hungary before 1526', *From Hunyadi to Rákóczi. War and society in late medieval and early modern Hungary*, ed. J.M. Bak and B.K. Király (Brooklyn, New York, 1982), pp. 63–80. I am indebted to Dr Ferenc Sebök of József Attila University, Szeged for the primary source references in this footnote and the last.

69 Nicholson, *Edward III and the Scots*, pp. 89, 136. This did not always happen: exhaustion or prudence (as after Crécy) frequently dictated that the English stood their ground or withdrew quietly from the field. At Lunalonge in 1349 the French carried off the English horses during the course of the battle and although the latter had successfully defended themselves, they were obliged to make for the safety of an English-held fortress on foot (*Scalacronica*, pp. 136–37). Sir Thomas Gray's account of the battle supplements that provided by the writer of the *Chronique Normande*, which was used by T.F. Tout, 'Some neglected fights between Crécy and Poitiers'.

70 For a variant on this, see *Scalacronica*, p. 62, where Sir Thomas Gray tells how, after a sortie on foot by the garrison of Norham castle had put the Scots to flight, the ladies of

were essential to the successful prosecution of a *chevauchée*; yet we must doubt whether the destrier – the true 'great horse', highly bred for battle – would be suitable for hard-riding over rough country. Nor were they suited to siege-camp conditions. When, as so often happened, an expedition petered out in a protracted siege, expensive warhorses became redundant and regularly fell victim to disease. Consequently, during the investment of Calais in 1346–47 we find men-at-arms securing permission to send their valuable *grauntz chivalx* back to England,[71] while the king, in requesting reinforcements, urged that 'it would not be necessary to bring large horses' nor, indeed, to wait for the assembly of horse transports.[72] If this stipulation was in part to ensure speedy arrival, it must also have been founded upon the recognition that warhorses would not be needed during the siege, nor in all probability in any engagement with Philip de Valois' forces. Horses were even more obviously redundant when the knightly community enlisted for naval expeditions. The increased emphasis on seaborne operations by the English high command following the defeat of the earl of Pembroke's convoy off La Rochelle in June 1372 can only have contributed further to the marginalisation of the warhorse in English military thinking.[73]

It is clear, then, that by the middle of the fourteenth century, the warhorse no longer occupied a place of primary importance in the military practice of the English. The impact of this change on the collective psyche of the aristocracy – and, indeed, on the military establishment – should not be underestimated, particularly as it was associated with a more broadly-based challenge to the aristocracy's social identity as the military class. As we have seen, the tactical revolution and the enhanced military reputation of the English which it brought about, encouraged the emergence of socially ambitious groups in the military community. The rise of the archer, his potency underscored by growing numerical dominance in royal armies, was accompanied by a correspondingly altered status for the aristocratic warrior. The scions of ancient gentry families were now locked into a tactical system based upon cooperation with bowmen; and they might well find themselves wielding the sword alongside men-at-arms who owed their status to ability and good fortune rather than birth. That the battlefield was no longer the arena which set the minor aristocrat apart from his social inferiors had no more telling facet than the diminished role of the warhorse in the English war effort. Until the tactical revolution, the warhorse had been the *sine qua non* of aristocratic

the castle brought out their menfolk's horses for the pursuit. In the event of defeat, the grooms could not always be trusted. After a skirmish at Pont-Vallain in 1370, they took flight on the horses in their care, leaving the men-at-arms to be taken prisoner by the French: *Froissart*, ed. Lettenhove, viii, p. 53.

71 C81/1710, no. 47.

72 *Crecy and Calais*, pp. 103, 121–22.

73 J.W. Sherborne, 'The battle of La Rochelle and the war at sea, 1372–75', *BIHR*, xlii (1969), pp. 17–29; idem, 'The English navy: shipping and manpower, 1369–1389', *Past and Present*, xxxvii (1967), pp. 163–75.

combat: as Noel Denholm Young has put it, it was 'impossible to be chivalrous without a horse'.[74] This was not merely the stuff of romance, for it
involved questions of military identity and, indeed, social identity. Military
service for the knightly class, whether in fulfilment of feudal obligations or
for the king's pay, was unthinkable without a barded warhorse. The armoured horse was a prerequisite of service; it was, as much as anything, what
defined a man-at-arms as far as muster officials were concerned, and it was
what set him apart as a member of the military class.

As a symbol of that martial caste, the warhorse had never been more
potent than during the early decades of the fourteenth century, for it was
these years which saw the emergence of the true *magnus equus*. Under pressure of a growing burden of armour and equipment for man and horse, 'the
size of the best warhorses [had increased] almost beyond recognition between
the eleventh and the fourteenth centuries'.[75] The most expensive horses were,
indeed, of formidable stature, as is suggested, for example, by the powerfully
built 'great horse' depicted in Uccello's fresco of Sir John Hawkwood in
Florence Cathedral.[76] Yet such destriers were the preserve of the upper echelons of the aristocracy,[77] and we must imagine the horses ridden by the
majority of Edwardian men-at-arms to have been of rather less imposing
stature; perhaps they should best be visualised as heavy hunters.[78] They
needed to be strong certainly, for the weight of a man-at-arms' armour and
equipment reached a peak during the fourteenth century;[79] but strength

[74] 'The tournament in the thirteenth century', *Collected papers of N. Denholm-Young*
(Cardiff, 1969), p. 95.

[75] R.H.C. Davis, *The medieval warhorse* (London, 1989), pp. 21–24, 69. On the early stages
of warhorse evolution, see idem, 'The warhorses of the Normans', *Anglo-Norman
studies X. Proceedings of the Battle Conference, 1987*, ed. R.A. Brown (Woodbridge,
1988), pp. 67–82. The development of the medieval warhorse is a subject which has
excited much debate. For example, dismissing the evidence offered by Davis as unconvincing, Robert Bartlett has argued recently that development of the man-at-arms' mount was
'slight' between the mid eleventh and the late thirteenth centuries: *The making of Europe.
Conquest, colonisation and cultural change, 950–1350* (London, 1993), pp. 62, 329.

[76] Davis, *The medieval warhorse*, plate 40 (page 97). Davis suggests that the 'great horse'
may have reached seventeen or eighteen hands in height (ibid., p. 69); but, as Matthew
Bennett has pointed out to me, the Uccello fresco actually shows a fifteen to sixteen hand
horse. For valuable comment on the size of horses, see Ann Hyland, *Equus. The horse in
the Roman world* (London, 1990), pp. 44, 67, 68–69.

[77] There is a danger of assuming that *all* late medieval warhorses were destriers: e.g. J.M.
Brereton, *The horse in war* (Newton Abbot and London, 1976), pp. 24–25; and P.
Edwards, *The horse trade of Tudor and Stuart England* (Cambridge, 1988), pp. 12–13 –
which is rather like assuming every saloon car to be a Rolls Royce.

[78] In Edward I's reign many of them were decribed as *runcini* in the horse inventories; and
throughout the period, the least expensive were valued at as little as £5.

[79] Davis, *The medieval warhorse*, pp. 22–24. While a complete suit of plate armour in the
fifteenth century would weigh about 50 to 60lb, the combined weight of mail haubergeon,
plastron de fer and other plate defences was greater for a fourteenth-century man-at-arms.
A mail shirt alone might weigh 30lb; a bascinet 6lb: G. Laking, *A record of European*

needed to be combined with mobility. Such are the powerful, yet agile, horses which are depicted in the literature of the fourteenth century; the horses on which King Arthur's knights achieve their sanguinary triumphs, a horse such as Gryngolet, Sir Gawain's inseparable companion.[80] By the middle decades of the century, the best of them were described as *coursers* in the military records, a term which underlines their strength, speed and stamina, all virtues required of a good hunter.[81]

The 'great horse' became the pride of the English aristocracy during the late thirteenth and early fourteenth centuries. R.H.C. Davis has shown that a shortage of suitable horses at a time of growing military commitments in Wales prompted Edward I to embark upon a serious warhorse breeding programme in the royal studs. Although, for reasons of economy, this activity slackened towards the end of Edward I's reign, his son, who had a keen interest in horsebreeding, 'revived the [royal] studs with the utmost vigour'.[82] It would seem that the crown's example was followed on the estates of the nobility and gentry. This can be seen as early as 1277, when following the king's acquisition of over 150 horses from continental sources, similar imporrts were made on behalf of the earl of Lincoln (thirty horses), Roger de Mortimer (twelve), Otes de Grandison (two), William de Beauchamp and others (twelve) and William de Valence (twenty-five).[83] Such men as these provided the heavy cavalry for the king's armies. None would wish to appear at muster with inferior horseflesh and the king was keen that none should do

---

armour and arms through seven centuries, 5 vols (London, 1920–22), ii, p. 179; J. Alexander and P. Binski, eds, *Age of chivalry* (London, 1987), p. 262; M. Vale, *War and chivalry* (London, 1981), pp. 184–85.

80 Gryngolet is 'gret . . . and huge' (line 2047), yet is no ponderous destrier (e.g. lines 2160–63): *Sir Gawain and the Green Knight*, ed. J.R.R. Tolkien and E.V. Gordon, 2nd edn (Oxford, 1967). The martial skills of an Arthurian knight very much depended upon his 'jambe stede', his swift-footed warhorse: see *The alliterative Morte Arthure*, ed. V. Krishna (New York, 1976); the expression is used in line 2894.

81 Some of the horses in the alliterative *Morte Arthure* are described as coursers: e.g. lines 1388, 2115, 2166, 4010. In *A Gest of Robyn Hode*, when Robin and his men re-equip 'a gentyll knyght that is fal in poverte' they provide him with a 'gray coursar' as most befitting the knightly rank (stanza 76): *Rymes of Robyn Hood*, ed. R.B. Dobson and J. Taylor (London, 1976), p. 84. Cf. *Canterbury Tales*, The Knight's Tale, line 2501; and *The Tale of Gamelyn: Middle English metrical romances*, ed. W.H. French and C.B. Hale (New York, 1930), p. 227.

82 Davis, *The medieval warhorse*, p. 87–89; this adds a little to R.H.C. Davis, 'The medieval warhorse', *Horses in European economic history: a preliminary canter* (Reading, 1983), pp. 9–11. On the role of imported Spanish horses, see T. Tolley, 'Eleanor of Castile and the "Spanish style" in England', *England in the thirteenth century*, ed. W.M. Ormrod (Stamford, 1991), pp. 173–75. For Edward II's purchase of Spanish horses, see W. Childs, *Anglo-Castilian trade in the later Middle Ages* (Manchester, 1978), pp. 120–21. Apart from the evidence discussed by Davis and Childs, Edward II's interest in horses is reflected in a document recording the purchase of nine palfreys at Ripon fair in May 1307: C47/3/52, no. 13.

83 *CPR, 1272–81*, pp. 171, 184, 194.

so. In May 1282, with a second campaign in Wales just beginning, writs were issued which ordered those holding land worth £30 or more to 'meet the scarcity of the great horses suitable for war, by procuring such a horse with appropriate horse-armour' and to keep it in readiness for active service.[84]

The extent to which the breeding of 'great horses' was actively pursued on the estates of the English aristocracy during the late thirteenth and early fourteenth centuries requires further research; but, as we shall see, the evidence of the horse inventories suggests a significant improvement in warhorse quality during the reigns of the first two Edwards, reaching a peak at the start of the Hundred Years War. Thus it was that the warhorse in England reached its apogee at the very time that it was being abandoned as a practical tool of warfare. The warhorses which were left in the baggage camp at Buironfosse in October 1339 may have comprised the most impressive collection of horse-flesh ever taken on campaign by the English. Yet the military revolution was soon to have a significant effect on the warhorse in England. By the time of the Reims campaign in 1359-60, the quality of warhorses employed by the English aristocracy had quite perceptibly declined. It seems that men saw less need for expensive warhorses if they were not to be put to vigorous use on the field of battle. The diminished status of the warhorse in the Edwardian fighting machine also had an unsettling effect on the terms of service, the bundle of obligations and benefits which formed the relationship between the king and the men-at-arms who served in his armies. The eventual result was the crown's abandonment of the system of horse appraisal and *restauro equorum*; but this is to anticipate.

---

[84] *Parl. Writs*, i, p. 226, no. 9. A concession allowed those owing service, but who lacked a suitable horse, to pay a fine in lieu. M. Prestwich, *Edward I* (London, 1988), p. 197, places this royal order in the context of developments in military obligation. Cf. the efforts of Philip III in France: V. Chomel, 'Chevaux de bataille et roncins en Dauphiné au XIVe siècle', *Cahiers d'Histoire*, vii (1962), p. 16; R-H.Bautier and A-M. Bautier, 'Contribution à l'histoire du cheval au Moyen Age', *Bulletin Philologique et Historique du Comité des Travaux historiques et scientifiques*, 1978, pp. 60–62.

2

The Warhorse and Aristocratic Society

The mounted, armoured knight is one of the most potent symbols of medieval civilisation, a persistent, ubiquitous image which springs from the folios of illuminated manuscripts and the texts of the chroniclers of chivalry. Man and warhorse formed a unified fighting unit: the horse was far more than simply a means of conveyance. 'There are horses', observed Diaz de Gamez, 'who are so strong, fiery, swift and faithful, that a brave man, mounted on a good horse, may do more in an hour of fighting than ten or mayhap a hundred could have done afoot'.[1] By the late thirteenth century, with both horse and man armoured, 'a fully equipped knight was like a moving castle',[2] the equivalent of the tank in modern warfare: able in the right circumstances to perform a decisive role, but by no means invincible on the field of battle. Indeed, the chinks in the mounted warrior's armour were exposed on a number of occasions in various parts of early fourteenth-century Europe, as infantry armies inflicted humiliating and bloody defeats on heavy cavalry;[3] but only in the case of the English aristocracy did a major battlefield catastrophe herald a complete and permanent re-appraisal of tactical methods. The explanation for this is no doubt to be found in the particular circumstances of campaigning in Scotland and France, combined with the tactical potency of massed archery. Yet it is indeed an arresting fact that after Bannockburn, for the remainder of the Middle Ages, there was scarcely a significant battle in which the English *chivalric* class fought on horseback. The English man-at-arms became renowned throughout Europe for his skill in dismounted combat and long remained so: in 1486 a company of English troops fighting in Granada were observed to be fighting on foot *a uso de sua*

---

[1] *The unconquered knight: a chronicle of the deeds of Don Pero Niño*, trans. and ed. J. Evans (London, 1926), p. 11.

[2] F.M. Powicke, *The thirteenth century, 1216–1307* (Oxford, 1953), p. 549.

[3] J.F. Verbruggen, *The art of warfare in western Europe during the Middle Ages* (Amsterdam, 1977), chapter 3: 'The foot soldiers'; C.J. Rogers, 'The military revolutions of the Hundred Years War', *The Journal of Military History*, lvii (1993), pp. 247–57. For a less well-known example, see C.C. Giurescu, 'Les armées Roumaines dans la lutte pour la défense et l'indépendance du pays, du XIVe au XVIe siècle', *Revue Internationale d'Histoire Militaire*, xxxiv (1975), pp. 6–7, for the defeat of King Charles I's Hungarian army in a defile at Posada (9–11 November 1330), which the author compares with the better known battle of Mortgarten (1315).

tierra. Three years earlier, Dominic Mancini commented that the English used horses simply 'to carry them to the scene of the engagement . . . therefore they will ride any sort of horse, even pack horses'.[4] Other European states, including England's adversaries, certainly experimented with similar tactics. The French had been dismounting their men-at-arms for some years before the battle of Poitiers in an effort to find an effective response to the English tactical system;[5] and the disaster which befell the crusader army at Nicopolis has been attributed to the eagerness of the western European contingents to fight on foot.[6] But this experimentation did not mark the end of heavy cavalry in continental Europe; far from it. With man and warhorse encased in armour and wielding a heavier, firmly supported lance, the mounted man-at-arms retained a place in the fore-front of military affairs until the sixteenth-century.[7]

Despite the practical requirements of the battlefield, the association of knight and warhorse was an enduring one in the minds of Englishmen, within both the aristocracy itself and society at large. It is an association which continually re-asserts itself in the visual and literary arts of the period. Perhaps the most striking representation of an equestrian warrior in a manuscript of late medieval English provenance is that of Sir Geoffrey Luttrell of Irnham, Lincolnshire, in the psalter which he himself commissioned at the end of the 1330s.[8] Although Sir Geoffrey appears to have been no longer militarily active at this time,[9] a scene such as that depicted, with a mounted knight about to leave for war, could easily have been played out with his son, Andrew, in the saddle.[10] Yet this is not a scene taken from life, but rather a

---

4   A. Goodman, *The Wars of the Roses. Military activity and English society, 1452–97* (London, 1981), pp. 175, 195. But Goodman considers that 'the Wars of the Roses probably produced a revival of English cavalry fighting': ibid., p. 179.

5   T.F. Tout, 'Some neglected fights between Crécy and Poitiers'.

6   The Franks 'leaped off their horses, as is their custom, intending to fight as foot-soldiers'; but the Hungarians were 'not yet acquainted with Frankish war strategy': János Thuróczy, *Chronicle of the Hungarians*, ed. F. Mantello and P. Engel (Bloomington, Indiana, 1991), pp. 57–58; see also A. Atiya, *The crusade in the later Middle Ages*, repr. (New York, 1970), pp. 453–55.

7   Vale, *War and chivalry*, pp. 100–28.

8   BL Additional MS 42130, fo. 202b. The best reproduction is the frontispiece of *The Luttrell Psalter*, ed. E.G. Millar (London, 1932). Sir Geoffrey, on horseback, is attended by his wife Agnes (d.1340) and daughter-in-law Beatrice. For recent views on dating, see L. Dennison, ' "The Fitzwarin Psalter and its allies": a reappraisal', *England in the fourteenth century*, ed. W.M. Ormrod (Woodbridge, 1986), pp. 58–59; J. Backhouse, *The Luttrell Psalter* (London, 1989), pp. 48–60.

9   Sir Geoffrey (d.1345) would have been in his early sixties in the later 1330s. His military career, which began in the late 1290s, appears to have ended in the 1320s: see *The Luttrell Psalter*, ed. Millar, pp. 3–4. He is, however, included on the Ashmolean Roll of Arms, dating in all probability from the midwinter of 1334–35 (Oxford, Bodleian Library MS Ashmole 15A), and on Cotgrave's Ordinary, c. 1340: *Rolls of arms of the reigns of Henry III and Edward III*, ed. N.H. Nicolas (London, 1829), p. 31.

10   Andrew Luttrell (d.1390) served in Scotland in 1337 (with warhorses valued at 12 marks

celebration of knightly status, an expression, by a member of the chivalrous class, of his position in society. As such, it is only to be expected that Sir Geoffrey would wish to be presented as a mounted warrior on a brightly caparisoned warhorse; indeed, it is just such an image which his peers, and society at large, would expect to see.

The martial equestrian figures represented on the seals of fourteenth-century noblemen offer a similar view of aristocratic status,[11] as indeed does the portrayal of the day of judgement in *The Holkham Bible Picture Book* (dated c.1325–30), which so strikingly distinguishes the mounted, knightly mêlée of 'le grant pouple' from the foot combat of 'le comoune gent'.[12] It is, moreover, this traditional image of the aristocracy as a mounted warrior class which is offered when the subject of illustration is an apparently realistic representation of military events, whether contemporary or from some time in the past. The combat scenes included in countless illuminated manuscripts almost invariably present the aristocratic warrior fighting in time-honoured fashion. There are, for example, many such tableaux in *The Romance of Alexander*,[13] a beautiful manuscript dating from the early years of the French war (and, therefore, an appropriate counterpart to the portrait of Sir Geoffrey Luttrell). Although the armour depicted is up-to-date,[14] the *Romance* shows no sign of an awareness of the tactical revolution of the mid fourteenth century – perhaps it is a little too early in date (it is not, of course, attempting to portray contemporary events). Yet the tendency of illuminators to show the aristocracy fighting on horseback, rather than on foot, is an enduring one. As Anthony Goodman has noted, in relation to contemporary

and 20 marks: E101/20/17, m. 10d; E101/388/5, m. 19) and then in the opening campaign in the French war (*Treaty Rolls, 1337–39*, no. 371). He is still to be seen in the king's service in 1359: E101/393/11, fos 71r, 83v. In his testimony before the Court of Chivalry in 1387 he claimed in addition to have taken part in the siege of Tournai and the duke of Lancaster's campaign in Caux: *Scrope-Grosvenor*, i, p. 243. See also Backhouse, *The Luttrell Psalter*, pp. 21, 28–36.

11 For example, Fowler, *The king's lieutenant*, plate 4 (duke of Lancaster; DL27/324). By the fourteenth century, the equestrian seal (which hitherto had been widely used) was largely the preserve of such noble houses as the Beauchamps and the Montagus: J.H. Bloom, *English seals* (London, 1906), pp. 139, 144; *Catalogue of seals in the Department of Manuscripts in the British Museum*, ed. W de G. Birch, 6 vols (London, 1887–1900), ii, pp. 235–373.

12 *The Holkham Bible Picture Book*, ed. W.O. Hassall (London, 1954), fo. 40r. Cf. the *Falling Knight*, the famous late-fourteenth-century misericord on the sub-dean's choir stall in Lincoln cathedral, which depicts a man-at-arms, wounded in the back by an arrow and falling from his horse: M.D. Anderson, *The choir stalls of Lincoln Minster* (Lincoln, 1967), fig. 10 and pp. 33, 36–7.

13 *The Romance of Alexander. A collotype facsimile of MS Bodley 264*, ed. M.R. James (Oxford, 1933). As with other collections of military scenes, the *Romance's* many illustrations of mounted mêlées are as reminiscent of the tourney-field as of the traditional aristocratic modes of fighting on the battlefield.

14 B. Thordeman, *Armour from the battle of Visby, 1361*, 2 vols (Stockholm, 1939), i, chapters 5–8.

battle illustrations of the Wars of the Roses, 'the artist has taken considerable licence with his text . . . suggesting that the battles were primarily cavalry engagements'.[15] This distortion may be in evidence in even the most valuable visual representations of battle. The selection of vivid, well-observed scenes from the military events of the early decades of the fifteenth century, presented by the (late fifteenth century) 'pictorial life' of Richard Beauchamp, earl of Warwick, also offers a view of the English man-at-arms as an essentially mounted warrior.[16] The illustrator seems aware that if he is to present the earl and his followers in the best chivalrous light, he must depict the closing stages of battle, at which point the English did, on some occasions, take to their warhorses.

Turning from the visual arts to literature, we find the same persistent emphasis on mounted combat. The alliterative *Morte Arthure*, for example, contains an enormous amount of battle detail; it is, indeed, an almost unremitting orgy of violence. Yet it is striking that, although apparently written in the second half of the fourteenth century,[17] the fighting depicted is entirely in the traditional chivalrous mode: men are described wielding lance and sword *from the saddle*. Despite achieving, in many respects, 'an aura of contemporaneity quite unique in fourteenth-century English romance',[18] there is no sign of the tactical methods which the English were employing in their military adventures all over Europe at this time. Archers are mentioned occasionally,[19] but their role is not associated with that of the knightly class and the latter are never shown to be fighting on foot. King Arthur's men, like their real counterparts, often find themselves facing long odds,[20] but unlike the English in France, their immediate response is to spur their warhorses forward in a headlong charge; they 'come flyeande before one ferawnte stedes' (line 2451). In fact the writer is presenting not an accurate portrayal of the conditions of war, but a projection of the methods of the tournament (i.e., the mêlée, in which the traditional forms of mounted combat were still employed) onto a

---

[15] Goodman, *The Wars of the Roses*, p. 179.

[16] *Pageant of the birth, life and death of Richard Beauchamp, earl of Warwick, K.G., 1389–1439*, ed. Viscount Dillon and W.H. St John Hope (London, 1914), plates 6, 7, 40 and 48. The artist appears to be well-informed about military affairs (e.g. armour, the role of archers).

[17] K.H. Göller, 'A summary of research', *The alliterative Morte Arthure: a reassessment of the poem*, ed. K.H. Göller (Cambridge, 1981), pp. 11–14. Elizabeth Porter argues for a late-fourteenth-century date: 'Chaucer's Knight, the alliterative *Morte Arthure*, and the medieval laws of war: a reconsideration', *Nottingham Medieval Studies*, xxvii (1983), pp. 56–78.

[18] Including 'the most mundane aspects of military organisation': J. Barnie, *War in medieval society. Social values and the Hundred Years War* (London, 1974), pp. 148–49.

[19] For example, *The alliterative Morte Arthure*, ed. V. Krishna (New York, 1976), lines 2095–2105.

[20] As in the final battle against Mordred, in which Arthur's knights ('Bot awghtene hundrethe of all, entrede in rolles') faced an army of 60,000 foreign mercenaries.

broader canvas. This is mortal combat certainly.[21] Yet, as the writer observes on one occasion, 'was never siche a justyng at journe in erthe' (line 2875); and when he comments on the *unfayre* strike which causes Sir Kayous to be mortally wounded (line 2171), he is surely revealing that his portrayal of warfare is based upon the *mores* of the tournament field, rather than the reality of the battlefield.[22]

It could, of course, be argued that the author of the alliterative *Morte Arthure* was writing romance not contemporary history and should not, therefore, be expected to reflect the most up-to-date modes of fighting. Yet turning to the *historical* writing of this period, we very often find a similar high regard for the exploits of the mounted warrior. For example, Froissart and Chandos Herald, whilst aware of prevailing tactical developments, delight in drawing attention to feats of arms of a traditional kind. Their descriptions of Sir William Felton's exploits during a skirmish before the battle of Nájera provide a good example of this. A small Anglo-Gascon force, confronted by a much larger body of Castilians, takes up a defensive position on a 'petit montaigne'. But Felton, in true Arthurian fashion, charges 'come home sanz sens & sanz avis, a chivall la lance baissie'. In terms very reminiscent of the tone of the alliterative *Morte Arthure*, he engages the enemy with great gusto; but 'son chival ont desoubz li mort' and he is finally killed.[23] The earl of Warwick's chivalrous escapade soon after the English landing in Normandy in 1346 was particularly notable because 'il monta sur ung povre et meschant cheval'. Undaunted, Warwick and a small group of followers charged into the *presse*, shouting 'Saint Jorge au bon roy d'Engleterre'.[24] It is a contrast, indeed, to turn to the family memoirs of a veteran soldier of the northern border country. Sir Thomas Gray's imagery may be less colourful than the chroniclers of chivalry, yet in his writing we see a more realistic portrayal of the relationship between a man-at-arms and his warhorse, with the latter being employed as a practical tool of warfare. On one occasion, Gray's father, finding himself stranded in the town of Cupar some distance from the safety of the castle, managed to force his way through a crowd who were barring his way by using his spurred horse as a battering ram.[25] Here, indeed, is Sir Maurice Powicke's 'moving castle' in action! If for Sir William Felton his warhorse was a means of achieving glory, for Sir Thomas Gray it was a means of escaping from a tight corner.

---

[21] It is reminiscent of Chaucer's vivid description of a tournament in *Canterbury Tales*, 'The Knight's Tale', lines 2605–19.

[22] Cf. A. Goodman's comments on Sir Thomas Malory's version of the Arthurian romances: *The Wars of the Roses*, p. 180.

[23] *Life of the Black Prince by the herald of Sir John Chandos*, ed. M.K. Pope and E.C. Lodge (Oxford, 1910), pp. 84–85; cf. *Froissart*, ed. Johnes, i, p. 366.

[24] Chronique de Valenciennes: *Froissart*, Lettenhove, iv, p. 486; cf. the version in the *Acta Bellicosa* of 1346: *Life and campaigns of the Black Prince*, ed. Barber, p. 28.

[25] *Scalacronica*, pp. 49–50. Sir Thomas Gray *senior*'s career, as related by his son, was punctuated by a series of hair-raising escapades: e.g. ibid., pp. 18, 24–26.

'Artistic and literary evidence', Anthony Goodman has observed, 'provide uncertain guides to the realities of the contemporary battlefield'.[26] What they do offer are insights into the complex of assumptions and attitudes which occupied the minds of artists, patrons and the wider receiving public. For the Englishman of the mid-late fourteenth century, the association of knight and warhorse was as strong as it had ever been. The tactical changes which helped to bring unparalleled successes and prestige to English arms on the continent do not appear to have shaken this association. To illustrate the point, let us consider one further piece of artistic evidence. In his description of the Knight's appearance in the General Prologue of *The Canterbury Tales*, Geoffrey Chaucer tells us nothing of his horses, except that they were *goode*.[27] But the early fifteenth-century illustrator of the Ellesmere manuscript of the *Tales* knew exactly what kind of horse would be appropriate for the Knight – and indeed for his son, the Squire. The horses portrayed are not those which would actually be used for travelling – these would be palfreys – but they are the types of horse which society would immediately associate with members of the aristocracy. The Ellesmere artist has therefore provided a most telling visual dimension to Chaucer's literary tapestry of late fourteenth-century English society.[28] Both the Knight and the Squire are shown astride large and powerful horses. The Knight's is particularly heavily built and is presumably intended to be a destrier. The artist has added a neat touch: a brand mark (a letter 'M') on the horse's flank underlines the military association and may perhaps reflect the Knight's service with the Teutonic knights.[29] Whilst his father is shown on a rather old-fashioned horse, as would be appropriate for a veteran who began his career in arms in the first half of the century, the Squire's horse is of lighter build and is depicted 'executing the high-school air known as *curvet* or *courbette*'.[30] This may well be intended to reflect Chaucer's words about the Squire's equestrian skill ('wel koude he sitte on hors and faire ryde');[31] but equally, the artist may have wished to depict a courser, a lighter, more agile form of warhorse, which had become popular with the well-to-do members of the aristocracy.

[26] Goodman, *The Wars of the Roses*, p. 180.

[27] *Canterbury Tales*, General Prologue, line 74.

[28] For reproductions of the Ellesmere manuscript illustrations, see A.A. Dent, 'Chaucer and the horse', *Proceedings of the Leeds Philosophical and Literary Society*, ix (1959–62), figs 1–13.

[29] Dent, 'Chaucer and the horse', p. 9; cf. T. Jones, *Chaucer's knight* (London, 1982), pp. 29–30. Jones' argument that the brand might be intended to suggest service in a mercenary company in Italy has little to commend it: one of the weaknesses in his controversial view of the Knight is the fact that the latter is *not* said to have served in Italy.

[30] Dent, 'Chaucer and the horse', p. 9.

[31] *Canterbury Tales*, General Prologue, line 94. In his tale, the Squire shows himself to be well versed in equestrian matters.

For the Ellesmere artist, then, a large and expensive warhorse was still very much the mark of a member of the knightly class. This is hardly surprising, for he would have been surrounded by powerful imagery which could only serve to reinforce the established view of the warrior class as a mounted élite. Despite the developments in military practice which, as we shall see later, appear to have had a depressive effect on the quality of warhorses employed on campaign, expensive and highly distinctive horses continued to occupy a prominent place in the lives of the nobility and gentry.

Horsemanship was an essential accomplishment for an active member of the knightly class, for the simple reason that a great deal of his life was spent in the saddle. Some men began their military careers at an early age,[32] yet for most, an association with horses which they had forged as boys would find many outlets before they were called upon to join a *chevauchée*; and for many, horsemanship remained a largely peacetime activity throughout their lives. A member of the aristocracy was distinguished not simply by the possession of good horses, but also by the way that he handled them.[33] He should combine a courtly demeanour with practical proficiency; and he should take an active interest in the welfare and management of his horses. In these respects, the *Gawain* poet offers his hero's relationship with his faithful companion, Gryngolet, as a model of true knightly behaviour.[34] Similarly, the eulogy of Don Pero Niño stresses that 'he knew all about horses; he sought for them, tended them and made much of them'.[35] It is certain that many of his English counterparts behaved similarly, for there is evidence enough to demonstrate the activities of a community of equestrian connoisseurs amongst the nobility and gentry. In 1332–33, for example, Sir Ralph de Neville made gifts of three and four year-old horses from his studs at Raby, Middleham and Ulgham to members of the lay and ecclesiastical aristocracies.[36] Horse traffic of this kind, whether involving gifts, loans, exchanges

---

[32] N. Orme, *From childhood to chivalry. The education of the English kings and aristocracy, 1066–1530* (London, 1984), pp. 190–91, citing evidence from the records of the armorial disputes in the Court of Chivalry in the 1380s. Many of the deponents revealed that they first bore arms in their mid-teens.

[33] On the enduring importance of horsemanship for the aristocracy, see J. Thirsk, *Horses in early modern England: for service, for pleasure, for power*, Stenton lecture, University of Reading, 1977 (Reading, 1978), especially pp. 6–7, 16–23; and A. Dent, *Horses in Shakespeare's England* (London, 1987), chapter 8.

[34] *Sir Gawain and the Green Knight*, ed. J.R.R. Tolkien and E.V. Gordon, 2nd edn (Oxford, 1967), e.g. lines 670–73, 2047–53, 2062–63. By contrast, the *parvenu* mercenary Crokart, of whom Froissart heartily disapproved, was killed in a riding accident as a consequence of failing to detect that his horse had been badly shod: *Society at war*, ed. C.T. Allmand (Edinburgh, 1973), p. 89.

[35] *The unconquered knight*, ed. Evans, p. 41.

[36] E101/507/14. Recipients included Sir Ranulph Fitzralph, Sir Alexander de Neville, Sir John le Sturmy and the Priory of Warter. Five mares were given to the bishop of Winchester and three to Sir William de Montagu. In July 1335 the king gave Montagu a warhorse

or purchases, was one of the major pre-occupations of the landholding class. Some of the horses would be destined for use on campaign, but we must also recognise the demands of the more mundane, and the purely recreational, aspects of aristocratic life.

The peripatetic life-style of the medieval landed classes ensured that they would spend a significant proportion of their time on horseback[37] and their principal outdoor recreation, their passion for hunting, contributed to the same end. David Crouch has reminded us recently that 'the image of the hunter is also the image of the aristocracy' and this no where better illustrated than on the obverse of Earl Simon de Montfort's great seal which shows 'the eminent soldier-earl riding through a wood blowing a horn, in hunting garb, a dog running at his horse's side'.[38] The chase was certainly a most appropriate pastime for the military class when not engaged in war. An exhilarating, aggressive pursuit and not without risk (especially when hunting boar), it tested endurance, horsemanship and one's eye for the lie of the land. It might also serve to forge bonds of comradeship which could be carried over into the testing arenas of war and politics.[39] But if hunting possessed undoubted military overtones, it was on the tournament field that the aristocracy could most effectively express its traditional martial role, short of actually going on campaign.

For many young men during the fourteenth century, the rigours of the tournament provided the first test of their martial prowess.[40] For older hands, experienced in war, it offered opportunities for the display of traditional mounted combat skills which from the mid fourteenth century were only infrequently employed on campaign. During the reign of Edward III such opportunities were very plentiful.[41] Detailed lists of participants, such as the Second Dunstable Roll of Arms,[42] are rare, but it is nevertheless clear that tournaments were popular and well attended.[43] 'Tourneying society' was,

---

caparisoned with his arms: *Knighton*, i, p. 472. For gifts of horses of all kinds by the prince of Wales in the 1350s, see *BPReg*, iv, pp. 67–73.

[37] For the travels of some members of the east Sussex gentry, see N. Saul, *Scenes from provincial life* (Oxford, 1986), pp. 174–76.

[38] D. Crouch, *The image of aristocracy in Britain, 1000–1300* (London, 1992), p. 305.

[39] Saul, *Scenes from provincial life*, pp. 187–92; Orme, *From childhood to chivalry*, pp. 191–98; *Sir Gawain and the Green Knight*, ed. Tolkien and Gordon, lines 1126–1923.

[40] Some of the deponents before the Court of Chivalry in the 1380s speak of the tournaments of their youth: e.g. John Garlek, who mentions an event at Thetford sixty years earlier (C47/6/1, no. 19).

[41] For a 'Provisional list of the tournaments of Edward III, 1327–55', see J. Vale, *Edward III and chivalry* (Woodbridge, 1982), appendix 12: fifty-five are listed.

[42] 'Roll of arms of the knights at the tournament at Dunstable, in 7 Edward III', *Collectanea, Topographica et Genealogica*, iv (1837), pp. 389–95; and see J. Barker, *The tournament in England, 1100–1400* (Woodbridge, 1986), p. 131 n. 75.

[43] There were about 250 knights at the Dunstable tournament of 1342 (*Murimuth*, pp. 123–24; *Le Baker*, p. 75). Indirect evidence for the identities of active tourneyers is to be found in inventories of goods and chattels. For example, an inventory of John, Lord

however, a closed community: although during the fourteenth century it came to include large numbers of esquires,[44] it did not by any means embrace the whole of the active military community. The tournament remained the violent and prestigious pastime of the traditional military class, and whether involving an old-fashioned *mêlée*-style combat between teams or, as was increasingly popular, jousting competitions between individuals wielding lances, the display offered could only serve to re-affirm society's vision of the knight as an élite mounted warrior.

As a contest between mounted men-at-arms, the tournament in its various forms bore little resemblance to the 'English' method of fighting which, from the mid fourteenth century, was employed in countless battles and skirmishes throughout Europe. This is not to deny the undoubted links between warfare and tourneying for the English. In the first place, the men who served in the king's armies were also the men who attended tournaments in England: 'military preoccupations and hastiluding went hand in hand'.[45] Some of them were bound to engage in both activities by the terms of indentures of retinue,[46] but it is clear that most, in any case, regarded warfare and tourneying as complementary aspects of a career in arms. Many of the deponents before the Court of Chivalry offered testimony which consisted of a mixture of tournament and campaign memories. A good example is William de Penbrigg esquire, who attended the *tourneamentz de Dunstable* and *certeins Joustes de Lonndres* and also served at Sluys, the siege of Calais and during the Reims campaign.[47] Keen tourneyers would find opportunities for combats *à outrance* during the course, or at the end, of expeditions in Scotland, France and elsewhere.[48] Such contests, whether arising from careful planning or chance encounters, were usually fought in traditional fashion, on horseback with lance; and fuelled by the bitterness of 'national' conflicts, they frequently resulted in fatalities. The contest, during the Crécy campaign, when Sir

Fitzwalter's goods, compiled in 1351, contains armour and saddles for tournaments and jousting, whilst that listing Sir Robert Marny's possessions includes receptacles 'plein de diverses choses pur justes': E199/10/16, m. 9; E199/10/18, mm. 1, 3. Cf. Sir Fulk de Pembridge's will, 1325: BL Stowe Charter 622.

44 Barker, *The tournament in England*, pp. 116–17. Many of the Court of Chivalry deponents who mentioned attendance at tournaments remained esquires throughout their lives: e.g. C47/6/1, nos. 7, 14, 19, 92. For Thomas Bezoun's tournament attendance in 1348, see G.H. Fowler, 'A household expense roll, 1328', *EHR*, lv (1940), pp. 630–34; the roll has been re-dated to 1348 by C.M. Woolgar.

45 Barker, *The tournament in England*, pp. 125–29.

46 Ibid., pp. 27–29; 120–23. Cf. Vale, *War and chivalry*, p. 67.

47 C47/6/1, no. 7; cf. the similarly mixed career of Sir Ralph de Ferrers, speaking on behalf of the Scropes: *Scrope-Grosvenor*, i, pp. 155–56.

48 Barker, *The tournament in England*, chapter 2; *Fernao Lopes: The English in Portugal*, ed. Lomax and Oakley, pp. 248–49, 276–79, for reports of jousts and dismounted single combat in Castile in 1387.

Thomas Colville killed a French knight who had insulted Edward III is good example.[49]

For the English, it was the tournament which was largely instrumental in keeping alive the traditional methods of chivalrous combat. On campaign, a bout of tourneying offered opportunities for the demonstration of individual prowess at a time when battle tactics required disciplined formation-fighting on foot, with the warhorse being used only for transport or the pursuit of a beaten enemy. Back in England, tourneying served to reinforce the established image of a mounted warrior aristocracy. Hastiludes, particularly the urban events, were well-attended spectator sports. The most lavish of them were great theatrical spectaculars, involving processions of masked riders through streets packed with onlookers.[50] The clamour of the crowds can be well imagined from Chaucer's vivid picture of a tournament in the *Knight's Tale* and the crowds will have included all sections of society. In 1386, John Durant, parson of Thelnetham, remembered how he had attended jousts at Bungay and Bury St Edmunds back in the 1340s.[51] Such colourful events can only have had a most potent effect on the popular imagination. For artists – illuminators and writers – it offered the most readily available experience of warlike activity[52] and we should not be surprised to detect, as we have earlier, a marked similarity between warfare as depicted in illuminated manuscripts and by romance writers, and the combat conditions and codes of conduct of the tournament field.

For the many participants who knew both the tourney field and the battle-field, the reality of the contrast between war and hastiludes was clear enough. If in the past there had been a close relationship between the *mêlée*-tournament and the conditions of cavalry warfare, with mounted knights fighting in closely-formed tactical units (*conrois*) on both the tourney field and the battlefield,[53] by the mid fourteenth century such an association was far less relevant to English military needs.[54] The disappearance of the *mêlée*-style tournament in the 1340s – during, it should be noted, a most active period of tourneying in England – has been explained in terms of the increas-

---

[49] Barker, *The tournament in England*, pp. 30–31; cf. *Anonimalle*, p. 22.

[50] There is a discernible 'gradual relocation of the sport' to towns: Barker, *The tournament in England*, p. 99.

[51] C47/6/1, no. 15.

[52] Even though domestic tourneying tended to be *à plaisance*, it was nevertheless a violent sport and casualties were commonplace: e.g. the hastiludes at Northampton in 1342, where 'multi nobiles fuerunt graviter laesi et aliqui mutilati, et perditi multi equi, et dominus J. de Bello monte occisis' (*Murimuth*, p. 124). The violence of the tournament field is conveyed by the excellent illustrations in R. Barber and J. Barker, *Tournaments* (Woodbridge, 1989).

[53] Barker, *The tournament in England*, pp. 19–22, 139–45; Verbruggen, *The art of warfare in western Europe during the Middle Ages*, pp. 32–39.

[54] Cf. J. Vale, who considers that 'the tournoi still provided essential training and experience of fighting': *Edward III and chivalry*, p. 59.

ing popularity of the 'smaller types of hastilude', which favoured the display of individual prowess.[55] But it must also, in part, have been prompted by the transformation in English tactical thinking which had occurred during the preceding years. Increasingly, in war and tourneying, we see two separate, but complementary, aspects of the military aristocracy's life. It is true that the later fourteenth century saw the emergence of the 'feat of arms', which usually included a significant element of dismounted combat,[56] was normally fought *à outrance* and which, therefore, 'reflected the changing expectations of the knight's role in warfare'. Yet it is equally clear that during the second half of the century, jousting became the most popular form of tourneying, particularly in a peacetime context; and that jousting and war had become very different forms of activity.[57] On one level, it was a question of different equipment. A greater weight of armour was used for the joust and this, combined with the specialised training demanded by the sport, prompted men to keep separate horses for jousting and for war.[58] But on a more profound level, these two activities involved different conditions of combat and codes of conduct, and altogether different attitudes of mind. The joust was a carefully regulated test of individual prowess and, with the exception of contests *à outrance*, killing was not the aim of the exercise. War was wholly unpredictable. A man's prowess could be neutralised by unfavourable terrain, the work of projectile weapons or the crush of a *mêlée*; and to survive he must be prepared to kill, though he would always be on the look out for rich pickings, which included warhorses as well as men.[59] 'The sport was quite distinct from real warfare';[60] this had always been the case, but in the English context, from the mid fourteenth century, the distance between jousting, even *à outrance*, and the customary English tactics of the battlefield, meant that a contrast in methods underlined the contrast in mentality.[61]

   Despite its distance from the reality of war, jousting acquired a popularity with both participants and spectators which ensured that the traditional form

---

[55] Barker, *The tournament in England*, p. 140. The Dunstable tournament of 1342, a large scale *mêlée*-style event, is 'the last recorded occasion of its kind in England'. On the survival of the *mêlée*-style tournament throughout the Middle Ages in continental Europe, see Vale, *War and chivalry*, pp. 63–87.

[56] Barker, *The tournament in England*, pp. 14–15, 23, 40, 156–58.

[57] Ibid., pp. 22–3, 145–48.

[58] Ibid., chapter 8 (on tournament armour); pp. 173–74 (on jousting horses). R. Barber and J. Barker, *Tournaments*, chapter 7.

[59] At the fight before the castle of *Albone* in August 1374, 'la somme des bones chivals nomes ionets Despaigne et autres chivals conquys amounent a ccviii': *Anonimalle*, pp. 76–77. The winning of warhorses was one of the primary aims of the old-style *mêlée* tournaments – *Murimuth* (p. 124) says of the Dunstable tournament of 1342 that 'x equi fuerunt perditi vel lucrati' (cf. Vale, *War and chivalry*, p. 70) – but this was not the case with jousting.

[60] Barker, *The tournament in England*, p. 42.

[61] Cf. Vale, *War and chivalry*, pp. 70ff, which argues for the continuing relevance of the tournament to continental warfare in the fifteenth century.

of mounted combat with lance maintained a prominent place in the training of the military class and an enduring hold on the imagination of society at large. In considering how the tournament helped to re-affirm the long-established association between the knightly class and the warhorse, we should not underestimate the ceremonial aspects of these colourful events. Tournament processions were an impressive and not infrequent sight in the main tourneying centres. The route from the Tower to the tournament site at Smithfield was used so regularly that it became known as *Knightriders Street*.[62] Ceremonial of this kind was an entertainment, but also a forceful demonstration of the reality of the social order. The 'great horse' which had originally been bred for the battlefield and which reached its peak of development in the mid fourteenth century could play a most effective role in such events. The warhorse, whose direct military function had diminished a good deal, continued nevertheless to stand as a potent symbol of the power and wealth of the aristocracy. In the stables of all wealthy members of the chivalrous class would be found not only horses for war, for hunting and for travelling, but also larger, heavier steeds needed for jousting and ceremonial activity.[63] It is no surprise to find that the greatest ceremonial warhorses graced the stables of the king: the great steed ridden by Richard II at his coronation cost £200.[64]

Colourful ceremonial processions associated with coronations, military triumphs and urban tournaments were events which many in England would never witness; yet most of the population would occasionally be exposed to displays with a similar message, though staged on a smaller scale. Perhaps the most arresting formal occasion in which the warhorse could play a central part in the re-affirmation of the knight's place in the social order was the funeral ceremony, an event in which the local context and the solemnity of the occasion would add greatly to the effectiveness of the symbolism. What function could the warhorse perform in such events? In one very striking way the warrior class in England failed to exploit the symbolic power of the warhorse at the point of their departure from this world. By contrast with, for example, late medieval Italy, which is noted for its equestrian statues[65] and *bas* reliefs,[66] the warhorse rarely figures in the sepulchral monuments of the aristocracy in medieval England. The inclusion of a horse's head on the

---

[62] Barker, *The tournament in England*, p. 99.

[63] Cf. Don Pero Niño, who trained his horses 'some for war, some for parade and others for jousting': *The unconquered knight*, ed. Evans, p. 41.

[64] M. McKisack, *The fourteenth century, 1307–1399* (Oxford, 1959), p. 239 n. 3.

[65] A splendid fourteenth-century example is the funeral monument of Cangrande I della Scala, lord of Verona: E. Arslan, 'La statua equestre di Cangrande', *Studie in onore di F.M. Mistrorigo*, ed. A. Dani (Vicenza, 1958); H.W. Janson, 'The equestrian monument from Cangrande della Scala to Peter the Great', *Aspects of the Renaissance: a symposium*, ed. A.R. Lewis (Austin and London, 1967), pp. 73–85.

[66] For example, the tombstone of the Beccadelli (1341) at Imola, of which there is an illustration in J. Larner, *The lords of Romagna* (London, 1965), frontispiece.

semi-effigal slab of a man-at-arms at Gilling-in-Ryedale (Yorkshire) is highly unusual.[67] If not incorporated in monuments, warhorses *were* frequently bequeathed, together with military equipment and heraldic achievements, as mortuary gifts – a gesture from which the Church benefitted financially, but which also marked its recognition of the continuing martial function of the aristocracy.[68] In the will made shortly before his death in 1345, Sir Geoffrey de Luttrell directed that 'for a mortuary I leave my best horse with the trappings of war as befits'.[69] We might reasonably imagine a caparisoned great warhorse very like that depicted in *The Luttrell Psalter*.

The horse intended as a mortuary gift would play a prominent part in the funeral ceremony. In 1308 Henry, Lord Grey, asked that the 'graunt piolé destrer', which he was giving to the burial church at Aylesford, Kent, should precede his body in the procession.[70] In 1347 John de Warenne, earl of Surrey, had more ambitious plans, for his corpse was to be preceded by four 'grauntz chivaux', caparisoned in his arms. Two of them, barded for war, were to be mortuary gifts for the church of his burial, St Pancras, Lewes.[71] If anything, it is possible to perceive an increase in the ceremonial role of the warhorse at the very time that its military role was diminishing: as Malcolm Vale has observed, 'the procession of chargers ridden by men dressed in the arms of the dead man became a striking part of the funeral ceremony in the second half of the fourteenth century'.[72] Few, perhaps, would match the grandeur of Arcite's funeral procession as depicted by Chaucer in the *Knight's Tale*;[73] but with an occasion such as Sir Brian Stapleton's funeral in the 1390s, which was

---

[67] The slab is illustrated in H. Lawrence, *Heraldry from military monuments before 1350 in England and Wales*, Harleian Soc., xcviii (1946), plate opposite p. 3.

[68] 'La monture était probablement revendue au profit du bénéficiaire mais l'équipment restait exposé dans l'église, près du mausoleé du défunt': C. Gaier, *L'industrie et le commerce des armes dans les anciennes principautés belges du XIIIe siècle à la fin du XVe siècle* (Paris, 1973), p. 73. Cf. Vale, *War and chivalry*, p. 88.

[69] For the will, see *The Luttrell Psalter*, ed. Millar, appendix I, pp. 52–56. For similar mortuary gifts, see J.T. Rosenthal, *The purchase of paradise* (London, 1972), pp. 86, 91, 92, 94.

[70] *Report of the MSS of Lord Middleton of Wollaton Hall, Nottinghamshire*. Historical Manuscripts Commission, lxix (London, 1911), p. 85.

[71] Vale, *War and chivalry*, p. 89. Eight horses ridden by armoured men were involved in Sir Ralph de Neville's funeral in Durham cathedral in 1355 (Barker, *The tournament in England*, p. 174). This kind of display was not to everyone's taste. Henry of Grosmont, first duke of Lancaster, wanted 'nothing vain nor extravagant, such as armed men, covered horses, nor other vain things' at his funeral (Vale, *War and chivalry*, p. 88). Cf. M. Vale, *Piety, charity and literacy among the Yorkshire gentry, 1370–1480*. Borthwick Papers, I (University of York, 1976), pp. 12–14.

[72] Vale, *War and chivalry*, pp. 89–90. For a different view, see J. Catto, 'Religion and the English nobility in the later fourteenth century', *History and imagination. Essays in honour of H.R. Trevor-Roper*, ed. H. Lloyd-Jones, V. Pearl and B. Worden (London, 1981), pp. 50–51.

[73] *Canterbury Tales*, Knight's Tale, lines 2871–904.

to include a man 'de bone entaile' wearing the deceased Garter knight's arms and helm, and riding a good horse,[74] we see a decidedly theatrical event, redolent of the traditional symbolism of a warrior aristocracy.

THE ENGLISH WARHORSE IN THE FOURTEENTH CENTURY: THE SOURCES

To confine oneself to the records generated by the owners and breeders of warhorses in late medieval England necessitates acceptance of documentary coverage which is both patchy and unsystematic. The one great exception to this picture of archival paucity concerns the king's studs and great horses, which are greatly illuminated by a series of detailed accounts.[75] For the English nobility and gentry, evidence is more fragmentary: occasional stud and equestrian expenses accounts,[76] and a miscellany of other references, to be found in such records as the Registers of Edward, prince of Wales and John, duke of Lancaster, in household and estate accounts,[77] and in a scatter of wills.[78] A certain amount of information can also be quarried from the

---

[74] The other participants in the event included a 'gathering of Stapleton's tenants and servants, dressed in gowns of blue cloth': Vale, *Piety, charity and literacy*, p. 12.

[75] The *Equitium Regis* accounts form a section of Exchequer Accounts, Various (E101). They have been examined most recently by R.H.C. Davis in *The medieval warhorse*, pp. 86–97. For a discussion of the king's horses during the first decade of Edward III's reign, see N. Neilson, 'The king's hunting and his great horses', *The English government at work, 1327–1336*, ed. J.F. Willard and W.A. Morris (Cambridge, Mass., 1940), i, pp. 435–44. For the officials in charge of the king's horses, see M.M. Reese, *The royal office of Master of the Horse* (London, 1976), chapters 4 and 5.

[76] For a stud account (Neville family), see E101/507/14. For an expenses account of the earl of Hereford's horses, July 1304, see E101/12/23. On the earl of Arundel's studs, see C. Given-Wilson, 'Wealth and credit, public and private: the earls of Arundel, 1306–1397', *EHR*, cvi (1991), p. 18 and n. 7.

[77] For the marshalsea costs of the earl of Cornwall's destriers in 1297, see *Ministers' accounts of the earldom of Cornwall, 1296–1297*, ed. L.M. Midgley, 2 vols, Camden Soc., 3rd ser., lxvi and lxviii (1942, 1945), i, pp. 63–64. Cf. Sir Hugh Luttrell of Dunster's stabling expenses: Sir H.C. Maxwell-Lyte, *A history of Dunster*, 2 vols (London, 1909), i, 97–99. For a discussion of the costs of keeping horses in aristocratic households, which amounted to about 10% of annual expenditure, see C. Dyer, *Standards of living in the later Middle Ages* (Cambridge, 1989), pp. 70–72. For examples of stable or marshalsea accounts, see *Household accounts from medieval England, part 1: introduction, glossary and diet accounts*, ed. C.M. Woolgar, Records of Social and Economic History, new ser., xvii (Oxford, 1992), p. 35 and n. 129–31.

[78] The evidence is usually imprecise. In 1379 Sir Roger de Beauchamp bequeathed to his grandson and heir 'deux de mez meillourz Chyvaux except mon principall Chivall' which was left to his wife: 'The Bedfordshire wills and administrations proved at Lambeth Palace and in the Archdeaconry of Huntingdon', ed. F.A. Page-Turner, *Bedfordshire Historical Record Soc.*, ii (1914), p. 8. Considerably more illuminating is Henry, Lord Grey's will of 1308 in which, apart from his mortuary gift, the testator bequeathed 'mon neir destrer, un bon rouncyn de vint mars ou de dis livres, le sor rouncyn de Estaumford, le ferraunt destrer de Fraunce, le ferraunt rouncyn ky est apele Dycoun' and 'le bay rouncyn de Estaumford': *Report of the MSS of Lord Middleton of Wollaton Hall,*

standard series of royal administrative records, in which can be found references to equestrian gifts,[79] thefts,[80] and forfeitures.[81]

Documentary materials of such varied provenance cannot provide reliable evidence for a systematic study of the late medieval English warhorse. Although the total haul seems substantial, the information is insufficiently consistent to allow a clear impression to emerge of developments over time. Much of the evidence is not about warhorses at all, but concerns horses needed for activities far removed from the noise of battle: palfreys for riding and cart-horses for haulage, for example. Frequently, indeed, the records fail to distinguish warhorses from those kept for non-military work. The inventory of Sir Edmund Appleby's property, drawn-up in 1374, lists, among a number of horses, his own grey worth 100s,[82] which might be a cheap warhorse, but – given Appleby's age – is probably a palfrey. Household accounts are usually no more specific in their references to 'the lord's horses'.[83] The greatest barrier to analysis, however, is not the ambiguity of terminology employed, but the lack of a consistent measure of horse quality. Warhorses are often referred to, and even described, but they are far less frequently

Nottinghamshire. Historical Manuscripts Commission, lxix (London, 1911), pp. 84–86. But even a detailed will, such as Grey's, offers only selective glimpses of a nobleman's stables; and the majority of the horses itemised are not valued.

[79] For presentations of horses to the crown, see the *Dona* section of royal household accounts, which record small royal gifts to servants bringing the horses to the king. The donors were quite often foreigners: for example, in 1359 John de Gistell, *scutifer* of Sir Wulfard de Gistell, presented a courser to Edward III (E101/393/11, fo. 71r); cf. gifts by Germans in the mid 1330s: BL Additional MS 46350, fos 6r, 7r. French and German knights made similar gifts to Henry of Bolingbroke during his stay in Prussia in the 1390s: *Expeditions to Prussia and the Holy Land made by Henry, earl of Derby in 1390–91 and 1392–93*, ed. L.T. Smith, Camden Soc., new ser., lii (1894), p. 105.

[80] For example, the theft of forty horses from the Yorkshire estates of John de Mowbray in 1342: *CPR, 1340–43*, p. 590; for numerous thefts of valued horses, see *The 1341 royal inquest in Lincolnshire*, ed. B.W. McLane, Lincoln Record Soc., lxxviii (1988).

[81] Thirty-four destriers, coursers and other horses, which had belonged to Sir Andrew de Harcla prior to his fall, were in the custody of Sir Anthony de Lucy from the end of February to early July 1323 (BL Stowe MS 553, fo. 32v; cf. E101/16/9). The livestock forfeited by some who had been on the losing side at the battle of Shrewsbury is discussed in Morgan, *War and society in medieval Cheshire*, pp. 82–83; Sir Hugh Browe, for example, forfeited thirty-nine horses.

[82] There are also three horses worth in all £5 and five cart-horses with a combined value of 10 marks. The inventory is printed, with a translation, in G.G. Astill, 'An early inventory of a Leicestershire knight', *Midland History*, ii (1973–4), pp. 274–83. There are few inventories of this kind for the fourteenth century and they do not always include details about horses.

[83] For example, see 'The earliest roll of household accounts in the muniment room at Hunstanton for the 2nd year of Edward III [1328]', ed. G.H. Holley, *Norfolk Archaeology*, xxi (1923), pp. 77–96, which refers simply to the 'horses' of the lord and his visitors. It does, however, distinguish stotts. Cf. a diet account for the earl of March's journey to Scotland in 1378, which distinguishes 'hakeneis': *Household accounts from medieval England, part 1*, ed. Woolgar, pp. 245–58.

valued. Many of the estimates of horse value which we do have come not from objective assessors, but from the horse-owners themselves in circumstances in which they might be expected to furnish inflated valuations. In 1331, for example, John de Aspale was allowed 100 marks, which he claimed represented the value of two horses confiscated as a result of his connection with Edmund, earl of Kent.[84] A few years earlier Isabel de Vernoun sought recovery of, amongst other things, a £20 courser, a 12 mark rouncy and a 4 mark sumpter, which had been taken into the king's hands at Carlisle castle at the time of Sir Andrew de Harcla's fall.[85] From the plea roll for Edward I's army in Scotland in 1296 we hear of a barded horse, value 8 marks, which was lost when it ran away from its groom; and a destrier, worth £50, which was roughly handled by horse-thieves.[86] Prices data of such unreliable origin is obviously unsatisfactory; the problem with more 'conventional' prices data, the records of actual sales of warhorses, is that there is not enough of them for worthwhile analysis.[87] Information concerning the king's purchases and sales is relatively plentiful,[88] but there are comparatively few data relating to the secular aristocracy's buying and selling of warhorses during this period.[89] The best that can be mustered is a miscellany of isolated references. The busy trading at fourteenth-century horse fairs has left only scattered traces of hard evidence in the records – such as the purchase for John of Gaunt of two coursers 'grey pomelez', costing £29 13s 4d, at Pontefract in 1381.[90] By no means all of the evidence is provided by financial accounts. For example, Reginald, Lord Grey of Ruthyn, stated before the Court of Chivalry in 1386 that his only personal contact with the Grosvenors had been through

---

[84] *CCR, 1330–33*, p. 105. Twenty years later John de la Rokele claimed that a horse worth £10 had been killed during an assault on his person: *CPR, 1350–54*, p. 277.

[85] *Northern petitions*, ed. C.M. Fraser, Surtees Soc., cxciv (1981), pp. 115–17.

[86] 'A plea roll of Edward I's army in Scotland, 1296', ed. C.J. Neville, *Miscellany XI*, Scottish History Soc., 5th ser., iii (1990), nos. 38, 184.

[87] Evidence of this kind forms the basis of analyses of livestock prices in medieval England: J.E. Thorold-Rogers, *A history of agriculture and prices in England, 1259–1793*, 7 vols (Oxford, 1866–1902); H.E. Hallam, ed., *The agrarian history of England and Wales, II, 1042–1350* (Cambridge, 1988), pp. 745–55 (D.L. Farmer). For the horse-market during the early modern period, see P. Edwards, *The horse trade of Tudor and Stuart England* (Cambridge, 1988).

[88] See, for example, Davis, *The medieval warhorse*, pp. 87–91. For horses bought from Spanish and Italian merchants during the mid 1330s, see BL Cotton MS, Nero C. VIII, fos 62r–62v. In 1342 six destriers and six coursers, with a combined value of £230, were shipped to England from Spain for the king's use: E403/326, mm. 14, 15.

[89] Dyer, *Standards of living in the later Middle Ages*, pp. 37, 71–2. Cf. France, for a similar situation: P. Contamine, *Guerre, état et société à la fin du Moyen Age* (Paris, 1972), p. 19.

[90] *JGReg, 1379–83*, ii, no. 744. In 1364, the prince of Wales' servant, John Pryme, was sent to purchase horses at Stamford fair in preparation for his master's departure for Aquitaine: *BPReg*, iv, p. 488. Cf. Thomas, Lord Morley's horse purchases, prior to leaving for France in 1416: Staffordshire Record Office, D 641/3/R/1/2 (I am grateful to Dr Philip Morgan of the University of Keele for showing me a copy of this document).

the purchase of a black horse from an Emma Grosvenor, costing £22 and more.[91] In 1319 Hugh de Neville' servants spent £20 on five horses for use by their master on campaign in Scotland, only to have them stolen by miscreants.[92]

Occasionally we find records of warhorse sales among the documentation associated with military administration, but usually there are good reasons for doubting the value of the evidence. For example, at the end of the short and dispiriting Weardale campaign in 1327, John of Hainault's substantial contingent of continental men-at-arms sold most of their horses to the English crown.[93] Little is known about this sale, but the re-sale of some of these horses to Englishmen is recorded in detail.[94] The prices secured by royal officials appear very modest. In all they raised only £920 2s 8d from the sale of 407 beasts,[95] whilst the Hainaulters claimed no less than £21,482 5s 6d for their lost and sold horses.[96] The discrepancy is not difficult to explain. John of Hainault had no doubt secured the values recorded in the official horse inventories drawn up at the time of muster,[97] whilst the English crown had to accept whatever it could get for horses which may have been in poor condition after a demanding campaign and which were being sold in a local market suddenly flooded with horseflesh.

Clearly the prices obtained for the Hainaulter horses in 1327 did not reflect their true value. A similar case, this time involving the horses of Englishmen, can be seen about twenty-five years later. Towards the end of 1352, some of the men-at-arms serving with the earl of Stafford delivered-up their warhorses to the constable of Bordeaux before leaving Gascony. But, as in 1327, rather than knowing the sums which the authorities paid for the horses, what we have is a record of prices secured when the horses were re-sold;[98] and, once again, the prices are very low. This is certainly not a reflection of the status of the men-at-arms who had been their owners: at least nine of these were knights, some with long and distinguished military careers. One of their number, Sir Richard de Merton, had been campaigning regularly for at least twenty years and we might reasonably expect his warhorse to have been

---

[91] *Scrope-Grosvenor*, i, p. 208.

[92] *CPR, 1317–21*, pp. 474–75.

[93] Some 672 of these animals were kept at York, in the castle and the archbishop's palace, during the second half of August: E101/18/5.

[94] The sale of ninety-eight of these horses (to sixty-five named persons) is itemised in John de Brunham's account book: E101/383/8, fos 8r–8v.

[95] E101/383/8, fo. 7r.

[96] E101/18/4.

[97] John of Hainault's company may have been the only section of the English army in 1327 to have had their horses appraised.

[98] E101/170/20, fos 19r–21v. In 1350 twenty-seven members of the earl of Lancaster's retinue sold their horses to the constable of Bordeaux before leaving the duchy and on this occasion the values are known: E403/355, m. 19.

worth rather more than the £6 for which it was sold by the constable of Bordeaux.[99]

It is fortunate, therefore, that we need not rely upon conventional prices data for systematic evidence on the fourteenth-century English warhorse. The horse inventories compiled at the start of periods of paid military service offer an excellent alternative source for the study of warhorse prices, and much else besides. It is perhaps only to be expected that the warhorses with which a knight or esquire served would tend to reflect his standing in both society and the military hierarchy. This can be seen clearly enough when the man is well known, his career well documented. But many members of the chivalrous community figure only fleetingly in the most readily accessible records. For the hundreds of faceless men-at-arms serving in Edwardian armies, the quality of their warhorses, as recorded in the surviving inventories, may offer our only means of assessing social and military status. Often a particular individual will appear only once in the inventories, a single 'snapshot' of man and warhorse, and it may be uncertain whether an accurate reflection of his military status is being offered. A series of records is obviously more revealing, for it will allow us to chart the course of a man's career, perhaps his rise and fall, as reflected in the quality of the horseflesh which he employed on campaign.

Some members of the military community are well known to history. Earlier, a fleeting glimpse was offered of Sir Andrew de Harcla's stock of horses at the time of his dramatic fall from power.[100] A series of horse inventories for the years 1313 and 1314 reveal a little more about this ambitious border fighter. Harcla, as leader of a retinue, is listed with warhorses ranging in value from 20 marks to 40 marks;[101] horses which were of significantly higher quality than those possessed by the men in his retinues and which demonstrate well his military standing in the western March. Admittedly, retinue captains form a small élite in the military community. Most names listed in horse inventories are far less familiar; many belong to shadowy figures who left little mark on the recorded past. Yet their association

---

99 This was, nevertheless, one of the most expensive horses to be sold. Merton had served at Halidon Hill (C71/13, m. 31), in Scotland in the later 1330s (C71/16, m. 32; C71/17, m. 20; E101/35/3, m. 1), at Buironfosse in 1339 (*Treaty Rolls, 1337–39*, no. 392), at Sluys in 1340 (C76/15, m. 24), in Brittany in 1342–43 (C76/17, m. 32) and at Crécy and the siege of Calais (*Crecy and Calais*, pp. 125, 145). He was still prepared to go on active service in 1359 (C76/38, m. 10).

100 See above, p. 40 n. 81. On Harcla's fall, see N. Fryde, *The tyranny and fall of Edward II, 1321–1326* (Cambridge, 1979), pp. 156–58. On his career, see J.E. Morris, 'Cumberland and Westmorland military levies in the time of Edward I and Edward II', *Transactions of the Cumberland and Westmorland Antiquarian and Archaeological Society*, iii (1903), pp. 315–25; and J. Mason, 'Sir Andrew de Harcla, earl of Carlisle', ibid., xxix (1929), pp. 98–137.

101 E101/14/15, m. 2 (destrier valued at 20 marks on an inventory dated 7 November 1314); m. 4 (horse: 40 marks; 16 January 1313); m. 5 (destrier: £20; 8 July 1314).

with a particular type and quality of warhorse gives them a measure of identity, which it may be possible to amplify through further research. Take, for example, Laurence de Streatley, who can be seen serving in Ireland in the mid 1340s in the retinue of Sir Ralph de Ufford. That he was a man-at-arms of very modest status is suggested by the fact that the horse which he lost during this expedition was valued at a mere 5 marks.[102] Although Streatley never really rose out of obscurity, his military status appears to have risen to some extent by the mid 1350s, for in December 1354 he can be seen claiming and receiving compensation for a horse worth £10.[103] For others, service with Ufford in Ireland in the mid 1340s represented a slightly more advanced stage in their careers. Sir Thomas Daniel claimed £13 for the loss of two horses.[104] This represents a modest improvement in warhorse quality – as an esquire, he had served regularly in Scotland in the later 1330s[105] – but he had further to go up the military ladder.[106] Sir Reginald Fitz Herbert seems to have ascended rather more quickly. Like Daniel, as an esquire, Fitz Herbert served in Scotland in the mid 1330s with modestly priced horseflesh.[107] But unlike Daniel, Fitz Herbert became actively involved in the French war from the outset, and by the time he joined Ufford's retinue in 1344, during a lull in continental campaigning, he had acquired a more elevated military status,[108] indicated not only by the substantial fee which he received for this term of duty, but also by the £20 warhorse which he lost whilst serving in Ireland.[109]

The upward course of many other careers can be charted in the inven-

---

102 The low fee which he received for two years' service, 10 marks, tends to confirm this suggestion: C260/57, m. 28.

103 E101/172/4, mm. 9, 10. His presence in Gascony was probably connected with that of Master John de Streatley, who had been appointed to his second term as constable of Bordeaux earlier in the year. In May 1348 Laurence had secured a letter of protection for service in Gascony with Master John at the start of the latter's first spell as constable: C61/60, m. 27. For John de Streatley, see Tout, *Chapters*, v, pp. 376 n. 5, 377 n. 1; vi, pp. 69–70.

104 One was probably a cheap 'second string' horse. Daniel's fee for nine months service was 20 marks: C260/57, m. 28.

105 1336: 10 marks (E101/19/36); 1337: £8 (E101/20/17); 1337–8: £5 (E101/35/3) – on each occasion serving in Sir Henry de Percy's retinue. Still an esquire, Daniel was a member of the Edinburgh Castle garrison in 1340–41: E101/23/1, m. 4.

106 He was serving in Gascony with Ralph, Lord Stafford in 1345: C61/57, m. 5. This, perhaps significantly, was the first occasion on which he can be seen to have received a letter of protection. He served in the prince of Wales' retinue during the Crécy-Calais campaign and captured the count of Tancarville at Caen: *The life and campaigns of the Black Prince*, ed. Barber, p. 33; *BPReg*, i, 45, 48.

107 In 1336 he served with a 10 mark warhorse in the retinue of the earl of Cornwall: E101/19/36. He had also been in Cornwall's retinue for the summer campaign of the previous year: C71/15, m. 32.

108 Cambrésis-Thiérache campaign: *Treaty Rolls, 1337–39*, nos 181, 365, 385. Sluys: C76/15, m. 22. Brittany, 1342–43: C76/17, m. 26. In 1345, after a year in Ireland, Fitz Herbert joined the earl of Pembroke's retinue for service in Gascony: C76/21, mm. 5, 6.

109 The fee was 40 marks for one year's service: C260/57, m. 28.

tories.[110] In some cases, however, a distinguished career in arms and consequent high esteem in the military community failed to confer permanent benefits. It will be recalled that, according to the inventory of his property, Sir Edmund de Appleby's most valuable horse in 1374 was worth a mere £5. Even allowing for undervaluation (which is to be expected in such documents),[111] this is indicative of a sad decline, for this aged and apparently impoverished country gentleman was a man with a long and varied military past, which had seen him in the company of some of the foremost captains in the kingdom.[112] In the year after Bannockburn he had served in Scotland with a horse valued at 10 marks.[113] In 1337–38, he was once more in the north, but now with a 20 mark warhorse. He was by this time a distinguished knight[114] and a prominent member of the earl of Gloucester's military retinue.[115] This was by no means the climax of his career, for he was to serve in several of the early campaigns of the French war.[116] By the 1370s, however, Sir Edmund de Appleby had little to show for a long career in arms: a striking reminder that regular service, sometimes in apparently profitable theatres of war, did not guarantee the accumulation of profits which could be converted into lasting wealth.

Using the evidence of the inventories as a barometer to measure the fortunes of an individual man-at-arms is most effectively done when the circumstances of the individual can be set against the collective experience of the wider military community. If Sir Andrew de Harcla's warhorses in 1313–14 are viewed in the context of the whole aristocracy at the time of Bannockburn, he begins to seem a captain of no more than moderate standing. He is an important, rising figure in the western March, but captains with greater political weight and from wealthier corners of England – and less attuned to

---

110 Many similar case studies are to be found in Chapter 6.

111 Cf. Dent, *Horses in Shakespeare's England*, pp. 119–20.

112 For his financial difficulties, see G.G. Astill, 'An early inventory of a Leicestershire knight', p. 277. For a man with similar problems, see N. Saul, 'A "rising" lord and a "declining" esquire: Sir Thomas de Berkeley III and Geoffrey Gascelyn of Sheldon', *Historical Research*, lxi (1988), pp. 345–56.

113 E101/15/6, m. 2; serving in the retinue of Sir Richard de Grey, as he was also to do in the War of Saint-Sardos (Astill, 'An early inventory of a Leicestershire knight', p. 275).

114 He is included on the Ashmolean Roll of Arms (Oxford, Bodleian Library, Ashmole MS 15A); and Cotgrave's Ordinary, of c.1340: *Rolls of arms of the reigns of Henry III and Edward III*, ed. N.H. Nicolas (London, 1829), p. 47.

115 E101/35/3, m. 1. He had served against the Scots in Audley's retinue in 1327, 1335 and 1336 (E101/383/8, m. 10; C71/15, m. 32; C71/16, m. 19).

116 1340: C76/15, m. 6. 1341: C76/16, m. 26. 1342: C76/17, m. 25. On each occasion he served in the retinue of the earl of Gloucester. An 'Edmund de Appleby' was in Gascony in the early 1350s with the earl of Stafford (E101/170/20, fo. 20v) and a knight of this name was at Poitiers (Hewitt, *Black Prince's expedition*, p. 196); but this Gascon service was probably performed by Sir Edmund's son, Edmund, who was later retained by John of Gaunt and who served on at least four expeditions with the duke from 1367–78 (Walker, *The Lancastrian affinity*, p. 262).

the practical realities of border warfare – will often be listed with horseflesh of considerably higher value.[117] A man's fortunes may rise or fall, but the development of individual careers needs to be set against a background in which the collective experience of the military community, as reflected in the general level of warhorse values, was also fluctuating. Here we must distinguish, on the one hand, trends of a long term nature, associated with the rise of the 'great horse' and, later, with the eclipse of the warhorse in English military practice; and, on the other, short term fluctuations associated with the circumstances of particular campaigns, which may include the nature of the theatre of war or the identity of the captain. Gathering the data and compiling the statistics so that these patterns are uncovered is a laborious task, but the end-product amply repays the labour expended. The results, summarised in Tables 6.1 and 6.2, represent something approaching a 'prices series' for warhorses. But, more importantly, the aggregated statistics allow us to look into the mental world of the aristocracy, enabling us to trace how they responded as a group to the changing circumstances of campaigning in the fourteenth century, as reflected in the quality of the horseflesh which they selected for active service. Thus, the warhorse of a particular knight or esquire, if viewed in the context of the body of data for the whole chivalrous community, can be seen as a reflection not simply of the man's military status, but also of his response to the conditions of a particular campaign. His response may be broadly in line with that of others, or spurred by the circumstances of his own career, it may be wholly divergent. Either way, the evidence of the horse inventories offers a means of gaining access, however fleetingly and imperfectly, to the thought processes of hundreds of faceless men.

The Edwardian horse inventories have largely escaped the attention of historians. There has not, hitherto, been anything approaching a systematic study of these records; but at least there have been a few attempts at summary analysis of selected inventories, most notably by the father of Edwardian military studies, J.E. Morris. He indicated the range of values which are to be found in the inventories and showed, in general terms, how the quality of horseflesh was related to a man's status, from 'barons and [the] richest bannerets' (80 – 120 marks), through knights (£15 – £30) to 'ordinary troopers' (£5 – £8).[118] Morris's figures seem to have formed the basis for much, if not

---

117 For example, the retinue commanders' warhorses in the earl of Pembroke's small army, campaigning in the Scottish borders during the summer of 1315: the earl himself (£100); Sir Richard de Grey (100 marks); Sir Robert de Mohaut (£80); Sir Bartholomew de Badlesmere (100 marks). E101/15/6.

118 J.E. Morris, *The Welsh Wars of Edward I* (Oxford, 1901), pp. 49, 53, 82 (based, in the main, on the rolls for the Falkirk campaign, 1298). For brief comment on other records, cf. idem, 'Cumberland and Westmorland military levies in the time of Edward I and Edward II', p. 311; idem, 'Mounted infantry in medieval warfare', *TRHS*, 3rd ser., viii

most, subsequent comment on the quality of the English warhorse.[119] His scale of values was used, for example, by N.B. Lewis to establish the rank structure of a small company which was to serve in Wales in the later 1280s.[120] In most cases, Morris's figures are simply re-stated; but the manner of re-statement is often misleading, for there has been a tendency to dwell upon horses of the highest quality, without giving a clear impression of what an ordinary man-at-arms would need to pay for a typical warhorse.[121] It may well be true that 'a good Edwardian *dextrarius* alone would fetch from £20 to £100',[122] but about 90% of the horses listed in the inventories for the Falkirk campaign were valued at *less* than £20.[123] In order to emphasise the scale of a

(1914), p. 85 n. 2; idem, *Bannockburn* (Cambridge, 1914), p. 33. For the analysis of similar materials of continental provenance, see M. Vale, 'Warfare and the life of the French and Burgundian nobility in the late Middle Ages', *Adelige Sachkultur des Spät-mittelalters* (Vienna, 1982), pp. 170–80; tables 1 and 2; and idem, *The Angevin legacy and the Hundred Years War, 1250–1340* (Oxford, 1990), pp. 110–11 (Gascon inventories from the 1290s and 1320s). P. Contamine, *Guerre, état et société*, annexe 12, A: 'Prix des chevaux d'armes d'après les estimations sur les rôles de montre: 1328–1368'; K.H. Schäfer, *Deutsche Ritter und Edelknechte in Italien während des 14. Jahrhunderts* (Paderborn, 1911), pp. 57–67; P. Blastenbrei, *Die Sforza und ihr Heer* (Heidelberg, 1987), pp. 181–87; L. Ménabréa, 'De l'organisation militaire au moyen-age, d'après des documents inédits', *Mémoires de l'Académie Royale de Savoie*, 2nd ser., i (1851), pp. 200–1, 220 (horses lost in Faucigny in 1355).

[119] But cf. J.S. Hamilton, 'Piers Gaveston and the royal treasure', *Albion*, xxiii (1991), p. 204 n. 15 for some independent calculations for Edward II's reign; and B. Lyon, 'The role of cavalry in medieval warfare: horses, horses all around and not a one to use', *Mededelingen van de Koninklijke Academie voor Wetenschappen, Letteren en Schone Kunsten van België*, xlix (1987), p. 86, for brief comment based upon the *restauro equorum* accounts for the Low Countries campaign of 1338–39.

[120] N.B. Lewis, 'An early indenture of military service, 27 July 1287', *BIHR*, xiii (1935), p. 88.

[121] For example: a knight's great warhorse was 'worth anything from £40 to £80' (Powicke, *The thirteenth century*, p. 549); for similar wording, see S. Harvey, 'The knight and the knight's fee in England', *Peasants, knights and heretics*, ed. R.H. Hilton (Cambridge, 1981), p. 170; 'the price of destriers is known to have risen as high as £80 in the thirteenth century' (Dyer, *Standards of living in the later Middle Ages*, pp. 71–72); 'a good war horse could cost up to £80': A.L. Brown, *The governance of late medieval England, 1272–1461* (London, 1989), p. 86. R.H.C. Davis shows us both ends of the spectrum: 'the best military horse . . . the warhorse or destrier [cost] £50–£100 or even more', whilst 'the horse ridden by the non-knightly man-at-arms was a rouncy costing £5–10 or slightly more': *The medieval warhorse*, p. 67.

[122] N. Denholm-Young, *History and heraldry, 1254–1310* (Oxford, 1965), p. 20.

[123] See Table 6.2. It is unfortunate that the other main source of evidence for Edwardian warhorse prices, the records of royal purchases, tends to reinforce this impression of highly-priced horseflesh still further (e.g. M. McKisack, *The fourteenth century* (Oxford, 1959), p. 239 n. 3); an impression to which many of the fragments of evidence from earlier periods, often concerned with the possessions of great men, lend further weight: e.g. R.A. Brown, 'The status of the Norman knight', *War and government in the Middle Ages*, ed. J. Gillingham and J.C. Holt (Woodbridge, 1984), p. 28; P. Contamine, *War in the Middle Ages* (London, 1984), p. 96. But for a balanced assessment of the warhorse

man's investment in his warhorses, it is unnecessary to dwell on the prices of the greatest destriers – which were, in any case, the preserve of commensurately wealthy men. To a member of the lesser gentry, a £10 horse represented a massive outlay. This was, after all, a horse of real quality, worth at least ten-times as much as an average cart-horse and twenty times as much as a plough horse.[124] It represented over six months pay for a man-at-arms serving in the king's army,[125] or, looked at another way, 25% of an annual income which in this period would usually be regarded as adequate for the support of knighthood, and 40% of the income which in 1344–5 qualified a man to be equipped as a man-at-arms.[126] And compared with many luxury goods upon which a knight or esquire could spend his disposable wealth, warhorses were perishable commodities.

Such men as these, the owners of warhorses worth £10, 10 marks or even as little as 100s, will often be taking centre stage in this book. Their role in the functioning of the Edwardian military machine was crucial and it is one of the great strengths of the horse inventories that they reveal the part played by the ordinary man-at-arms rather more clearly than most military records. They and their warhorses will be considered in due course; but first we must turn our attention to the documents, the horse inventories and related records, and the administrative processes which gave rise to them.

price-range in eleventh-century Normandy, see J. Campbell, 'Was it infancy in England? Some questions of comparison', *England and her neighbours, 1066–1453*, ed. M. Jones and M. Vale (London, 1989), p. 12 and n. 79. Cf. M. Bennett, 'The status of the squire: the northern evidence', *The ideals and practice of medieval knighthood*, vol. I, ed. C. Harper-Bill and R. Harvey (Woodbridge, 1986), p. 9.

124 Hallam, ed., *The agrarian history of England and Wales, II, 1042–1350*, pp. 749–50 and table 7.4: 'Livestock prices by decades, 1160–1356'. Cf. Vale, 'Warfare and the life of the French and Burgundian nobility in the late Middle Ages', pp. 173–75, 178.

125 Cf. Vale, *War and chivalry*, p. 126; Contamine, *War in the Middle Ages*, p. 97.

126 Saul, *Knights and esquires*, pp. 37–47; *CPR, 1343–45*, p. 495.

3

The Horse Inventories: Documents and Administrative Processes

INVENTORIES AND *RESTAURO EQUORUM* ACCOUNTS

At the core of this study are two distinct, though closely related, types of document: horse inventories and *restauro equorum* accounts. The former were working records, drawn up as an army's warhorses were appraised at the start of a period of paid military service and designed to be consulted and annotated during and after the campaign. The latter, consisting of lists of horses lost on active service, were based on information contained in the full horse inventories, but were usually compiled long after the dust of the campaign had settled, as part of a formal set of accounts.[1] Although the product of different administrative exercises – and despite consequent differences in appearance and layout – horse inventories and *restauro equorum* accounts are similar in their essential content. They both consist of lists of men-at-arms grouped into retinues, with each man having a horse, described and valued, against his name. Although horse inventories and *restauro equorum* accounts provide the most substantial body of information on the Edwardian warhorse, a range of other materials also contribute to our knowledge of these animals, their owners and their place in the organisation and conduct of war. These include the documents subsidiary to *restauro equorum* accounts, such as claims and warrants for compensation payments, together with many scattered entries on the Issue Rolls and Chancery Rolls. Such records supplement the evidence of the horse inventories and broaden our understanding of the administrative processes at work.

Horse inventories and *restauro equorum* accounts are highly distinctive sources. As far as English medieval history is concerned, they are unique to the period of the three Edwardian kings: there is nothing remotely similar for

---

[1] The great majority of Edwardian horse inventories, together with a miscellany of related materials, are to be found in Exchequer, Accounts Various (E101) and Chancery, Miscellanea (C47, bundle 2) at the Public Record Office. The most important *restauro equorum* accounts for the reigns of Edward II and III are included in the Wardrobe Books of the royal household, held at the PRO (E36 and E101) and the British Library (e.g. Cotton MS, Nero C. VIII; Stowe MS 553). A few of these documents are available in printed editions. For the horse inventories compiled at the start of the Falkirk campaign in 1298, see *Gough*, pp. 160–237; for *restauro equorum* accounts for the period 1299–1300, see *Topham*, pp. 155–87, and for those arising from the Low Countries campaign of 1338–39, see *Norwell*, pp. 309–25.

either the period prior to the later thirteenth century, or for that which followed the passing of Edward of Woodstock.[2] The earliest surviving inventories date from the second Welsh war of Edward I (1282) and the latest from the duke of Clarence's expedition to Ireland in 1361–64. They are available in substantial quantities for the Scottish expeditions of the English kings from the 1290s until the late 1330s. For their overseas enterprises, including those in Ireland, there are good materials rather more intermittently from the later 1290s until the 1360s. Within this time span of rather less than a hundred years, the coverage of these records is far from consistent. They are available for only a proportion of Edwardian campaigns, either because of changes in the terms of military service, or as a consequence of the vagaries of documentary survival. The continuous modification of the terms of military service, and their complete overhaul towards the end of Edward III's reign, will be discussed in detail in the next chapter. Suffice to say here that there were many military operations, during the period c.1280–c.1370, for which no horse inventories were compiled. Only a proportion of the inventories which *were* drawn up have survived the rigours of the intervening centuries. Rarely do we encounter the kind of embarrassment of documentary riches which have made the English expeditions to Gascony in 1324–25 amongst the best documented of the fourteenth century. Often, the full inventories have entirely disappeared, and it is necessary to rely upon *restauro equorum* accounts (as, for instance, for the campaigns of 1322, 1338–39 and 1342–43), files of compensation warrants (e.g. Gascony in the mid 1350s) or less revealing materials, such as the aggregated warhorse casualty figures embedded in the *vadia guerre* accounts for the Reims campaign of 1359–60. Even when full horse inventories are available for a particular army, they rarely provide anything like a complete record; usually only a selection of retinues are covered. A *restauro equorum* account, on the other hand, will include only those horses which have been lost on campaign. It will offer, therefore, only a sample from the full inventory, though an invaluable one if the original lists have not survived.

THE APPRAISAL OF WARHORSES

How did these documents come into being? The compilation of horse inventories usually formed part of the mustering process at the start of a period of paid military service.[3] The assembly of the feudal host traditionally involved

---

[2] For horse inventories from fourteenth-century France, see Dom P.H. Morice, *Mémoires pour servir de preuves à l'histoire ecclésiastique et civile de Bretagne*, 3 vols (Paris, 1742–46), i, cols 1469–72; P. Contamine, 'Les compaignies d'aventure en France pendant la guerre de cent ans', *Mélanges de l'École Française de Rome*, lxxxvii (1975), pp. 390–96.

[3] For brief comments on the appraisal process, see Prince, 'The indenture system under Edward III', p. 294; Hewitt, *The organisation of war under Edward III*, pp. 87–88; Hewitt, *The Black Prince's expedition*, pp. 32–33. Bryce Lyon's comments in his 'Introduction' to *The Wardrobe Book of William de Norwell* are not wholly reliable: *Norwell*, pp. xciii–xciv.

an inspection of the contingents offered by tenants-in-chief, to ensure that the required numbers of men-at-arms were present and that their horses and equipment were of suitable quality.[4] Proffer rolls, compiled at feudal musters by the Constable and Marshal or their deputies, have survived for several early fourteenth-century armies.[5] They list, for each tenant-in-chief, the names of the men-at-arms who were to serve in the host, together with the total number of 'covered' horses (or in certain circumstances 'equi discooperti') brought by each feudal contingent. The advent of paid service, and with it *restauro equorum*, complicated the mustering procedure to a certain degree in that it was now necessary not only to inspect warhorses, but also to compile a written record of their descriptions and values. Like the proffer rolls, the horse inventories were often compiled over a period of weeks rather than on a single day, new contingents being added as they arrived and were taken into the king's pay. In 1322, for example, the *vadia guerre* accounts show that horse valuation occurred on ten different days between 4 and 16 August.[6] In the case of this particular army, it is likely that the Constable and Marshal, or their lieutenants, supervised horse valuation as well as the receipt of proffers.[7] The task was frequently performed by officers of the royal household. This was no doubt the consequence of the wardrobe's continuing involvement in the financing of campaigns, but it was also entirely natural, given the origins of *restauro equorum* in royal household practice.[8] With smaller expeditionary forces, horse appraisal was usually the responsibility of 'a king's clerk trained to the work and a capable knight',[9] the latter probably the marshal of the army. For Henry of Lancaster's army serving in Scotland in the spring and early summer of 1336, the task was undertaken by Sir Ralph de Neville of Raby, the leader of a substantial retinue in the army, and John de Houton, clerk.[10] More often, perhaps, a larger team of appraisers was employed, sometimes working in more than one location.[11]

---

4 For a discussion of the mustering process, see H.M. Chew, *The ecclesiastical tenants-in-chief and knight service* (Oxford, 1932), pp. 83–94.

5 For an analysis of these rolls and in particular those for 1300, 1310 and 1322 see M. Prestwich, 'Cavalry service in early-fourteenth-century England', *War and government in the Middle Ages*, ed. J. Gillingham and J.C. Holt (Woodbridge, 1984), pp. 148–51.

6 BL Stowe MS 553, fos 56v–63r. The gradual build-up of Aymer de Valence's small army during the summer and autumn of 1315 is clearly shown by annotations in the surviving inventory: E101/15/6.

7 Henry de Beaumont was Constable and Thomas of Brotherton, earl of Norfolk, was Marshal of England (C47/5/10). Proffers were received on five of the ten days on which horse appraisal occurred and in the same locations.

8 In 1338 the appraisers for the continental campaign were Sir John Darcy, seneschal of the household and Richard de Nateby, controller of the wardrobe (*Norwell*, p. 309).

9 Prince, 'The indenture system under Edward III', p. 294.

10 BL Cotton MS, Nero C. VIII, fos 280v–82r. John de Houton's rolls for this army are largely intact: E101/19/36.

11 As in 1305–6, when the 'main unit', operating from Carlisle, consisted of two knights, Sir Thomas Paynell and Sir Robert de Felton, and a clerk, James de Dalilegh. Some horses

As horse appraisal formed an integral part of the muster process, we usually find with overseas expeditions that it took place at the port of embarkation. When contingents were to sail from a number of ports, a team of horse appraisers would be needed. The records rarely offer more than glimpses of this sub-division of responsibility, but for the Breton expeditions of 1342–43 it is possible to see a number of different men being sent to Plymouth, Portsmouth, Southampton and Winchelsea to appraise the horses of several magnate captains.[12] They are all clerks, so we must assume that they collaborated with military men, or local officials, on the spot.[13] On occasion, it was necessary or desirable to delay the process of horse appraisal until reaching France.[14] In 1345, for example, the earl of Derby's retinue was paid from the day of arrival at Southampton, but their horses were only appraised after they had reached Bordeaux.[15] It is quite likely that many of them were bought in the duchy, thus avoiding the potential hazards of a long voyage from England, as well as making it easier to assemble an adequate transport fleet.

were valued at Berwick by John de Sandale, clerk, and the records sent to Dalilegh at Carlisle (E101/612/15).

12 William de Dalton, clerk, was sent to Portsmouth and Southampton to appraise the horses of the earl of Northampton's company, whilst William de Cusance and Thomas de Baddeby, clerks, were despatched to Winchelsea to deal with the horses in the companies of the earl of Salisbury and other magnates (E36/204, fo. 79r). Also sent to value the horses of the earl of Northampton's troops were William de Stury and William de Huggate, clerk (C76/17, m. 31). On 20 October 1342 John de Pitte and John de Baddeby, clerks, were appointed to appraise the horses of the earl of Gloucester's retinue at Plymouth (C76/17, m. 17), but a few days later William de Northwell and John de Kermond, clerks, were assigned to the same task (C76/17, m. 18); and it is clear that the latter pair actually went to Plymouth, for an account exists outlining the expenses incurred by their journey (E101/23/36; the account is incorrectly dated: cf. E403/327, m. 6). Master Richard le Ferrour accompanied them, together with three esquires, seven grooms and nine horses. Kermond was also responsible for paying the wages of some of the troops and seamen assembled at Plymouth (C76/17, m. 18; E101/23/22). Gloucester's retinue is not included in the *restauro equorum* account for this campaign.

13 In 1337 Roger Turtle, mayor of Bristol, was one of two men appointed to supervise the appraisal of the horses of Sir John de Norwich's retinue, assembling in his town for the voyage to Gascony: C61/49, m. 17. The horses of Aymer de Valence's company, mustered at York in July 1315, were valued by three men, including the mayor of the city: E101/15/6.

14 Cf. the earl of Stafford's indenture of 1361 which allowed for the appraisal of his horses in either England or upon arrival in Ireland, in case 'les chivalx que serront achatez p[er]dela': E101/28/27, m. 4; CCR, 1360–64, p. 198.

15 E101/25/9. The terms of Derby's indenture allowed him a choice: his men could either have their horses valued 'devant lour eskippeson en manere acustumee', or they could acquire them in Gascony where they would be appraised by the constable of Bordeaux (Fowler, *The king's lieutenant*, pp. 230–31). They were, in fact, appraised by three men: Sir Thomas Cok, marshal of Lancaster's army (though only a knight), John de Wawayn, constable of Bordeaux and Bernard Brocas, controller of Bordeaux. The prince of Wales was given similar terms in 1355: Hewitt, *The Black Prince's expedition*, p. 33.

As regards the actual procedure of horse appraisal, we are almost wholly reliant on the evidence of the inventories themselves. Other record sources cast very little light on this subject and, as H.J. Hewitt observed, contemporary illuminators were not usually attracted by such routine aspects of military organisation as the appraisal of horses.[16] One or two observations can be made, however. The order in which the horses were inspected seems to be preserved in the order of the entries in the surviving inventories. Most of the documents which have come down to us are the original working records, drawn-up at a time and place noted at the head of the document and subsequently amended 'in the field'. It may have been usual to make duplicates or copies rearranging the order of the originals, but few such records have survived the passage of the centuries.[17] The retinues were dealt with one by one; sometimes they are each given a separate membrane, sometimes they appear in sequence on a single roll. In most cases the order of appraisal within a retinue appears to have followed the dictates of military precedence. The captain is followed by his knights and then his esquires in two separate blocks. Although knights banneret are not always distinguished from knights bachelor, there will usually be no danger of confusing bachelors with ordinary men-at-arms, as there often is with other military records.[18]

Sometimes the order of appraisal within a retinue was a little different: the horse of each knight was followed by those of his esquires, with the result that the inventory provides a clear impression of the internal company structure of the retinue. Several of the retinues included in the bundle of inventories compiled during the winter of 1337–38 offer good examples of this approach.[19] Not only do inventories of this kind provide glimpses of military

---

[16] Hewitt, *The organisation of war under Edward III*, pp. 154–55.

[17] Normal practice seems to have been to make several copies of the original inventory: copies of the whole inventory for administrative use, and also sections of it for the retention of individual captains. It is probable, therefore, that more than one clerk was at work during horse appraisal. Given that two men were likely to record slightly different versions of an essentially verbal proceedings, this might also explain some of the apparent discrepancies between surviving inventories and *restauro equorum* accounts. The four versions of the horse inventory for the first (western) fleet which sailed for Gascony in 1324 differ from one another in a number of respects. Two copies are identical except for the fact that one is in Latin and the other in French (E101/17/2); the third is basically the same, but with some changes to the order of the material (E101/16/38); this applies also to the fourth, although this is clearly the latest version as it incorporates a number of last-minute corrections (E101/13/35). These documents exhibit spelling differences which appear to have arisen from the dictation process.

[18] In particular, in enrolled lists of letters of protection, but also *restauro equorum* accounts.

[19] E101/35/3: in particular, the retinues of the earls of Gloucester, Arundel and Salisbury, and Sir Giles de Badlesmere. The terms *esquier* and *vallet* are used interchangeably on this roll: see Saul, *Knights and esquires*, pp. 11–20. The contrast between the quality of a knight's horse and those of his esquires is brought out very strikingly when the inventory is arranged in this fashion. Some inventories appear to have a random order of names

structures which are otherwise all too rarely revealed by the records;[20] they also offer evidence of associations between individuals which may indicate the existence of retaining or tenurial ties, or at least links of a less formal kind. For example, the inventory of the earl of Salisbury's retinue in 1338 includes companies led by members of the Berkeley and Ufford families, together with those of a number of other knights with whom they were closely associated.[21] At times, a connection of a particularly interesting kind is suggested. Sir Thomas West contributed a company of six *vallets* to the earl of Salisbury's retinue in 1338, but the man immediately following West's name in the inventory, Sir Richard Penlee, is described as 'son compaignon', a term of association which suggests friendship, and perhaps brotherhood in arms.[22] Although there is no evidence that West and Penlee served together before this time, they *were* both members of the earl of Pembroke's retinue in Brittany in 1342–43, shortly before West's death.[23]

Each man-at-arms would come forward, declare his identity[24] and present

(e.g. the earl of Warwick's retinue in 1337: E101/20/17, m. 7), simply because the personal ties between knights and esquires are not explicitly supplied.

20 The company structure of a retinue is sometimes revealed by collections of subcontracts (see, for example, A. Goodman, 'The military subcontracts of Sir Hugh Hastings, 1380', *EHR*, xcv (1980), pp. 114–20), but such documents are somewhat scarce. Some muster rolls are arranged so as to reveal the existence of component companies (e.g. Henry, Lord Percy's retinue in 1337: E101/20/17, m. 5), but most are simply grouped according to rank; and their survival is in any case very patchy for the earlier fourteenth century.

21 E101/35/3, m. 2d. Such 'indirect' sources as this are our only guide to the Berkeley affinity (see Saul, *Knights and esquires*, pp. 69–73). A rising star of this phase of Edward III's reign, Sir Ralph de Ufford, had a small company in Salisbury's retinue. One of his *vallets*, Robert Tanc, and one of those in the company of the *Sire de Ufford*, Thomas de Hertford, also served with him in Ireland during the mid 1340s: *CPR, 1343–45*, p. 244; C260/57, m. 28.

22 E101/35/3, m. 1d. We may, however, be seeing nothing more than clerical etiquette: a term reserved for a man who is serving in the company of another man of equal rank (the equivalent phase in Latin inventories, like the Falkirk rolls, is *socius eiusdem*). An unusually complete set of enrolled letters of protection, dated about a month after the inventory, suggest that Penlee and the six *vallets* (and one further man) were all serving *with* (i.e. under) Sir Thomas West, but Chancery roll terminology cannot be said to be unambiguous (C71/18, m. 23). On brothers in arms, see K.B. McFarlane, 'An indenture of agreement between two English knights for mutual aid and counsel in peace and war, 5 December 1298', *BIHR*, xxxviii (1965), pp. 200–8; idem, 'A business-partnership in war and administration, 1421–1445', *EHR*, lxxviii (1963), pp. 290–308; M. Keen, 'Brotherhood in arms', *History*, xlvii (1962), pp. 1–17.

23 C76/17, m. 27. Sir Thomas West was a very experienced soldier, having served in Scotland in 1322, 1327, 1333, 1335 and 1338 (*CPR, 1321–24*, p. 186; E101/383/8, fo. 12r; C71/13, m. 28; C71/15, m. 30) and the Low Countries in 1338–39 (*Treaty Rolls, 1337–39*, nos. 401, 404, 714; C76/14, m. 3) before going to Brittany in 1342. He died overseas in November 1343 (*GEC*, xii, part 2, pp. 517–18). Sir Richard Penlee was to play an active role in the Crécy-Calais campaign (*Crecy and Calais*, pp. 85, 91, 137).

24 That the names were almost certainly transmitted verbally, rather than in writing, is suggested by the extremely variable spelling of surnames in the inventories (far more so,

his horse for inspection. The appraisers were required to determine the type of the horse, its colour (together with any distinctive markings) and its value. All were written down in the inventory next to the name of the owner. There is much uniformity in the basic layout of these documents, irrespective of whether they are written in Latin or French. All are in list format with a single line of information for each man-at-arms and his horse: Symond de Lulleford – *un chival ferant pomele* – 10 m.[25] The appraisers rarely included any additional information about either horse or man-at-arms; never, for instance, the height or age of the horse.[26] Sometimes the valuation was omitted. This was usually because the horse was a gift from the king and would not qualify for compensation if lost.[27] As we have seen, it is likely that several copies of an inventory would be drawn-up at the time of appraisal. The survival of duplicate inventories, such as those for the War of Saint-Sardos, is unusual; but we know that on some occasions at least indented copies were made for the retention of retinue commanders and something along these lines may well have been normal procedure.[28]

In addition to making a written record of their inspection, the appraisers would ensure that each horse was branded. Next to nothing is known about this aspect of the appraisal process,[29] but English practice was probably similar to that of continental states. John II's ordinance of 1351 states that all

for example, than in lists of letters of protection, which are based upon written warrants) and the occasional inclusion of unusual name forms: e.g. 'Sire d'Ufford'; 'Mons. de Asslarton' (E101/35/3, mm. 1d, 2).

[25] In some parts of the early inventories (in the 1280s) the order of the information is reversed: e.g. 'un chival ferant pomele pour Symond de Lulleford – 10 m' (C47/2/6 and 7).

[26] Cf. fourteenth-century France: 'le pelage est parfois decrit, sans allusion malheureusement à l'âge ou à la race' (Chomel, 'Chevaux de bataille et roncins en Dauphiné au XIVe siècle', p. 12). In Italy, more detail might be recorded about the owner: his father's name and his place of birth (Contamine, *War in the Middle Ages*, p. 131). Sometimes the man-at-arms' county of origin is supplied in English inventories (e.g. occasionally in the Falkirk rolls). The omission of height and age from the horse descriptions is perhaps surprising; cf. sixteenth-century practice in England: C.G. Cruickshank, *Elizabeth's army*, 2nd edn (Oxford, 1966), p. 34 n. 1.

[27] For example, Sir Pain Tibetot's *destrier ferrand*: E101/14/15, m. 9; cf. a number of examples in E101/15/6. It is not clear why there are no values at all in the earl of Warenne's inventory dating from 1325 (E101/17/31); but this may simply represent incomplete work. The last section of the household inventory for the Falkirk campaign, dated 21 July 1298, also lacks values, apparently because the task of appraisal had not been completed before the battle on the 22nd (*Gough*, pp. 204–5).

[28] For example, in 1364 for William de Windsor's expedition to Ireland (CCR, *1360–64*, pp. 507–8); but only one inventory has survived: E101/29/5. The inventory for the winter campaign of 1337–38 is indented down its left side, suggesting that two identical copies were made in the manner of an indenture for service: E101/35/3.

[29] Hewitt's reference to the 'usual' branding instructions is a little misleading (*The organisation of war under Edward III*, p. 87 n. 3), for they are often omitted from the orders appointing horse appraisers during the early years of the Hundred Years War. For an example, dating from July 1342 and referring to troops in Gascony, which *does* include

warhorses were to be branded on the thigh, a separate brand-mark, decided upon by the muster official, being used for each company.[30] In Italy, warhorses were branded with the condottiere's emblem; as in France, this helped prevent 'improper substitution' at musters.[31] Although probably designed to emphasise the continental origin of the horse depicted, the brand-mark shown on the flank of the Knight's mount in the Ellesmere manuscript of *The Canterbury Tales*, apparently in the form of a capital *M*, may well resemble the kind of marking employed at musters of English royal armies earlier in the century.[32]

The valuation of horseflesh was probably the most time-consuming task facing royal and military officials as an army gathered at a muster point or port of embarkation. The appraisers sent to value the horses of the earl of Gloucester's men at Plymouth in November 1342 stayed for eight days.[33] The assembly of a really large army might involve the examination of several thousand horses, a task which would have taken weeks. It should be remembered, however, that only a proportion of an army's horses would be submitted for appraisal. As a general rule it was only the warhorses of men-at-arms which were eligible for valuation. As with all rules, very occasional exceptions can be found. The inventory of the earl of Salisbury's retinue which was drawn-up early in 1338 includes a 100s horse for an unnamed archer.[34] Rather more frequently encountered are appraised horses for non-combatants, such as the clerks who figure in Salisbury's *restauro equorum* account from the Low Countries campaign of 1338–39.[35] But the vast majority of horses listed in the inventories and compensation accounts were destined for a military role and belonged to men-at-arms. As a consequence

these instructions, see C61/54, m. 2; cf. for the Black Prince's expedition of 1355, *Rymer*, III, i, p. 310.

30 '[Le chival sera] marque en la cuisse d'un fer chaut, a tel saing comme il plaira a ceulx qui en auront afaire, & seront touz les chevauls d'icelle Route marquiez d'un mesme fer & saing': *Ordonnances des roys de France de la troisième race*, ed. D.F. Secousse et al. (Paris, 1734; repr., 1967), iv, p. 68. The branded part of the horse's hide was usually required as proof of loss: Contamine, *Guerre, état et société*, p. 104.

31 Mallett and Hale, *Military organisation of a Renaissance state*, p. 138. Cf. Jones, *Chaucer's knight*, pp. 29–30, quoting the 'Rules for the foreign mercenaries in the employment of the Republic of Florence' of 1337; and C.E. Bosworth, 'Recruitment, muster and review in medieval Islamic armies', *War, technology and society in the Middle East*, ed. V.J. Parry and M.E. Yapp (London, 1975), p. 71.

32 On the Ellesmere MS brand-mark: A.A. Dent, 'Chaucer and the horse', *Proceedings of the Leeds Philosophical and Literary Society*, ix (1959–62), p. 9; Jones, *Chaucer's knight*, pp. 29–30. Leger Brosnahan has suggested that the *M* probably stands for *miles*: 'The pendant in the Chaucer portraits', *The Chaucer Review*, 26 (1992), p. 430 n. 7.

33 E101/23/36.

34 E101/35/3, m. 1d; instead of a name, are the words 'pur Archour'. Similarly, in Valois France it is exceptional to find archers receiving *restor* payments: Contamine, *Guerre, état et société*, p. 104.

35 *Norwell*, p. 312.

of this, comparatively little is known about the animals ridden by the non-chivalrous elements of an Edwardian army, particularly those of the mounted archers. When specifically mentioned in the records, the archer's mount is usually referred to as a *hakeneye*:[36] a horse for the march rather than the battlefield. Such documentary evidence as there is suggests that a typical hackney cost a good deal less than the cheapest warhorse. In 1335 John de Bikenor, king's archer, received a gift of 20s from the crown in compensation for a horse lost in Scotland.[37] Eleven years later, Sir Thomas Dagworth claimed 20s in compensation for each of the 120 hackneys lost by his mounted archers during a year of service in Brittany, whilst the corresponding figure for horses lost by men-at-arms was £10.[38]

A more fundamental deficiency of the horse inventories is the fact that, in the great majority of cases, only one horse has been recorded for each serving man-at-arms.[39] As an indenture of war between Edward III and three foreign knights in May 1346 put it, it was 'la custume Dengleterre' for each man-at-arms to have '*un* chival prise'.[40] But, once again, there are exceptions. It was not uncommon for captains of retinues to have more than one horse appraised. This privilege was sometimes written into indentures, as we find in 1361 when Ralph, earl of Stafford was allowed to have 'deux chivalx pris pur son corps'.[41] In his retinue's horse inventory, drawn-up at Bristol on 18 August 1361, Stafford duly appears with a destrier and a *trotter*, worth 80 marks and £20 respectively.[42] The inventories compiled during the winter of 1337–38 allow two destriers for the earl of Gloucester, three horses each for the earls of Arundel and Salisbury, two for Sir Hugh le Despenser and several *chivals* for Sir Richard Talbot.[43] A captain might also have a horse valued for 'son baner':[44] the earl of Stafford's in 1361 was borne by 'une Lyard de Burbache', valued at 20 marks.

Although the great majority of men who appear in inventories have been allowed only one appraised warhorse, we can be sure that they had more than one mount with them.[45] As the theoretical 'unit' of the feudal host, a knight

---

[36] As in a memorandum concerned with the garrisons in Ponthieu in 1366: SC1/41, no. 154.

[37] BL Cotton MS, Nero C. VIII, fo. 273v.

[38] E101/25/17.

[39] On one occasion at the end of Edward I's reign, Sir Robert de Clifford was specifically disallowed from having a second appraised horse: E101/612/15, mm. 1, 2.

[40] E101/68/3, no. 64.

[41] E101/28/27, m. 4.

[42] E101/28/11, m. 3.

[43] E101/35/3. By contrast, the inventories for the Scottish campaigns of 1336–37 list only one horse for the captains of retinues (E101/19/36, E101/20/17).

[44] Including most of the above-mentioned captains in 1337–38. Of these, only the earl of Salisbury's banner-bearer is named.

[45] Cf. France: Contamine, *Guerre, état et société*, pp. 17–18; and the horse allowances for the military orders: A. Forey, *The military orders from the twelfth to the early fourteenth centuries* (Basingstoke and London, 1992).

traditionally served with two 'covered' horses.[46] In addition to these war-horses, he would probably have had a palfrey for himself to ride on the march, a rouncy for his servant and a sumpter for his baggage.[47] Records for Edward II's Scottish campaigns duly show knights serving with two or more 'covered' horses,[48] even though related horse inventories would record only one for most men. Despite the consistent emphasis on dismounted combat by the middle of the fourteenth century, there is no evidence of a decline in the number of warhorses accompanying English armies under Edward III or his successors. An English man-at-arms in the mid fourteenth century would still need several good horses for both his peacetime pleasures[49] and the more serious business of war. Some indication of the numbers of horses taken on campaign is provided by the allowances paid to captains for the transport-ation of their retinues by sea. In 1340 the crown was willing to pay the cost of the passage of 4,614 horses from Sluys to England: five horses were allowed for bannerets, four for knights and three for esquires.[50] The same scale was employed for Sir James Audley's retinue on its outward voyage to Gascony in 1345, with the additional allowance of one horse for each mounted archer.[51]

[46] Chew, *The ecclesiastical tenants-in-chief and knight service*, p. 90; S. Harvey, 'The knight and the knight's fee in England', *Peasants, knights and heretics*, ed. R.H. Hilton (Cambridge, 1981), p. 150.

[47] R.A. Brown, 'The status of the Norman knight', *War and government in the Middle Ages*, ed. J. Gillingham and J.C. Holt (Woodbridge, 1984), pp. 28–29; Matthew Bennett, 'The status of the squire: the northern evidence', *The ideals and practice of medieval knighthood*, vol. I, ed. C. Harper-Bill and R. Harvey (Woodbridge, 1986), pp. 4–5. Cf. an indenture of 1310, which makes specific reference to a knight's *chivaus, palefroi, somer* and *Rouncyn*, as well as his *vadlet*'s *hakeney* and *somer*: M. Jones 'An indenture between Robert, Lord Mohaut, and Sir John de Bracebridge for life service in peace and war, 1310', *Journal of the Society of Archivists*, iv (1972), p. 391.

[48] The proffer roll for the 1322 campaign assumes two 'covered' horses for each knight: C47/5/10. A roll of Sir John de St John's retinue (*temp*. Edward II) lists most of the knights with two *chivaux covertz*, with some having three and one with as many as five: E101/17/32.

[49] On the need for re-mounts on the tournament field, see R. Harvey, *Moriz von Craûn and the chivalric world* (Oxford, 1961), pp. 222, 226, 235, 237, 254.

[50] *Norwell*, pp. civ–cv, 386–92. Cf. the terms for the shipment of horses (allowing three horses per knight) in Henry I's reign: B. Lyon, 'The feudal antecedent of the indenture system', *Speculum*, xxix (1954), p. 506. The horse shipment allowances appear more generous in the early fifteenth century: R.A. Newhall, *The English conquest of Normandy, 1416–1424* (New York, 1924), pp. 191 n. 7, 194 n. 27. This may suggest an increase in the size of the 'lance', or basic fighting unit, a development which certainly occurred in several European states during the late fourteenth and fifteenth centuries. The growing weight of armour for man and horse necessitated a larger number of re-mounts for combat and, consequently, more support personnel for the man-at-arms. See Contamine, *War in the Middle Ages*, pp. 126–28, cf. 67–68, 91; Vale, *War and chivalry*, pp. 121–25; Mallett, *Mercenaries and their masters*, pp. 148–50.

[51] E101/24/20. The same horse passage allowances were in force in 1347 (ships ordered for the transport of thirty men-at-arms and thirty archers, together with 120 horses: C76/24, m. 10) and for the Irish expeditions of the 1360s (E101/28/21, fo. 13v).

Roger Mautravers' indenture of war with the earl of Salisbury, dated 1372, stipulated that he was to be provided with 'eskipeson resonable' for four *chivaux* (for himself) and two *hakkneys* for his two *vadlet* archers.[52] Evidence of a similar kind can be found in the terms of an indenture, drawn-up in May 1347 between the prince of Wales and Sir Thomas Fournival, which included the provision that in wartime the prince would supply hay and oats for four horses in the case of Sir Thomas and a knightly companion, and three for each of two esquires.[53] Given that such allowances probably underestimate the numbers of horses actually transported or stabled (and accepting the presence of 'non-combatant' horses), all this evidence strongly suggests that knights certainly, and esquires very probably, took more than one real war-horse on active service. Some *vadia guerre* accounts from the mid fourteenth century record pay cuts for men-at-arms who served with insufficient war-horses; and a few further fragments of evidence point firmly to the same conclusion. In October 1346 during the siege of Calais, the king gave per-mission for Sir Roger de Huse 'denvoyer en Engleterre trois garsouns ove trois grauntz chivalx', presumably to escape the unhealthy conditions of the siege camp; the same order also allowed Robert Alwyne to send three horses home.[54] It is clear from the horses sold by members of the earl of Lancaster's retinue shortly before leaving Gascony in 1350, that some at least of the earl's men had served with *several* expensive horses. Sir Stephen de Cusington sold one destrier for 100 marks and three other horses with a combined value of £43 6s 8d.[55]

At any single moment, only one of Cusington's horses would have been appraised and, therefore, eligible for compensation; but in the event of the loss of this horse, a replacement could be offered to the appraisers for valu-ation. The indenture of war between Edward III and the prince of Wales, drawn up on 10 July 1355, is unusually explicit on this point, stipulating that the constable of Bordeaux would 'value any horses purchased from time to time by men-at-arms to make good the loss of horses previously valued';[56] and the process is sometimes mentioned by *vadia guerre* accounts when wage payment is dependent upon the possession of an appraised horse. In theory, the sequence of equestrian loss and new valuation could occur several times during the course of a campaign. The results will be seen if a *restauro*

52 E101/68/5, no. 107.
53 *BPReg*, i, p. 128. An indenture between Sir John de Wylughby *le fitz* and the prince, apparently drawn-up at the same time, provided for similar horse stabling arrangements: ibid., p. 129. The stabling allowances outlined in Sir John de Sully's indenture of March 1353 are rather more generous. In wartime he and his esquire were to have livery for nine horses between them: *BPReg*, ii, pp. 45–46.
54 C81/1710, no. 47. Sir Roger de Huse was an experienced campaigner, having served in Scotland in 1333, 1335 and early 1338 – on the last occasion, with a £10 horse (C71/13, m. 24; C71/15, m. 32; E101/35/3).
55 E403/355, m. 19.
56 *BPReg*, iv, pp. 143–45.

equorum account has survived. During the Cambrésis-Thiérache campaign of 1338–39, four of the members of the earl of Northampton's retinue each lost two warhorses.[57] All of the replacement mounts were of good quality; but since they could have been bought locally – or acquired in other ways – such evidence cannot be used with any confidence as an indicator of the quality of English men-at-arms' second-string warhorses. The fact is that the re-mounts remain resolutely in shadow; we know they were there, but were they usually of similar, or inferior, quality to the warhorses presented to the appraisers? Assuming at least one re-mount per man-at-arms, it is clear that no more than a half, and probably nearer a third, of the warhorses taken on campaign would have been appraised and, therefore, potentially available for our scrutiny. If we further assume that a man would usually present his best horse for valuation, then it follows that this group of appraised horses is unlikely to constitute a sample which truly reflects the quality of all war-horses. That we are seeing only the best horses in aristocratic stables is a possibility which should be borne in mind when compiling statistics from the valuation data.

If, even with the most completely documented fourteenth-century army, it is necessary to be content with seeing only a sample of its warhorses, then how certain can we be that the data in the sample are a reliable body of evidence, presenting an accurate record of the quality of the appraised horses? How confident can we be in conclusions which are based upon com-parative analysis of a series of such collections of valuation data? All de-pends, clearly, on how the horse appraisers carried out their duties. Horse appraisal cannot have been an exact science – much would depend upon the knowledge and experience of the appraisers – and is impossible now to determine how skilled or fastidious particular men were at their task. We might reasonably expect that the appraisers who were militarily active mem-bers of the aristocracy would have considerable relevant experience to draw upon; they will have spent much time assessing the merits of particular horses for their own use. Some men, like Sir Thomas Cok, were called upon to supervise appraisal on a number of occasions.[58] The clerks involved would probably have less specialised equestrian knowledge, but their primary func-tions would have been administrative: ensuring that the regulations surround-ing appraisal were fully adhered to and that the inventories were correctly drawn-up. They might also be responsible, simultaneously, for overseeing the muster of men-at-arms and archers.[59] It is uncertain how far the appointed appraisers went about their task independently, or whether the owners of the

---

57 John de Clepton, Sir Richard de Denton, Sir Hugh de Neville and Sir John de Wauton: *Norwell*, pp. 309–10.

58 Sir Thomas Cok was an appraiser of Henry of Lancaster's horses on at least two occa-sions, in 1345 and 1350: E101/25/9; E404/508, nos. 51–79.

59 Letters of appointment often combined horse appraisal and manpower mustering duties: see, for example, C76/16, m. 6; C76/17, mm. 18, 31.

horses under inspection were called upon to offer information. The greater captains may have been keen to place their own records at the disposal of the appraisers; some will have compiled their own inventories for their retainers' horses before reaching the muster centre.[60] It is easy to see how this could lead to a conflict of interests and a decidedly tense atmosphere. The owners, after all, would have sought the highest possible valuations, whilst the royal clerks may have been briefed to keep the valuations as low as possible. The pressures would be particularly great if heavy pre-campaign demand had induced a surge in warhorse prices. The knightly appraiser was often not without a personal interest in the proceedings. He would usually not only be marshal of the section of the army being inspected, but also a serving soldier in his own right: a man with horseflesh of his own, perhaps a retinue, certainly friends and rivals – all of which could influence his decisions. However impartial the appraiser might strive to be, we must suspect that the opinions of the mightier captains concerning the quality of their mens' horses could not always be entirely excluded.

If this kind of interference could have served, on occasion, to disrupt the consistency of horse appraisal, then we must in any case suspect that real consistency was impossible to achieve, because valuation was often conducted in more than one place, by a number of different appraisers. It has been noted already how a team of clerks was despatched to the ports of embarkation during the summer and autumn of 1342. However seamless the *restauro equorum* account for the Breton expeditions might appear, it is clear that it was based upon a substantial and varied collection of inventories: records drawn-up by a number of different men over a period of several months. The horse inventories for a Scottish campaign might be confined to a single roll, but they will often have been compiled over a period of weeks, or even months. The inventory of the four retinues comprising Aymer de Valence's army serving in Scotland during the summer of 1315 shows that valuations were made on twenty separate days from July to October. What is more, the 'knightly' appraiser changed during the course of the campaign.[61] If a degree of inconsistency in the valuation process is to be suspected for a single expedition, then how much more likely is it that the appraisers for one army would bring to the task of describing, classifying and valuing the horses which came before them, criteria which differed to some extent at least from those applied to the next? How far are the apparent contrasts in the types of

---

60 Sir William Latimer's indenture with the earl of Lancaster (May 1319) stipulates that his warhorses would be appraised at the commencement of hostilities 'par les gentz le dit Counte': G.A. Holmes, *The estates of the higher nobility in fourteenth-century England* (Cambridge, 1957), p. 123. Cf. *BPReg*, i, pp. 69–70, for the valuation of the horses of the prince of Wales' bachelors.

61 E101/15/6. Sir John de Pabenham, the mayor of York and John de Percy, clerk, made the initial valuations, whilst those conducted 'in Marchia versus Scotiam' were undertaken by Sir William de Felton and John de Percy. Pabenham was a member of Valence's retinue, whilst Felton appears to have commanded a small independent company.

warhorses employed and their quality, which emerge from an analysis of a series of inventories, reflecting real changes and how far do they arise simply from shifting terminology and differences in standards of judgement?

It is indeed a salutary thought that the modern historian can discover far more about the appearance of Edwardian warhorses than about that of the men who rode them. There are certainly no muster rolls for English armies to match that which has survived for a Provençal army of 1374, which includes descriptions of the principal physical features of individual soldiers.[62] Although the English horse inventories do not include the height of the animals appraised, they do provide descriptions of the colour and distinctive features of the horses. Vivid colour combinations are employed[63] and there is much attention to pertinent detail. After the horse's basic colouring, the clerk might add, for example, 'cum stella in fronte et iiii pedibus albis'. A one-eyed (*monoculus*) horse, like Peter de Nutle's £10 rouncy in 1282, is unlikely to have gone unnoticed.[64] All this testifies, to some degree, to the diligence and expertise of the inspectors, but what of their judgements concerning the quality of the horses coming before them?

However experienced the horse evaluators, assessment of quality would always have been to some extent a subjective exercise. In the first place, they had to decide what type of horse was before them. In the surviving inventories for Edward III's reign the great majority of warhorses are described simply as *equi* or *chivals*. Of the 1,250 horses listed in the inventories and *restauro equorum* accounts for the later 1330s, over 90% were so described, in either the Latin or French forms. The *restauro equorum* accounts for the early campaigns of the French war offer a figure of very similar magnitude.[65] The umbrella term *equus* or *chival* could be applied to horses of very different quality; but there were some warhorses which could not satisfactorily be embraced by this term. Some, like destriers and coursers, were superior in quality, whilst others, also apparently distinguishable from *equi*, were considered to be inferior.

The word 'destrier' (or *dextrarius*) is commonly regarded as synonymous with 'warhorse': according to popular imagination, destriers were 'the chargers who carried the mounted knights to war'.[66] Yet, as far as the men whose task it was to classify and appraise horses at the start of a campaign

---

62 M. Hébert, 'L'armée Provençale en 1374', *Annales du Midi*, xci, (1979), pp. 5–27; cf. C.E. Bosworth, 'Recruitment, muster and review in medieval Islamic armies', p. 71.

63 For a glossary of the colours used to describe horses in medieval sources, see Davis, *The medieval warhorse*, pp. 137–38; cf. A-M. Bautier, 'Contribution à l'histoire du cheval au Moyen Age: II. La robe des chevaux', *Bulletin Philologique et Historique du Comité des Travaux Historiques et Scientifiques* (1976) pp. 237–46.

64 C47/2/7, m.3; cf. *Gough*, p. 227; Vale, 'Warfare and the life of the French and Burgundian nobility in the late Middle Ages', p. 176.

65 For the sources, see Table 6.1.

66 M.M. Reese, *The royal office of Master of the Horse* (London, 1976), p. 53; cf. G. Parker, *The military revolution* (Cambridge, 1988), p. 69, for similar wording.

were concerned, only a small minority of warhorses were true destriers.[67] Less than 5% of the warhorses listed in the *restauro equorum* accounts for the campaigns of 1338–39 and 1342–43 are described as destriers, whilst the proportion for the immediately preceding Scottish campaigns of the later 1330s is even smaller: thirteen out of a total of 1,250 warhorses.[68] In fact, destriers had never been numerous; they had always been the preserve of a small élite amongst the chivalrous class.[69] The other category of warhorse to be found regularly in the inventories of Edward III's reign is the 'courser' (or *cursarius*).[70] This is often characterised as a horse for the chase or the tournament field,[71] but the inventories show quite clearly that it was also regarded as a high quality warhorse, clearly a cut above the ordinary *equus* and second only to the destrier in value.

The *chival*, the destrier and the courser were the main categories of warhorse employed by the horse appraisers of the 1330s and '40s. Occasionally, however, they felt the need to use a different term. In the case of the *trotter*, listed as the earl of Stafford's second appraised horse in 1361,[72] we are not seeing a warhorse; but most of the less usual terms which are to be found in the inventories do concern horses with a military function. On eleven occasions while compiling the horse inventories during the early summer of 1336, Sir Ralph de Neville and John de Houton, clerk, felt that the horse before them was really a 'hobby', rather than a conventional *chival*. The hobby is

---

67 The term was used more loosely in other records and had a long history (see Davis, *The medieval warhorse*, chapter 4). It was gaining ground in French literary circles during the central Middle Ages (J. Frappier, 'Les destriers et leur épithètes', *La technique littéraire des chansons de geste* (Paris, 1959), 85–104); and some late medieval writers in England used it as a generic term for warhorse: e.g. *Le Baker*, p. 52.

68 Numbers were to remain at this low level. Only one of the horses sold by Henry of Lancaster's men in March 1350 was a destrier: Sir Stephen de Cusington's mount, valued at 100 marks (E403/355, m. 19). Similarly, only one of the horses listed in the surviving inventories for service in Ireland in the 1360s is a destrier: the earl of Stafford's mount, valued at 80 marks (E101/28/11, m. 3).

69 Fewer than 5% of the horses listed in the Falkirk campaign inventories (1298) are destriers. Cf. the rolls for the 1297 Flanders expedition: only ten destriers are listed on one roll (E101/6/37) and six on another (E101/6/28).

70 They do not appear in great numbers: there are fifty-three (about 5% of all warhorses) on the Scottish campaign horse rolls from the later 1330s (generally in the possession of retinue commanders and wealthy knights), but rather fewer (twenty-six in all) are listed in the *restauro equorum* accounts for the early French campaigns.

71 The courser: 'the best horse for hunting . . . [it was] large as well as swift but for some reason does not seem to have been used for fighting' (Davis, *The medieval warhorse*, p. 67); 'employed as a hunter and as a racehorse but never for military purposes' (A.A. Dent, 'Chaucer and the Horse', p. 5); 'not a racehorse but one that ran a course at jousts' (Hewitt, *The horse in medieval England*, p. 2). Shakespeare knew better: 'the officer's charger throughout the works is most often called a courser': Dent, *Horses in Shakespeare's England*, pp. 74, 155.

72 E101/28/11, m. 3; cf. E101/29/33 for documents concerning the passage of *chivals*, *coursers*, *trotters* and *hakeneys* to Ireland in the 1360s.

usually regarded as a 'light cavalry' horse, ridden by hobelars,[73] and yet here we see them being used by men-at-arms and in most cases the valuation suggests a horse of good quality. Two of the hobbies, indeed, were valued at £10, which was rather higher than the mean value for *equi* in this army.[74] The one *frison* to be found in the inventories of 1336 (and, indeed, the whole period) was valued at only 100s. It is not clear what distinguished it from the ordinary *chival* – or, indeed, the hobby – except its place of origin.[75] Also rather enigmatic is the *hengst*.[76] Neville and Houton included one of these in their inventories in 1336: a spotted bay valued at £8 for Robert Fermer.[77] Once again it is not certain what distinguished this kind of horse from the fourteen *equi* in the earl of Oxford's retinue. There are only two other *hengsts* mentioned in inventories of English retinues during this period and both are rather more valuable animals. Sir Giles de Badlesmere's was appraised at £24 during the winter of 1337–38 and Philip le Despenser lost an impressive 40 mark *hengst* during the Breton campaign of 1342–43.[78]

That specialist types or breeds of horse were occasionally noted in the inventories may lend some weight to the view that the appraisers were knowledgeable and discriminating men whose work can be relied upon. But there remains the suspicion that the horse classifications and descriptions are not always correct; that some amongst the multitude of *equi* and *chivals* in the inventories should actually have been classified as coursers or destriers. There would be conflicting influences at work at the time of appraisal. Warhorse owners would want their mounts to be accurately, indeed flatteringly, classified and described. On one level, it was a matter of personal prestige: the captain of a major retinue would not wish to be recorded with anything less than a courser; but the classification of the horse might also affect its valuation, for a destrier or courser was likely to secure a higher value than an

---

[73] Davis, *The medieval warhorse*, pp. 26, 67; J.F. Lydon, 'The hobelar: an Irish contribution to medieval warfare', *The Irish Sword*, II, v (1954), pp. 12–16.

[74] Owned by Alan de Clavering and William de Nafferton – both, perhaps significantly, members of Sir Ralph de Neville's retinue (E101/19/36, m. 3d). Three of the eleven hobbies were valued at less than £5, however; and their mean value (£6.4) was rather less than that for *equi* (£8). The most valuable hobby in the inventories for this period is a 20 marks horse lost by Thomas Gisors during the 1338–39 Low Countries campaign (*Norwell*, p. 311).

[75] It was probably imported from Friesland (cf. the *freson* mentioned in the alliterative *Morte Arthure*, line 1365). It was owned by Thomas de Rodhom and it may be significant that two other members of the Rodhom family, both called John, were also serving with unconventional horses – hobbies. E101/19/36, mm. 3, 5.

[76] Davis, *The medieval warhorse*, p. 136; it may be a warhorse of German origin. A groom is occasionally termed a *henxstmann*: e.g. E101/393/11, fos 63v, 72r.

[77] E101/19/36, m. 6.

[78] E101/35/3, m. 1; E36/204, fo. 87r. There is a further *hengst*, valued at 10 marks, recorded as having been lost by one of Henry of Flanders' men-at-arms in 1339: *Norwell*, p. 316. In 1339 the king bought two *hengsts* costing £22 10s from Sir Reginald de Cobham: *Norwell*, p. 215.

equus. Horse owners would no doubt offer suggestions to the appraisers and it may be that the amendments to horse classifications which can be seen in some inventories[79] arose from such prompting, combined perhaps with subsequent reflection and re-consideration by officials. Indeed, it may have been the owners who were responsible for those cases of unusual terminology which we occasionally find in the inventories. Sir Giles de Badlesmere's *hengst* is described in such terms – 'un chival appele hensk' – as to suggest that the appraisers were not familiar with this particular type of warhorse. Given such pressures at the time of appraisal (and the ever-present possibility of clerical error), it is not difficult to see how mistakes could occur. That they did occur is clear enough. The surviving roll of inventories for the Scottish campaign of 1337–38 consists of a list of over 350 *chivals*, punctuated by only three destriers.[80] The absence of coursers from this roll stands in stark contrast with the inventories for 1336 and 1337, which list coursers for many bannerets and some of the more prominent knights.[81] But even more telling is the appearance of eleven coursers amongst the *restauro equorum* accounts for the winter 1337–38 campaign.[82] Most of them must have been drawn from inventories consisting of a more balanced range of horse types, but which have long since disappeared; but in several cases there is at least a suspicion that the lost *coursers* correspond to *chivals* in the surviving inventory. With the records for the winter of 1337–38 the evidence for a change in terminology between inventory and *restauro equorum* account is not conclusive,[83] but if we turn to the materials for the summer 1336 campaign, a number of clear-cut examples can be found. Sir Henry de Beaumont heads his retinue's inventory with a courser valued at £40, but in the *restauro equorum* account, this horse is described as a destrier. Similarly, two of Beaumont's knights have *equi* in the inventory, which become coursers in the compensation account;[84] and there are further examples from other retinues.[85] How have these changes occurred? They may be simply the result of scribal carelessness. Comparison of the records shows that the clerks drawing up compensation accounts abbreviated the often very detailed horse descriptions as a matter of course. Alternatively the 'changes' may derive from a third document which no longer exists: perhaps a slightly different version of the inventory, compiled

---

[79] E.g. E101/14/15, m. 9.

[80] Two for the earl of Gloucester and one for the earl of Arundel: E101/35/3, mm. 1, 2d.

[81] There are, nevertheless, individual retinues in the bundles for 1336 and 1337 which also present a suspiciously uniform list of *equi*. The earl of Cornwall's roll (8 September 1336) is a good example of this: E101/19/36, m. 1.

[82] E101/388/5, mm. 19–20.

[83] In three cases the descriptions and values do not match exactly.

[84] Sir Robert de Saltmarsh and Sir Edmund Barde: E101/19/36, m. 2; BL Cotton MS, Nero C. VIII, fo. 281r.

[85] For example, Sir John de Tibetot's *equus*, which was lost during a passage of the Forth, becomes a courser in the *restauro equorum* account: E101/19/36, m. 5d; BL Cotton MS, Nero C. VIII, fo. 281v.

at the time of horse appraisal, or an intermediate document listing only those horses which have been lost. The latter could take the form of a bundle of warrants authorising compensation payment or a single summary roll of losses. Such a roll has survived for Henry of Lancaster's retinue from the Scottish campaign of 1336 and it is striking that the sequence of information and degree of abbreviation exhibited by this roll is reproduced exactly in the corresponding section of the *restauro equorum* account for this expedition.[86]

Whilst drawing attention to transcription errors and the consequences of clerical abbreviation, an exploration of inconsistencies in horse classification should also take account of the fact that equestrian terminology, as used in the inventories, was in a state of flux in the first half of the fourteenth century. That the term 'courser', for example, was not used consistently in the horse inventories of the 1330s is probably due in part to the fact that it had only recently been admitted to the practical vocabulary of the horse appraiser. It does not appear at all in the inventories of the first two Edwards. As late as the mid 1320s, there is not a glimpse of it in the substantial collection of horse rolls arising from the War of Saint-Sardos.[87] Then, coursers appear quite suddenly in the inventories drawn-up during the late spring of 1336. They immediately become a favoured type of warhorse amongst the upper echelons of the aristocracy and, indeed, remain so until the early 1360s, when the inventory evidence dries up.[88]

The question which must be asked is whether the appearance of the courser in the military records marks the emergence of a new type of warhorse (or the first use of an existing type of horse in the military sphere), or simply a new usage: an attempt to differentiate a type which had long existed or which was only gradually emerging, but which previously had been described simply as *equus*. In considering this question it is necessary to look beyond the immediate circumstances of the courser, to take account of broader trends during the period of the three Edwardian kings. It was during this period, as we have seen, that the warhorse reached the peak of its development in England. We would expect this to be mirrored in the horse inventories, and indeed it is: not only in the emergence of the 'great horse', the true destrier and, perhaps also, in the evolution of the *courser*, a swift, but heavy, hunter; but also (as we shall see in Chapter 6) in a general improvement in the quality of horses used by all men-at-arms. The earliest surviving

---

[86] E101/15/12; for a fuller discussion of this document, see below pp. 77–79.

[87] The surviving inventories list nearly 700 different horses, of which all are described as *equi*, with the exception of fifteen destriers. For sources, see Table 6.1. This is not to suggest that the term 'courser' was not in general use, but that it was not used in specialised military records. For coursers in the *Equitia* accounts of the English crown prior to 1336, see Davis, *The medieval warhorse*, pp. 88–89.

[88] Of the forty-four horses listed on the most readily legible inventories from the Irish expedition of 1361–64, thirteen are classified as coursers. This includes Sir Thomas de Hoggeshawe's small company in which all five men served with coursers. E101/28/11, mm. 1–2.

inventories, from the Welsh war of 1282, show the numerically dominant horse to be the rouncy (or *runcinus*).[89] About three quarters of the horses listed are rouncies, whilst the remaining, rather higher grade, warhorses are described simply as *equi*. The roll includes not a single destrier.[90] Edward I's efforts, from the early 1280s, to encourage the breeding of 'great horses' in England were discussed in Chapter 1. The results of this policy were beginning to be seen in the inventories by the later 1290s. The rolls for both the Flanders expedition of 1297 and the Falkirk campaign of the following year continue to show rouncies and *equi* in a roughly three to one balance; but there are now also sixteen destriers amongst the nine hundred *runcini* and *equi* in the Flanders inventories,[91] and a rather larger proportion of these great horses (though still less than 5%) on the Falkirk rolls.[92] In some retinues, destriers figured more prominently. In 1305–6, for example, of the eighteen horses appraised for Sir Henry de Percy's retinue, four were destriers; of Sir Robert de Clifford's nineteen horses, six were destriers.[93] Such cases were unusual, however, for (as we have seen) destriers were never more than a small minority of all English warhorses. Nevertheless, by the early years of Edward II's reign, the terminology of the inventories had undergone a major transformation. The rouncy had disappeared and the great majority of horses not classified as destriers were described simply as *equi*.[94]

As with the appearance of the courser in the 1330s, so with the virtual disappearance of the rouncy from the inventories in the first decade of the century, it must be asked whether a real change in the horseflesh employed by men-at-arms has occurred, or whether we are merely witnessing a shift in terminology, in response, perhaps, to changing fashion or official directives. Statistical analysis of the valuations data suggests that the reigns of Edward I and Edward II did indeed witness a general improvement in warhorse quality. Yet are we to believe that a type of horse which served the majority of men-at-arms under Edward I had been abandoned so completely and so abruptly? Were all the *equi* of the 1310s, 1320s and 1330s, which comprised 90% of all warhorses, really of a quality comparable with the *equi* of the

---

[89] The roan cy was by no means an insubstantial horse, as it had to be capable of carrying an armoured man and barding. It would surely, therefore, be inappropriate to compare this modest grade of warhorse with the 'rounseys familiar to us from Chaucer' (as does Morris, *The Welsh wars of Edward I*, p. 53), or indeed those listed in Little and Exon. Domesday. Cf. J. Langdon, *Horses, oxen and technological innovation* (Cambridge, 1986), p. 296.

[90] C47/2/7. The absence of destriers does not mean that there were no expensive warhorses at this time: forty-six of those listed in this inventory were valued at £20 or more.

[91] E101/6/28; E101/6/37.

[92] *Gough*, pp. 161–237.

[93] E101/612/15, m. 1.

[94] As early as 1301, the rouncy has all but disappeared from a horse roll of the prince of Wales' *comitiva* – nearly all the warhorses listed are *equi*, except for a sprinkling of highly priced destriers: E101/9/23.

1280s and 1290s, which amounted to only 25% of appraised horses? It seems unlikely. More probable is that changes were occurring in equestrian terminology. The word *equus* (or *chival*), as used in military records, has broadened in meaning to become the standard term for a man-at-arms' warhorse. *Magnus equus* is a term reserved for higher quality animals, like the horse lost by Sir Richard de Grey at Bannockburn.[95] At the same time, the word 'rouncy', as used in the inventories, has also shifted in meaning. From being the standard term for the 'fighting' horse of the typical man-at-arms – the type ridden by three out of four men-at-arms, including a number of knights, at Falkirk – it has become, by the early years of the fourteenth century, the description of a horse used primarily for transport; a little closer, therefore, to the Chaucer's usage in *The Canterbury Tales*. A royal proclamation issued prior to the Weardale campaign in 1327 asks that all who intend to serve against the Scots should bring 'swift, strong and hardy rouncies to ride and pursue' the enemy.[96] The rouncy is now presented as the optimum horse, not for the battlefield, but for the march, for rapid movement over rough terrain. As such, rouncies would not be presented for appraisal at the start of a campaign, and it is the *equus* – the man-at-arms' warhorse – which appears in great numbers in the inventories of the 1310s, '20s and '30s. It must be doubted, however, whether the more moderately valued *chivals* and *equi* of this later period differed very significantly as horses from the more highly priced *runcini* of the 1290s: a view which is reinforced by the discovery that, of the eight *runcini* (ranging in value from 100s to 20 marks) which appear unexpectedly in the *restauro equorum* accounts for the War of Saint-Sardos (1324–25),[97] six can be traced in surviving inventories, where each of them is recorded as an *equus* or a *chival*.

In interpreting the evidence compiled by the horse appraisers, it is necessary, therefore, to take account of developments in horse-breeding and changes in terminology. If the former 'was a very slow business, extending over scores of years'[98] or longer, the latter could occur quite suddenly, with established terms changing their meaning or being used for the first time in a specialised military context. In addition, the personal factor should be not be over-looked. The horse appraisers came from a variety of social, occupational and geographical backgrounds and would bring different levels of knowledge and experience to their task. This element of subjectivity would have given rise to a degree of inconsistency in horse classification, but, more significantly perhaps, it would also have influenced valuation.

According to an indenture of the mid 1340s, the warhorses of the

---

[95] E404/482, file 31, no. 9.
[96] 'Runcinos veloces fortes et asperos': *Rot. Scot.*, i, p. 208.
[97] BL Additional MS 7967, fos 104r, 105r, 105v, 106r.
[98] Davis, *The medieval warhorse*, p. 8.

contracting captain's retinue were to be 'prisez a covenable pris'.[99] The 'appropriate' valuation for a particular warhorse would be strongly influenced by a combination of forces, including prevailing economic conditions and the balance of supply and demand. But the value which was entered in the horse inventory was the decision of the appraisers, determined by their standards of judgement, as well, perhaps, as the influence of the owner of the appraised horse. The 'personal' mark of the appraisers, or the influence of others, can be detected in the warhorse valuations in a number of ways. Sometimes a value has been crossed out and a higher or lower figure substituted. In the inventory for the Scottish campaign of 1336, Sir Henry de Beaumont's courser was given a value of £20 at first, only subsequently to be altered to £40.[100] Moreover, if the values are examined in bulk, some intriguing insights into 'valuing policy' can be gained. For some campaigns a clear-cut minimum valuation can be detected: £5. On several occasions during the 1340s clerks appointed to the task of horse appraisal were ordered to restrict their attention to horses worth 100s or more.[101] It is not clear how often this ruling was applied, but the weight of evidence suggests that it was a customary regulation for fourteenth-century continental campaigns. It is equally uncertain how the minimum value rule was applied in practice. Were horses which were considered to be worth less than 100s simply passed-over by the appraisers, or were they all given the minimum valuation and included in the inventory? The latter is a real possibility, as there are always substantial numbers of £5 horses in the inventories.[102] Some expeditionary forces during this period were quite clearly not subject to this valuation restriction. The inventories arising from the Scottish campaigns of 1336–37 include considerable numbers of horses with low valuations, the lowest being Walter de Thomaston's *equus*, valued at a mere 30s on 14 May 1336.[103] The inventories for the winter 1337–38 campaign list very few low-value warhorses[104] and whilst this contrast might in part result from genuine differences in warhorse quality, it probably also reflects contrasting approaches to valuation by different teams of appraisers.

99 The earl of Derby's indenture with Edward III, 15 March 1345, printed in Fowler, *The king's lieutenant*, p. 230.

100 E101/19/36, m. 2.

101 Brittany, 1342: C76/17, mm. 17, 18; Scotland, 1347: *Rot. Scot.*, i, 694.

102 The *restauro equorum* accounts for the Breton campaign of 1342–43 list thirty-five £5 horses (15%); those for the Cambrésis-Thiérache campaign of 1339, forty-two (11%). The inventories for the War of Saint-Sardos include seventy-three (11%).

103 E101/19/36, m. 5. He was one of fifteen men (out of thirty) in the earl of Angus' retinue with horses worth less than £5. Most of the inventories for the Scottish campaigns of Edward I and Edward II contain numerous *runcini* and *equi* valued at under £5 (a notable exception is Aymer de Valence's roll in 1315: E101/15/6), but the absolute minimum value appears to be £2.

104 There are only eight horses valued at less than £5 in 1337–38, as compared with sixty-seven in 1336 and fifty-five in 1337.

A global view of the values in the inventories reveals further differences of approach. As a general rule, the horse appraisers were not concerned with minute gradations of valuation: the great majority of warhorses were assigned values from a comparatively limited selection. During the 1320s, '30s and '40s they would usually choose from the following: £5, 8 marks, £6, 10 marks, £8, £10, £12, 20 marks, £20, 40 marks, £30, 50 marks, £40, £50, 100 marks and £100.[105] They were not, therefore, attempting to provide a precise valuation for each horse – a valuation which offered a true reflection of its strengths and weaknesses – so much as seeking to assign it to one of a small selection of numerical pigeon holes. As a result, some horses would be undervalued and others over-priced; the more valuable the horse, the less precise the valuation category. Whilst this rough and ready approach is the norm for most inventories, in some cases there are clear signs of a more subtle and flexible attitude to valuation. Two examples will serve to demonstrate the point very clearly.

The *restauro equorum* accounts for the Breton campaign of 1342–43 allow for twenty-two different valuations. It adds only six categories to the normal selection and these additional values account for only eleven of the 228 horses on the roll. By contrast, the corresponding accounts for the Cambrésis-Thiérache campaign of 1338–39 make use of a total of fifty-one different values, with thirty-six categories beyond the normal selection and sixty-three of the total of 376 horses falling into these additional categories. The accounts for 1338–39 list a larger number of horses than those for 1342 and this certainly serves to heighten the contrast, but the fact remains that the appraisers responsible for the original inventories in the summer and autumn of 1342 were far less flexible in their approach to valuation than their counterparts had been in 1338–39.

Turning to the three collections of original inventories from the period 1336–38, a similar significant contrast in valuing policy can be seen. The rolls for 1336 and the summer of 1337 have a restricted selection of values. In 1336, well over five hundred horses are grouped into only eighteen value categories, with those worth £5 or more (the great majority) allocated to no more than twelve. The treatment of the 341 horses in the 1337 inventories is broadly similar, but with the winter 1337–38 inventories (and associated *restauro equorum* accounts) we see a marked contrast. The latter, as we have seen, contain very few low-value warhorses; they also exhibit an interesting *spread* of higher values. About two-thirds of the 367 horses on the roll have, it is true, been slotted into eight standard value pigeon holes,[106] but thirty-two other values are also used to provide more subtle indications of equestrian quality. The 1337–38 materials are particularly distinctive in that they favour

---

105 Of the lower values, 8 marks and £6 are prominent in some inventories, but not others; £5 and 10 marks are consistently the most frequently occurring low values. The same limited selection of values dominate the inventories under the first two Edwards.

106 £5, 10 marks, £8, £10, 20 marks, £20, 40 marks and £40.

several values which are seen far less often in the other inventories of this period. Thirty-two horses are valued at eight marks, whereas only four and seven are assigned this figure in 1336 and 1337 respectively.[107] Two other values, 16 marks and 24 marks, are also employed with greater than usual frequency in the 1337–38 materials.

Why the appraisers responsible for the winter 1337–38 inventories should show an unusual preference for valuations of 8 marks (and, indeed, multiples of eight) is not clear; it is always far easier to draw attention to such phenomena than to explain them. This is, however, a neat illustration of the subjectivity of the appraisal process. Two appraisers, with equal experience of equestrian affairs, may well propose different values for a particular horse. This would, perhaps, be most likely to happen if one of them was more inclined to favour subtle gradations of value. It is probable, for example, that the great majority of the horses valued at 8 marks (£5 6s 8d) in the 1337–38 inventory would have been assigned a £5 or a 10 marks valuation by a different, more conventional team of appraisers. But the effects of subjectivity – and, indeed, the tendency to force horses into a modest range of value categories – on the quality of the evidence should be placed in proper perspective. It should perhaps be borne in mind when examining individual horses, particularly highly priced animals, where the scope for wayward valuations must have been greatest; but it becomes a far less important consideration in global-level analysis of horse values, when individual valuations are absorbed in broad summary statistics. As we shall see in Chapter 6, if some inventories are tinged with the character of their compilers, they seem to be far more profoundly coloured by economic conditions and prevailing military attitudes.

COMPENSATION FOR LOSSES

> You could see horses here and there lying in the meadow and letting out their last breath; others, wounded in the stomach, were vomiting their entrails, while others were lying down with their hocks severed.[108]

Horse inventories were working records. Admittedly, some show no sign of use, perhaps because they were 'clean' copies, preserved for reference only, or because their active life had been very short.[109] Most, however, were consulted by army marshals and annotated by clerks throughout the course of a campaign. The marginal notes and textual emendations, made during the weeks following muster, add an extra, often very useful, dimension to these records. Deletions of names, substitutions and late arrivals provide an

---

107 '8 marks' appears regularly in the inventories for the War of Saint-Sardos, but far less often in the *restauro equorum* accounts for the early campaigns of the French war.

108 Extract from William the Breton's *Philippiad*, quoted in G. Duby, *The legend of Bouvines*, English trans. (Cambridge, 1990), p. 200.

109 For example, the inventory for the earl of Cornwall's retinue in 1336, drawn up only a few days before the earl's death: E101/19/36, m. 1.

indication of changes in army size and structure, whilst the dates and places mentioned in the clerical notes can allow the historian to build up a detailed impression of an army's movements.[110] The majority of annotations concern horse losses. In many cases the word 'mortuus', 'perditus' or 'interfectus' is followed by the date and place of loss, and sometimes the precise circumstances, thereby providing glimpses of the course of the campaign and the intensity of the fighting; and also, perhaps, indications of changes in an army's military effectiveness. A great battle could leave an indelible mark on the inventories, as the two major horse appraisal rolls for the Falkirk campaign so eloquently demonstrate. Rather more than a hundred of the 1,350 or so horses listed are noted as having been lost in the battle on 22 July 1298. This does not take account of losses by the unpaid sections of the army, nor of fatalities amongst the second string mounts of those men-at-arms who were paid, so the total number of English warhorses that perished on that day must, indeed, have been considerable.[111] The Falkirk rolls offer an unusually vivid picture of equestrian losses on the battlefield; but large-scale battles were not an everyday event and for few do we have really detailed records of horse casualties (there is only fragmentary evidence for warhorse losses at Bannockburn, for example).[112] Moreover, many of the horse fatalities from combat arose from skirmishes rather than set-piece battles.[113] Even after the English had abandoned the regular tactical use of heavy cavalry, an event such as the ambush of Sir Ralph de Ufford's column in the Moiry Pass (Ireland) in 1345 could give rise to heavy equestrian casualties.[114]

For most campaigns a very significant proportion, if not the majority, of warhorse losses arose from the rigours of the march: from accidents, exhaustion, disease or malnourishment.[115] The inventories for the Scottish campaign of 1336 provide good examples of this. Several horses are said to have been killed 'in montibus' during Edward III's raid into the Highlands in July, whilst two horses in Henry, Lord Percy's retinue died of murrain at Elgin on

---

110 E.g. see J.R.S. Phillips, *Aymer de Valence, earl of Pembroke 1307–1324* (Oxford, 1972), pp. 89–90, for a reconstruction of Pembroke's operations in the Scottish Marches during the summer and autumn of 1315, based upon the dated notes in the army's horse inventory: E101/15/6.

111 *Gough*, pp. 160–237; M. Prestwich, *Edward I* (London, 1988), p. 481. For the losses of individual retinues, see J.E. Morris, *Bannockburn* (Cambridge, 1914), p. 46.

112 Wardrobe debentures: E404/482, files 31 and 32. Cf. the evidence for the heavy warhorse losses at the battle of Montecatini in 1315: L. Green, *Castruccio Castracani* (Oxford, 1986) pp. 68–69. For glimpses of the horse losses at Cassel, Crécy and Poitiers, see Contamine, *Guerre, état et société*, p. 105.

113 For example, in the 1310s fights at *Faringley*, *le Redecros* and *Penresax*: Morris, 'Cumberland and Westmorland military levies in the time of Edward I and Edward II'.

114 C260/57, m. 28.

115 On the daily amounts of feed required by warhorses, see M. Prestwich, 'Victualling estimates for English garrisons in Scotland during the early fourteenth century', *EHR*, lxxxii (1967), pp. 536, 539. Hyland, *Equus. The horse in the Roman world*, chapter 9: 'Hazards and health', is an illuminating discussion.

the 19th of the same month and Sir John de Tibetot's £20 horse was 'submersus' during a passage of the Forth on 7 September.[116] Had a more plentiful supply of original inventories survived for Edward III's continental campaigns, we would surely have found a similar story of sickness and misadventure. The narrative sources often draw attention to the heavy equestrian losses suffered by the English during their *chevauchées*. The Black Prince's raid of 1355 cost the English many horses, due to the difficulty of the terrain and inadequate supplies of water.[117] Even if the French chronicle estimates for English horse casualties during John of Gaunt's 'Great *Chevauchée*' are exaggerated (80% of over 30,000 horses),[118] there is unimpeachable record evidence for the loss of well over a thousand *appraised* warhorses during the Reims campaign of 1359–60.[119] In addition to the hazards of the march, the dangers arising from protracted occupation of unhealthy siege-camps should also be recognised. It is hardly surprising that men were keen to send their expensive horseflesh back to England during the siege of Calais.

The other major cause of equestrian losses, at least where continental campaigns are concerned, arose from the necessity of transporting large numbers of warhorses by sea; but once again, in the absence of annotated inventories, it is necessary to rely in the main upon the narrative sources for evidence of maritime disasters. For example, the *restauro equorum* accounts for the Breton campaign in 1342–43 reveal nothing about the circumstances behind the loss of well over two hundred appraised warhorses. It would be safe to assume that the siege camp at Vannes would have taken its toll; but several chronicles also draw attention to equestrian losses incurred during the turbulent passage back to England.[120] In addition to the loss of ships in stormy weather, which was an occasional, if devastating, occurrence,[121] we should also recognise the damaging effects of long, debilitating voyages during which horses would get no exercise, as well (in all probability) as being subjected to an inadequate or inappropriate diet.[122] There would be

---

116 E101/19/36, mm. 3, 3d, 5d, 7d.

117 *The life and campaigns of the Black Prince*, ed. Barber, pp. 61, 66, 68, using the chronicle of Geoffrey le Baker. The horses were given wine to drink, with disastrous results.

118 G. Holmes, *The Good Parliament* (Oxford, 1975), pp. 26–28.

119 E101/393/11, fos 79r–116v. Cf. the French royal army in 1340, which lost over 3,000 warhorses: Contamine, *Guerre, état et société*, p. 106.

120 *Murimuth*, p. 135; *Melsa*, iii, pp. 51–52.

121 For the effect of the elements on Thomas, duke of Gloucester's voyage to Prussia in 1391 (his losses included 'equos optimos'), see *Westminster*, pp. 482–85. In December 1379 a fleet bound for Brittany was devastated by storms and nineteen horse transport vessels were wrecked on the Cornish coast: J. Sherborne, 'Indentured retinues and English expeditions to France, 1369–1380', *EHR*, lxxix (1964), p. 731.

122 For a most illuminating discussion of the problems of transporting horses by sea, as relevant to the Middle Ages as for the period in which it was written, see M.H. Hayes, *Horses on board ship. A guide to their management* (London, 1902). Also useful are B.S. Bachrach, 'On the origins of William the Conqueror's horse transports', *Technology and*

equestrian casualties even during tranquil voyages,[123] and after a long journey many horses would be unfit for immediate service. Such considerations seem to have encouraged many men serving in Gascony to purchase their horses upon arrival in the duchy, rather than risk bringing them from England. The stipulation, in the agreement between the king of Portugal and the earl of Cambridge for the service of English troops in Portugal in 1381, 'that the king should provide a mount for every Englishman, but discount its value from his pay' appears to be founded upon similar wholly justified anxieties.[124]

A horse need not actually be killed for its owner to qualify for a compensation payment. A man-at-arms was occasionally the victim of sharp practice by the enemy. On 23 June 1337 Sir Henry Fitz Henry's courser, valued at 20 marks, was stolen in the night by the Scots.[125] But more frequently, we find men receiving compensation when their appraised warhorses become unfit for service, through injury, lameness, exhaustion or disease. In such cases, the clerk responsible for keeping the inventories up-to-date would usually note that the horse had been delivered to the army 'caravan' or baggage train: 'redditur ad karvannum'.[126] Some horses were evidently well cared for in the caravan,[127] for we occasionally see animals being discharged with their health fully restored. But in these circumstances no compensation payment was due;[128] and the same applied if the injury which had caused the horse's incapacity had been noticed at the time of appraisal.[129]

There are several further forms of marginal annotation which appear to indicate that a horse has been withdrawn from service. The most common is 'redditur ad Elemosinam', but we also occasionally find 'redditur ad Garderoba'. In both cases a location (e.g. Newcastle) is often specified. It

Culture, xxvi (1985), pp. 505–31; and J.H. Prior, 'Transportation of horses by sea during the era of the crusades: eighth century to 1285 A.D.', *The Mariner's Mirror*, lxviii (1982), pp. 9–30; 103–25.

123 For example, the Black Prince's voyage to Gascony in September 1355: Morgan, *War and society in medieval Cheshire*, p. 110, drawing on the evidence of John Henxteworth's *Journal*.

124 *Fernao Lopes: The English in Portugal*, ed. Lomax and Oakley, pp. 68–69.

125 E101/20/17, m. 7d.

126 Cf. the Templar Rule, which allowed for the return of difficult mounts ('pullers', 'stoppers' and 'throwers') to the 'caravanne': M. Bennett, '*La Règle du Temple* as a military manual or how to deliver a cavalry charge', *Studies in medieval history presented to R. Allen Brown*, ed. C. Harper-Bill, C.J. Holdsworth and J.L. Nelson (Woodbridge, 1989), pp. 10–11.

127 On medieval veterinary science, in the development of which England appears to have played very little part, see Davis, *The medieval warhorse*, pp. 100–7.

128 E.g. the case of two knights whose horses joined the caravan on the day after the battle of Falkirk. For each, the clerk added in the margin: 'Non habebit restaurum quia equus restituitur sanus apud [Durham/Newcastle]'. *Gough*, p. 196.

129 E.g. the appraisers in 1282 noticed that Sir Hugh de Doddinseles' 12 mark horse had various injuries and recorded that no compensation should be paid if these defects proved to be the cause of death: C47/2/7, m. 2.

must be admitted that the meaning of these phrases is not entirely clear.[130] The experience of other European states may tempt us to look for unexpected and very precise explanations,[131] but the weight of evidence suggests that, far from representing wholly distinct and separate concepts, they are in fact interchangeable with one another and, indeed, with the phrase 'redditur ad karvannum'. For example, the *restauro equorum* account for the Scottish campaign of 1322 states that two of the horses attached to Sir Thomas de Ughtred's retinue have been rendered 'ad Elemosinam' at Newcastle on 12 September, whilst the corresponding *vadia guerre* account records that these two horses have in fact been delivered to the caravan at Newcastle.[132] In 1327, after the Weardale campaign, the warhorses of John of Hainault's contingent of men-at-arms were delivered 'ad karvannum',[133] but here we are seeing horses which were being *sold* to royal officials. In the inventories for the Scottish campaign of 1336 there are five horses marked 'ad Elemosinam' and three 'ad Garderoba'. Yet there are seven other horses which are simply assigned to a location (for example 'redditus apud Perth', 3 September) and there are no annotations 'ad karvannum' in any of the inventories for this expedition, which also include no fewer than ninety (out of 542) horses marked 'mortuus', with varying amounts of additional information.[134] A contrasting, and indeed perplexing, situation is to be found in a set of inventories for a small army serving in Scotland in 1315. In these rolls there are no 'mortuus' annotations at all, but over two dozen horses (*all* of the 'losses' in the inventory) are marked 'redditur ad Elemosinam'.[135] Did this army not suffer a single equestrian fatality, or has the clerk responsible for the inventory simply used a single form of annotation for all circumstances of horse loss?

It is clear from this selection of cases that a clerk might use one of several different short-hand phrases to identify a horse which had been delivered into the king's custody; and, moreover, that a horse which had been *killed* may not

---

130 They imply that the horse has been transferred, perhaps sold, into royal custody. The phrase 'redditur ad Elemosinam' is particularly problematic: it might indicate that the horse is being treated as a *deodand* (the cause of a person's death which has been 'handed-over to the king and devoted by his almoner to pious uses': Sir F. Pollock and F.W. Maitland, *The history of English law before the time of Edward I*, 2 vols, repr., (Cambridge, 1968), ii, p. 473). Alternatively, it might suggest that compensation was being offered as 'as alms, not as a matter of obligation': *Topham*, p. 364.

131 In Spain, for example, a knight who neglected his military duties suffered the humiliation of having his horse's tail cut off. As a consequence, a man automatically received *restauro equorum* if his horse accidentally lost its tail in battle, thus enabling him to avoid embarrassment amongst his peers. J.F. Powers, *A society organised for war. The Iberian municipal militias in the central Middle Ages, 1000–1284* (London, 1988), pp. 199–200.

132 BL Stowe MS 553, fos 60v, 70r.

133 E101/383/8, fo. 7r.

134 E101/19/36. The three 'ad Garderoba' cases are all to be found in Sir Ralph de Neville's retinue and all are dated 'Berwick, 14 December'.

135 E101/15/6.

always be distinguished from one which had simply been withdrawn from service. However, the important point is that all of these clerical usages, the enigmatic ones as well as the unambiguous cases of 'mortuus', indicated that the horse had been 'lost' and that its owner was eligible for compensation. This is most clearly shown when a *restauro equorum* account offers full details of the circumstances of loss. For example, the horse compensation list associated with the Scottish campaign of 1322 and its immediate aftermath includes eleven fatalities from the battle of Byland, but also fifteen horses which had been rendered 'ad Elemosinam' in various places.[136] The *restauro equorum* accounts for the continental campaigns of 1338–39 and 1342–43 do not provide this kind of detail, but given the inconsistency and ambiguity of clerical usages, we should not, perhaps, be unduly concerned about the detail that has been obscured.[137] We should not allow the limitations of the *restauro equorum* accounts to outweigh their strengths. They only list losses among appraised horses, but such accounts are, nevertheless, likely to give a more comprehensive view of losses than the original inventories, which usually provide only partial coverage and may not be completely up-to-date. For example, the inventories for the 1336 Scottish campaign, although an un-usually full set, do not offer quite as complete a picture of equestrian casual-ties as the corresponding *restauro equorum* accounts.[138]

The relationship between the information supplied by horse inventories and that contained in *restauro equorum* accounts is best explored by refer-ence to the administrative processes set in motion when a captain claimed compensation for the losses sustained by men in his retinue. Such claims were handled by the marshal of the army and/or the clerk who had been associated with the marshal in the appraisal process.[139] They would require proof of loss. In normal circumstances this would probably involve the presentation of the branded portion of the dead horse's hide.[140] Sometimes this would not be

---

136 BL Stowe MS 553, fos 70r, 71r.

137 Cf. the *restauro equorum* accounts for the War of Saint-Sardos, in which, although the time and place of most horse losses are specified, all are regarded simply as 'mortuus': BL Additional MS 7967, fos 104r–106v.

138 E101/19/36; BL Cotton MS, Nero C. VIII, fos 280v–282r. Although all of the horses listed in the *restauro equorum* account are to be found in the surviving inventories, four of them are *not* marked as casualties in the original lists. Conversely, Robert de Longvill's 10 mark hobby, 'mortuus' at Perth on 6 September (m. 2d), has *not* been included in the compensation account. These *restauro equorum* accounts are more detailed than those for subsequent French campaigns; they record all the horses as simply 'mortuus', but do attempt to summarise information about the time and place of death.

139 See, for example, *Bain*, v, p. 213 (1306–7); BL Cotton MS, Nero C. VIII, fo. 280v (1336).

140 This was the usual practice of several continental states: Contamine, *Guerre, état et société*, p. 104–5; Mallett and Hale, *The military organisation of a Renaissance state*, p. 139. It is sometimes suggested that the ears and tail of the dead animal were presented as evidence of its death (e.g. *List of documents relating to the household and wardrobe, John-Edward I* (London, 1964), p. 59); but this would provide far less certain proof than the brand-mark.

possible – a horse's carcass would not always be recoverable – and in these cases it is likely that 'une simple déclaration de perte affirmée sous serment'[141] would suffice. The captain's coordinating role in such *restor* claims ensured that the less clear-cut cases at least received the backing of a retinue commander. Injured animals would present the greatest problem to the army marshal. He would need to determine whether they were unfit for further service and thus qualified their owner for compensation. This would inevitably involve difficult decisions, for we may be sure that the more expensive an animal, the more likely that the slightest injury would be seen by its owner as justification for a compensation claim.

Each *restor* claim would be verified against the description in the horse inventory. The inventory was also the absolute authority for the sum which was due in compensation. Occasionally we are allowed a glimpse of this consultative process. In the early 1360s Sir Thomas Dale wrote to Walter Dalby asking him to 'enserchier les prises' of two horses from Sir Eustace d'Auberchicourt's retinue which 'sont tuez sur les guerres' in Ireland, so that their owners 'purront estre duemont restorez de la prise des chivalx'.[142] Once the check had been made, the details of the loss would be noted in the inventory in one of the ways which we have considered[143] and a warrant authorising payment would be issued.[144] Retinue captains would present these *restauro equorum* warrants when they accounted for their men's wages.[145] The authorisation process has sometimes left a trace in the surviving documentation. The horses listed in the *restauro equorum* account for the Scottish campaign of 1336 qualified for compensation 'by witness' of Sir Ralph de Neville, marshal of the army and John de Houton, clerk.[146] In the case of Henry of Lancaster's retinue in 1336, the documents involved in the process of making account have survived: a roll which includes a muster list for Lancaster's men-at-arms and a list of the warhorses lost by Lancaster's

---

[141] As in France: Contamine, *Guerre, état et société*, p. 104.

[142] E101/28/27, m. 10. These were the only horse losses sustained by d'Auberchicourt's retinue: E101/28/21, fo. 14v. Both Dale and Dalby had been appraisers of d'Auberchicourt's horses early in 1363: E101/28/11, m. 1.

[143] Separate lists might be made of horses delivered to the army caravan: see, for example, E101/7/21 (1298–99: 'ad karvannum' and 'ad Elemosinam'); E101/612/12, m. 7 (1304–5: 'Rotulus de karvannum').

[144] For a similar warrant issued to Millet le Buef, esquire, for a horse killed during the battle of Crécy, see Contamine, *Guerre, état et société*, p. 105 n. 101.

[145] See, for example, the detailed records for the Scottish campaign of 1322, which frequently give the date and place of account for both *vadia guerre* and *restauro equorum*: BL Stowe MS 553, fo. 56r; cf. fo. 70r. An individual presenting his own compensation warrant would be at an advantage if supported by the authority of a prominent captain: see, for example, Aymer de Valence's letter supporting Hugh de Whaplode's bid to recover the cost of his *rounscin darmes*, thereby confirming the letter of authorisation by the appraiser, Sir James de Dalyleye (SC1/48, no. 114).

[146] BL Cotton MS, Nero C. VIII, fos 280v–82r.

retinue during the campaign.[147] The latter is a most interesting document. The entries in the list are in the standard horse inventory form, but unlike the original inventory[148] they are arranged chronologically according to the date of loss (from the first on 27 May to the last on 4 November), and they also appear in a more abbreviated form. The horse descriptions are shorter and whilst the date and place of loss *are* noted, there is no attempt to reproduce the distinction between 'mortuus' and 'ad Elemosina' which we find in the original inventory. If Lancaster received individual warrants for each of the twenty-one horses which were lost by members of his retinue, then they appear to have been enrolled into a single list. It is this list, moreover, which formed the basis of Lancaster's entry in the *restauro equorum* account for this campaign.[149] The order is the same (i.e. very different from that of the inventory) and the content is identical, with the exception of a few further abbreviations of the horse descriptions and slight variation in the spelling of the names of individuals.

It seems likely, then, that it is an intermediate stage of documentation which holds the key to the disparities which are so often to be found between associated inventories and *restauro equorum* accounts. But such intermediate documents, compiled in the field and presented at the time of making account, must have taken a variety of forms. A comparison of the annotated inventories and the *restor* accounts for the 1336 campaign suggests that the chronological ordering of the information displayed by Lancaster's roll was not the norm. The majority of retinue-sections in the *restauro equorum* account reproduce the order of the original inventory, but whether this arose from rolls like Lancaster's (but differently ordered), or from the sorting of bundles of *restor* warrants into the order of the inventories, is unclear.[150] Although Lancaster's roll may not in some respects have been a typical document, the evidence that it offers for the process whereby the information of the inventories was abbreviated and simplified is nevertheless very valuable. The 'intermediate' document retains the date and place of horse losses, but is unspecific about the precise cause of loss, with the result that the final

---

[147] E101/15/12. There are, in fact, two muster rolls (though the second is truncated), one for each of the two accounting periods specified in the *vadia guerre* accounts (1 May to 7 September; 8 September to 16 November): BL Cotton MS, Nero C. VIII, fo. 240r.

[148] E101/19/36, m. 7.

[149] BL Cotton MS, Nero C. VIII, fo. 280v.

[150] The only exception is the section concerned with the earl of Warwick's losses (ibid., fo. 281r). In this case, the order is by rank, but the information within each rank-grouping *does* follow the order of the inventory. This unusual, though entirely logical, arrangement was in all liklihood based upon a horse roll similar to Lancaster's. The materials for other campaigns suggest that the order of the inventories was frequently preserved in the corresponding *restauro equorum* account: e.g. the earl of Gloucester's retinue in 1337–38 (E101/35/3, m. 1; E101/20/25, m. 3). In the case of the *restauro equorum* account for the Breton campaign of 1342–43, the horses within most of the retinue-sections are listed in decreasing value order: E36/204, fos 86v–88r.

restauro equorum account, though summarising the information about time and place (and adopting the abbreviated horse descriptions of the intermediate record), simply regards all the horses listed as 'dead'.[151] The other differences which are occasionally found between associated inventories and compensation accounts (as, for example, when an *equus* becomes a *courser*)[152] are also most likely to be the result of changes, conscious or unconscious, made at the point of drawing up the warrants to authorise *restauro equorum* payments.

A discussion of the influence of authorising warrants on the form and content of *restauro equorum* accounts will necessarily be tentative, for supportive evidence is not abundant. It is not clear, for example, how far the reticence of the *restauro equorum* accounts for the early campaigns of the French war is the consequence of heavily abbreviated 'intermediate' records or of clerical conciseness at a later stage. Nor is it clear whether the clerks responsible for the *restauro equorum* accounts made use of the original inventories. It would certainly be unwise to assume consistency of clerical method, just as it would be prudent to expect a sprinkling of clerical errors. A glance at two versions of part of the *restauro equorum* accounts for the winter 1337–38 campaign in Scotland will show how two attempts at the same clerical exercise, but not necessarily drawing on the same materials, could produce slightly different results.[153] Comparison of the two rolls, Walter de Westons's and William de Kellesey's, with the original inventory reveals a certain amount of abbreviation in the horse descriptions; but in the case of two of the horses in the earl of Salisbury's retinue, Weston's roll offers colourings which are quite different from those given in the inventory.[154] With the earl of Gloucester's retinue, on the other hand, we find that it is Kellesey's roll which differs from the inventory, this time with respect to the horse valuations. The most interesting discrepancy concerns Sir Adam de Everingham's horse, which Kellesey's roll records with a value of 28 marks, as compared with 25 marks in the inventory. Weston's roll has the latter figure, but '28 marks' can clearly be seen to have been erased.[155] Whether the explanation of this particular case lies in the influence of an 'intermediate' record or a different version of the inventory (the only surviving one is wholly

---

[151] E.g. John de Wetwang's £6 horse which was stolen by the enemy at Stirling (E101/19/36, m. 5d) is presented as a fatality in the *restauro equorum* account: BL Cotton MS, Nero C. VIII, fo. 281v.

[152] E.g. Sir John de *Tybbetoft's equus*, drowned in the Forth between Cambuskenneth and Stirling on 7 September 1336 (E101/19/36, m. 5d), becomes Sir John *Tibetot's courser* which died at Stirling on 7 September (BL Cotton MS, Nero C. VIII, fo. 281v).

[153] Some of the *restauro equorum* materials appear in both Walter de Weston's roll (E101/20/25) and the 'duplicate' roll of his controller, William de Kellesey (E101/20/26).

[154] E101/20/25, m. 3; cf. E101/35/3, mm. 2d–1d and E101/20/26, m. 2. Kellesey's roll, but not Weston's, notes that Nicholas Webbele, who lost a 10 mark horse, was the '*vallet* of Sir Roger Huse', a usage which seems closely related to the appraiser's roll.

[155] E101/20/26, m. 2; cf. E101/35/3, m. 1 and E101/20/25, m. 3.

unannotated), or in clerical error, its implications are clear enough. It provides a concrete example of how the process of drawing up a set of *restauro equorum* accounts could give rise not merely to loss of detail, through abbreviation and the frequent need to translate from French into Latin,[156] but also to the recording of horse valuations different from those in the inventories. It is necessary to be aware of this potential flaw in the *restauro equorum* data, but we should not be unduly dismayed by it. Firstly, such errors are unlikely to be numerous; and though disruptive on the level of the individual, they would have no more than a minimal effect upon a statistical analysis of horse values. Secondly, the inventories should not be assumed to be infallible. Disparity between inventory and *restauro equorum* account may arise from the earlier document being incompletely annotated.

In general, the crown's liability for compensation was based squarely upon the information contained in the horse inventories. This meant, on the one hand, that only those warhorses which had been appraised were eligible for compensation in the event of loss: in most cases, only one horse per man-at-arms at any one time. A man would indeed be unfortunate if the horses he lost were those which had *not* been valued, but this must have been a very common occurrence. On the other hand, the crown would accept liability for the *full value* of the appraised horses which were lost. Only in exceptional circumstances was a system of flat-rate compensation payments adopted, though such a system was normal in some continental states.[157] In emphasising that it was only appraised horses which were eligible for compensation, we must recognise that there *were* exceptions to the rule. The group most likely to secure special treatment from the king were his own household servants. Under Edward III, gifts to cover the cost of unappraised horses, lost during a campaign or whilst pursuing the king's business in England, are a commonplace of the records; but these, assuredly, are not warhorses and the gifts were made at the modest standard rate of 40s per horse, as we see in November 1343 when William de Bolton, clerk, received this sum 'pro restauro unius somerii sui . . . apud Vanes perditi'.[158] Evidence of similar gifts for the compensation of unappraised *warhorses* is far less frequently encountered. Clearly the king's closest confidants were in the best position to

---

[156] The process of translation also has an effect upon name forms. This is reinforced by the tendency of clerks drawing up final accounts to employ standard forms, rather than the eccentric spellings used in the inventories, which were, no doubt, the result of oral communication at the time of appraisal.

[157] Sir Thomas Dagworth's *restauro equorum* claim following a year's service in Brittany in 1346 was based upon a flat-rate of £10 per warhorse lost: E101/25/17. By contrast, in fourteenth-century France, it was usual to pay a fixed rate of 25 livres tournois for each lost horse (Contamine, *Guerre, état et société*, p. 105); cf. a contract between Louis de Nevers and a household knight from 1338 (Vale, *War and chivalry*, p. 67).

[158] E403/331, m. 11. For many such 40s payments, see *Norwell*, pp. 320–25. Cf. M.C. Hill, *The king's messengers, 1199–1377* (London, 1961), pp. 39–40.

secure special favours of this kind, as William de Montagu appears to have done in 1336;[159] but deserving cases also stood a reasonable chance of receiving fair treatment. In December 1369 the king and council agreed to a gift of 200 marks for a group of nine Scottish esquires who had incurred losses during a period of service in France.[160] We should not imagine, however, that the crown agreed to all such compensation requests; there was a limit to the king's generosity. Thierry, lord of Fauquemont's retinue lost thirty-four horses during the Low Countries campaign of 1338–39, and this, combined with 'diversis equis perditis in via versus domum una nocte que non potuerat habere hospicium nec pabulum', amounted to a total of £600. But Fauquemont's claim was disallowed 'by oral order of the king at Brussells' because the horses concerned could not be found amongst the lists of those appraised for the campaign.[161]

It was one thing for a captain's compensation claim to be accepted by the crown; but actually securing payment was quite another matter. As so often with royal disbursements for military service, *restauro equorum* payments were rarely made promptly.[162] A captain might wait months, and not infrequently years, for full payment of the cost of his retinue's lost horses. Sir John Darcy *junior* received a payment of £16 in July 1344 for a horse which had been lost by a member of his retinue, John de Sautre, during the Breton campaign of 1342–43;[163] but Sir Reginald de Cobham was still receiving instalments to cover losses from the same campaign throughout the following

---

159 Montagu received £100 in compensation for unappraised horses which had been lost on campaign: BL Cotton MS, Nero C. VIII, fo. 282r. In June 1353 the king authorised the payment of £500 to the earl of Stafford to cover the cost of horses lost by his men in Gascony during the previous year: E101/26/25.

160 *Issue Roll of Thomas de Brantingham*, ed. F. Devon (London, 1835), pp. 410–11.

161 *Norwell*, p. 324. For the *fief-rente* which Fauquemont received from Edward III, see *Treaty Rolls, 1337–39*, no. 39; see also H.S. Lucas, *The Low Countries and the Hundred Years War, 1326–1347* (Ann Arbor, 1929), p. 218. Others among the foreign lords in Edward III's army successfully secured compensation for losses: e.g. Henry de Flanders (*Norwell*, p. 316), who had been promised in his indenture that warhorse losses would be paid for 'solonc ceo qils serront loialment & en bone foi prisez': E101/68/3, no. 43.

162 The receipt of a compensation payment could involve several administrative steps. Captains accounting for their losses at the wardrobe would be issued with a debenture for presentation at the Exchequer of Receipt (see, for example, the debentures arising from horse losses at Bannockburn: E404/482, files 31, 32). The eventual payment would be recorded on the Issue Rolls. In some circumstances, however, it is clear that *restauro equorum* payments *were* made very rapidly. In Gascony during the 1350s it was not uncommon for only a day or two to elapse between the issue of a warrant for *restauro equorum* by the seneschal and the receipt of payment from the constable of Bordeaux: for a file of warrants and receipts, see E101/172/4. Of the seventeen cases in which we have both warrant and receipt, all except two involve an intervening period of less than a week, and for two men the whole process was completed in a single day. It should perhaps be added that all these cases concerned individuals and that the sums involved were not large.

163 E403/332, m. 16; cf. E36/204, fo. 88r.

year.[164] The sums involved could be quite substantial,[165] and even the smaller debts might not be satisfied within a few years, though the fact that it took twenty years to meet the cost of a horse lost at Bannockburn seems extraordinary.[166] Many of the men seeking *restauro equorum* payments from the crown were captains whose claims were mainly made up of warhorses lost by men in their retinues. Thus, although Sir Reginald de Cobham had lost his own horse, valued at 100 marks, during the Breton expedition in 1342–43, this was less than a third of his total compensation claim for the campaign.[167] How promptly did captains compensate their men for their losses? Occasionally, we find an indenture which includes an undertaking by the captain to pay compensation in full within a fixed period from the time of loss. In Aymer de Valence's agreement with Sir Thomas Berkeley in 1297, the period was a generous forty days;[168] but in 1350, Richard, earl of Arundel was only prepared to guarantee payment 'dedeinz lan' for horses which had been 'mort ou mayneinez'.[169] It is quite unusual for indentures, whether of a long- or short-term nature, to be as specific as this,[170] and we are left wondering whether captains were inclined to pay their men and wait for eventual recompense from the crown, or whether they kept their military retainers waiting until they received payment themselves. The terms of some military subcontracts of the later fourteenth century tend to suggest that the latter is most likely.[171] One might imagine that men who were more permanently attached to a captain would receive prompt compensation, but the retainers of great magnates can often be seen waiting a year or two for *restauro equorum* payments, and sometimes much longer.[172] Sir Maurice de Berkeley, who was

---

164 E403/335, mm. 21, 27; E403/336 m. 6.

165 For example, Hugh Audley *senior*, who in 1327 was owed £410 6s 8d for horses lost some years earlier in the Scottish war: *Calendar of Memoranda Rolls, 1326–27* (London, 1968), p. 304.

166 Geoffrey de Mildenhale, who lost a horse valued at £20 13s 4d: E404/482, file 31, no. 18 (Wardrobe debenture, dated 25 September 1314); E403/270, m. 20 (Exchequer issue in 1334). Cf. Sir John de Bures, whose company at Bannockburn lost horses with a total value of £106 13s 4d, but who had still not been paid most of this in November 1331: E404/482, file 31, no. 4; *CPR, 1330–34*, p. 221.

167 £213 6s 8d: E36/204, fo. 87r.

168 Indenture printed in facsimile in B. Lyon, 'The feudal antecedent of the indenture system', *Speculum*, xxix (1954), pp. 503–11. It is interesting to note that the earl of Pembroke secured similar terms from the crown in an indenture of war drawn up twenty years later: E101/68/2, no. 42D.

169 Indenture between Arundel and Sir Gerard de Lisle: Berkeley Castle, Select Charter 526. I am indebted to Professor Michael Jones for supplying a transcript of this document.

170 For a variant, see N.B. Lewis, 'An early indenture of military service, 27 July 1287', *BIHR*, xiii (1935), pp. 85–89.

171 S. Walker, 'Profit and loss in the Hundred Years War: the subcontracts of Sir John Strother, 1374', *BIHR*, lviii (1985), p. 102.

172 E.g. in February 1372 Sir John Cresy received 25 marks for a horse lost during the campaign in Normandy and Picardy in 1369: *JGReg, 1371–5*, ii, no. 908. On Gaunt's cash-flow problems and the arrears owed to his men, see S. Walker, *The Lancastrian*

owed £80 for horses lost in Gascony in 1355, was still awaiting full payment from the prince of Wales in the mid 1360s.[173] In 1358 William Trussell, who describes himself with some justification as the prince of Wales' 'povre bachelor', was seeking compensation for no fewer than six horses which he had lost in the prince's service.[174]

affinity, 1361–1399 (Oxford, 1990), pp. 58–63, 69–70; and A. Goodman, *John of Gaunt* (Harlow, 1992), pp. 220–21.

[173] *BPReg*, iv, p. 516; but for a case of more rapid payment, see *BPReg*, i, 57.

[174] BL Cotton MS, Caligula D. III, no. 30.

4

Restauro Equorum, Vadia Guerre and the Profits of War

The horse inventories generated by the administrative machinery of the English crown are available for a period of rather less than a hundred years, from 1282 to the mid 1360s. Within this period, the coverage is uneven, with a notable thinning of the evidence during Edward III's reign. Contemplation of this corpus of documents gives rise to a number of questions. Does the spread of surviving records accurately reflect the time-span during which horse appraisal and compensation operated? What were the origins of *restauro equorum*? Was it a regular, or merely an occasional, element in the terms of service offered to men-at-arms during this period? Why did it cease to operate?

PAY AND THE APPRAISAL OF WARHORSES: THE REIGNS OF EDWARD I AND EDWARD II

The essential criterion for inclusion in a horse inventory drawn up by the agents of the English crown was established long ago by J.E. Morris, the pioneer of Edwardian army studies: 'inventories, it is clear, were only taken of the horses of stipendiary troops . . .; this was not done in the case of the feudal quotas which served as a duty'.[1] Men performing military service in royal armies as a consequence of their feudal obligations supplied their own arms and horses, and made good any losses themselves, as part of those obligations.[2] Men serving for pay also supplied their own equipment and horses, but their relationship with the crown was rather different. Their service was not obligatory, their resources were only temporarily at the

---

[1] Morris, *The Welsh wars of Edward I*, p. 78.
[2] Some of the military costs of the feudal aristocracy would eventually be met by the collection of scutage, but initially the cost of service was borne by the military tenants' own resources. During King John's reign a means of 'subsidising' feudal service was devised. The crown would issue 'an advance to a feudal tenant [to help him meet the cost of equipping for war] which was ultimately repayable in cash, if not previously pardoned'. Such *prests*, therefore, enabled military tenants 'to anticipate their scutage': *Praestita Roll, 14–18 John*, ed. J.C. Holt, Pipe Roll Soc., new ser., xxxvii (1964), pp. 79–80. Warhorses and military equipment were, moreover, exempt from taxation: see S.K. Mitchell, *Taxation in medieval England* (New Haven, 1951), pp. 139, 146, 148; J.F. Willard, *Parliamentary taxes on personal property, 1290 to 1334* (Cambridge, Mass., 1934), pp. 77, 79.

disposal of the royal paymaster and it was only reasonable and prudent for the crown to ensure that the heaviest costs, and particularly the replacement cost of lost warhorses, were met.[3] If pay 'was rather more like a return on an investment than wages in the modern sense',[4] that investment needed to be insured against loss.

Whilst discussing the inventories for the second Welsh war of 1282, Michael Prestwich observed that it was 'customary' for the crown to offer *restauro equorum* to those in royal pay.[5] But it is far from clear when the association between paid military service and horse appraisal actually began. The English crown had certainly been employing paid troops for several centuries prior to the Edwardian period,[6] and we know that compensation for warhorse losses had frequently been extended, along with wages, to men who had been recruited by means of *fiefs-rentes*.[7] But whether *restauro equorum* was normally made available to all paid men-at-arms is far less certain. Stephen Brown has drawn attention to the rarity of compensation payments for mercenaries in twelfth-century accounts.[8] As late as Henry III's reign there is no firm evidence for the operation of a formal system of warhorse appraisal embracing all men-at-arms entering the king's pay. The crown might contribute to the cost of a man's equipment at the outset of a campaign[9] and at a later stage would make gifts to individuals to help with the replacement of lost warhorses.[10] But the evidence does not necessarily suggest the operation of a carefully regulated mechanism of warhorse appraisal of a kind similar to that which was to become a familiar feature of Edwardian expeditions. In the middle decades of the thirteenth century it seems more a matter of royal favour.[11] Moreover, no horse inventories are available for the period

---

[3] The contrast between, on the one hand, obligatory unpaid feudal service and, on the other, voluntary paid service is a simplification. Men obliged to perform military service as a consequence of money fiefs (*fiefs–rentes*) received daily wages and their costs, including lost warhorses, were met (see n. 7 below).

[4] M. Keen, *Chivalry* (New Haven and London, 1984), p. 225.

[5] Prestwich, *War, politics and finance under Edward I*, pp. 50–51.

[6] See J.O. Prestwich: 'War and finance in the Anglo-Norman state', *TRHS*, 5th ser., iv (1954), pp. 19–43.

[7] For examples from John's reign, see B. Lyon, 'The feudal antecedent of the indenture system', *Speculum*, xxix (1954), p. 510; idem, *From fief to indenture* (Cambridge, Mass., 1957), pp. 232–43. An early example is the treaty of 10 March 1101 between Henry I and Count Robert of Flanders: *Diplomatic documents, i (1101–1272)*, ed. P. Chaplais (London, 1964), no. 1.

[8] S.D.B. Brown, 'Military service and monetary reward in the eleventh and twelfth centuries', *History*, lxxiv (1989), p. 36.

[9] R.F. Walker, 'The Anglo-Welsh wars, 1217–1267', D.Phil. thesis, University of Oxford, 1954, p. 82; e.g. *CLR, 1240–45*, p. 316.

[10] For example, *CLR, 1240–45*, pp. 269, 305, 325; *CLR, 1245–51*, p. 26. These are payments to *individuals*, not to *captains* for the warhorses lost by their men – as we find so often under the Edwardian kings.

[11] Gifts were made for the replacement of all kinds of horses (sometimes several lost by a single man), for all types of personnel: e.g. Baudechun the crossbowman, in 1243 (*CLR,*

prior to the Edwardian wars (although this is by no means decisive, given the relative sparsity of military records from Henry III's reign).[12] Indeed, the first inventories to have survived were compiled during the second Welsh war of 1282;[13] and bearing in mind that this campaign is notable for Edward I's attempt to raise a wholly paid army, it is tempting to see this as the first occasion in which pay and a formal system of *restauro equorum* had been combined on a large scale. The form and content of the inventories drawn-up for the 1282 campaign certainly suggest a military institution in the process of development. They lack the consistent layout which we find in later horse rolls. In some sections, the individual entries take the form: 'Un cheval . . . pour . . .', or 'Un cheval . . . pris de . . .', rather than in the standard 'name – description – value' form which was to become the established norm with records of this kind by the later 1290s.[14]

All this is not to argue that men-at-arms would be unable to secure compensation for lost horses unless they served in an army, or at least a contingent, which was receiving the king's pay. The crown might not extend *restauro equorum* to the feudal host or, indeed, to those offering voluntary unpaid service;[15] but many men serving in feudal or unpaid contingents would doubtless have received *restor* payments, or equivalent benefits, from their immediate lord,[16] perhaps as a consequence of membership of magnate households or in fulfilment of the terms of military subcontracts. The evi-

---

1240–45, p. 197). Such gifts continued to be made during the Edwardian period, but were quite separate from the *restor* of appraised warhorses lost by men-at-arms.

12 On these military records, see I.J. Sanders, *Feudal military service in England* (Oxford, 1956), pp. 108–35; J.S. Critchley, 'Summonses to military service early in the reign of Henry III', *EHR*, lxxxvi (1971), pp. 79–95.

13 C47/2/5, 6 and 7, assigned to the second Welsh war by Prestwich, *War, politics and finance*, pp. 50–51. A further fragment (C47/2/21, m. 29) may also derive from this campaign.

14 A similar impression is provided by the few other fragmentary horse inventories to have survived from the 1280s and early 1290s (e.g. C47/2/2, m. 19 [12–13 Edw. I] and C47/3/48, mm. 16, 17 [13–17; 20–22 Edw. I]); and by a subcontract for service in Wales in 1287, a very early survival, which gives 'minute attention . . . to the question of compensation for horses lost on service': N.B. Lewis, 'An early indenture of military service, 27 July 1287', *BIHR*, xiii (1935), pp. 85–89.

15 For example, the Falkirk campaign, when more than half of the armoured cavalry were not paid and therefore excluded from the inventories: Prestwich, *War, politics and finance*, pp. 68–69. Cf. the employment of *restor* in France during the thirteenth and fourteenth centuries: 'on le trouve servant de complément au service à gages, mais ailleurs il était employé pour alléger le service gratuit, et on ne saurait douter que ce fût bien son usage primitif' – P. Guilhiermoz, *Essai sur l'origine de la noblesse en France au Moyen Age* (Paris, 1902), pp. 284–85.

16 For some continental parallels see: V. Chomel, 'Chevaux de bataille et roncins en Dauphiné au XIVe siècle', *Cahiers d'Histoire*, vii (1962), pp. 5–23; C. Gaier, *L'industrie et le commerce des armes dans les anciennes principautés belges du XIIIe siècle à la fin du XVe siècle* (Paris, 1973), pp. 74–75 and n. 42; B. Arnold, *German knighthood, 1050–1300* (Oxford, 1985), p. 84.

dence is admittedly patchy and much of it is of late provenance. The military contractors employed by tenants-in-chief to perform their feudal service[17] would not necessarily have *restauro equorum* written into their terms of service, but the lump sum payments which they received would probably have included some allowance for possible horse losses. In 1327 Sir Robert Constable of Flamborough was engaged by the archbishop of York to provide 'dis hommes darmes as chevaux coverts' (i.e the service of five knights). For twenty days service with this company, Constable was to receive £100, which seems a very generous rate of payment, but which included £20 'pur son travaille, et pur son apparaille'.[18] A similar allowance was probably included in the £100 agreed between the bishop of Salisbury and Sir Robert de Sapy for the latter's provision of five knights for the king's army in 1322.[19] Although documentary evidence is slight for the period prior to the fourteenth century, we can be sure that members of magnate households would have had their major military costs, including lost warhorses, met by their lord.[20] There are indications that the Lord Edward compensated members of his household for horses lost during the crusade of 1270–72.[21] At the very end of the century a small group of indentures of retinue show similar

[17] On this subject, see M. Prestwich, 'Cavalry service in early fourteenth–century England', *War and government in the Middle Ages*, ed J. Gillingham and J.C. Holt (Woodbridge, 1984), p. 149; J.M.W. Bean, *From lord to patron. Lordship in late medieval England* (Manchester, 1989), p. 134.

[18] N.B. Lewis, 'The summons of the English feudal levy, 5 April 1327', *Essays in medieval history presented to Bertie Wilkinson*, ed. T.A. Sandquist and M. Powicke (Toronto, 1969), pp. 242–49. Lewis notes that Constable's 'fee of £20 for raising and equipping the troop would have been at about the normal rate of *regard* paid in Edward's reign': ibid., p. 246 n. 40.

[19] The £100 was to be paid in two instalments. If the campaign was cancelled after the payment of the first £50, Sapy would return two–thirds of this sum, keeping £13 6s 8d 'pur les custages qil avera mys': *The registers of Roger Martival, bishop of Salisbury, 1315–30*, ed. K. Edwards, C.R. Elrington, S. Reynolds and D.M. Owen, Canterbury and York Soc. (1959–65), iii, pp. 97–98.

[20] For a discussion of the origins and shadowy early history of indentures of retinue, see Bean, *From lord to patron*, chapter 4; an analysis of surviving indentures of retinue from the late thirteenth and early fourteenth centuries is to be found on pp. 41–56. S. Waugh's careful study of the mainly indirect thirteenth-century evidence led him to conclude that, in Henry III's reign, the majority of contracts were prompted by administrative and legal, rather than purely military, needs. Facing 'new military demands' in Edward I's reign, lords 'simply adjusted the system of contractual retaining which they had developed for administrative service to military needs'. S. Waugh, 'Tenure to contract: lordship and clientage in thirteenth-century England', *EHR*, ci (1986), pp. 811–39.

[21] S. Lloyd, *English society and the crusade, 1216–1307* (Oxford, 1988), p. 119 n. 30. The contracts which record the expansion of Edward's household for the crusade are, however, 'lamentably vague' with respect to the terms of service employed; no mention is made of *restauro equorum* (ibid., pp. 118–19). H.G. Richardson and G.O. Sayles, *The governance of medieval England* (Edinburgh, 1963), appendix 6, pp. 463–65, prints the contract between Edward and Adam of Jesmond.

privileges being extended to the retainers of several non-royal magnates.[22] Evidence from the later 1290s may not, of course, be a reliable guide to normal practice earlier in the century. By the time of Edward I's Scottish campaigns, most magnates were, after all, receiving royal pay for some at least of the men which they brought on campaign and so the *restauro equo-rum* payments which they made to their retainers would, to some degree, be re-couped from the crown. In this respect, the evidence offered by a small group of indentures drawn up during the 1310s is particularly useful, for the superior contracting party is Thomas, earl of Lancaster, a magnate who may never have accepted pay for the troops which he contributed to royal armies, and certainly never during the period in which these contracts operated. The indenture between Lancaster and Sir William Latimer offered the latter 'mon-ture por son corps du dit Counte come affiert por un Baneret'; in addition, 'ses chevaux darmes [serront] prisees al entre des dites guerres *par les gentz le dit Counte*, et avera restor de ses chevaux darmes perduz en les dites guerres en le service le dit Counte selonc le dit pris'.[23] Great magnates like Lancaster were obviously well placed to offer generous benefits to their retainers and yet the practice of their households would doubtless have been copied by many smaller establishments. In this respect, the foremost exemplar was the crown. Although the earliest detailed records of horse valuation and compensation date from the late thirteenth century,[24] it had become customary for members of the military household of English kings to be compensated for their losses as early as the reign of Henry I.[25] It was the long-established methods of the royal household which provided the solid bedrock of administrative experience needed when horse appraisal and compensation were extended to *all* men-at-arms in the paid service of king.[26]

During the early decades of the fourteenth century an increasing proportion of troops serving in the king's armies were drawn within the embrace of royal pay. Unpaid contingents, whether based on obligatory or voluntary service, made only a modest contribution to Edward III's armies.[27] For the

---

22 Bean, *From lord to patron*, pp. 43–48, 138–39.

23 Indenture printed in G.A. Holmes, *The estates of the higher nobility in fourteenth-century England* (Cambridge, 1957), pp. 122–23. The other three indentures also make provision for horse loss compensation. All four are analysed by J.R. Maddicott, *Thomas of Lancaster, 1307–1322* (Oxford, 1970), pp. 41–48 and Bean, *From lord to patron*, pp. 48–50, 139–40.

24 For the relevant records from Edward I's reign, see *List of documents relating to the household and wardrobe, John–Edward I* (London, 1964), pp. 59–61. On Edward I's military household, see Prestwich, *War, politics and finance*, chapter 2.

25 J.O. Prestwich, 'The military household of the Norman kings', *EHR*, xcvi (1981), p. 8.

26 On the growth of *restor des chevaux* from household practice, see Contamine, *Guerre, état et société*, pp. 103–4.

27 These developments are unravelled with great clarity in Prestwich, *War, politics and finance under Edward I*, chapter 3; idem, 'Cavalry service in early fourteenth-century England', pp. 147–58.

English military machine, this was a most significant development; and yet its effects may have been but little felt by the ordinary man-at-arms. If he lost a warhorse whilst on active service the man-at-arms would receive compensation from the captain of his retinue irrespective of whether that retinue was providing paid, voluntary unpaid or feudal service. Thus, although the growing universality of paid military service served very rapidly to institutionalise *restauro equorum*, drawing it completely within the orbit of royal administration, the main impact of this change would have been felt, not so much by the ordinary man-at-arms, as by those who were in direct contact with the royal paymaster: the magnates and lesser retinue captains. Some magnates had been vigorously opposed to the idea of receiving royal pay, refusing 'to descend to the level of stipendiaries'; 'but this was only a temporary stand . . . in little more than a generation they all had succumbed'.[28] The financial advantages – wages for all combatant retinue members and compensation payments for lost warhorses – were too great to be eschewed for very long. As far as the crown was concerned, it was money well spent,[29] for a wholly paid army was, in a number of respects, far preferable to one consisting of a shifting balance of paid, feudal and voluntary unpaid elements. Paid armies, whose size, structure and length of service could be predicted and regulated, offered new strategic possibilities, such as those explored during the first phase of the Hundred Years War.

If, through the provision of pay, the crown gained in terms of military flexibility and reliability, it also wished to preserve, indeed enhance, the quality of the armies mustered. Pay would be supplied only for those men-at-arms who arrived at muster 'covenablement mountez & apparaillez';[30] that is, the man must have the necessary armour and equipment and his warhorse must be of suitable quality, and 'covered' or barded.[31] These requirements

[28] Morris, *The Welsh wars of Edward I*, p. 158; K.B. McFarlane, 'Bastard feudalism', *BIHR*, xx (1945), p. 163.

[29] Part of the expenditure would be re-couped because a paid army was obliged to surrender to the crown a proportion of its profits of war. Such considerations may have influenced Edward I's attempt to raise a wholly paid army in 1282: Prestwich, *War, politics and finance*, pp. 71–72.

[30] A stock phrase with many variants; this version appears in an indenture for the garrison of Mitford castle, Northumberland, in 1316: E101/68/2, no. 36. Sometimes the tone is a little more forceful: 'bien & suffisaument mountez & apparaillez' (E101/68/3, no. 47; indenture, 1321).

[31] The dependence of the man-at-arms' full daily rate of pay (12d) on possession of a barded horse is evident before Edward I's reign (e.g. from 1269: *CLR, 1267–72*, no. 738). The horse armour of Edward I's reign was of mail or boiled leather resting on padding: Morris, *The Welsh wars of Edward I*, pp. 52–53; Chew, *The English ecclesiastical tenants-in-chief and knight service*, pp. 89–90. Plate armour for horses (chamfron, peytral, flanchards, crupper) appears in the fourteenth century: C. Blair, *European armour* (London, 1958), pp. 184–87. As far as the English armies of the mid to late fourteenth century are concerned, it is not certain whether horse armour was still deemed essential to a

had, of course, applied at musters of the feudal host;[32] but, as Michael Prestwich has shown, a very substantial proportion of the combatants in late thirteenth- and early fourteenth-century armies were providing voluntary, unpaid service and it is not clear how well they were equipped.[33] The provision of pay for most or all men-at-arms enabled the crown to demand a uniform standard of equipment for both man and warhorse. Seen in this light, horse appraisal represents not simply a privilege for men-at-arms taking the king's pay, but in fact a prerequisite of receiving pay. The receipt of pay was actually *dependent* upon prior horse appraisal: this is made plain in records of various kinds, including military contracts and letters appointing appraisal officials. In 1318 the indenture of retinue between Edward II and Sir John de St John established that in wartime, St John's 'chevaux serront prisez le premier jour de sa venue & adonques meintenant prendra gages pour lui & pour ses gentz tantz come il amenera'.[34] In April 1325 William de Oterhampton was ordered to pay *vadia consueta* to men-at-arms 'a tempore quo equos suos per [Sir Richard Damory] appreciari'.[35] Thus, at the start of a campaign, warhorses were inspected and valued to ensure that the correct level of compensation could be paid in the event of loss, but this inspection also formed an essential part of the muster process and a formal record was made of those men-at-arms whose equipment and warhorses were of a sufficient standard to entitle them to receive the normal rate of pay. The detailed descriptions in the inventories and the branding of horses would make it easy, at subsequent musters, to check for improper substitution.[36]

The connection between the valuation of warhorses and the receipt of pay is made explicitly in many pay-rolls from the reigns of Edward I and Edward II. A good example is the *vadia guerre* account for the English army serving in

---

man-at-arms' pay; there appears to be at least as much concern with the number and quality of horses taken.

[32] Helena Chew (*The English ecclesiastical tenants-in-chief and knight service*, pp. 87–88) shows that the feudal 'ostensio equorum et armorum' was a serious business: 'the constable and marshal were empowered to reject the services of all inadequately equipped knights or sergeants and to compel the lords to substitute others "lege militari decenter armati"'. Cf. R.F. Walker, 'The Anglo-Welsh wars, 1217–1267', D.Phil. thesis, University of Oxford, 1954, pp. 40–41, who also draws on Matthew Paris' description of a mid-thirteenth-century muster in *Chronica majora*.

[33] Prestwich, 'Cavalry service in early fourteenth–century England', pp. 147–58. The equipment specifications of the Statute of Winchester (1285) make no mention of horse armour: *Select charters*, ed. W. Stubbs, 9th edn, repr. (Oxford, 1957), p. 466.

[34] E101/68/2, no. 42C. Cf. an indenture drawn up during the previous year between Edward II and Aymer de Valence: 'touz ses chevaux darmes [serront] prisez le primer jour qil serra venuz': E101/68/2, no. 42D.

[35] C61/36, m. 6.

[36] A Pisan military code of 1327–31 laid down penalties for all involved in the selling or bartering of horses which had previously been registered for pay (quoted in Jones, *Chaucer's knight*, pp. 25–56).

Scotland during the summer of 1322.[37] For the men-at-arms in this army, pay commenced on the day that their horses were appraised: entry after entry makes this clear. Thus, the ninety-five *homini ad arma* in the earl of Pembroke's retinue were paid from the 5 August, 'quo die equi sui appreciabantur in guerra Scocie'.[38] What this particular *vadia guerre* account does not reveal is whether any men-at-arms were *not* taken into the king's pay at the standard rate, because their horses and equipment failed to pass muster – either because inadequate or because they did not appear at the appointed time.[39] That this was a common enough occurrence is made clear by many other pay-rolls. The *vadia guerre* account for the Flanders campaign of 1297 includes men who were paid 8d per day rather than 12d, 'quia sine equo appreciato'.[40] In July 1311, whilst John de Enefeld received wages at 12d per day 'quia cum equo appreciato', his fellow sergeant-at-arms, William Ferraunt, was paid only 8d 'quia sine equo appreciato'.[41] For the English forces in Gascony in 1324–25, the penalty for serving without an appraised horse was rather more severe: many company commanders were paid only 6d per day for men in this predicament.[42] It is possible that, on occasion, men were obliged to serve without an appraised horse – that is, in the eyes of the crown, *not* as a man-at-arms at all – because they had missed an official muster. It is more likely, however, that in most cases they appeared at muster, but were excluded from the horse inventory, because their horses and/or equipment were not of the standard required for the receipt of the man-at-arms rate of pay.[43] The fault might lie with the horse itself. English appraisers would surely be guided by principles similar to those stipulated by the Pisan military code for the employment of mercenaries (1327–31), which required

---

[37] BL Stowe MS 553, fos 55v–63r.

[38] The first retinue listed on the pay-roll. There are a number of variant formulae: e.g. '[date] quo die equi sui appreciati fuerunt'. Less explicitly, men are serving 'cum equis appreciatis' or 'cum equis ad arma', the latter serving to emphasise that the horses were barded.

[39] It is unlikely that significant numbers of men went unpaid for any length of time as a result of missing official musters, for the *vadia guerre* account suggests that the horse appraisers were regularly at work from 4 to 16 August. Changes in the size and structure of retinues are, therefore, probably to be explained in terms of actual movements of men, rather than changes in accounting totals. Thus, the fifty-one men-at-arms who on 15 August were added to the existing numbers of Sir Hugh le Despenser's retinue were probably new arrivals, rather than the victims of missed musters or stringent horse evaluation at an earlier date: BL Stowe MS 553, fo. 61r.

[40] BL Additional MS 7965, fo. 72r.

[41] BL Cotton MS, Nero C. VIII, fo. 97r.

[42] For example, Sir John de Felton who, as marshal of the army, was one of the three men responsible for horse appraisal at Plympton: BL Additional MS 7967, fo. 31v. It is not always clear whether a man's horse has yet to be appraised, or whether he has no horse at all.

[43] See, for example, James de Dalilegh's instructions, when sent to appraise the horses of the garrison at Lochmaban castle in 1302: *Bain*, v, no. 299.

officials to reject horses which were 'broken-winded, obstinate, affected by rheum or otherwise sick'.[44] Alternatively, the horse might not be properly 'armoured',[45] or the man's personal equipment might be considered to be that of a hobelar rather than a man-at-arms. There were bound to be disputes about what exactly constituted a man-at-arms equipment. In 1317 the keeper and chamberlain of Berwick were faced by a dilemma when, having been ordered to pay the wages of a company of fifty hobelars, twenty-eight arrived at muster 'covenablement mountez et armes Daketoun Hauberioun et bacinetz'. They were better equipped than some of the men-at-arms in the garrison, and their captain, John le Hircis, felt aggrieved that they were not paid 12d per day.[46]

Those who aspired to be men-at-arms, but who lacked an appraised horse, would usually be paid at a reduced rate. At times they appear to be receiving no pay at all. In 1322, according to the *vadia guerre* account, the earl of Louth served with the king's army in Scotland from mid August until the beginning of November with a force of seventy-four men-at-arms (including himself, four bannerets and six knights), 189 hobelars and ninety-three foot soldiers.[47] A separate retinue roll gives the names and ranks of the earl's men-at-arms, and reveals the retinue's internal company structure.[48] The most interesting feature of this roll is that there are *two* lists of names for each of the six companies: one listing men with valued horses, the other those with unvalued horses.

There is a close correspondence between the number of men-at-arms with valued horses and the number for whom the earl of Louth was allowed pay in the *vadia guerre* account; that is only to be expected. What is striking, however, is that so many men – about half of the earl's men-at-arms – were not allowed pay, apparently because their horses were unvalued. We must assume that their wages came out of the earl's own pocket.[49]

---

44 Quoted in Jones, *Chaucer's knight*, p. 122. Some men would doubtless arrive at muster with either no warhorse at all, or at least an inferior beast, but with every intention of acquiring one. They would be paid a reduced rate until they did.

45 Morris, *The Welsh wars of Edward I*, p. 53. Some records make the distinction between *equis coopertis* and *equis discoopertis* quite clear: e.g 'Account of military expenses in Cardiganshire (E101/4/9)', *Records of the wardrobe and household, 1286–1289*, ed. B.F. Byerly and C.R. Byerly (London, 1986), pp. 467–76. Cf. France in the 1290s: a man-at-arms with a barded horse received 12s 6d *tournois* a day, whilst those with unarmoured mounts were paid only 5s: J.F. Verbruggen, *The art of warfare in western Europe during the Middle Ages* (Amsterdam, 1977), p. 26.

46 *Northern petitions*, ed. C.M. Fraser, Surtees Soc., cxciv (1982 for 1981), pp. 62–63.

47 BL Stowe MS 553, fo. 56r.

48 E101/13/35, m. 8. The roll, headed *Hibn'*, is one of a bundle of miscellaneous military materials dated *temp.* Edward I by the PRO, but the identification offered here is very firmly based upon internal evidence.

49 It is possible that the seventy-four men-at-arms without valued horses were regarded as hobelars for the purposes of pay, and are therefore included among the 189 hobelars recorded by the *vadia guerre* accounts. Although this is consistent with pay policy at other

Table 4.1: Retinue of Sir John de Bermingham, earl of Louth:
Scottish campaign, 1322.

| Company commander: | Men-at-arms with: | |
	Valued horses	Unvalued horses
Earl of Louth	29	13
Sir Nicholas de Verdon	11	28
Sir John de Cusak	9	15
Sir Herbert de Marshal	8	2
Walter de Burgh	14	1
E. de Bermingham	4	15
Totals:	75	74

Does a chance documentary survival provide a glimpse of a phenomenon which, by the very nature of the pay records, would usually go unnoticed? Were significant numbers of men-at-arms regularly excluded from pay because, for whatever reason, their horses were not appraised? Not necessarily, for the circumstances of the earl of Louth's retinue were unusual. Not leaving Ireland until 18 August, the earl's men cannot have joined Edward II's army until long after the horses of the other retinues had been appraised and it is possible that Louth's men were treated rather differently from the rest of the army. There is no explicit reference to the valuation of their horses in the *vadia guerre* account, but this is not surprising because their period of paid service began when they set sail from Ireland and not upon completion of a muster in Northumberland. Their horses may have been valued at the time of embarkation or after their arrival in England. Either way, the evidence for these horses provided by the *restauro equorum* account for the campaign suggests a simpler method of evaluation than that employed for the rest of the army.[50] Four horses were lost, but rather than being separately costed, a suspiciously neat combined total is supplied: £20. It appears that they have been valued at 100s each, a value which, at a slightly later date, became the minimum acceptable for a man-at-arms' warhorse.

How far the treatment of Louth's retinue followed, or differed from, normal practice is not clear. The scheme of compensation payment for his retinue seems suspiciously neat and is certainly out of line with standard procedure at this time. But the apparent total dependence of his men's wages on prior horse evaluation does give pause for thought. There is no other surviving record quite like Louth's retinue roll, but there are fragments of evidence from other quarters which also show that a man-at-arms might

times, it is difficult to produce a total of 189 from these seventy-four men and the numbers of hobelars allocated to each company by the retinue roll.

[50] BL Stowe MS 553, fo. 70r. It may be significant that the *restauro equorum* entry dealing with the horses lost by Louth's retinue does not employ the normal formula for horses valued at the start of the campaign.

receive no pay at all until his horse had been valued. It was for this reason that Sir William de Fissheburn received nothing for one of his *scutiferi* for the first five days of August 1324, whilst Sir Nicholas de Stradeset lost over a month's pay for failing to secure an appraised horse for one of his men.[51] But few pay-rolls offer evidence of this kind. For most armies we can but speculate how many retinues were partly paid for by their captains because of difficulties arising from horse valuation, and by how much a calculation of army size based upon the evidence of the *vadia guerre* accounts will under-estimate the numbers of men-at-arms actually serving.[52]

There is another way of interpreting the evidence of the earl of Louth's retinue in 1322. It may be that the earl had contracted to supply a paid contingent of a fixed size, or a mixed force of paid and unpaid troops. Interpreted thus, the seventy-four men-at-arms listed in the earl's retinue roll who do not have appraised horses would be those who were not going to be paid for by the crown: the earl would know all along that he would be paying their wages himself. Contracts from this period do occasionally make provision for paid and unpaid men-at-arms.[53] In November 1316 Sir Robert de Welle agreed to garrison Brough castle with fifteen men-at-arms and twenty hobelars, of whom five men-at-arms and ten hobelars were to be 'a ses custages', the rest being paid for by the crown. Only the ten men-at-arms in the king's pay were to have their 'chevaux . . . prisez par les ministres notre seigneur le Roy & averont restor de ceux que se perdront en le service le Roy'.[54]

A man-at-arms received the standard rate of pay from the day that his warhorse was appraised and recorded on an inventory. But what happened if this appraised horse was killed or became unfit for service? We might reasonably expect the man's pay to be reduced until he acquired a replacement or had one of his other warhorses valued; yet the records provide evidence which is ambiguous and inconsistent. Take, for example, the pay-rolls for the Scottish campaign of 1322. On the one hand, there is the case of the earl of Louth's retinue. According to the *restauro equorum* account, the earl's retinue lost four horses at the battle of Byland on 14 October 1322.[55] Appropriately

---

51 BL Additional MS 7967, fos 34v, 35r.
52 Note also that a substantial number of foot soldiers in the 1322 army were serving at the expense of their home communities rather than the crown: see Morris, 'Mounted infantry in medieval warfare', pp. 87–91; M.R. Powicke, 'The English commons in Scotland in 1322 and the deposition of Edward II', *Speculum*, xxxv (1960), pp. 559–61; and idem, *Military obligation in medieval England*, pp. 151–53.
53 But making a contract did not in itself disqualify a man from horse appraisal: cf. one of N. Denholm-Young's more eccentric ideas in *History and heraldry, 1254 to 1310* (Oxford, 1965), p. 104.
54 Morris, 'Cumberland and Westmorland military levies in the time of Edward I and Edward II', pp. 320–22.
55 BL Stowe MS 553, fo. 70r. In all, seven valued and four unvalued horses were lost at Byland.

enough, on the earl's retinue roll, the four men-at-arms concerned are to be found amongst those having valued horses and receiving pay, but the *vadia guerre* account shows no changes in the numbers of the earl's retinue receiving pay at the time of Byland, or indeed at any other time. Further comparison of the pay-roll and the horse compensation account indicates that this case is far from exceptional. There are, admittedly, a few instances where an entry in the *restauro equorum* list is mirrored by an explicit statement in the *vadia guerre* accounts. Thus, Sir John de Norwich's *scutifer*, William de Banham, lost his horse at Norham on 1 September and his pay stopped immediately.[56] Similarly, when Sir Robert de Swyneborne lost his horse on 19 August his retinue captain, the earl of Arundel, henceforward received pay for one knight less. But Arundel's company lost one further horse and no allowance is made for this in the pay accounts, and the same applies to losses by other retinues, both large and small.[57] The pay-rolls for the army in Gascony in 1324–25 offer equally inconsistent evidence. Often it is quite clear that pay has not been adjusted following the loss of warhorses. Sir Roger de Hegham lost his £20 horse in March 1325, yet according to the *vadia guerre* account he received pay uninterruptedly for himself and two *scutiferi* for 499 days from August 1324.[58] On the other hand, it is possible that Sir Fulk Fitz Warin's loss of pay for his son (eight days) and Sir William de Wauncy (three days) was directly connected with the death of their warhorses.[59] In some sets of pay records, horse losses interfere quite regularly with the receipt of pay, but the penalties might not be uniform. Pay was stopped completely for two of Sir John de Crumwell's *scutiferi* who lost horses in Scotland in November 1310, whilst for others, serving about the same time, the loss of a horse resulted in a drop of pay to 8d per day.[60]

If taken at face value, the evidence suggests a lack of consistent practice from one campaign to the next and, indeed, in the treatment of personnel within a single army. How can this be explained? Some of the inconsistency may be more apparent than real. It is quite possible that in cases of unaffected wage payment, the loss of an appraised horse was followed immediately by the valuation of a new one. Many men-at-arms, and certainly those of knightly rank, would have served with at least one additional warhorse, so

---

[56] Ibid., fos 60v, 70r.
[57] Ibid., fos 56r, 70r. Sir Richard Damory's retinue lost three horses but no account of this is taken in the pay-roll: ibid., fos 56r, 70r.
[58] BL Additional MS 7967, fos 34r–34v, 106r.
[59] Valued at £20 and 40 marks respectively: ibid., fos 30r, 105r.
[60] BL Cotton MS, Nero C. VIII, fos 3v, 97r–97v. In this particular case those who received only 8d per day 'quia sine equo appreciato' were king's sergeants-at-arms. Such a reduction is specified in the 'Household Ordinances of York', 6 December 1318: a king's sergeant-at-arms would receive 12d per day if serving with 'un chivall darmez . . . Et si cel chiaul soit revenuz en garder[obe], ou moerge en le servise le roy, li serront alloez en . . . le roulle [de marechal] viii d. le jour pour gagez, tanque il eit autre chivall darmez'. T.F. Tout, *The place of the reign of Edward II in English history* (Manchester, 1936), p. 253.

the only practical obstruction to immediate re-appraisal would have been the availability of the necesary officials. Occasionally the pay accounts record when re-valuation has occurred, but it is usual for days, or even weeks, to have elapsed. For example, on 12 September 1322, the horses of two of Sir Thomas de Ughtred's three *scutiferi* were delivered 'ad carvannum' at Newcastle; but the whole company was back in service by early October 'cum equis de novo appreciatis'.[61] It may be that, for some expeditions or indeed for some privileged sections of the military community, a certain amount of flexibility was allowed: a man-at-arms who had suffered a loss might be allowed a period of grace before his pay was affected, in order to allow a replacement to be presented for appraisal.[62] This would explain why so many horse losses appear to have no impact on the *vadia guerre* accounts. On the other hand, it is probable that some at least of the cases where pay has stopped completely following an equestrian fatality arise not so much from the horse's death, as from that of the man-at-arms himself. So much about Edwardian pay-rolls remains uncertain; and, as we shall see in Chapter 5, many *vadia guerre* accounts survive only in condensed, summarised versions, thus complicating matters still further. Whilst a degree of experimentation with the terms of service is only to be expected, it is clear that much of the inconsistency of practice is more apparent than real, the product of a skein of circumstances which it is difficult now to disentangle.

A PERIOD OF EXPERIMENT: THE REIGN OF EDWARD III

By the end of Edward II's reign it had become the norm for the non-feudal contingents of men-at-arms serving in royal armies to be in receipt of the king's pay. Voluntary, unpaid service, so important for some of Edward I's Scottish expeditions, had largely disappeared.[63] At the same time as providing pay, the crown had shouldered responsibility for *restauro equorum*, but from the point of view of the man-at-arms, or perhaps more accurately the retinue captain, horse appraisal was at once a privilege and a prerequisite of paid military service. To what extent did the close relationship between horse appraisal and the receipt of wages continue into the reign of Edward III?

An examination of mid-fourteenth-century military records suggests a loosening of the link between pay and the valuation of warhorses. Admittedly, some military contracts from early in Edward III's reign do continue to associate the commencement of paid service with the appraisal of warhorses. A group of indentures for service in the Scottish Marches in 1342 provide a

---

[61] BL Stowe MS 553, fos 60v, 70r.
[62] Cf. the utopian efficiency envisaged by a Bolognese *condotta* of 1294: compensation payment within ten days of the claim being made, with the recipient purchasing a replacement warhorse within four days: D.P. Waley, 'Condotte and condottieri in the thirteenth century', *Proceedings of the British Academy*, lxi (1975), p. 344.
[63] Prestwich, 'Cavalry service in early-fourteenth-century England', pp. 147–58.

good example of this. In each case it is established that the contractor would muster at Newcastle (or Carlisle) on 15 July, on which day 'il entrera au gages et avera ses chivaux darmes prisez'.[64] Entering the king's paid service and horse appraisal are deemed to be simultaneous events, but one is not necessarily *dependent* upon the other. In practice, moreover, by the early 1340s they would probably no longer be simultaneous events. To see this it is necessary to turn to records of a different kind. Rarely in the *vadia guerre* accounts of Edward III's reign do we find an explicit association between horse appraisal and the commencement of paid service.[65] The pay-rolls for Henry of Lancaster's army serving in Scotland during the early summer of 1336 provide, it seems, the last significant example. The earl's retinue of one hundred men-at-arms drew royal pay from 1 May, on which day their horses were appraised; and the same explicit link is made with seven other captains serving under Lancaster's overall command.[66] In the majority of cases these were not empty words: the survival of the original dated inventories for most of the retinues in Lancaster's army demonstrates this clearly.[67] Although the pay accounts for most retinues serving in Scotland in 1336 make no reference to horse valuation, this may well be because valuation did not actually take place: the surviving inventories relate almost entirely to Lancaster's independent command.

---

[64] E101/68/3, nos. 49–58. Cf. indentures for the custody of Berwick in 1340–41, which stipulate that horses will be valued 'a la venue' of the contractor: E101/68/3, nos. 45, 48.

[65] By the end of the 1330s, explicit references to horse appraisal are no longer made in the pay-rolls. This reticence may in part be a product of the more abbreviated style adopted by the later accounts. The two most substantial sets of *vadia guerre* accounts from the 1320s, those for the War of Saint-Sardos and the Scottish campaign of two years earlier, are models of their kind (BL Additional MS 7967, fos 30r–93v; Stowe MS 553, fos 56r–63r), detailing every change in the composition of often very small retinues and making many incidental remarks about the terms of service of individuals. The pay-rolls for the Scottish campaigns of 1336–37 preserve some elements of this comprehensive approach. They often tell us who presented a particular captain's account: Sir John de Segrave's was presented by his clerk, John de Overton (BL Cotton MS, Nero C. VIII, fo. 240v). By comparison, subsequent pay accounts, for example those for the Low Countries expedition of 1338–39 (*Norwell*, pp. 325–56), are altogether more concise. They appear meticulous enough in their detailing of changes in retinue size, but they supply little additional detail about the comings and goings of individuals and say nothing about horse valuation. A greater economy of words is a feature not only of the pay accounts, but also of the corresponding *restauro equorum* accounts. Details supplied by the account for horses lost in 1322, such as the precise circumstances of each horse's demise and the date and place of account, are not to be found in the record listing equestrian losses in Brittany in 1342–43: BL Stowe MS 553, fos 70r–71r; E36/204, fos 86v–88v.

[66] BL Cotton MS, Nero C. VIII, fos 240r–41r. The usual formula is: '[commencing date] quo die equi sui fuerunt appreciati'.

[67] The relevant information is tabulated in Appendix 1. What is more, in the case of Lancaster's own retinue, an original muster roll seems further to underline the dependence of pay upon horse appraisal. The roll was originally dated 23 April, but this has been crossed out and '1 May', the date of the inventory, written-in instead: E101/15/12.

Moving on to the military operations which took place during the early summer of 1337, we find a rather different situation. The *vadia guerre* account explicitly mentions horse appraisal in the first of the retinue entries, that of the earl of Warwick, but in none of the others. Yet we know, from the survival of a bundle of original inventories, that the warhorses of at least six other retinues were valued.[68] The loosening of the link between horse valuation and the commencement of pay is not just semantic: the dates given on the seven inventories do not match those at which pay is said to have begun. In nearly all cases horse appraisal took place after the start of paid service; for one retinue a month separates the two dates.[69] The most striking case concerns the earl of Warwick's retinue. Although the *vadia guerre* account suggests that sixty-three men-at-arms presented their horses for valuation on 7 May, the surviving inventory shows that only twenty-two men actually had their horses appraised on that particular day, with a further thirteen, including the earl himself, being 'processed' the following day and the remaining thirty-three appearing before the appraisers on the 20th of the same month.[70] Either the *vadia guerre* accounts are offering a wholly inaccurate impression of the size and duration of service of the personal retinue of the 'capitaneo & duci' of the king's army in Scotland, or the dependence of pay upon horse appraisal no longer has the force in the later 1330s that it had in the 1310s and '20s. A comparison of the surviving inventories and pay-rolls for the winter 1337–38 campaign provides further evidence of a similar kind. The earl of Gloucester's retinue, consisting in all of ninety-two men-at-arms, took the king's pay from 1 December, whilst the inventory for his company, listing only fifty-four names, was drawn up several weeks after this date.[71] On the rare occasions that this kind of documentary correlation is possible for later armies, we find that the impression conveyed by the earlier evidence – of loosened links between horse appraisal and the commencement of pay – is further reinforced. According to the pay-roll for the duke of Clarence's expedition to Ireland in the early 1360s, the earl of Stafford drew the king's shilling for his retinue from 4 August 1361, the day of their arrival at Bristol;[72]

---

68 BL Cotton MS, Nero C. VIII, fos 245r–47r; E101/20/17, mm. 7–10d.

69 Sir Thomas de Wake's retinue: pay began on 7 May, but the inventory was compiled on 6 June. It names only twenty-five of the forty men who were supposed to be receiving pay, so it is possible that an earlier, partial inventory has been lost.

70 BL Cotton MS, Nero C. VIII, fo. 245r; E101/20/17, m. 7. The survival of muster rolls reveals that although the horses of Sir Ralph de Neville's retinue were only appraised on 2 June, part of the company did muster on 7 May, the day on which pay began; the rest of the retinue mustered on 17 May and 1 June (E101/20/17, m. 6). By contrast, Sir Henry de Percy also drew pay for forty men-at-arms from 7 May, but his muster roll shows that he did indeed appear at Newcastle with his complete retinue on that day: E101/20/17, m. 5.

71 E101/388/5, m. 13 (specifying two bannerets, seventeen knights and seventy-two *homini ad arma*): cf. E101/20/25, m. 3 (two bannerets, nineteen knights and seventy *scutiferi*). Gloucester's horses were *preisez* at Newcastle on 21 or 30 December: E101/35/3, m. 1.

72 E101/28/21, fo. 5r.

but the date on Stafford's horse inventory shows that appraisal did not take place until 18 August.[73]

If this evidence does indeed indicate a more relaxed attitude towards the timing of horse appraisal, how is this to be explained? In part it must have been a response to military and administrative pressures. On the northern borders we see the horses of garrison troops being valued not from the first day of paid service, but immediately prior to embarking upon a foray,[74] thereby enabling both man-at-arms and royal administration to make economies. But it was the start of a major continental war that actually *necessitated* a more flexible view of horse appraisal. With the establishment of paid service as the norm and with a war strategy demanding large-scale overseas expeditions, a re-evaluation of the function of horse valuation in the muster process was a practical necessity. It became customary practice for captains to receive the king's pay from the day of their arrival at the port of embarkation or the muster headquarters.[75] Pay could not be withheld if the appraisal officials were not ready and waiting; and such were the administrative and logistical problems presented by expeditionary forces gathering at several different locations that we can be sure that mustering for pay purposes and horse appraisal were rarely simultaneous events. In 1342, for example, the earl of Gloucester's retinue had been in paid service for six weeks before horse appraisal officials were even appointed. They actually arrived in Plymouth over eight weeks after Gloucester and his men.[76] On some occasions, as we have seen, horse appraisal was delayed until arrival in France,[77] and here the contrast between the conditions of service of the 1320s and those of the 1340s can be seen most strikingly. In 1324–25, a man-at-arms who left England without an appraised warhorse was paid only 6d per day until the deficiency was rectified.[78] By the mid 1340s, the crown was only too happy for men to acquire warhorses at their destination and there was no question of paying a reduced rate of pay as a result. This change of view was certainly influenced by practical considerations. Purchase and valuation in, for example, Bordeaux would reduce the administrative burden in England, ease pressure on a perennially inadequate supply of shipping and save the crown

---

[73] E101/28/11, m. 3.

[74] Sir Thomas de Musgrave, who secured custody of Berwick early in 1347, was to have his mens' horses 'prisez quant il chivachera de guerre': E101/68/3, no. 66.

[75] Indentures of war frequently state this explicitly: Prince, 'The indenture system under Edward III', p. 292.

[76] E36/204, fo. 106r; C76/17, m. 18; E101/23/36.

[77] Or Ireland: Sir William de Windsor's indenture in 1362 allowed for his men-at-arms' horses to be 'prisez a leur arrivaille au Irlande': E101/68/4, no. 82. Some of his retinue's horses were indeed valued in Dublin on 7 November 1362, whilst pay for his retinue had started in England on 24 June: E101/28/11, m. 2; E101/28/21, fo. 7v.

[78] For example, five of Sir John de Felton's *scutiferi* were on half-pay for a period of seventy days prior to 15 October 1324, when they all presented warhorses for appraisal in Bordeaux: BL Additional MS 7967, fo. 31v.

the cost of horses lost during the long, debilitating voyage to Gascony. But it may also be illustrative of a shift in attitude towards horse valuation itself. Rarely do we now find any direct association between horse appraisal and the receipt of pay in *vadia guerre* accounts or indentures of war; the two have become separate aspects of military service. The crown seems now to be viewing appraisal rather less as a requirement of paid military service, a prerequisite of receiving the standard rate of pay, and rather more as a customary privilege for those in the king's pay, as a means of insuring against one of the greatest hazards of campaigning.

The crown's altered view of the function of horse appraisal can be seen as but one aspect of a wider change in outlook during the 1330s and '40s. Here were the beginnings of a complete overhaul of the man-at-arms' conditions of service, prompted at least in part by the changing role of the warhorse in the functioning of the English military machine. Some of the evidence is admittedly fragmentary and by no means conclusive, and there are signs that the traditional requirements persisted during the Scottish campaigns of the later 1330s. During the autumn of 1336, Sir John de Ufford, newly appointed as admiral of the northern fleet and presumably serving at sea, received (along with a *scutifer*) pay at two-thirds the normal rate 'quia sine equis ad arma'.[79] Further entries in the same *vadia guerre* account also stress the dependence of the standard man-at-arms' pay upon the possession of an 'armoured' horse. Such an association had been central to the concept of the man-at-arms in the earlier fourteenth century, when the strength of a contingent of men-at-arms was frequently expressed as a number of 'covered horses';[80] but it is found much less often after the start of the French war. Records relating to horse appraisal – indentures and the appointment of officials – do occasionally make reference to 'armoured horses', but it is doubtful whether horse armour was still a prerequisite of appraisal. It seems more likely that the term *chivaux darmes* had become a synonym for 'warhorse' (the term *chivaux de guerre* is sometimes employed): the horses of the *gentz darmes*.[81] It is, indeed, by no means clear how usual it was for horse armour to be employed by English knights and esquires in the mid to late fourteenth century. Where contemporary illustrations show horse armour being worn – and this is certainly not invariably the case – it is usually confined to head, neck and chest defences (*chamfron*, *crinet* and *peytral*).[82] Pieces of horse armour are occasionally mentioned in inventories of

---

[79] BL Cotton MS, Nero C. VIII, fo. 243v; Ufford received 1s 4d per day and his esquire 8d.

[80] See, for example, BL Cotton MS, Vespasian F. VII, no. 1 (correct date: 29 Edward I); *Bain*, v, no. 480 (1307).

[81] For examples of such usage, see Dagworth's indenture with Edward III, 1346 (Prince, 'The strength of English armies', p. 371); Sir John de la Hyde's with the Black Prince, 1347 (*BPReg*, i, p. 127); and the duke of Lancaster's with the king, 1369 (E101/68/4, no. 87).

[82] E.g. *The Romance of Alexander*, ed. M.R. James (Oxford, 1933), fos 66r, 74r, 78r.

aristocratic property[83] and wills,[84] but the bulk of it was probably for use on the tournament field or for ceremonial purposes.[85]

If, by the 1340s, the receipt of a man-at-arms' rate of pay no longer depended upon the possession of horse armour, it was still necessary for the man-at-arms to possess a minimum standard of equipment: those 'qui sount ordeynes a prendre gages a xiid le jour soient suffisantement armes et montes'.[86] The man-at-arms' own armour would be scrutinised at muster. Roger Trumwyn, entrusted with the raising of troops in North Wales in 1345, reported to the prince of Wales that whilst some men claimed to be men-at-arms, it was likely that the prince 'will not find them of such condition as they make themselves out to be' and their pay would need to be adjusted accordingly.[87] Moreover, the records of the early campaigns of the continental war show that the number and quality of horses employed by a man-at-arms could still affect his pay. The *vadia guerre* accounts for the Low Countries expedition of 1338–39 suggest that each man-at-arms was expected to be accompanied on campaign by at least three horses. Several groups of men-at-arms are recorded as serving at half the normal rate of pay 'quia minus sufficientibus ad equos', or more explicitly, 'quia quilibet non habuit nisi duos equos'.[88] Presumably only one of these two horses was a warhorse, whereas the crown expected all men-at-arms to have at least one serviceable re-mount. Linking pay rates to particular numbers of horses was clearly very sound policy, and a logical continuance of longstanding practice; and in doing this the English crown was very much in line with continental practice.[89] In fact, the *vadia guerre* accounts, if they can be taken at face value,

[83] E.g. L.F. Salzman, 'The property of the earl of Arundel, 1397', *Sussex Archaeological Collections*, xci (1953), p. 47.

[84] E.g. that of John de Warenne, earl of Surrey: *Testamenta Eboracensia or the wills registered at York . . . from the year 1300 downwards, part 1*, ed. J. Raine, Surtees Soc., ii (1836), p. 43.

[85] Barker, *The tournament in England, 1100–1400*, pp. 175–76; S.J. Herben, 'Arms and armour in Chaucer', *Speculum*, xii (1937), pp. 484–85. For the use of *barded* horses in a mid-fourteenth-century funeral in England, see Vale, *War and chivalry*, p. 89. Little original horse armour has survived from the fourteenth century (J. Alexander and P. Binski, eds, *Age of chivalry* (London, 1987), pp. 264–65) and this, combined with the relative scarcity of helpful pictorial evidence, means that 'our knowledge of the subject is somewhat patchy'; but see C. Blair, *European armour*, 3rd impr. (London, 1979), pp. 184–87; and G. Laking, *A record of European armour and arms through seven centuries*, 5 vols (London, 1920–22), iii, chapter 21.

[86] SC1/41, no. 154: memorandum concerning garrisons in Ponthieu in 1366.

[87] *Calendar of Ancient Correspondence concerning Wales*, ed. J.G. Edwards (Cardiff, 1935), pp. 246–47.

[88] *Norwell*, pp. 351, 353. The allowances for the passage of part of this expeditionary force from Sluys to England assume that each man-at-arms was returning with three horses, each knight with four and each banneret with five. Thirty-eight men, each with only two horses, stand out starkly at the end: ibid., pp. 386–92.

[89] For fifteenth-century examples, see M. Vale, *War and chivalry*, pp. 121–22.

suggest that it was rarely necessary to reduce pay rates for this particular reason,[90] and it is likely that most knights and esquires in English armies brought more horses than were strictly necessary.[91] If few could claim, like Buonaccorso Pitti, that they 'had gone [on campaign] with fourteen horses, but received pay for four',[92] then it was probably because such extravagance for continental expeditions would have made intolerable demands on English shipping.

The quality of the horses brought on campaign had always been important and the records of the mid to late fourteenth century continue to emphasise that men-at-arms should be 'assez suffisaument mountez et apparaillez',[93] but they are rarely specific about the quality required. In Gascony during the late 1330s, men-at-arms were paid at the standard rate if they were serving with a warhorse (*equus*), but received only half pay if they had a palfrey ('cum palaffredis').[94] No direct evidence of this kind is provided by either the *vadia guerre* or the *restauro equorum* accounts for the Breton campaign of 1342–43,[95] but a useful clue to warhorse quality *is* offered by the letters of appointment of several of the clerks charged with horse appraisal for this expedition. They were required to restrict their attention to horses worth 100s or more.[96] This seems to be a statement not of the minimum standard of warhorse required for receipt of a man-at-arms pay, but rather of the minimum value which the crown was willing to recognise for purposes of compensation.[97] Appropriately enough the *restauro equorum* accounts for this expedition include thirty-five horses valued at 100s, but none worth less than that amount. What cannot be determined is the number of warhorses which were adjudged to be worth less than 100s and therefore excluded from the original inventories. It is unlikely that this 'minimum value' regulation was unique to

---

90 But cf. conditions in Lancastrian Normandy: R.A. Newhall, *Muster and review* (Cambridge, Mass. 1940), pp. 32 n. 65; 82–83.

91 In 1417 119 men in the earl of Suffolk's retinue had a total of 624 horses: twenty-four horses for each of five knights, six horses for each of twenty-four esquires and four horses for each archer (Newhall, *Muster and review*, p. 32 n. 65).

92 *Two memoirs of Renaissance Florence: diaries of Buonaccorso Pitti and Gregorio Dati*, ed. G. Brucker, trans. J. Martines (New York, 1967), p. 79.

93 A statement concerning the garrison of Cockermouth castle in 1337: E101/20/41, m. 5.

94 E101/166/11, m. 15; E101/167/3, m. 12. The difference was between 6s and 3s *bordelais* per day. Although the distinction here appears to be between two types of horse, it is possible that the term *equus* is being used to denote an 'armoured' horse.

95 Some of the letters appointing horse appraisers in 1342 do, however, make reference to the recording of horse *numbers* as well as *values*: e.g. C76/17, m. 31.

96 C76/17, mm. 17, 18.

97 But cf. continental practice. In France, John II's ordinance of 1351 laid down a minimum standard of horse acceptable for appraisal: for a man-at-arms, it was thirty pounds *tournois*, for varlets, twenty pounds *tournois*: *Ordonnances des roys de France de la troisième race*, ed. D.F. Secousse (Paris, 1734; repr., 1967), iv, p. 68; Contamine, *Guerre, état et société*, pp. 19–20. The Pisan military code of 1327 employed a similar scale of minimum acceptable values for paid troops: Contamine, *War in the Middle Ages*, p. 128.

the arrangements for the Breton expeditions in 1342–43. Looking forward from 1342 to the rather patchy inventory evidence of subsequent decades we find that 100s is the lowest valuation used by horse appraisers right up to the 1360s.[98] Looking back, on the other hand, we find that only one horse valued at less than £5 appears in the *restauro equorum* account for the Cambrésis-Thiérache campaign of 1338–39, and similarly only one in the inventories for the War of Saint-Sardos.[99] In between, however, the inventories arising from the Scottish campaigns of 1336–38 contain 130 horses valued at less than 100s; and similarly large numbers are to be found in most Scottish campaign inventories from the reigns of Edward I and Edward II. It may well be that an experiment tried out during the mid 1320s for the war in Gascony was re-adopted at the start of the French war in the late 1330s, perhaps to encourage the employment of warhorses of rather higher quality than those which had been used in the recent Scottish expeditions.

The changes in the conditions of service associated with *restauro equorum* that have been considered here, and in particular the loosening of the traditional ties between pay and horse appraisal, occurred during a period strongly characterised by administrative and institutional experimentation in a number of areas of military organisation.[100] Where the experimentation concerned the terms of service offered to men-at-arms, it usually had some bearing directly or indirectly upon the operation of *restauro equorum*. There has been a tendency to describe the system of horse appraisal and compensation as though it operated uninterruptedly and uniformly throughout the early decades of Edward III's reign,[101] but this was not the case. The only campaigns prior to the outbreak of the French war for which significant horse inventories have survived are the comparatively small-scale operations in Scotland during the years 1336–38. In this particular case documentary survival appears broadly to reflect documentary production. The English armies which conducted the Weardale campaign and fought the battle of Halidon Hill are very imperfectly illuminated by the surviving records.[102] We have only a rough idea of their size and structure, and the terms of service offered to retinue commanders are also by no means clear. There is sufficient evidence to be sure that, with the exception of feudal contingents in 1327,

---

98   See, for example, materials for Gascony in the 1350s (E101/172/4) and Ireland in the 1360s (E101/28/11; E101/29/5). The list of horses lost during Sir Ralph de Ufford's term as Justiciar of Ireland (1344–46) contains many valued at less than 100s, but this document (C260/57, m. 28) is unusual in a number of respects and many of the horses listed were not warhorses.

99   For references, see Table 6.1.

100 E.g. military obligation: Powicke, *Military obligation in medieval England*, pp. 194–98; G.L. Harriss, *King, parliament and public finance in medieval England to 1369* (Oxford, 1975), pp. 383–400.

101 E.g. A.E. Prince, 'The army and navy', *The English government at work, 1327–1336*, ed. J.F. Willard and W.A. Morris (Cambridge, Mass., 1940), i, pp. 337–38.

102 For the available records, see p. 140 n. 6.

both armies served for royal pay, but rather less certain is the form that the pay took[103] and whether the receipt of wages was accompanied by warhorse valuation. The administrative records make no reference to horse *appraisal* for either campaign, whilst the mentions of horse *losses* should be treated with caution. Horse losses during the Weardale campaign cost an extraordinary £28,076,[104] or in other words about two and a half times the cost of *restauro equorum* for the Reims campaign of 1359–60, during which well over a thousand appraised horses perished. Such an exorbitant figure might well have caused the crown to re-consider its position concerning horse appraisal if all the losses had been sustained by the retinues of English magnates. In fact the bulk, if not all, of this sum was owed to John of Hainault's company.[105] The cost of Hainault's horses lost during the campaign, or sold to the royal household afterwards, amounted to £21,482 5s 6d, and if to this is added his men's losses in 1326 (£7,380 2s 3d) we have a figure very similar to that mentioned in Robert Wodehouse's wardrobe account. No such interpretative difficulties exist for the campaign in 1333, since the only losses which can be observed in the records were sustained by members of the royal household.[106]

In the absence of concrete evidence for the armies of 1327 and 1333, would it not be reasonable to assume that the standard rates of pay and the usual right to *restauro equorum*, which had been on offer for earlier expeditions, were also likely to have been available for Edward III's first two campaigns? Although an enticing assumption, we should be wary of it, for the two major royal expeditions following Halidon Hill, which *are* thankfully very well documented, exhibit terms of service of a decidedly unconventional nature. Magnate captains serving in Scotland during the winter of 1334–35 with retinues of men-at-arms received from the crown, not the normal daily rates of pay graduated according to rank, but a payment based upon a simple formula: £100 for twenty men-at-arms for a quarter of a year's service.[107] This was not a favourable rate of pay;[108] and there appears, moreover, to have been no provision for the valuation of warhorses, not even for the periods of

---

103 The most detailed of a very thin array of records merely assign lump sums to individuals; they very rarely mention numbers of combatants, rates of pay or precise periods of service. For 1327, see E101/383/8; for 1333, BL Additional MS 35181. *Vadia consueta* had been promised before the campaign in 1333: *Rot. Scot.*, i, p. 225.

104 A.E. Prince, 'The payment of army wages in Edward III's reign', *Speculum*, xix (1944), p. 138.

105 E101/18/4.

106 BL Additional MS 35181.

107 BL Cotton MS, Nero C. VIII, fos 233r–35v. The period of service ran from mid November to mid February (the precise dates varied a little). See Nicholson, *Edward III and the Scots*, chapter 12, for an analysis of these pay-rolls.

108 Captains were receiving a little more than 1s per day for each man-at-arms, but *they* would presumably pay their knights at the standard rate of 2s per day. The earls of Angus and Surrey received a reduced rate of pay (100 marks for twenty men-at-arms for a quarter of a year) because they had property in Scotland, but the king's household knights were given normal rates of pay for their companies.

service preceding and following the Roxburgh campaign, for which captains were paid the standard wage rates.[109] The same system of remuneration was in operation for the great Scottish expedition during the following summer,[110] and once again there is no evidence that horses were valued or *restauro equorum* paid. Whilst the *vadia guerre* accounts occasionally refer to the muster process at the start of a period of service, they never mention horse appraisal.[111] We considered earlier how the first two decades of Edward III's reign witnessed a loosening of the ties between horse appraisal and the receipt of pay. That process was no doubt hastened by a period of experiment in the mid 1330s, a period during which these ties appear, for a time, to have been wholly severed.

Restauro equorum was not only dropped from the terms of service for field armies in 1334 and 1335; it was, for a rather longer period, only sporadically offered for garrison service. That there is no sign of *restauro equorum* in the garrison records of southern English castles and towns during the 1330s might not appear particularly surprising.[112] But in Scotland and the borders, where patrolling and raiding were essential aspects of garrison service, equestrian casualties were commonplace; and yet the *vadia guerre* accounts for these northern garrisons in the 1330s make no reference to horse appraisal or compensation for losses.[113] On occasion, we might suspect that the silence of the accounts is concealing something. Sir Richard Talbot's indenture for the custody of Berwick in 1340 makes provision for horse appraisal, yet his accounts include no hint of either valuation or losses; and the same applies with respect to Robert de Leyburn's indenture and accounts as captain of Cockermouth Castle in 1336–8.[114] There are, however, enough cases during this period where indenture and accounts can be compared,[115] but where neither refer to *restauro equorum*, to suggest that the broader corpus of garrison accounts are not providing a misleading impression. This stands in

---

109 A horse inventory fragment does survive from the period of this campaign, listing thirteen horses valued at Newcastle or Roxburgh, but the personnel concerned appear to be members of the king's household: E101/101/14, m. 2. The two legible names on the list, Gailard de Savynak and Richard de Grimesby were king's sergeants at arms: BL Cotton MS, Nero C. VIII, fo. 225v.

110 Ibid., fos 236r–39r; for the exceptions to these terms, see Nicholson, *Edward III and the Scots*, pp. 199, 220.

111 E.g. the earl of Cornwall drew pay from 23 June 1335 'quo die primo visi fuerunt [at Newcastle] per ministros Regis': BL Cotton MS, Nero C. VIII, fo. 236r. William de Montagu joined Edward III's army on 11 June 'quo die p(er)ati (prearmati?) fuerunt': ibid., fo. 237v.

112 In 1339, for example: Dover (E101/22/15: accounts), Southampton (Southampton Record Office, S.C. 13/3/2: keeper's indenture; E101/22/11: accounts) or Windsor (E101/21/22: accounts)

113 For 1334–37, see BL Cotton MS, Nero C. VIII, fos 248r–51r; or the more leisurely 'particulars' for Roxburgh (E101/19/27) and Stirling (E101/19/40) from these years.

114 Berwick: E101/22/21, mm. 1–2; Cockermouth: E101/20/41.

115 E.g. Edinburgh and Stirling castles, 1335–40: E101/19/21; E101/19/24; E101/23/1.

stark contrast with the two preceding reigns which offer many examples of garrison troops benefiting from horse appraisal.[116] But equally, garrison service in the Scottish border country *had* been subject to experimental terms of service in the past. In November 1310, Sir Roger de Mowbray contracted to provide twenty men-at-arms for the Perth garrison in return for an all inclusive fee of 300 marks.[117] In this and a number of other cases, the fee is said to include pay, *restauro equorum* and other costs. In some instances in the 1330s, the garrison captain's wages were supplemented by a fee, which may have been intended to cover such costs as horse losses. It should be said, however, that very few of Sir John de Strivelyn's sixty men-at-arms at Edinburgh castle in 1335-36 would need to have lost their horses for his annual fee of £20 to have been exhausted.[118]

The motives lying behind the experimentation with the terms of service in the 1330s are not entirely clear. It is possible that the crown was simply attempting to wage war more economically, in terms not only of expenditure, but also of administrative effort.[119] The concession, announced before the Roxburgh campaign, that those serving in Scotland would be allowed to keep any booty which they might acquire[120] may have been intended as a partial substitute for horse appraisal: the opportunity of gain to set against the possibility of loss. The crown may well have been attempting to formulate a better package of terms of service, a package more favourable to both the royal administration and the ordinary man-at-arms. Reforming motives of this kind certainly seem to have been behind the changes made to the terms of service for continental expeditions in the 1340s, and again in the 1370s. But where the experiments of the 1330s are concerned, a further interpretation is possible. In this case, it seems that the crown was endeavouring to establish a new principle which involved the modification of the terms of service for a certain kind of expedition. It was not that the right to horse compensation was being withdrawn from those receiving royal pay; this was to continue for several more decades for at least some forms of military service. It was rather

---

116 E.g. the surviving inventories for 1311–12 (printed in *Bain*, iii, pp. 413–32) and the *restauro equorum* section of the Carlisle garrison accounts for July–November 1314 (ibid., no. 403).

117 Ibid., no. 173.

118 E101/19/24, m. 5 (indenture, which envisages forty men-at-arms), m. 27 (account, which shows that there were sixty). At a slightly later date, the fee is quite explicitly described as a personal bonus for the captain, the 'regard de son corps' (e.g. indenture for the custody of Pembroke castle, 1377: E101/34/29).

119 Cf. Henry IV's Scottish expedition of 1400, where a single lump sum of 20s was paid for each man-at-arms and 10s for each archer. The king was 'desperately short of money' at this time and these unfavourable terms were part of an 'attempt to mount an honourable expedition economically'. A.L. Brown, 'The English campaign in Scotland, 1400', *British government and administration: studies presented to S.B. Chrimes*, ed. H. Hearder and H.R. Loyn (Cardiff, 1974), pp. 48–49.

120 Nicholson, *Edward III and the Scots*, p. 174. A similar proclamation was made in 1327: ibid., p. 17.

that *restauro equorum* was no longer to be offered for service in armies led by the king in person within the shores of Britain. The crown no doubt wished to encourage the use of lighter and cheaper horses, more suited to the campaigning conditions in the north. At the same time, the prospect of royal leadership would guarantee a level of support from the military community which would not be seriously dented by a rather less than generous array of service benefits. But the 'pay without appraisal' principle for campaigns in Scotland headed by the king in person rested essentially on considerations of military obligation. It was established by the three expeditions of 1333–35, for which captains were summoned individually on their allegiance to serve with contingents of mounted troops. The nature of the summonses, 'mandatory though non-feudal',[121] enabled the crown quite reasonably to withhold *restauro equorum* whilst offering pay. Similar terms operated for Edward III's later expeditions in Scotland: this is made manifest by a solid corpus of supportive evidence, beginning with the materials for the campaigns of 1336–38.

The importance of the English expeditions to Scotland in the later 1330s as preparation for the demands of the war in France has not gone unnoticed by historians.[122] In the context of the present discussion, these well-documented military operations, illuminated as they are by a substantial collection of original inventories, pay-rolls and *restauro equorum* accounts, demonstrate with utmost clarity the resumption, after a period of experiment, of a system of service resting upon standard rates of pay and horse compensation. Yet to suggest that the terms of service in Scotland provided a model for those which were subsequently employed in France would be misleading, for the operation of *restauro equorum* in these two campaigning areas was founded upon different criteria. The reappearance of horse appraisal in the Scottish theatre of war seems to have arisen from the king's personal withdrawal from the struggle. He appointed lieutenants to conduct the military operations and although in 1336 this was a temporary expedient until he arrived in person,[123] in 1337–38 his only appearance in the north was fleeting and unplanned.[124] The retinues which served for pay, with appraised horses, were those in armies commanded by the king's lieutenants: Henry of Lancaster in 1336, the earl of Warwick during the summer of 1337 and the earls of Salisbury and Arundel during the winter of 1337–38. Horse inventories have not survived

---

121 N.B. Lewis, 'The feudal summons of 1385', *EHR*, c (1985), p. 739. In 1335, for example, 136 magnates were summoned on their 'fealty, allegiance and affection' to serve 'with horses and arms as adequately as possible': Prince, 'The army and navy', p. 351.

122 For example, N.B. Lewis, 'The recruitment and organisation of a contract army, May to November 1337', *BIHR*, xxxvii (1964), pp. 1–19; Morgan, *War and society in medieval Cheshire*, pp. 41–42.

123 Fowler, *The king's lieutenant*, pp. 32–33; Lewis, 'The recruitment and organisation of a contract army', p. 3 n. 5.

124 For details of the king's movements, see Lewis, 'The recruitment and organisation of a contract army', p. 1 n. 4.

for all of these retinues; but more significant is the lack of evidence of horse appraisal for the contingents which came north with the king during his lengthy stay in Scotland in 1336 and his 'flying visit' in June 1337.[125] When Edward III once more assumed direct command of an expedition to Scotland, during the winter of 1341–42, horse appraisal and *restauro equorum* disappeared from the records. There is a good set of *vadia guerre* accounts, showing pay to be based upon the standard daily rates, but no accompanying inventories or *restauro equorum* materials.[126] Gifts were made to cover the equestrian losses of selected individuals.[127] By contrast, the captains who had custody of the Scottish March during the following summer contracted to serve for pay which *was* accompanied by horse appraisal.[128] Unfortunately there is no trace of the inventories which would have been drawn up; but this is often the case with such periods of contract service. We find the same problem with Sir John de Segrave's forty-seven days of service in the Scottish March during the summer of 1340. Segrave's account includes no evidence that horse appraisal took place, but his indenture with the king (which is referred to in the account) stipulates that the horses of his forty men-at-arms 'serront prisez al entre de la terre ou devant & [il] avera restor de ses chivaux ensi prises & perduz'.[129]

The early years of the French war witnessed further experimentation with the terms of service. Of the occasional schemes which envisaged the use of all-embracing lump-sum payments to meet wage bills and other costs, a good example was the plan dating from the summer of 1341, according to which

125 Of these troops, there is evidence of horse appraisal for only one small company in 1336, that led by Sir Geoffrey de Mortimer: BL Cotton MS, Nero C. VIII, fos 243r, 282r; E101/101/14, m. 4.
126 For the crown's instructions that *vadia consueta* should be paid, but no mention of horse appraisal, see *Rot. Scot.*, i, 611–12. The pay-roll for this very brief Scottish campaign is E36/204, fos 102r–4r. The roll for the Breton campaign of 1342–43, included in the same Wardrobe Book, does have an accompanying set of *restauro equorum* accounts. The terms of service for Edward III's Scottish expedition during the winter of 1355–56 were probably similar to those of 1341–42, but unfortunately the records offer only glimpses: see, for example, E101/26/33 and Fowler, *The king's lieutenant*, p. 148 n. 16. By the time of the Scottish expedition of 1385, *restauro equorum* had been abandoned for all forms of military service. Yet the essence of the 'pay without appraisal' principle was maintained, in that *regard* – which was closely associated with warhorse costs and which by the 1380s operated for continental campaigns at *double* the customary rate – was not offered for service in Richard II's army in Scotland.
127 E.g., *CPR, 1340–43*, pp. 383, 384.
128 E101/68/3, nos. 49–58; the calendared versions of some of these indentures (*Bain*, iii, pp. 253–54) omit the horse appraisal and compensation clause. The service of some of the contractors is attested by a wardrobe pay-roll of retinues engaged in the defence of the Scottish March during the summer and autumn of 1342: E36/204, fos 104v–105r. Some captains accounted separately: Sir Thomas Wake of Lydel's pay account for the same period makes reference to an indenture with Edward III, but this has not survived (E101/23/25).
129 Account: E101/612/2; indenture: E101/68/3, no. 46.

captains would receive assignments of wool in *lieu* of wages (and other payments) for the first forty days of the campaign.[130] But these were merely experiments prompted by the financial difficulties of the government and the perceived potential of wool; and there is no evidence that the crown seriously considered withdrawing *restauro equorum* from the terms of service for overseas campaigns prior to the Treaty of Brétigny. Indeed, from the late 1330s to the late 1350s, horse appraisal was a regular feature of Edward III's continental expeditions and it is not difficult to see why. Service on the continent, particularly if involving a feudal levy, had been the cause of much friction between king and magnates in the past:[131] the knightly class in England, it was said, 'did not give a bean for all of France'. Such attitudes were not to be changed overnight. Edward III failed to secure the wholehearted backing of the nobility for his Scottish expeditions (these depended upon the support of a group of 'self-interested northerners and personal friends')[132] and it must have been with some trepidation that the king embarked upon a continental war, particularly as his strategy of German alliances did not enjoy the universal support of his closest advisers.[133] It is hardly surprising, therefore (though contrary to the 'value for money' tone of the Walton Ordinances), that Edward and his advisers felt compelled to offer unusually generous terms of service at the start of the French war, in order to ensure a respectable level of support. For the expedition which left the shores of England in July 1338, men-at-arms served, with appraised warhorses, at *double* the customary rates of pay: an ordinary esquire received 2s a day, a knight 4s and a banneret 8s.[134] The quest for manpower also resulted in 'exeedingly generous terms', in the form of *fiefs-rentes*, being offered to continental allies.[135] Men-at-arms continued to receive double rates of pay (and *restauro equorum*) during the Sluys-Tournai campaign of June to September 1340;[136] but thereafter,

---

130 M. Prestwich, 'English armies in the early stages of the Hundred Years War: a scheme in 1341', *BIHR*, lvi (1983), pp. 102–13.

131 Sanders, *Feudal military service in England*, pp. 53–56; Prestwich, *War, politics and finance under Edward I*, pp. 75–77.

132 W.M. Ormrod, *The reign of Edward III* (New Haven and London, 1990) p. 100.

133 *Scalacronica*, p. 104; J. Sumption, *The Hundred Years War: trial by battle* (London, 1990), p. 221.

134 *Norwell*, pp. 325–62 (*vadia guerre*); 309–25 (*restauro equorum*). Mounted archers and infantry received the usual rates of pay. M. Powicke interprets the double pay rates in 1338–39 as 'perhaps the product of over-confidence and novelty': *Military obligation in medieval England*, p. 210.

135 M. Vale, 'The Anglo-French wars, 1294–1340: allies and alliances', *Guerre et société en France, en Angleterre et en Bourgogne, XIVe–XVe siècle*, ed. P. Contamine et al. (Lille, 1992), p. 20.

136 E101/389/8, mm. 11–16: *vadia guerre* account; neither inventories nor *restauro equorum* accounts have survived. Expenditure on wages was only about a quarter of what it had been for the preceding campaign: £23,368 10d as compared with £93,916 17s 4d; compensation for lost warhorses in 1340 cost the crown no more than half what it had in 1338–39. Prince, 'The payment of army wages in Edward III's reign', p. 150.

whether prompted by financial considerations or increased confidence in the aristocracy's commitment to the war, *vadia guerre* was reduced to more realistic levels. That the customary terms of service were once again in operation for the expeditions to Brittany in 1342–43 can be seen in the pay and *restauro equorum* accounts.[137]

Where the terms of service for all of these continental campaigns differed from those operating during the Scottish wars, was in their additional provision of *eskippeson*, sea transport for men and horses at royal expense. A captain would no doubt prefer to find ships ready and waiting for him at the port of embarkation; ships which would have been impressed by the king's agents, fitted out as 'fighting platforms' or horse transports and which would be paid for directly by the crown.[138] In the summer of 1338, nearly 350 ships were hired by the crown to transport the English army to Antwerp.[139] If the royal authorities were unable to assemble a transport fleet, captains would be obliged to make their own arrangements, but for this they would be paid a fixed sum for each horse in their retinues, with the number of horses allowed to each man being determined by his rank.[140] The return to England in January and February 1340 of a large proportion of Edward III's army was financed in this fashion.[141]

A great many horse inventories and *restauro equorum* accounts were compiled between the truce of Malestroit in 1343 and the Treaty of Brétigny in 1360, for horse appraisal was the invariable accompaniment of paid service on major overseas expeditions during this period. Yet, to our great loss, comparatively few have survived the intervening centuries. What the records do show, however, is that this period also witnessed a broadening of the terms of service normally offered to captains leading retinues in overseas ventures. It is to this development that we must now turn.

One element in the man-at-arms' terms of service which is usually included in discussions of military organisation in Edward III's reign has not yet been mentioned: *regard* (or *reward*), a payment intended as a contribution towards the expenses of preparing for war. The standard quarterly rate was 100 marks for the service of thirty men-at-arms, but there was always a certain amount of flexibility in the rates offered to captains.[142] The term 'regard'

---

137 E36/204, fos 105v–110v (*vadia guerre*); 86v–88v (*restauro equorum*). There were important exceptions to this scheme of remuneration: see Appendix 2.

138 Hewitt, *The organisation of war under Edward III*, chapter 4.

139 *Norwell*, pp. 363–86; these *vadia nautarum* accounts include fourteen royal vessels.

140 For the treatment of this in indentures of war, see Prince, 'The indenture system under Edward III', pp. 294–95.

141 *Norwell*, pp. 386–92.

142 Prince, 'The indenture system under Edward III', pp. 293–94; Sherborne, 'Indentured retinues and English expeditions to France, 1369–1380', p. 743 n. 6. Prince implies that the *regard* payment was a bonus for the captain, but Sherborne is quite insistent that it was 'divided among all the men-at-arms in a retinue'. It may be unsafe to generalise on this point: recent studies have shown that subcontractors would not necessarily receive

appears for the first time in the mid 1340s, but it was the term rather than the form of payment that was new. Although it has a passing resemblance to the 'lump-sum' payments employed by the English crown for the Scottish campaigns in 1334–35 and for many periods of garrison service, regard was in fact a different type of payment. It was not a substitute for pay and restauro equorum, but a supplement to them. In the sense of forming one element in a package of actual and potential payments, regard is rather more closely associated with the annual fees stipulated by indentures of retinue[143] and fiefs-rentes[144] and is directly descended from the terms of some early-fourteenth-century military contracts. In 1316–17 Sir William la Zouche contracted to provide the crown with the services of thirty men-at-arms for one year. Zouche would receive 'gages acustomez' and 'restor de chevaux' and 200 marks 'por fee e por toute manere dautres choses'.[145] The latter looks very like the regard payment of the later fourteenth century, though it represents only half the standard regard rate. Rather more generous was the feodum paid to the earl of Salisbury for a half year's service in Scotland from December 1337 to June 1338: 1,400 marks for 140 men-at-arms.[146] He also received wages for his men and was allowed £155 in compensation for eight lost horses. Here, then, is a balanced scheme of remuneration: pay, regard and restauro equorum. It was not, however, the norm at this time. Salisbury appears to have been the only English captain during Edward III's Scottish wars to have received such an advantageous package of payments. Nor does

the customary rates of remuneration (Sherborne, 'Indentured retinues and English expeditions to France, 1369–1380', pp. 743–44; Goodman, 'The military subcontracts of Sir Hugh Hastings', pp. 118–20). The regard which Sir John Strother received from the earl of March in 1374 represented a payment of about £9 for each of the subcontractor's thirty men-at-arms, but included a 'personal' regard of £60 for Strother himself (Walker, 'Profit and loss in the Hundred Years War', 103–4).

143 For example, the indenture of retinue between Aymer de Valence and Thomas, Lord Berkeley (1297) stipulates that the latter, for serving with his company overseas, should receive an annual fee of 100 marks, plus standard wages and restauro equorum: B. Lyon, 'The feudal antecedent of the indenture system', Speculum, xxix (1954), pp. 504–5. According to his indenture with John of Gaunt, Sir John de Neville was to receive, in addition to customary wages and restauro equorum, a wartime fee of 500 marks per year for the service of twenty men-at-arms and twenty mounted archers. Neville was, therefore, receiving a fee which was rather higher than the standard rate of regard: JGlndRet, p. 89.

144 See Lyon, From fief to indenture (Harvard, 1957). This is not, of course, to suggest that the purpose of the retaining fee or money fief was to supplement vadia guerre: 'It established the claim to military service, though it did not constitute the payment for such service. Payment was made separately in the form of subsidies, wages and maintenance.' (J.O. Prestwich's review of From fief to indenture, History, xliv (1959), p. 49).

145 N.B. Lewis, 'An early fourteenth-century contract for military service', BIHR, xx (1944), pp. 111–18.

146 E101/20/25, m. 3. This is equivalent to a quarterly rate of 150 marks for thirty men-at-arms, 50% higher than the standard rate of regard. Salisbury's wage account shows that he did not actually maintain 140 men-at-arms throughout this six month period.

regard figure in the records for the earliest campaigns of the French war; but it does appear, now actually called *regard*, in the indentures drawn-up during the spring of 1345 between the king and the captains who were to mount an ambitious multi-front offensive on France that coming summer.[147] For his 250 men-at-arms, Henry of Lancaster secured *regard* at three times the rate which was later to become the standard; and this formed part of a balanced, and very favourable, package of payments and benefits.[148] The terms of the earl of Northampton's indenture for service in Brittany are less detailed than Lancaster's, but he too can be seen to have served in return for a combination of wages, *regard* and *restauro equorum*.[149]

The captains serving under Edward III's two principal lieutenants in 1345 secured the same balanced scheme of benefits as their superiors,[150] and perhaps as a consequence of such widespread usage, this combination became established as the norm for field campaigns. Despite the patchiness of the surviving records for the Crécy-Calais expedition, the consequence of the loss of Walter de Wetwang's original accounts,[151] it is nevertheless possible to see the operation of both *regard* and *restauro equorum* through entries on the Issue Rolls (and related records)[152] and in the provisions of military contracts. In the latter, *regard* payments are termed 'fees'. Sir Thomas Ughtred's contract with the king, to provide twenty men-at-arms and twenty archers for a

---

147 Fowler, *The king's lieutenant*, pp. 49–52, and appendix 1.

148 Lancaster's indenture, dated 13 March 1345, is printed in Fowler, *The king's lieutenant*, pp. 230–32 (the half-yearly rate of *regard* was 5000 marks for 250 men-at-arms, and not 500 marks as printed there). Lancaster's account shows that his wage bill amounted to over £14,500, whilst he was also to receive £10,000 for *regard* and £1,384 13s 4d for the loss of forty-three warhorses: E101/25/9. Early in 1347 Ralph, Lord Stafford, formerly Seneschal of Aquitaine, received £611 13s 4d for horses lost by his men in the duchy: E404/496, no. 500.

149 E101/68/4, no. 72 (dated 27 April 1345), printed in *Rymer*, III, i, p. 37.

150 For the earl of Pembroke's indenture, for service with Lancaster in Gascony, see E101/68/3, no. 60. On 9 December John Charnels was ordered to pay *regard* for the 'second quarter' to Northampton and his captains in Brittany: 3,400 florins to Northampton, 1,333 to the earl of Oxford, 166 to Sir Michael de Poynings, 166 to Sir Edward de Montagu and 133 to the earl of Devon's men. C76/21, m. 3; E101/167/5.

151 There are a number of manuscripts, dating from the fifteenth to seventeenth centuries, which appear to be extracts from, or summaries of, Walter de Wetwang's original *vadia guerre* accounts. Despite much variety in appearance and content, all of these transcripts purport to show the English army at the siege of Calais; but they are little more than abbreviated lists of retinues, lacking indications of duration of service or amounts of money owing in wages. There is also much disparity between the manuscripts. Of the numerous printed editions of the Wetwang transcripts, the best known and the most detailed is that offered by Wrottesley in *Crecy and Calais*, pp. 193–204 (from College of Arms MS 2, M. 16); the earliest appears to be Robert Brady, *A complete history of England* (London, 1700), ii, pp. 86–88 (own extracts from the original accounts). The Wetwang transcripts are discussed more fully, with detailed bibliographical references, in A. Ayton, 'The English army and the Normandy campaign of 1346', *England and Normandy in the Middle Ages*, ed. D. Bates and A. Curry (London, 1994).

year's service, stipulated a fee of £200 (along with wages and compensation for lost horses), which represented a payment well above the normal rate of *regard*.[153] Terms of service might not be as favourable at subcontract level. When on 16 March 1347 Sir Hugh Fitz Simon contracted to serve for a year in Ralph, Lord Stafford's retinue with twelve men-at-arms, he secured a fee of only 100 marks, whereas payment at the usual royal rate would have amounted to 160 marks.[154]

The Crécy-Calais expedition was, therefore, the first under direct royal leadership in which conventional pay, *regard* and compensation for lost horses were offered simultaneously. It was a 'package' of benefits which was to be employed repeatedly in the coming years. For example, the indenture drawn up between the king and the prince of Wales prior to the latter's departure for Gascony in 1355 allows, in addition to the customary provision of shipping, for standard wages and *regard*, and the valuation of warhorses either at the port of embarkation or on arrival in Bordeaux.[155] Lesser captains taking part in this expedition obtained similar terms,[156] and advances of wages and *regard* were made to a number of captains for other expeditions in 1355.[157]

By the mid 1350s, then, a degree of stability had been established in the terms of service offered by the crown to captains serving in continental field campaigns. There was, of course, room for flexibility in individual cases, both in the terms offered and in their actual implementation; and there was, more-over, some experimentation before the system became firmly established. This is neatly illustrated by Sir Thomas Dagworth's period of service in Brittany in 1346. His indenture, dated 28 January 1346, allows for *gages usueles, regard* and the valuation of his warhorses.[158] These are quite conven-tional terms, but his account for just under a year's service from the date of

[152] *Regard* is only irregularly mentioned in either the Issue Rolls or Wetwang's book of receipts (E101/390/12); but that *regard* is included in general *vadia guerre* payments is strongly suggested by such sums as £92 15s 11½d, recorded in the wages debenture for Sir Alan la Zouche ('before Calais', 21 November 1346: E404/496, no. 28). *Restauro equorum* payments: 24 November 1347, for horses lost in Normandy and France by Sir Thomas de Bourn and his retinue (E404/496, no. 86); 27 February 1348, for similar losses by Sir John Stryvelyn's retinue (E403/340, m. 34).

[153] E101/25/33, m. 3 ('devant Caleys', 1 April 1347): printed in Lewis, 'An early fourteenth-century contract for military service', p. 118.

[154] *Crecy and Calais*, p. 192.

[155] *BPReg*, iv, pp. 143–45. For discussions of the wage and *regard* payments, and the valu-ation of horses, for this expedition, see Prince, 'The strength of English armies', pp. 366–67; idem, 'The payment of army wages in Edward III's reign', pp. 155–56; Hewitt, *The Black Prince's expedition*, chapter 2.

[156] A separate account has survived for Sir Thomas de Hoggeshawe's retinue, stipulating standard rates of pay and *regard*: E101/26/34.

[157] Prince, 'The payment of army wages in Edward III's reign', pp. 154–55.

[158] E101/68/3, no. 62: printed in Prince, 'The strength of English armies', pp. 370–71.

the contract contains some far from conventional features.[159] The wages section is unexceptional, but that concerned with *reward* shows Dagworth claiming 100 marks for himself, 20 marks for each of his fourteen knights and £10 for each of his sixty-five *armigeri*. These rates were very favourable, given that the standard rate of *regard* would yield about £9 per man-at-arms for a year's service; moreover, Dagworth's *regard* claim was graduated in the same way as pay. Whilst a captain might well employ differentials of this kind when dividing his retinue's *regard* among his men-at-arms, the payment he received from the crown would not itself be affected by the rank structure of his retinue. The *regard* section is not the only unusual aspect of Dagworth's account. Compensation for the loss of sixty-six warhorses is claimed at a fixed rate of £10 per horse. This strongly suggests that the horse valuation stipulated in Dagworth's indenture was not actually carried out. It may be, however, that Dagworth was trying to bend the rules (by including second-string horses, for example), for his retinue's losses are heavy even allowing for the intensity of his military operations in 1346. This possibility is supported to some degree by the fact that he also attempted to secure £120 for the loss of 120 archer hackneys, whilst simultaneously claiming in his wages account that not one of the 240 men in his company missed a single day's service during a period of 346 days. There was no precedent for the compensation of archer mounts and this part of the account has been crossed out, but like so many others, Dagworth's wages claim appears to have been accepted without demur.

Whatever the correct interpretation of Dagworth's intriguing account, this case does serve as a reminder that the terms of indentures, if not corroborated by evidence of performance, should be approached with more than a little caution. Unforeseen circumstances of various kinds could intervene to disrupt the smooth implementation of indenture provisions. In April 1352 the earl of Stafford was no doubt expecting to have his retinue's warhorses appraised at Southampton prior to departure for Gascony,[160] but as his expenses account shows, his expedition was disrupted by a common logistical problem. A shortage of horse transports forced a substantial number of the earl's men to leave their warhorses in England, thereby obliging them to buy suitable mounts on arrival in Gascony. Stafford's account indicates that the crown agreed to reimburse the cost of these purchases (£686 13s 4d), whilst also paying Stafford £500 in compensation for lost horses.[161] The latter looks

---

159 E101/25/17.
160 The original indenture has not survived and the details supplied in Sir William le Neve's collection of indenture abstracts are obviously not complete (BL Stowe MS 440, fo. 9r); but there is no reason for thinking that horse appraisal was not envisaged when the indenture was drawn up on 3 March.
161 E101/26/25. Cf. the provisions of Stafford's indenture for service in Ireland in 1361, which include the crown's guarantee of re-imbursement of the cost of horses bought on arrival: E101/28/27, m. 4.

suspiciously like a lump sum, an estimate not based on the evidence of inventories, and it is likely, therefore, that none of Stafford's horses were valued either in England or Gascony.[162] None of this improvisation affected the operation of the standard rates of pay or *regard*, however.[163]

Of the benefits which captains offering their services for field campaigns in the 1350s might reasonably expect to receive, horse appraisal was the one most prone to disruption and the most costly in terms of administrative effort. As we shall see, these considerations may have contributed significantly to the crown's decision to abandon *restauro equorum* in the 1370s. In the preceding decades horse appraisal was withdrawn from some forms of military service. On occasion, this was because a very different form of payment had been adopted, as for example with the all-inclusive annual fees paid to keepers of the town of Berwick.[164] But even when a garrison commander was paid on the basis of standard daily wage rates, together with *regard*, it will often be found that his men were serving without the insurance of horse appraisal. This is perhaps not particularly surprising in the case of the Isle of Wight garrison in 1352.[165] But that *restauro equorum* is not mentioned in the terms of service of the captains of Calais in the 1350s is more worthy of comment, since such a garrison was not intended to be an immobile force, a fact that the crown recognised by providing *eskippeson* for horses at the start of a contracting period.[166] But, then, by the 1350s the great majority of English garrisons in France were not on the king's pay-roll at all: there were insufficient resources available and 'increasingly the authorities had to allow troops to live from the uncontrolled proceeds of ransom districts'.[167]

---

[162] Similarly suspicious is the payment of 1,000 marks to Sir John Chandos for 100 'coursers' lost whilst implementing the terms of the Treaty of Brétigny in 1360–61: Prince, 'The strength of English armies', p. 368; idem, 'The indenture system under Edward III', p. 294 n. 4.

[163] The wage bill totalled £3,614 11s 8d, whilst the cost of *regard* was £828: E101/26/25.

[164] Thomas de Musgrave served as keeper of Berwick from February 1347 to October 1349 for an annual fee of 2,000 marks: E101/25/30. Later keepers received annual fees as low as 400 marks (e.g. 1369: E101/73, nos. 17 and 18); 1000 marks (e.g. 1351 and 1367: E101/68/3, no. 70, E101/68/4, no. 86) or as high as 4000 marks (e.g. 1356: E101/68/4, no. 75).

[165] E101/26/24: discussed by S.F. Hockey, *Insula vecta. The Isle of Wight in the Middle Ages* (London and Chichester, 1982), pp. 95–96.

[166] These are the indenture terms for Sir Robert de Herle, appointed captain of Calais in 1351, and Sir John de Beauchamp in 1356: *Rymer*, III, i, pp. 222, 324. The terms of the latter indenture are confirmed by the accounts of the treasurer of Calais (E101/173/7) where *regards* are termed *feoda*. Cf. the treasurer's accounts of 1371–72, which display a variety of pay and *regard* rates for the cluster of garrisons around Calais (John Rylands Library, Latin MS 240, fos 3r–4r). Some *scutiferi* serving at Guines and Ardres received 18d per day, whilst others were paid 12d. At the castle of Hames the higher rate was paid to 'homini ad arma equitum' and the lower to 'homini ad arma peditum'. A similar distinction between mounted and foot 'lances' can be seen in the muster rolls of the garrison at Neufchâtel-en-Bray in 1363: BL Additional MS 41567, Q, fos 250r–55r.

[167] Fowler, *The king's lieutenant*, pp. 165–70, which draws on the same author's article, 'Les

The balanced scheme of remuneration which had emerged for continental expeditions – pay, *regard*, *restauro equorum* and shipping – was also in due course employed in that rather less fashionable centre of Edwardian military activity: Ireland. The turning point came with the duke of Clarence's expedition in 1361, for it was the first of five over a period of fifteen years which were financed, in the main, from England and consequently subject to the terms of service which operated for English campaigns in France.[168] Before 1361 the justiciar in Ireland was appointed to serve with a retinue of stipulated proportions, and the wages of these men, together with his fee (from which he was required to maintain a further twenty men-at-arms), were paid by the Irish exchequer.[169] An unusual documentary survival from the term of office of Sir Ralph de Ufford in the mid 1340s allows us to see how one particularly resourceful justiciar endeavoured to make the system work.[170] Ufford was required to employ a retinue of forty men-at-arms and two hundred archers,[171] but it is clear that he had more than forty men-at-arms at his disposal for most of his period of duty.[172] It must have been difficult for a justiciar like Ufford to hire good men for a lengthy term of service in Ireland. Initial recruitment in 1344 was probably made easier by a lull in the French war, but the Irish exchequer was only willing to pay 12d per day for each of Ufford's men-at-arms, irrespective of the fact some of them were knights. It was probably in order to facilitate recruitment that Ufford issued fees to

finances et la discipline dans les armées anglaises en France au XIVe siècle', *Les Cahiers Vernonnais*, iv (1964), pp. 55–84. Some towns and castles in Brittany were farmed out to captains: for three such agreements in 1359, see *Rymer*, III, i, pp. 427, 429, 432. For Sir Walter Bentley's memorandum to the king's council, which outlined with great clarity the impossibility of maintaining military discipline amongst the English troops in Brittany without regular pay, see *Froissart*, ed. Lettenhove, xviii, 'Pièces Justificatives, 1319–99', no. lxxix, pp. 339–43. The council's responses included, in effect, a definition of the terms of service for garrisons in France: customary pay rates and a fee for the captain.

168 P. Connolly, 'The financing of English expeditions to Ireland, 1361–1376', *England and Ireland in the later Middle Ages*, ed. J. Lydon (Blackrock, Co. Dublin, 1981), pp. 104–21.

169 For example, in 1349 Sir Thomas Rokeby was required to bring twenty men-at-arms and forty mounted archers, in addition to the company (twenty men-at-arms and twenty archers) which he supported from his £500 fee: *CCR, 1349–54*, pp. 47–48.

170 R. Frame, 'The justiciarship of Ralph Ufford: warfare and politics in fourteenth-century Ireland', *Studia Hibernica*, xiii (1973), pp. 7–47; idem, *English lordship in Ireland, 1318–61* (Oxford, 1982), pp. 263–78.

171 *CCR, 1343–46*, p. 304; *CPR, 1343–45*, p. 227.

172 Exactly forty men-at-arms received pay without fluctuation from July 1344 to December 1345, which suggests that there were in fact rather more than forty in service, thus enabling gaps in the retinue, arising from departures or fatalities, to be filled immediately. Ufford would have been required to maintain at least twenty further men-at-arms from his fee as justiciar. For a summary of the pay accounts, see Frame, 'The justiciarship of Ralph Ufford', p. 44, table B. Dr Frame takes the personnel numbers at face value, despite the fact that the nominal records for Ufford's retinue, even allowing for a steady turnover of manpower, strongly suggest a larger number of men-at-arms.

sixty-nine of the men who served with him in Ireland, together with the prospect of *restauro equorum* should they lose any horses. Judging by the respectable number of knights and veteran esquires listed in the fee roll, this added inducement appears to have had the desired effect.[173] Whether Ufford was setting a precedent in providing supplementary benefits of this kind is not clear; certainly the *restauro equorum* list exhibits a number of decidedly unconventional features. If it *was* an experiment, then it was nevertheless drawing on long-established practices. The terms on offer – fees, *restauro equorum*, as well as wages – resemble those of many indentures of retinue. But the financing of this exercise in retinue formation came not from the personal resources of the captain, but from those of the Irish exchequer. It seems that Ufford had perceived the inadequacy of existing rewards for service in Ireland and, with a certain amount of improvisation, created a scheme of payments which resembled more closely those which were beginning to be paid by the crown for campaigns in France. This was essential if a retinue of respectable quality was to be maintained in Ireland at a time when altogether more attractive conflicts were taking place elsewhere.[174]

It is, therefore, perhaps surprising that it was only during the Peace of Brétigny that the system of remuneration which had been developed for campaigns in France also came to be applied to the Irish theatre of war. Walter de Dalby's *vadia guerre* accounts for the duke of Clarence's expedition (1361–64) show all the English captains to have been in receipt of the normal rates of pay and *regard*.[175] Less certain is whether all of the men-at-arms who participated in this expedition did so with appraised horses. The surviving indentures of war stipulate *restauro equorum*, along with 'gages acoustumes de guerre', 'le regard acustume' and shipping allowances,[176] but the collection of inventories for this expedition is obviously very incomplete.

---

[173] C260/57, m. 28. Eighteen knights and fifty-one esquires received fees for varying lengths of time from two years (twenty-nine men, but only four knights) to six months (ten men in all). The annual fees awarded to knights ranged from £10 to 40 marks; those for esquires from £2 10s to 10 marks. The largest fees may have been awarded to those bringing small companies with them. Sir John de Carreu, who received 40 marks, had served with a small retinue in Brittany in 1342–43 and was to bring one to Ireland in 1361 (E36/204, fo. 107r; E101/28/21, fo. 6v). Of the men named in the *restauro equorum* list, all except one were recipients of fees. Of those receiving or requesting letters of protection (of whom some would have been non-combatants), about half (thirty-five) appear on the fee roll. There were at least nine knights in Ufford's retinue who did not receive fees. For the protections, see *CPR, 1343–45*, pp. 244–45, 255, 257, 259–60, 301, 310; C81/1741, nos. 5, 7, 8; SC1/41, no. 102. For discussions of the backgrounds of the men in the retinue, see Frame, 'The justiciarship of Ralph Ufford', pp. 13–15; idem, *English lordship in Ireland*, pp. 265–66.

[174] Thirty-five, or about half, of the fee-recipients were in service for one and a half years or longer. There was a steady exodus of personnel from Ufford's command in 1345 and 1346, balanced to some extent by late arrivals.

[175] E101/28/21, fos 3v–10v. For the passage and re-passage allowances, see ibid., fos 13v–14r.

[176] E101/28/27, mm. 4, 6, 10, 11.

Not only are some important retinues not represented, but of those which are, several have only partial coverage.[177] It is possible, of course, that many of the original inventories, including that for the duke of Clarence's retinue, have long since perished. This is unlikely to provide a complete explanation, however, for of the thirty-five horses included in the *restauro equorum* section of Dalby's account book, only one (that of Sir Thomas de Nauton) does not appear in one of the surviving inventories.[178] The natural conclusion to be drawn from this is that horse appraisal, and thus *restauro equorum*, had been extended to only a proportion of the men-at-arms serving in Ireland in the early 1360s. Given that this was the first time that the full package of service benefits had operated in Irish conditions, it is perhaps not altogether surprising that they were not uniformly applied. It comes as rather more of a surprise to find that they were inconsistently applied for the last major continental campaign of the 1350s.

At first glance, the *vadia guerre* accounts for the Reims campaign of 1359–60[179] appear to provide the clearest possible evidence of the extent to which the terms of service offered to English captains had broadened since the experimental days of Edward III's early Scottish campaigns. Captains received payments under five headings: wages, *reward*, *restauro equorum*, outward sea passage and return sea passage.[180] Yet closer examination of the accounts reveals that only a minority of retinue commanders benefited from all five payments. The irregular allocation of funds to support 'passage' and 're-passage' does not present a problem, for such payments were made only to those retinues which could not be transported by requisitioned vessels. The apparently irregular incidence of *restauro equorum* is less easily accounted for. Although we might reasonably expect some retinues, particularly the smaller ones, to have come through the campaign without losing any appraised warhorses, it is difficult to believe that the earl of March's retinue, consisting of 300 men-at-arms, suffered no equestrian losses; and the same doubts must exist for other companies, such as those of Sir Walter de Mauny and Sir William Latimer.[181] Even if we are to conclude that warhorse appraisal was not universal in 1359, might we not reasonably expect that every retinue which included paid men-at-arms would qualify for a *reward* payment? This, however, does not seem to have been the case. Indeed, no mention is made of *reward* for the majority of separately accounting companies,

177 E101/28/11; E101/29/5.
178 E101/28/21, fo. 14v. Conversely, only one of the retinues included in the original inventories (Sir Thomas de Hoggshawe's) does not appear in the *restauro equorum* account.
179 Contained in the Wardrobe Book of William Farley, Keeper of the Wardrobe: E101/393/11, fos 79r–116v.
180 The earl of Northampton, for example, served for 259 days with 159 other men-at-arms and 200 mounted archers. His wage bill amounted to £3,893 12s 8d and he was allowed £1,008 8s 10d in *reward*, £312 6s 8d for the loss of forty horses, £56 for the 'passage' of 336 horses and £117 for the 're-passage' of 702: ibid. fo. 79v.
181 E101/393/11, fos 79v, 80v, 81r.

and whilst most of these are small, size *per se* does not appear to have been the essential criterion for receiving *regard* – nor, indeed, does the period of service, whether *restauro equorum* was being paid, or whether the captain was receiving a fee as a household banneret or knight. Thus, the retinues of Sir Michael de Poynings and Sir Thomas de Ughtred both included twenty men-at-arms, they served for similar periods (266 and 254 days respectively) and they both lost horses (five and nine); but Poynings received *regard* and Ughtred did not.[182] Sir Richard de Pembridge served with two *scutiferi* and received *regard*, whilst Sir Thomas de Berkeley served with three and did not. Once again, their periods of service and equestrian losses were similar; and both were household knights.[183] It is possible that Farley's accounts omit payments which were in fact made; but it is more likely that the terms of service had not been fixed and that some captains had negotiated a more favourable 'package' than others.[184] The case of Sir Thomas de Beauchamp is a good example of the diversity of terms in operation. Whilst in most cases the captain was included in the total of men-at-arms for which *regard* would be provided, Sir Thomas received *reward* only for his two *scutiferi*.[185] Flexibility of terms can also be seen in the *restauro equorum* payments. Sir William de Granson was allowed £600 for unspecified losses and Sir Frank Hale received 1000 marks for the loss of forty-three warhorses. In both cases, the payment appears to be a lump sum, based upon an estimate of the value of the losses rather than the precise evidence of inventories.[186]

By the time of the Treaty of Brétigny, a balanced scheme of remuneration, involving wages, allowances for costs incurred and compensation for losses sustained, had become firmly established as the normal terms of service for English men-at-arms serving in royal armies on the continent.[187] Whether it was a particularly advantageous scheme of benefits, representing a significant improvement upon those available for paid military service earlier in the century, is open to question. Standard wage rates in 1360 were at the same levels as under Edward I. *Restauro equorum* was still the norm, though expenditure on warhorses may now have been less crippling than had hitherto been the case.[188] *Regard*, or an equivalent type of fee, had not normally been offered as a supplement to pay prior to the 1340s; this, therefore, was new – apparently a response to the increasing cost of armour and warhorses. But *regard*, as we have seen with Farley's *vadia guerre* accounts, might not be

---

[182] E101/393/11, fos 81r, 81v.

[183] E101/393/11, fos 82r, 82v.

[184] Cf. M.J. Bennett, *Community, class and careerism* (Cambridge, 1983), pp. 175–76.

[185] £12 13s for 264 days service: E101/393/11, fo. 83v.

[186] E101/393/11, fo. 86v.

[187] The terms offered to foreign mercenaries serving in these royal armies might well be much less favourable. Farley's *vadia guerre* accounts for the Reims campaign suggest that the 'German' contingents received pay, but not *regard* or *restauro equorum*.

[188] See Chapter 6 for a discussion of the trend in warhorse prices in the second half of the century.

extended to all captains participating in an expedition and it is uncertain how far the ordinary man-at-arms, at a lower level of the military hierarchy, benefited from it.

THE END OF *RESTAURO EQUORUM*

For the Reims campaign, *regard* had been paid at the standard rate – 100 marks for thirty men-at-arms for a quarter of a year's service – and the long-established scale of wages had continued to operate. The same rates applied to the duke of Clarence's Irish expedition of the early 1360s,[189] but the resumption of the French war was accompanied by a change. For John, duke of Lancaster's expedition in 1369, both *regard* and wages were offered at one and a half times the normal rates, whilst horse appraisal and *restor* of losses, and provison of shipping, continued 'en manere acustumee'.[190] These terms of service appear generous, but those which were secured by Lancaster and Sir Walter Hewitt for service in Gascony in 1370–71 were still more favourable: double *regard* and double the usual wage rates, as well as the normal arrangements for horse appraisal and sea transportation.[191] Such generosity was not to be repeated; indeed, these two expeditions under Lancaster's command were the last for which the crown was to offer the well-balanced package of payments and benefits which, over the preceding twenty years, had become the norm for field campaigns. The most significant change was the abandonment of *restauro equorum*. Sir John atte Wode and William de Humberstane, who had been sent to Calais 'pur preiser les chivalx' of the retinues of the duke of Lancaster and the earl of Hereford,[192] were the last royal officials to supervise warhorse appraisal for a major English army; and it is particularly to be regretted therefore that the inventories which they compiled, or indeed those drawn-up for the much smaller expedition to Gascony in 1370, have not survived.[193] The end of horse appraisal was,

---

[189] E101/28/21, fos 3v–6v, 7v–9r, 10r–10v.

[190] The terms of service are laid out in two surviving indentures, those of the duke of Lancaster himself, and Henry de Percy: E101/68/4, nos. 87, 88. The detailed pay–roll for this expedition has not survived, but other records (including a file of privy seal letters ordering Henry de Wakefield, Keeper of the Wardrobe, to account with individual captains: E101/396/13) show the operation of the usual 'package' of benefits: wages, *regard*, *restauro equorum* and *eskippeson* payments. On Lancaster's expedition, see Sherborne, 'Indentured retinues and the English expeditions to France, 1369–80', pp. 720–23; idem, 'John of Gaunt, Edward III's retinue and the French campaign of 1369', *Kings and nobles in the later Middle Ages*, ed. R.A. Griffiths and J. Sherborne (Gloucester, 1986), pp. 41–61; Goodman, *John of Gaunt*, pp. 229–32.

[191] BL Stowe MS 440, fo. 10v; *Issue Roll of Thomas de Brantingham*, p. 99; J. Sherborne, 'The cost of English warfare with France in the later fourteenth century', *BIHR*, l (1977), pp. 138–39.

[192] E101/396/13, m. 1.

[193] Lancaster's *Register* offers glimpses of some of the horses lost by men under his com-

indeed, sudden and it was final.[194] The major expedition of 1370, jointly led by Sir Robert Knolles and three other captains, was experimental in its financial arrangements, so it is not surprising to find no mention of horse compensation.[195] But it is not to be found in the records for any subsequent expedition by an English army in France, Scotland or, indeed, elsewhere.

Why did the English crown – and, indeed, several continental states – abandon *restauro equorum* at this time?[196] Was it simply a question of cost? Although at times the cost was very great, indeed prohibitive,[197] it was more usual for *restauro equorum* payments to constitute only a small proportion of total campaign expenses. The total value of appraised horses lost during the Breton campaign in 1342–43 amounted to about 11% of payments due to captains in Edward III's army.[198] For the Reims campaign, the corresponding figure is 9%,[199] whilst for the Low Countries expedition of 1338–39, it is as low as 6%.[200] Clearly, by comparison with the crown's expenditure on wages, the outlay demanded for the replacement of lost warhorses was not that burdensome and although the heavy financial demands of the renewed war effort in 1369–70 (combined with a consequent political crisis in the 1371 parliament)[201] may have prompted a review of military expenditure, it is unlikely to have been on grounds of cost alone that the English military

mand: e.g. *JGReg, 1371–75*, nos. 896 (1370, Gascony), 908 (1369, Normandy and Picardy).

[194] But for a much later period, see C.H. Firth, *Cromwell's army*, 3rd edn, repr. (London, 1962), pp. 244–45.

[195] Knolles' indenture stipulates double wages and *regard* at one and a half times the normal rate, but only for the first quarter of a year: E101/68/4, no. 90. For this expedition, see Sherborne, 'Indentured retinues and the English expeditions to France, 1369–80', pp. 723–25.

[196] France: 'les derniers exemples d'estimation et de description des chevaux datent respectivement de 1375 et 1380' (Contamine, *Guerre, état et société*, p. 146 n. 46); cf. Mallett and Hale, *Military organisation of a Renaissance state*, pp. 17–18.

[197] For example, the cost of the horses lost or sold by the company of Hainaulters in England in 1327 amounted to nearly £21,500, which represents over half of the total bill presented by John of Hainault for this period of service (E101/18/4, m. 1) and is roughly twice the size of the total *restauro equorum* cost for the Reims campaign of 1359–60. Cf. Italy in the 1320s: L. Green, *Castruccio Castracani* (Oxford, 1986), pp. 132–33.

[198] £3,407 6s 8d was due for *restauro equorum* and £30,472 11s ½d for wages: E36/204, fos 88v, 110v. Cf. the war in Gascony in 1294–99: total expenditure was £249,079, of which £25,816 was spent on *restor* (M. Vale, *The Angevin legacy and the Hundred Years War*, appendix II).

[199] The value of lost horses added up to £11,658 and the total of all payments due to captains (which included wages, *regard*, *restauro equorum* and some sea transport) was £133,820 16s 6½d. The latter figure appears at the foot of the last folio of the *vadia guerre* section of Farley's accounts: E101/393/11, fo. 116v.

[200] Out of a total outlay of nearly £120,000 (wages, *restauro equorum* and a modest amount for re-passage) only £6,656 was owed for horses lost during the campaign: Prince, 'The payment of army wages in Edward III's reign', p. 150.

[201] C. Given Wilson, *The royal household and the king's affinity: service, politics and finance, 1360–1413* (New Haven and London, 1986), p. 139.

establishment was moved to abandon *restauro equorum*. A further contributory factor may have been the reduced role of the warhorse in English military practice. By the 1370s, with the Edwardian military machine no longer primarily based upon the service of men-at-arms on armoured steeds, horse appraisal and *restor de cheval* must have seemed far less important than they had a hundred years earlier. The great majority of equestrian casualties for which the crown was paying compensation were being sustained not in combat, but as a consequence of the rigours of the march; and as men-at-arms employed less expensive horses, so *restauro equorum* came to occupy a less central place in the terms of service than it had earlier in the Edwardian period.

Given the transformation in English military practice, the cost of *restauro equorum* may well have become less acceptable; but it is likely that the crown was as much concerned with the weight of the administrative burden which horse appraisal entailed. As we have seen, the valuation of warhorses and the recording of losses were technically demanding and time-consuming tasks; and they could constitute a major administrative headache where continental campaigns were concerned. They had, moreover, very often been shouldered by wardrobe personnel. But from the middle of the century, the king's wardrobe had been taking only an intermittent role in the financial and logistical organisation of war as, increasingly, captains prosecuting the king's multi-front strategy were recruited by indenture and accounted directly with the Exchequer.[202] The absence, from all except the major royal expeditions, of the elaborate administrative machinery and reservoir of experience in dealing with horse appraisal which the royal household could provide (and the fact that appraisal was not one of the bureaucratic responsibilities which could simply be handed-over to contracting captains) will have added weight to the arguments in favour of abandoning *restauro equorum*.

A militarily inactive king and dependence upon the 'indenture system' for the raising of armies may have made the end of warhorse appraisal in the 1370s inevitable, but the administrative motives underlying the abandonment of *restauro equorum* amounted to more than a simple desire to remove a major bureaucratic burden. Behind the changes of the 1370s can be perceived a positive determination to formulate a better package of terms of service; a package which was more attuned to prevailing military conditions and which covered the costs of campaigning more effectively. At first glance, the abandonment of *restauro equorum* might seem to be to the ordinary man-at-arms' financial disadvantage; his warhorse, after all, was a major investment. But, as we have seen, horse compensation was not offered for all forms of military service; and even when it was, only one of a man-at-arms' warhorses would be embraced by the appraisal process at any one time. Thus, as a means of

---

[202] See Prince, 'The payment of army wages in Edward III's reign', pp. 137–60; Prestwich, 'English armies in the early stages of the Hundred Years War: a scheme of 1341', p. 107.

meeting the cost of equestrian casualties it was far from comprehensive and it did not provide a mechanism enabling men to acquire immediate replacements for lost horses. The full value of a prized warhorse which had died on campaign would usually only be forthcoming long after the dust of the *chevauchée* had settled.

The shortcomings of the system of horse appraisal and compensation must have played a part in urging the crown to embark upon a complete overhaul of the terms of military service. Administratively cumbersome and offering less than satisfactory coverage for equestrian costs, *restauro equorum* was to find no place in the re-fashioned 'package' of terms offered by the crown from the early 1370s. The operation of the new package can be seen clearly enough in indentures of war and pay accounts. In essence, it involved improved rates of *regard* and more advantageous terms for the division of spoils – both, essentially, to offset the withdrawal of *restauro equorum*.[203] The indentures of war drawn up in February 1372 show the reformed package in operation. They specify standard wage rates, together with double *regard* for *gentz darmes*; but they also emphasise very firmly that the captain 'ne demandera . . . pur lui ne pur nul de ses gentz restor de chivalx perduz en dit viage'.[204] The indentures of March 1373, for captains accompanying Lancaster to France, offer the same terms: 'gages de guerre acustumez' and 'regard acustumez double sanz priser de chivalx'.[205] The emergence of these new terms would be a little easier to detect were it not for a certain amount of continued experimentation in the 1370s, for Knolles' expedition in 1370 and the Breton campaign in 1375.[206] Indeed, the new terms of service may have

---

[203] The connection between *restauro equorum* and *regard* has been commented upon by Prince ('The indenture system under Edward III', p. 294) and Sherborne ('Indentured retinues and English expeditions to France, 1369–1380', p. 743 n. 6); but they did not notice the end of horse compensation in the early 1370s, nor did they make the further connection with the division of spoils. For N.B. Lewis, the increases in the rates of pay and *regard* from 1369 were 'special financial attractions', necessary for recruitment at a time when the pool of manpower had been 'drastically reduced' and the war was becoming less popular; he does not perceive the end of *restauro equorum*: N.B. Lewis, 'The last medieval summons of the English feudal levy, 13 June 1385', *EHR*, lxxiii (1958), pp. 9, 12.

[204] E101/68/4, nos. 92–94. The earl of Warwick's indenture (no. 93) is reproduced in facsimile in K. Fowler, *The age of Plantagenet and Valois*, repr. (London, 1980), p. 99. For the earl of March's, see *Sir Christopher Hatton's book of seals*, ed. L.C. Loyd and D.M. Stenton (Oxford, 1950), no. 227. Lancaster's indenture with Edward III (1 July 1372) specifies the same terms and employs identical wording with respect to the disallowance of *restor de chivalx*: *JGReg, 1372–76*, i, no. 51.

[205] For example, Edward, Lord Despenser's indenture (E101/32/26, m. 3); for his account, see m. 4. Lancaster's own indenture with the king employs similar wording: *JGReg, 1372–76*, i, no. 52.

[206] For the Breton campaign in 1375 wages and *regard* were paid for six months only: Sherborne, 'Indentured retinues and English expeditions in France, 1369–1380', p. 730 n. 6.

been intended as an experiment when they were introduced for the 1372 campaign. They had been tried out some years earlier. The indenture drawn up in September 1360 between Edward III and Thomas de Holand, earl of Kent, for the latter's service as 'captain and lieutenant in France and Normandy' stipulated standard wages and double *regard*, and made no reference to horse appraisal.[207] But the withdrawal of the wardrobe's administrative machinery from the prosecution of the war, following the re-channelling of military finance through the hands of a separate war treasurer from the end of 1372,[208] would have reinforced the need for a permanent change in the terms of service in favour of a package involving minimal administrative overheads.

The new terms of service, introduced in 1372 and 1373, became the normal package for continental land campaigns.[209] The withdrawal of horse appraisal was compensated for by the doubling of *regard* and, thus, an insurance cover of very restricted scope and offering little prospect of speedy pay-outs had been replaced by an assured fixed payment, part of which was issued in advance of service.[210] The sum involved was admittedly not that large: 'single' *regard* was worth about £9 a year to a man-at-arms, assuming that he was in receipt of crown rates. Yet whilst *restauro equorum* had only been available following the loss of an appraised warhorse, *regard* could be used to cover a wider range of campaign costs, including those incurred in preparing for expeditions which were cancelled at the last minute.[211] In as far as it was applied to equestrian expenses, it could contribute to the purchase price of a horse at the start of an expedition, or help to finance an immediate replacement during the course of a term of duty. It is significant that the English

---

207 C76/40, m. 5. Cf. the terms offered to the earl of Warwick, serving as king's lieutenant in Normandy from May to September 1360: double pay, standard *regard*, *restauro equorum* and return passage (E101/393/11, fo. 87r).

208 Given-Wilson, *The royal household and the king's affinity*, pp. 122–3.

209 E.g. the Breton expedition of 1380 (see Goodman, 'The military subcontracts of Sir Hugh Hastings', p. 118) and the earl of Cambridge's expedition to Iberia in 1381 (BL Stowe MS 440, fo. 7r). Less generous terms of service were offered in other theatres of war. For Richard II's expedition of 1385, *regard* was only paid in exceptional cases: N.B. Lewis, 'The last medieval summons of the English feudal levy, 13 June 1385', *EHR*, lxxiii (1958), pp. 9, 12–13, 21–22. Given the close connection between the *regard* payment and warhorse costs, and the fact that no allowance for *restauro equorum* had been made for royal expeditions to Scotland since the 1330s, the absence of *regard* in 1385 appears rather less 'a departure from tradition' than has been thought: cf. J.J.N. Palmer, 'The last summons of the feudal army in England (1385)', *EHR*, lxxxiii (1968), pp. 773–74.

210 It was usual for half a year's *regard* to be paid in advance, with subsequent payments at quarterly intervals: Prince, 'The indenture system under Edward III', p. 293. The earl of Hereford's indenture in 1372 emphasises the importance of prompt pre-payment: double *regard* was to be delivered 'hastivement en main pur la moite du dit an' (E101/68/4, no. 92).

211 In the event of cancellation, captains retained advance payments of *regard*: Prince, 'The indenture system under Edward III', p. 293.

crown chose to increase *regard* rates, for in the case of some continental states the abandonment of *restauro equorum* was accompanied by an increase in wage rates.[212] In England, however, from the time of its general introduction in the 1340s, *regard* had been intended as a contribution to campaigning costs, including the replacement of *unappraised* horses, and so it was natural that it, rather than wages, should have been increased in the 1370s.

The association between *regard* and warhorse costs is made explicit in some the indentures for continental land campaigns of this period; and records relating to maritime activity emphasise the point still further. For naval expeditions, such as that led by the earl of Salisbury during the winter of 1372–73, *regard* was paid at only one and a half times the standard rate, presumably because horses were not required for military operations of this kind.[213] In the case of expeditions to Gascony, on the other hand, a captain might be offered a special level of *regard*, higher than the normal double rate.[214] This may have been in recognition of the high risk of equestrian casualties during the long sea voyage, but it was also no doubt intended to encourage men to buy their warhorses upon arrival in Bordeaux, rather than transport them from England. Given the difficulties involved in raising large expeditionary fleets, the preponderance of horse transports in such fleets and the increased cost of mobilising naval forces after the introduction of *tontyght* in 1380,[215] it was natural that ways would be sought to transport English armies without their horses. In 1381, for example, it was formally agreed that the earl of Cambridge's troops would be shipped to Portugal without horses. These would be supplied on arrival and paid for by the English Exchequer.[216] There is, then, a real possibility that in the re-fashioning of the terms of service in the early 1370s, the general switch to *pre-payment* of costs, as represented in the bolstering of *regard*, was intended, in part at least, as a response to the perennial logistical problems involved in the

---

[212] In Venice, for example, the end of *restauro equorum* was accompanied by a 33% pay increase: Mallett and Hale, *The military organisation of a Renaissance state*, pp. 17–18; but cf. 138–39. For minor variations in English wage-payment practice, see Prince, 'The indenture system under Edward III', pp. 291–93.

[213] BL Additional MS 37494, fos 10r–11r. Thus, Edward, Lord Despenser's retinue received 1½ *regard* for naval service in 1372 and double *regard* for a land campaign the following year (E101/32/26, m. 4). The frequency of naval expeditions during this phase of the war, as compared with the years prior to Brétigny, is particularly striking. Quite apart from strategic considerations, such 'horseless' operations may have been attractive because they did not require the assembly of large numbers of horse transports – the cause of regular, acute problems for Edwardian military administrators.

[214] See, for instance, the clause included in the earl of Hereford's indenture in March 1372: E101/68/4, no. 92.

[215] J. Sherborne, 'The English navy: shipping and manpower, 1369–1389', *Past and Present*, xxxvii (1967), p. 165.

[216] P.E. Russell, *The English intervention in Spain and Portugal in the time of Edward III and Richard II* (Oxford, 1955), pp. 299, 304 n. 2; cf. *Fernao Lopes: The English in Portugal*, ed. Lomax and Oakley, pp. 68–69.

assembly of transport fleets. If so, then the scale of the conflict as it unfolded during the two decades after 1369 certainly showed this to have been a shrewd decision, for these were years of almost unremitting warfare, 'a long war of attrition',[217] with armies being shipped to the continent regularly.

By abandoning *restauro equorum* and concentrating on a general contribution to costs through the *regard* payment, the crown had reduced the magnitude of the administrative and logistical problems attendant upon the raising of an army, whilst at the same time improving the terms of service of men-at-arms. In effect, there had been a shift in responsibility with respect to campaign expenses from the crown to the individual man-at-arms, or more accurately, perhaps, to the individual captain. The onus was now rather more on the combatant to decide on the quality and numbers of warhorses which he brought on campaign. This can be seen in the changed terms relating to horse shipment which emerged in the 1370s. Hitherto, men had been allowed a fixed sum (for example, 6s 8d in early 1340) for *each horse* accompanying them, usually a prescribed number, determined by their rank.[218] But in the mid 1370s we find a shift to providing a fixed sum for *each man*, irrespective of his rank, military status or the number of horses he actually had with him. Thus, Lancaster was allowed 7s per man for the return from Gascony in 1374, whilst for the repassage of the English army from Brittany in 1375, the allowance was 13s 4d for each man *cum equo*.[219] Admittedly, the crown did maintain a minimum acceptable equestrian standard and captains continued to insist in their subcontracts that troops should be well mounted and arrayed, so as to avoid 'loss or reproach' at muster.[220] That possession of suitable horseflesh *was* still important to the English man-at-arms is indicated by the Ordinances of Durham of 1385, which laid down that forfeiture of horse and harness should be the penalty for a range of offences, the implication being that this would bring about expulsion (at least temporarily) from the military community.[221] But if the abandonment of *restauro equorum* did not give rise to an immediate, dramatic slump in warhorse quality, it is likely nevertheless to have been responsible for some decline – in fact, a *further* decline – in the value of horseflesh used on active service. For although a man might participate in several campaigns without incurring any equestrian

---

[217] J.J.N. Palmer, *England, France and Christendom, 1377–99* (London, 1972), pp. 1–2.

[218] Prince, 'The indenture system under Edward III', pp. 294–95.

[219] Prince, 'The payment of army wages in Edward III's reign', p. 159 n. 1; E101/34/5; E101/34/6, m. 4.

[220] For example, Sir John Strother's subcontracts of 1374–75 (Walker, 'Profit and loss in the Hundred Years War', p. 102) and Sir Hugh Hastings' of 1380 (Goodman, 'The military subcontracts of Sir Hugh Hastings', p. 115). Cf. the stipulation in many Lancastrian indentures of retinue, following the abandonment of *restauro equorum*, that the retainer should be 'bien et covenablement mountez, armez et arraiez pur pees et pur guerre come a soun estat partent': *JGIndRet*, nos. 10–14, 19, 22, 27–42.

[221] *Monumenta juridica: the Black Book of the Admiralty*, ed. Sir T. Twiss, 4 vols, Rolls Ser. (London, 1871–76), i, pp. 453–58.

casualties, the death or disablement of horses was always a very real possibility; and the loss of even one, if reasonably priced, would serve to negate the effect of the doubling of *regard*, allowing a man, at best, to break-even at the end of a long campaign (it would take rather more than a year's 'single' *regard* to pay for a £10 warhorse). It may, indeed, have been to offer a further incentive to potential recruits, by extending the opportunities for individual gain, whilst cushioning the impact of horse losses and other costs, that the reformed package of terms of service offered by the crown in the 1370s included a further significant change: an adjustment to the established arrangements for the division of the spoils of war in order to offer rather more favourable terms to the combatant.

What were the normal arrangements for the division of spoils prior to the reforms of the early 1370s? It is clear that the crown had an established right to the ransoms of the most important and valuable prisoners of war. Such captives were to be delivered into the king's custody and their original captors would receive reasonable compensation.[222] But before the last quarter of the fourteenth century, the terms relating to the sharing out of profits from the ransoms of lesser prisoners and from booty are rarely specified precisely in surviving indentures of war, whether between the king and his captains, or between captains and lesser combatants; and such transactions are not the concern of the *vadia guerre* accounts. The evidence for the size of the 'portions' in the division of spoils is therefore patchy, but not so sparse as to preclude the formulation of secure conclusions.

In general terms the crown had an undoubted right to a proportion of the profits of those troops who were receiving pay and other benefits for serving in a royal army. The size of the 'royal' portion certainly varied in different parts of Europe, and very probably also within each individual state, as different levels of remuneration would be accompanied by different terms for the division of spoils. Often, of course, the rules would be disregarded: 'men simply took what they wished, their actions undoubtedly beyond the control of their commanders'.[223] It is no wonder, therefore, that Honoré Bouvet, writing in the 1380s, considered that 'the law on the matter is involved and by no means clear, and expressed opinion is doubtful'.[224] Yet, largely as a consequence of an influential article published in the 1950s by Denys Hay,[225] much

---

[222] Prince, 'The indenture system under Edward III', p. 295; D. Hay, 'The division of the spoils of war in fourteenth-century England', *TRHS*, 5th ser., iv (1954), pp. 99–101.

[223] M.C. Bartusis, *The late Byzantine army. Arms and society, 1204–1453* (Philadelphia, 1992), p. 249. Cf the precise arrangements stipulated in some thirteenth-century *condotte*: D.P. Waley, '*Condotte* and *condottieri* in the thirteenth century', *Proceedings of the British Academy*, lxi (1975), p. 341.

[224] *The Tree of Battles of Honoré Bonet*, ed. G.W. Coopland (Liverpool, 1949), p. 150.

[225] Hay, 'The division of the spoils of war in fourteenth-century England'; and see also idem, 'Booty in border warfare', *Transactions of the Dumfriesshire and Galloway Natural History and Antiquarian Society*, 3rd ser., xxxi (1952–53), especially pp. 157–63. K.B. McFarlane's brief treatment of the division of spoils in his second 1953 Ford lecture

of the recent secondary literature concerned with military matters in late medieval England offers a deceptively confident view of the division of spoils. Hay felt that the evidence, though far from abundant, pointed very clearly to one conclusion. By the 1350s, he argued, 'we have . . . proof that troops in royal pay were liable to surrender a third' of their profits to the king; and in all probability, the third, 'of old standing in the royal household', had been extracted from captains leading retinues in royal armies for a not inconsiderable period before this.[226] Some magnates, it was admitted, can be seen during the first phase of the French war to be claiming a half rather than a third of the profits amassed by their retainers. But the 'royal system of taking only a third was gradually adopted [by English captains] during the period after the Peace of Brétigny, and was pretty universal by the last decade of the reign.'[227] Thus, by the time of the Ordinances of Durham of 1385, the 'system of thirds' was firmly in place.[228] It had become normal practice for a superior contracting party to claim a third of the total spoils accumulated by immediate subordinates. A captain would seek, from each of his subcontractors, a third of the value of the ransoms and booty which they had amassed during the course of a campaign. The king in his turn would claim from each of his captains a third of the total spoils which they had asssembled (i.e. their own, combined with that which they had gained from their men).[229]

Denys Hay's neat chronological scheme for the development of uniform practice in the division of spoils has been widely accepted: it has been echoed regularly in both detailed articles and textbooks.[230] Although it is possible to

must have been composed at about the same time (*The nobility of later medieval England*, p. 28). The subject had attracted little previous attention, apart from a short discussion by A.E. Prince ('The indenture system under Edward III', pp. 295–96).

[226] Hay, 'The division of the spoils of war', pp. 104, 105. For speculation on the origins of the royal third (perhaps connected with the customary practice of the Welsh, the Scots and the marcher lords – and 'the mists of Celtic antiquity'), see ibid., pp. 108–9; idem, 'Booty in border warfare', pp. 158–63. For further early evidence of 'thirds', see L. Alcock, *Economy, society and warfare among the Britons and Saxons* (Cardiff, 1987), p. 291 (Laws of Hywel Dda); J. Campbell, 'The sale of land and the economics of power in early England: problems and possibilities', *The Haskins Society Journal*, i (1989), pp. 35–36. Cf. the penitential *dicta* of Archbishop Theodore (A.D. 669–90) which stipulate that a third of the profits of war should be granted to the Church or to the poor: J.M. Wallace-Hadrill, *Early germanic kingship in England and on the continent* (Oxford, 1971), p. 69.

[227] Hay, 'The division of the spoils of war', pp. 105–6. The gradual, but ultimately uniform, adoption by the English military community of royal household conventions on the division of spoils is seen to be the consequence of the 'growth of the indentured army'.

[228] *Monumenta juridica: the Black Book of the Admiralty*, ed. Twiss, pp. 456–57. For the stipulation of 'thirds' in Henry V's Ordinances of War, see ibid., pp. 463–64; *The essential portions of Nicholas Upton's 'De re militari' before 1446*, trans. John Blount, ed. F.P. Barnard (Oxford, 1931), pp. 45, 57, 60 (n. 37).

[229] Hay, 'The division of the spoils of war', pp. 95–96.

[230] For example, C. Given-Wilson, 'The ransom of Olivier du Guesclin', *BIHR*, liv (1981), p. 24; Prestwich, *The three Edwards*, p. 202; C. Allmand, *The Hundred Years War*

point to a sprinkling of aberrant cases[231] – and although it is uncertain how far the crown was actually receiving its portion[232] – there is certainly no doubt that the 'system of thirds' had indeed become 'pretty universal' at all levels of the English military community by the mid 1370s. From this time forward references to thirds and 'thirds of thirds' become commonplace in indentures of war for service on the continent. In 1381, for example, Thomas de Felton, leading a substantial force to Brittany, was to receive 'la tierce partz de touz les prouffis gaignez par la personne du dit [subcontractor's name] et la tierce part du tiers du prouffit de sa retenue'.[233] But what of the division of spoils prior to the 1370s? As far as non-aristocratic combatants are concerned – infantry and mounted archers – Hay's argument that the 'rule of thirds' had long been the norm may well be correct; but with regard to men-at-arms, his analysis is far less reliable. Hay has misinterpreted the evidence for the 1350s and '60s, because he did not see how arrangements for the division of spoils fitted into a broader 'package' of terms of service; and as a consequence of this, he failed to perceive how the widespread adoption of the 'system of thirds' in the 1370s formed an integral part of a general reform of this package of terms. At the centre of these changes, as we have seen, was the abandonment of *restauro equorum*. Prior to this, the certainty of receiving compensation for warhorse losses had rested squarely upon an acceptance that *half* of the profits of war should be surrendered to the authority supplying *restauro equorum*. Captains would render this substantial portion to the king; subcontractors would deliver it to their captain. Thus, men-at-arms had a measure of security for their principal warhorses which could cost them nothing, or a very great deal, depending upon the fortunes of war. When warhorses were not appraised at the start of a campaign, as was the case with various forms of military service under Edward III, the portion of profits surrendered to the superior contracting party was a third, rather than a half.[234] It was, therefore, entirely consistent with earlier practice that the

---

(Cambridge, 1988), p. 128. H.J. Hewitt is, however, very cautious on this matter: *The organisation of war under Edward III*, pp. 107–10. For a recent critique of the 'Hay thesis', see Bean, *From lord to patron*, pp. 238–44.

[231] See, for example, Given-Wilson, 'The ransom of Olivier du Guesclin', pp. 24–25; Walker, 'Profit and loss in the Hundred Years War', pp. 102–3.

[232] 'It is doubtful whether the Crown was receiving . . . 'thirds and thirds of thirds' from profits in France at this time': J. Sherborne, 'The cost of English warfare with France in the later fourteenth century', pp. 142–43.

[233] E101/68/8, nos. 195–96, 200; E101/68/9, nos. 201–12. Cf. Goodman, 'The military sub-contracts of Sir Hugh Hastings', p. 116; and N.H. Nicolas, *History of the battle of Agincourt*, 3rd edn (London, 1833), appendix, pp. 10–12 (indenture between the earl of Salisbury and William Bedyk, 1415). For further fifteenth-century examples, see Hay, 'The division of the spoils of war', p. 97.

[234] J.M.W. Bean's recent suggestion that 'a retainer paid over a third of his winnings to his lord if he provided his own horse, but gave up a half if his horse was provided by his lord' (*From lord to patron*, pp. 238–44) has little to commend it, as far as men-at-arms

crown's complete abandonment of *restauro equorum* in the 1370s should be accompanied not only by the doubling of *regard*, but also by a reduction in the 'royal portion' of the spoils of war from a half to a third. If the near uniform employment of the 'system of thirds' from the last years of Edward III's reign is to be explained in terms of 'the growth of the indentured army',[235] then it was only in as much as that development was itself a contributory factor to the abandonment of *restauro equorum*.

At the heart of Hay's thesis was a process of increasing uniformity of practice; a progression from a state of affairs where 'the methods of dividing the spoil varied from magnate to magnate' to a general acceptance of 'the royal third' at all levels of the military community. But it is in his discussion of the 'variety of usages' in the mid fourteenth century that the principal flaw in Hay's thesis lies.[236] In the first place, the bulk of the evidence at subcontract level suggests that there was, in fact, a remarkable degree of uniformity in the arrangements for the division of spoils. The evidence is admittedly not abundant. Many military subcontracts and indentures of retinue make no mention of the spoils of war.[237] Yet prior to the 1370s, all of the examples which *do* refer to the division of winnings stipulate that, when engaged in service with horses which have been appraised and are therefore eligible for compensation, the retainer should surrender a *half* of his profits to his captain. Thus, an indenture between Edward, prince of Wales and Sir Thomas Fournival, dated 1 May 1347, makes provision for the latter's warhorse losses and the handing over of half of any ransoms secured whilst in the prince's service.[238] A decade later Sir Warin de Bassingbourne was reminded that half of the 500 marks

are concerned. Bean's case is actually supported by only one piece of evidence: the terms of a military indenture of 1420 which is concerned with the service of *archers*; and it is flatly contradicted by a miscellany of fourteenth-century indentures (e.g. ibid., p. 243 n. 12, dismissed as 'special circumstances'). In fact, the evidence overwhelmingly suggests that the great majority of men-at-arms supplied their own warhorses and that if these mounts were appraised and thus eligible for compensation, the captain's portion of profits would be a half. The same portion would be due from those who were supplied with a warhorse by their captain, but if the horse was appraised by the crown and subsequently lost, it would be for the captain to decide what to do with the money. In the case of a gift from the king, the horse would not be appraised. Bean's suggestion may well be valid with respect to the service of horse archers, but there is no known supporting evidence from the fourteenth century.

[235] Hay, 'The division of the spoils of war', pp. 105–6.

[236] Ibid., pp. 99, 103, 105.

[237] For example, the indenture of 1340 whereby the earl of Northampton retained Sir William Talemache for life: DL25/32. Similarly, the indenture of retainer between Henry, earl of Lancaster and Sir Edmund de Ufford (1347): printed in Fowler, *The king's lieutenant*, p. 234.

[238] BPReg, i, pp. 128–29. The majority of the surviving indentures issued by the prince of Wales make no reference to the division of spoils: e.g. BPReg, i, pp. 83, 127–28; BPReg, ii, pp. 45–46; *Report of the MSS of Lord Middleton of Wollaton Hall, Nottinghamshire.* Historical Manuscripts Commission, lxix (London, 1911), p. 98.

which he had secured from a prisoner of war should be surrendered to the prince, 'as he well knows'.[239] The prince of Wales might have been particularly well placed to demand a substantial proportion of his retainers' winnings; but all the evidence indicates that lesser magnates were also insisting upon a half during the 1340s and '50s. An indenture, dating from March 1347, whereby Sir Hugh Fitz Simon agreed to serve with a company of men-at-arms for a year in Ralph, Lord Stafford's retinue allows Hugh *gages accustumez* (or *bouche de court*), a fee of 100 marks and valuation of his *grantz chivalx*; but it also requires that 'des prisoners qui serront priz del avantdit Hugh, ou de ses gentz, le avantdit Monsieur Raufe aura le moytie des proffitz de lour ransom'.[240] A further contract, drawn up in March 1350 between Richard, earl of Arundel, and Sir Gerard de Lisle, stated that if Sir Gerard 'ou nul des soens ascun prison[er] preignent le dit conte avera la moyte del raunson et le dit mons. Gerard lautre moyte'.[241] Although aware of most, if not all, of these cases, Denys Hay felt that it would be 'premature' to conclude 'that the normal procedure in the 1340s, at any rate in continental campaigns, was for the spoils to be divided by half'.[242]

If Hay's was an unduly cautious view, even for the state of knowledge in the mid 1950s, then it is now surely untenable, for 'fresh evidence' as it comes to light serves only to augment the group of mid-fourteenth-century magnate captains who can be seen demanding half of their subordinates' winnings.[243] Thus, the indenture drawn up in July 1347 between William Montagu, earl of Salisbury, and Geoffrey Walsh stipulates that the latter's 'chival darmes sera preise & encas qil sera perdutz en le service le dit counte, le dit Geffrei avera restitucioun'; and, appropriately enough, the earl would be given half of any ransoms which came Walsh's way 'par fortune de guerre'.[244] Moving on twenty-five years to another of the same earl's military subcontracts, we find that the terms of service were now rather different. The intended continental expedition of 1372 was, as we have seen, the first for which the crown employed the reformed package of terms of service: the indentures between the king and the captains of major retinues explicitly exclude the provision of *restauro equorum*.[245] At the subcontract level, the indenture between the earl

---

239 *BPReg*, iv, p. 249; cf. also *BPReg*, iii, 251–52, 294–95.

240 *Crecy and Calais*, p. 192.

241 Berkeley castle, Select Charter 526.

242 Hay, 'The division of the spoils of war', p. 102.

243 Cf. in late thirteenth-century Ireland, 'horses and animals seized by those serving at Geoffrey [de Joinville]'s expense should be divided equally between him and his men, unless the horses were actually taken from Irish enemies who had been felled by Geoffrey's men with lances': R. Bartlett, *The making of Europe* (London, 1993), pp. 27–28.

244 E101/68/3, no. 68.

245 Although the 1372 expedition eventually took the form of a naval operation, the original intention was for a *chevauchée* in France: the indentures include, for example, provision for the shipment of horses to the continent.

of Salisbury and an esquire of modest status, Roger Mautravers, simply omits to mention the valuation of warhorses; but it, unlike those between the king and his captains, *does* make specific provision for the division of spoils. Now, without the potentially heavy financial burden of *restauro equorum* to worry about, the earl claims only a third of Mautravers' profits of war.[246]

The earl of Salisbury's subcontracts are particularly valuable because they straddle the change in the terms of service in the early 1370s and they, unlike the bulk of indentures between Edward III and his captains, are explicit about arrangements for the division of spoils. For the largest body of evidence of a similar kind, we must turn our attention to the records which illuminate the retinue of John of Gaunt and in particular to the texts of over 130 of his indentures of retinue.[247] The problem with this material, of course, is that Gaunt cannot in any sense be regarded as a typical captain. The greatest magnates were likely to be more independently minded, more able to stand aloof from developments occurring around them and perhaps simply slower to change established practices, than their less elevated contemporaries. Indeed, one of the most interesting features of the collection of Gaunt's indentures is the way that, apparently unlike the earl of Salisbury and the other captains whose short-term subcontracts have survived,[248] the duke continued to offer *restauro equorum* to his retainers well into the mid 1380s, despite the crown's abandonment of it a decade earlier. The registered indentures of retinue from the period 1379–83 generally include provision for horse valuation and compensation[249] and the last indentures surviving in any form to do

---

[246] E101/68/5, no. 107. The earl's indenture with the king for this expedition is E101/68/5, no. 102.

[247] Eighty-eight life indentures in Gaunt's surviving chancery registers (*JGReg, 1372–76*; *JGReg, 1379–83*), forty-two in the Patent Rolls (*JGIndRet*) and a handful in private archives: Goodman, *John of Gaunt*, pp. 213, 376–77; and Walker, *The Lancastrian affinity*, appendix 3. See also Bean, *From lord to patron*, appendices 2 and 3. Appendix 3 provides a list of the surviving indentures (fifty-six for knights and 102 for esquires), together with tabulated summaries of some aspects of their contents.

[248] The surviving military subcontracts (as distinct from indentures of retinue) from the 1370s and '80s make no mention of *restauro equorum*; and many display terms which allow a margin of profit for the captain: the subcontractor's lump sum for a year's service is less than would be realised by standard pay and double *regard*. The subcontractor also agrees to surrender one third of profits to his captain. See Sherborne, 'Indentured retinues and English expeditions to France, 1369–1380', pp. 743–44; Goodman, 'The military subcontracts of Sir Hugh Hastings', pp. 118–19; Walker, *The Lancastrian affinity*, pp. 70–71. Some subcontractors negotiated favourable deals, however. Sir John Strother, serving with a company in the earl of March's retinue in 1375, secured a 'personal *regard*' of £60 in addition to normal wages and double *regard* for his men (Walker, 'Profit and loss in the Hundred Years War', p. 103). The fees offered in some indentures of retinue represented a rate of remuneration substantially higher than even double *regard* (e.g. *JGIndRet*, no. 3: Sir John de Neville, 1370).

[249] *JGReg, 1379–83*, i, nos. 23–52, 55.

so date from 1384 and 1385.[250] So, with respect to *restauro equorum*, it seems that the duke took over ten years to bring his household arrangements into line with royal policy.

The evidence for the division of spoils is less clear-cut. Although the majority of Lancastrian indentures prior to the mid 1380s refer to both warhorse appraisal and the apportionment of spoils, only in a minority of cases is the duke's portion specified precisely. Generally speaking a retainer will be treated as 'autres esquiers ou bachelers de son estat et condicion'.[251] The exceptions to this seem, at first glance, to lend support to Denys Hay's view of the matter. Only six of the registered indentures are specific about the duke's portion (five from the early 1370s and one from 1381), but of these, five stipulate that the duke 'avera la tierce partie' of the retainers' gains of war, whilst also offering *restauro equorum* in the usual manner.[252] We should, however, be wary of concluding from these cases that the duke of Lancaster usually offered so advantageous a package of terms of service to his retainers. Firstly, it is inherently unlikely that the greatest of secular magnates, whose lordship would always be greatly sought after, would feel the need to offer terms which were markedly more favourable than the norm. Secondly, the fact that the great majority of the registered indentures imply the operation of established and well-understood terms for the division of spoils may well suggest that the duke's portion is spelled out only when the terms concerned deviate from the norm. We may reasonably expect that some individuals would negotiate better terms than others, often for reasons that are difficult now to fathom.[253] But it may also be significant that three of the

---

[250] Life indentures for Sir Thomas de Wennesley, 10 December 1384 (*JGIndRet*, no. 6); Sir Ralph de Bracebridge, 4 April 1385 (Historical Manuscripts Commission, lxix, pp. 99–100); and Richard Rixton, 30 April 1385 (Walker, *The Lancastrian affinity*, appendix 3, no. 3). N.B. Lewis regards the dropping of warhorse appraisal and compensation as but one aspect of 'a general tendency towards standardization and simplification of the substance of the contracts, generally in a way that leaves the duke with more latitude to use his discretion and the retainer with less specific guarantees for his rewards or allowances': *JGIndRet*, p. 80. Cf. the 'restore' payments which Grace Stetton noticed in Bolingbroke's accounts for his crusading expeditions in the early 1390s, though these are New Year's gifts to minor household personnel and not authentic *restauro equorum* payments for warhorse losses: G. Stretton, 'Some aspects of medieval travel, with special reference to the wardrobe accounts of Henry, earl of Derby, 1390–93', *TRHS*, 4th ser. vii (1924), p. 81.

[251] Sir John de Neville's indenture of 1370 adds 'et selonc le manere de pais': *JGIndRet*, no. 3. This is significant, for terms of service might vary according to the theatre of war concerned.

[252] *JGReg, 1372–76*, i, nos. 782, 788, 789; ii, no. 868. *JGReg, 1379–83*, i, no. 45.

[253] Janekyn Pole de Hertyngton, who was retained in September 1381, appears to have been just such a favoured individual, for he was allowed normal horse appraisal and shipment terms, but of his 'profites de guerre' the duke 'avera ses tiercez': *JGReg, 1379–83*, i, no. 45. The same balance of arrangements are outlined in John de Swynton's indenture of 1372, but in his case the tailoring of terms for a particular individual is further

five cases where *restauro equorum* is accompanied by the duke's third are found in indentures drawn up in January or February 1372, shortly before the first continental expedition for which the crown implemented its revised package of terms of service.[254] At such a time of transition we might reasonably expect a degree of flexibility in terms offered, as magnate captains made adjustments in response to the crown's initiative.

If the handful of Lancastrian indentures of retinue which allow for both 'thirds' *and* warhorse appraisal can with reasonable certainty be dismissed as special cases, there is fortunately some evidence to suggest that Lancaster *did* offer the normal balance of terms to his men, both before and after his final abandonment of *restauro equorum* in the mid 1380s. Six of the twelve surviving indentures from the second half of the 1380s, whilst omitting any reference to the valuation of horseflesh, stipulate that the duke's portion of 'profitz de guerre' would be a third.[255] After 1390 none of the remaining enrolled indentures make specific reference to the duke's third, probably because it had by then become the established and well-understood norm. For an insight into normal practice before the abandonment of *restauro equorum*, it is necessary to rely upon two indentures with unusually detailed provisions. That for Sir William de Beauchamp, drawn up in February 1373, outlines in customary fashion that the warhorses of Beauchamp's company will be 'covenablement preisez, et selonc le dit pris restor ly serra fait si nulles de eux soient perduz en le service de nostre dit seigneur'. The price of this security for his horseflesh would be 'la moitie des profitz de guerre' secured by Beauchamp and his immediate entourage, but only 'la tierce partie' of the profits of his other men 'si nulles de leur chivaux ne soient perduz'.[256] Nicholas de

emphasised by the fact that *restauro equorum* and the surrendering of a third, rather than a half, are once again explicitly stipulated just over two years later when Swynton, now a knight, entered into a new retaining agreement with the duke (*JGReg, 1372–76*, i, no. 789; ii, no. 868). S. Armitage-Smith (*JGReg, 1372–76*, i, p. xxii) asserted that 'the proportion [of profits] taken by the lord varies with the rank of the retainer', but the evidence does not support this view.

254 *JGReg, 1372–76*, i, nos. 782, 788 and 789. The other Lancastrian indentures dating from this period make reference to *restauro equorum*, but are unspecific about the division of spoils. Simon Walker places the 1372 indentures, generous also for the scale of their fees, in the context of Gaunt's planning for 'the invasion of Castile to which his recent alliance with Portugal had committed him': recruitment at a time of heavy demand for manpower obliged the duke to 'bid high': Walker, *The Lancastrian affinity*, p. 69.

255 *JGIndRet*, nos. 10–14, 18.

256 *JGReg, 1372–76*, i, no. 832. The wording of this indenture is a little ambiguous. The intention may have been to offer a reduced 'ducal' portion to the whole of Beauchamp's company in the event of no *restauro equorum* claim being made. Such concessions would no doubt have been more readily available to men of Sir William's status (the son of an earl); cf. Bean, *From lord to patron*, pp. 240–41. The other unusual feature of Beauchamp's indenture is that it seems to suggest that the duke would take a direct third of the profits of Beauchamp's men, rather than a third of Beauchamp's third. For a similar arrangement, see Walker, 'Profit and loss in the Hundred Years War', pp. 102–3.

Atherton's indenture of March 1370 underlines the crucial relationship between warhorses and the division of spoils in a slightly different way. Atherton's *chivaux de guerre* would be appraised and in the event of loss, *restor* would be paid 'come reson demande'; but in return the duke was to receive 'la moitie des prisoners et gayns de guerre prisee et gaynez par le dit Nicholas'. So much was entirely conventional, but the indenture adds: 'si null' des chivaux lavantdit Nicholas ne soient prisez, alors aura le dit duc sinoun' la tierce partie des profitz de guerre issint par le dit Nicholas gaynez'.[257] In Beauchamp's case, then, 'thirds' would apply if no *restauro equorum* claims were made; in Atherton's, if his warhorses were not appraised. These two cases can perhaps be attributed to the prevailing conditions of the period of transition in the early 1370s. But although representing deviation from, or at least elaboration upon, customary practice, they are nevertheless extremely valuable. In order to allow for unusual provisions, it has been necessary to outline the normal package of terms – *restauro equorum* and half profits to the superior contracting party – and thus has been revealed what in the great majority of John of Gaunt's indentures goes unstated because it is taken for granted.

Prior to the abandonment of *restauro equorum*, then, it was normal for the king and his magnate captains to demand a half of the spoils of those who served with appraised warhorses. But what of the cases of 'thirds' during the 1350s and 1360s, to which Hay has drawn attention? The evidence for 'thirds' from this period is not in fact abundant (certainly not 'fairly plentiful'). What is more, all of the cases which Hay cites arise not from mainstream royal expeditions, but from garrison service (Brittany and Normandy during the 1350s) and the Nájera campaign.[258] If there was 'a variety of usages' with respect to the division of spoils in the mid fourteenth century, the diversity arose not so much from differences at the level of the magnate household, as from the particular circumstances of certain forms of military service. As we have seen, the package of terms of service as it developed during the course of Edward III's reign varied according to the theatre of war and military context concerned; and as an element in the package, arrangements for the division of spoils need to be viewed in the same light. When *restauro equorum* was offered, as with major expeditions to France, the superior contracting party would receive half of his immediate subordinates' profits. When it was not, as we often find with garrison service, it would be reasonable to expect the portion surrendered to have been a third. At times it is clear that it was.[259]

---

257 *JGIndRet*, no. 2.

258 Hay, 'The division of the spoils of war', pp. 103–6.

259 But it is equally clear that no single set of terms for the division of spoils amassed by garrison personnel existed. Indeed, the terms operating for the garrison of a particular town or castle might fluctuate with changes of captaincy or even during the course of a single captain's period of command. During the 1370s, for example, a captain of Brest might be required by the terms of his indenture to surrender all, half or none of the

Thus, Sir Walter Bentley, as king's lieutenant in Brittany in the early 1350s, sought a third of the profits of men who, though in receipt of the king's pay, were serving without the benefit of appraised horses or *regard*.[260] It is doubtless this type of minimal package of remuneration which explains the 'thirds' which garrisons in Normandy during the 1350s were expected to surrender during periods of formal warfare.[261] Garrison service in Scotland appears to have involved similar arrangements. Since at least the start of Edward III's reign, *restauro equorum* had not normally been offered to the personnel of English royal garrisons in Scotland and the border country. The financial arrangements were often very simple, with a captain agreeing to maintain an adequate garrison in return for a fixed annual fee. From the late fourteenth century, the wardens of the Scottish Marches were usually engaged on similar terms.[262] There is rarely any mention of the division of spoils, so the detail supplied in the indenture concerning the Lochmaben garrison in the early 1370s is very valuable; and it may well be representative of widespread practice. The new constable from March 1371, William de Stapleton, who was serving for a fixed fee (initially £200 *per annum*), agreed to deliver a third of his 'gayne', including a third of the third which he would secure from his men, to the superior contracting party, the earl of Hereford and Essex.[263]

If, for the continental theatre of war prior to the early 1370s, the arrangements for the division of spoils depended upon the form of military service being undertaken, in the case of operations in Scotland the 'system of thirds' had probably been the norm for *both* royal expeditions and garrison service since the start of Edward III's reign. As we have seen, *restauro equorum* had not been offered to armies led by the king himself since the 1320s. As a consequence of this, and in complete contrast with expeditions to France, it was natural for the crown to demand a third rather than a half of the winnings of war. Seen in this light, the provisions for the division of spoils in the 'Ordinances of Durham', issued for Richard II's Scottish expedition of 1385, were outlining terms of service which had been in operation for half a

---

profits derived from ransoms: M. Jones, *Ducal Brittany, 1364–1399* (Oxford, 1970), pp. 149–50. Cf. Cherbourg: Given-Wilson, 'The ransom of Olivier du Guesclin', p. 25.

260 Bentley was authorised to take a third of the profits of both paid and unpaid troops: Hay, 'The division of the spoils of war', pp. 103–4.

261 Hay, 'The division of the spoils of war', p. 104. In 1361 Thomas Fog delivered £800 to the Chamber in part fulfilment of his obligation to surrender a third of the gains accumulated whilst serving as a captain in Normandy and elsewhere: *CPR, 1361–64*, p. 126.

262 R.L. Storey, 'The wardens of the marches of England towards Scotland, 1377–1489', *EHR*, lxxii (1957), pp. 593–615.

263 *Bain*, iv, no. 178. But, as in France, garrisons in Scotland were probably subject to a variety of terms. In the later 1340s Lochmaben captains surrendered two-thirds of their profits to the earl of Northampton: *Bain*, iii, no. 1459. D. Hay used the arrangements at Lochmaben to support his argument for the gradual adoption of 'the third' at all levels of the military community during the mid fourteenth century: Hay, 'Booty in border warfare', p. 158.

century. Denys Hay was, therefore, right to regard these Ordinances as a 'statement of existing practice rather than an innovation',[264] but he failed to recognise that, with respect to the treatment of spoils, this 'existing practice' had been long established only for campaigns in Scotland. The clause concerned with the 'system of thirds' may appear 'curiously matter of fact', but it had been applied to major expeditions to France for little more than a decade.

In part, then, the 'variety of usages' in the division of spoils (and, indeed, other terms of service) as experienced by the ordinary man-at-arms arose from diversity at the level of the individual magnate household; captains did not always offer the same terms to their subcontractors. But if it would be to misrepresent the evidence to insist upon uniformity of practice at all levels of the military community, it is nevertheless important not to obscure the essential rules to which the bulk of the evidence conforms. Most captains, it is clear, were more like the earl of Salisbury than the duke of Lancaster; they would be strongly influenced by the terms offered to them by the crown and would adjust the terms which they extended to subordinates accordingly. The nature of these terms would depend upon the theatre of war and whether the service involved a field campaign or garrison duty (or, indeed, a naval expedition). Thus, when an indenture stipulates the treatment of spoils in the manner 'which was customary in the French wars', or which was accorded to others of the same rank, it is referring not to a single custom, a single fraction of booty, but to a range of practices which were closely associated with the 'le manere de pais'[265] and type of military service involved.

---

[264] Hay, 'The division of the spoils of war', pp. 96–97.
[265] This phrase is used in the indenture of retinue between John of Gaunt and Sir John de Neville, 10 November 1370: *JGIndRet*, no. 3.

5

The Personnel of Edwardian Armies:
An Assessment of the Sources

A documentary source of great, though insufficiently utilised, potential, the horse inventories reveal much about the character and composition of Edwardian armies and the military events in which they were involved. A bundle of inventories will open-up the structure of an army, exposing its framework of retinues, their component companies and a multitude of personal relationships; and there will often be vivid evidence of those processes of structural change which affected all armies – the late arrival, early departure, fragmentation or regrouping of retinues and companies during the course of a campaign. Some changes in army composition were the direct result of the rigours of warfare: the loss of manpower through combat, disease or desertion. As we have seen, when they include details of horses killed or injured, the inventories can provide a most telling impression of the intensity of battle or the slow, continuous attrition of the march. Invaluable as these insights undoubtedly are, for the historian of Edwardian armies the inventories are perhaps *primarily* of use as a source for the names and status of serving men-at-arms, from notable bannerets to esquires of obscure origins. They are one of the most important types of nominal record available to us, particularly since they contain much more than merely lists of names. By associating named individuals with warhorses of specified quality, they offer a unique insight into the character and attitudes of the military aristocracy in fourteenth-century England. But before turning to this aspect of the subject, it is important to establish where this most distinctive type of record source fits into the overall corpus of documentation relating to late medieval military service. The personnel listed in the inventories are a sample of the militarily-active community of late medieval England; but what kind of sample is this and how does the profile of the military community which the inventories offer compare with that furnished by other records?

THE *VADIA GUERRE* ACCOUNTS
Although much scholarly attention has been focused on the impact of war on fourteenth-century England, there has been comparatively little systematic, detailed work on the personnel of English royal armies and the composition of the military community in general. Whilst the patchiness of the records may make this understandable where the non-aristocratic personnel are

concerned, it is rather the sheer bulk and inaccessibility of the manuscript sources which have discouraged reconstruction of the military lives of knights and esquires on anything other than a local level. But a serious study of military service requires that these voluminous records be confronted, for only by attempting a quantitative approach will it be possible to perceive change or continuity in the composition of armies and to gauge the size and character of the military community of fourteenth-century England. It will soon be apparent that the task of reconstructing the military community – of determining the number and identity of 'strenuous' knights, esquires and archers in the military pool, and establishing the nature and extent of their careers – can never be more than partially achieved. There are several dimensions to this problem. First, we cannot be sure of the overall numbers of men who took-up arms during this period. Second, of this uncertain number of militarily-active men, only a proportion of their names can be recovered. Third, the reconstitution of individual military careers from the named fragments of evidence offered by our sources, the process of linking items of information relating to the same person, is a most problematic task, yielding imperfect results. What we are left with is information about *parts* of the careers of a *proportion* of the military community.

Let us begin by examining the records which can contribute to the establishment of global figures for military service. Since paid service became firmly established as the norm during the course of the first half of the fourteenth century, it would be natural to assume that the *vadia guerre* records, the pay-rolls for armies, would be the essential source for this task, with other types of records, like indentures of war and the views of chroniclers, performing no more than useful supporting roles. The historian of fourteenth-century English armies is indeed fortunate in having at his disposal a substantial collection of *vadia guerre* records, each offering a systematic captain by captain schedule of an army's retinues, with details of personnel numbers, periods of service and pay due. They are an unusually rich source; but, like all records, they have limitations which must be understood by those who use them.

Given the range of martial opportunities open to Englishmen in the fourteenth century, we must accept from the outset that the task of assessing the extent of military service will be very far from straightforward. Even if service with the Teutonic knights in *Pruce* or in the companies of *condottieri* in Italy is set aside – for quantifying such service must surely defy the efforts of the most determined researcher – and attention is focused primarily on those who joined the king's expeditions or served in his garrisons, it is rarely possible to determine with any precision how many men were performing military service during a prescribed period. There are two reasons for this. On the one hand, the collection of source materials, and in particular the collection of pay-rolls, is incomplete; on the other, those records which *are* available pose a variety of interpretative problems.

The incompleteness of the records is nicely illustrated by the period from the battle of Boroughbridge (1322) to the Treaty of Brétigny (1360). In many ways this is a period well served by surviving pay-rolls.[1] As far as the major royal expeditions are concerned, there are excellent series of *vadia guerre* accounts for the Scottish campaign of 1322, the War of Saint-Sardos in 1324–25,[2] the Scottish expeditions of 1334–38,[3] the Low Countries campaign of 1338–39, the Sluys-Tournai campaign of 1340, those in Scotland in 1341–42 and in Brittany in 1342–43, and Edward III's last expedition to France in 1359–60.[4] To supplement the records for these major enterprises, there is a substantial corpus of pay-rolls for military activity on a smaller scale. The English garrisons in Scotland and the borders during the 1330s are, for example, well served by such materials.[5] However, there *are* important expeditions during this period for which no systematic pay materials are available. Much has been written about the Weardale campaign of 1327, from the vivid eye-witness account of Jean le Bel to the meticulous research-based studies of modern historians. But for this campaign and the next, which culminated in the dramatic English victory at Halidon Hill, no systematic pay records have survived. What we have is a collection of miscellaneous financial accounts, which are either very detailed but of restricted coverage, or wide-ranging but too imprecise. For the Weardale campaign, for example, a great deal is known about the bishop of Ely's retinue and the London contingent, but John de Brunham's account book, which offers glimpses of *vadia guerre* advances and debts for some captains, is inadequate for forming an impression of the army as a whole.[6] Although the first twenty years of the

---

1   Although corrected and supplemented in many points of detail, Prince, 'The strength of English armies', remains a valuable guide to the records for the 1330s, '40s and '50s.

2   BL Stowe MS 553, fos 55v–63r; BL Additional MS 7967, fos 30r–97v.

3   The controller's copy of Richard Ferriby's Wardrobe Book includes pay-rolls for the armies sent to Scotland in 1334–37: BL Cotton MS, Nero C. VIII, fos 233r–47r; 252r–63v. For 1337–38 there are *vadia guerre* accounts in two separate places: Walter de Weston's roll (E101/20/25) and Edmund de la Beche's account (E101/388/5, mm. 12–17). For these armies, see: Prince, 'The strength of English armies', pp. 353–60 and idem, 'The army and navy', *The English government at work*, i, pp. 332–93; Nicholson, *Edward III and the Scots*, chapters 11–14; Lewis, 'The recruitment and organisation of a contract army, May to November 1337'.

4   For the 1338–39 campaign, see *Norwell*, pp. 325–62; for Sluys-Tournai, see E101/389/8, mm. 11–16 and Tout, *Chapters*, iv, pp. 106–107. For the expeditions to Scotland and Brittany in 1341–43, see E36/204, fos 102r–110v and Appendix 2; for the Reims campaign, see E101/393/11, fos 79r–116v.

5   See E101, bundles 19–23 and BL Cotton MS, Nero C. VIII, fos 248r–51r.

6   Bishop of Ely's retinue: E101/18/6. London contingent: E101/35/2, m. 1 and E101/18/7. Brunham's account book: E101/383/8. These and other materials are discussed by V.B. Redstone, 'Some mercenaries of Henry of Lancaster, 1327–1330', *TRHS*, 3rd ser., vii (1913), pp. 154–57; A.E. Prince, 'The importance of the campaign of 1327', *EHR*, l (1935), pp. 299–302; Nicholson, *Edward III and the Scots*, chapters 2 and 3; N.B. Lewis, 'The summons of the English feudal levy: 5 April 1327', *Essays in medieval history presented to Bertie Wilkinson*, ed. T.A. Sandquist and M.R. Powicke (Toronto, 1969), pp. 236–49; N. Fryde, *The tyranny and fall of Edward II, 1321–1326* (Cambridge, 1979), chapter 15. The

Hundred Years War are generally well served by royal army pay-rolls, there are major gaps in the series. The Black Prince's expedition of 1355–57 is patchily documented;[7] but even more unfortunate is the disappearance of the original pay-rolls for the momentous Crécy-Calais campaign of 1346–47.[8] This is particularly frustrating, since we *do* have detailed knowledge of some of the much smaller expeditionary forces commanded by Edward III's lieutenants at this time. Pay accounts and some muster rolls reveal a great deal about the expeditions led by Henry, earl of Derby in Gascony in 1345,[9] Sir Thomas Dagworth in Brittany in 1346,[10] and Edward Balliol for a raid into Scotland in 1347.[11]

Given the survival of apparently full and detailed *vadia guerre* accounts for many of the major, and a proportion of the minor, expeditions from Boroughbridge to Brétigny, it is often not necessary to rely too heavily on the other records documenting the performance of paid service during this period. These include, most notably, the long series of Exchequer of Receipt Issue Rolls, the associated files of warrants for issue, together with various books recording payments for military purposes. On the Issue Rolls can be found numerous instances of retinue captains receiving advances of money (or 'prests'), the first installment of their men's wages and *regard*, as well as *post bellum* payments of arrears. Admittedly, for expeditions in the early and mid fourteenth century, the Issue Rolls have limited utility. Although confirming the participation of some retinue commanders (and leaders of companies, serving in the retinues of greater men) for those expeditions for which no pay-roll has survived, the Issue Rolls will rarely provide a complete register of captains; and amongst the recipients of prests and arrears will be many non-combatants – minor officials of the royal household, for example. Since arrears payments will often be spread over several years, during which there may well be gaps in the series of rolls, gathering all the relevant data for a particular army will be a difficult task. Moreover, the wage payments data assembled are unlikely to include much specific information on manpower numbers, periods of service completed or, in the case of *ante bellum* prests, the period for which the advance is being made. Of all the prests recorded on the Issue Roll before the Crécy campaign, only that received by the earl of Oxford, 800 marks, mentions that it is a first quarter payment.[12] If we could

only surviving financial document casting any light on the Halidon Hill expedition (BL Additional MS 35181) supplies no more than isolated details. For this campaign, see Nicholson, *Edward III and the Scots*, chapters 8 and 9.

7   Prince, 'The strength of English armies', pp. 366–67; Hewitt, *The Black Prince's expedition*, pp. 20ff.

8   See above, p. 112 n. 151.

9   E101/25/9; see Fowler, *The king's lieutenant*, appendix 1.

10   E101/25/18; see Prince, 'The strength of English armies', pp. 364–65.

11   E101/25/10; see Morris, 'Mounted infantry in medieval warfare', p. 100.

12   E403/336, m. 42; on the Issue Rolls and associated records for the Crécy-Calais campaign, see Ayton, 'The English army and the Normandy campaign of 1346', especially n. 42–44.

be sure of this with regard to the other prests, it would at least be possible to establish an order of precedence in the size of retinues. But many of the payments prior to the Crécy campaign are clearly lump sums, not precisely calculated for a particular period of time. Some captains received a series of lump sums over several weeks: the earl of Northampton, for example, received payments of £1000, £50, £200 and 20 marks.[13] Fortunately, later in the fourteenth century, with service now based upon formal indentures of war, the Issue Rolls become an altogether more useful source, giving details of manpower numbers, sometimes with the men-at-arms defined by rank, less often with precise information about length of service.[14] Typical are the prests made to Sir Walter Hewitt in 1370 for the service of thirty knights, 170 men-at-arms and 300 archers in Aquitaine.[15]

The unfortunate disappearance of the original *vadia guerre* records for the Crécy-Calais campaign highlights one of the biggest obstacles to calculating the size of the active military community during the mid fourteenth century. Where evidence for the size and structure of a particular army during the reign of Edward III is lacking, this will almost certainly be because the *vadia guerre* records have failed to survive the intervening centuries, rather than because such records were never compiled. During Edward I's reign, a royal army would often include many men serving 'voluntarily at their own expense'; they would appear, therefore, on neither feudal muster roll nor in the *vadia guerre* accounts and can only be detected with the aid of less conventional sources.[16] Unpaid service, whether voluntary or in response to feudal summons, can also be perceived during Edward II's reign. The pay-roll for the army which served in Scotland in the late summer of 1322 suggests a force of about 1,250 men-at-arms, but this does not include the feudal contingents listed on a proffer roll (over 500 men), not to mention an indeterminate number of men-at-arms paid for by retinue captains rather than by the crown.[17] By the 1330s, however, the attraction of voluntary, unpaid service appears very largely to have disappeared,[18] whilst the Weardale campaign of

---

13 E403/336, m. 41; E101/390/12, fos 7v, 8r, 8v.

14 See, for example, Sherborne, 'Indentured retinues and English expeditions to France, 1369–1380', pp. 718–19 and *passim*; Lewis, 'The last medieval summons of the English feudal levy, 13 June 1385', p. 6 and appendix 2; *Chronicles of the revolution, 1397–1400: the reign of Richard II*, ed. C. Given-Wilson (Manchester, 1993), appendix A: 'The duke of York's army, July 1399' (pp. 247–51). Cf. Powicke, 'Lancastrian captains', which draws heavily on the evidence of Exchequer of Receipt warrants for issue.

15 *Issue Roll of Thomas de Brantingham*, pp. 119, 130, 141–42.

16 Prestwich, 'Cavalry service in early-fourteenth-century England', pp. 147–48 (on Edward I's army in Scotland in 1300, which is illuminated by the *Song of Caerlaverock*). Cf. Prestwich, *War, politics and finance under Edward I*, chapter 3, which considers unpaid voluntary and feudal service for the whole reign.

17 BL Stowe MS 553, fos 55v–63r, 79v–83v; for the estimate of paid men-at-arms, see N. Fryde, *The tyranny and fall of Edward II, 1321–1326* (Cambridge, 1979), p. 128 and n. 45; for the proffer roll, see C47/5/10; on the other unpaid troops, see above pp. 92–94.

18 There are a few traces of voluntary, gratuitous service. For example, in 1337 the

1327 was to be the only expedition of Edward III's reign in which unpaid feudal contingents were to play a part. Can it be safely assumed, then, that the pay accounts from the 1330s onwards will present an accurate picture of army size and structure, even if the precise terms of payment might vary from one campaign to the next? Can we rely upon the *vadia guerre* accounts during the Hundred Years War to provide us with a comprehensive and undistorted view of English armies?

As we shall see, that question cannot be answered wholly in the affirmative. Even so, the evidence of pay-rolls will certainly be far more reliable than that offered either by narrative sources or by records which present only pre-campaign projections of personnel numbers, such as indentures of war. It is usual now to be critical of chroniclers' estimates of personnel numbers, often with very good reason.[19] Admittedly, some mid-fourteenth-century narrative sources do offer army size figures of the correct order of magnitude. It is possible, moreover, that chroniclers' figures may often have been inflated by the inclusion of non-combatants who do not appear in pay-rolls.[20] But what even the most well-informed and careful of chronicles will lack is the detailed breakdown at the retinue level provided by *vadia guerre* accounts. This kind of structural detail is usually to be found in indentures of war; but these records, for all their scrupulous attention to the terms of service, can only give us the *proposed* dimensions of individual retinues. The men actually mustered might fall some way short of the contracted numbers. Although noting, for the period 1369–80, that 'when deficiencies occurred they were only small', James Sherborne added that there was a 'widespread inability by captains to find the numbers of knights to which they had agreed'.[21] On the other hand, more men might be mustered, and allowed wages, than had been stipulated in an indenture.[22] The limitations of indentures of war are, of course, common to all records which offer projections for recruitment rather than the numbers of men who actually muster. This is certainly the case with the county-level arraying targets, frequently encountered on Edwardian

Hospitallers supplied ten men-at-arms for the king's army (Lewis, 'The recruitment and organisation of a contract army', p. 13 n. 6); but, as Lewis observed, they 'had special reasons for wishing to be in the king's favour'. Another exception concerns the military community of the Scottish Marches, who would mobilise to defend the northern counties without pay, as during the brief Neville's Cross campaign in 1346: Morris, 'Mounted infantry in medieval warfare', pp. 98–100.

[19] See, for example, J.H. Ramsay 'The strength of English armies in the Middle Ages: estimates of chroniclers and modern writers', *EHR*, xxix (1914), pp. 221–27.

[20] C. Gaier, 'Analysis of military forces in the principality of Liège and the county of Looz from the twelfth to the fifteenth century', *Studies in Medieval and Renaissance History*, ii (1965), pp. 209–11; P. Contamine, 'Froissart: art militaire, pratique et conception de la guerre', *Froissart: historian*, ed. J.J.N. Palmer (Woodbridge, 1981), pp. 134–35, 138–39.

[21] Sherborne, 'Indentured retinues and English expeditions to France, 1369–1380', pp. 744–45.

[22] Prince, 'The indenture system under Edward III', p. 290.

Chancery rolls;[23] and also with the unusual 'working draft' document listing retinues proposing to serve in Scotland in 1337.[24] Such records are of value as a guide to government aspirations, what was considered possible or desirable. That they cannot be relied upon as firm evidence of actual service is often demonstrable when correlation with pay-rolls is possible.[25]

No one, then, would prefer the testimony of a chronicler, or indeed the personnel numbers offered by an indenture of war, to the evidence of *vadia guerre* accounts. But, for all the riches they provide, the pay-rolls contain many pitfalls for the unwary. Non-combatants can be a source of difficulty. Whilst some civilian personnel, including engineers, craftsmen and others engaged in militarily-related duties, do appear in the pay-rolls, there will be many camp-followers and servants who do not.[26] This deficiency can be allowed for, though not quantified; altogether more problematic are the *fighting men* who have been hidden from view. How might such concealment have occurred? A *vadia guerre* account, whilst giving the impression of completeness,[27] might actually cover only part of an army's *paid* personnel. On occasion, more than one paymaster operated simultaneously, with the result that more than one set of pay accounts was produced. This occurred, for example, with the English forces in Scotland in 1337–38.[28] Sometimes, part of an army was financed in an unconventional way, with the result that it has not found a place in the *vadia guerre* accounts. Robert de Artois and William de Kildesby contributed substantial retinues (in all, perhaps 170 men-at-arms and 220 archers) to the second expeditionary force sent to Brittany in 1342, but they are not included in the pay-roll for this campaign, apparently because both Artois and Kildesby had been granted assignments of wool to cover their wage bills.[29]

Also apparently excluded from the *vadia guerre* accounts for the Breton campaign of 1342–43 are several hundred fighting men who were serving in return for charters of pardon.[30] The terms whereby 'service pardons' could be

---

23 The writs of array for two momentous campaigns are discussed by Morris, *Bannockburn*, pp. 40–41; and Ayton, 'The English army and the Normandy campaign of 1346'.

24 Lewis, 'The recruitment and organisation of a contract army, May to November 1337'.

25 E.g. for the 1335 campaign: R. Nicholson, *Edward III and the Scots*, pp. 194, cf. 200.

26 Goodman, 'The military subcontracts of Sir Hugh Hastings', p. 120; J. Gillingham, *The Wars of the Roses* (London, 1981), pp. 43–44; 'A plea roll of Edward I's army in Scotland, 1296', ed. C.J. Neville, *Miscellany XI*, Scottish History Soc., 5th ser., iii (1990), pp. 26–27. Cf. Contamine, *Guerre, état et société*, pp. 20–21, 24–25; A. Curry, 'Sex and the soldier in Lancastrian Normandy, 1415–1450', *Reading Medieval Studies*, xiv (1988), pp. 17–18.

27 Sometimes the gaps in the accounts are fairly obvious: for the Roxburgh campaign, see Nicholson, *Edward III and the Scots*, p. 177 and appendix 3.

28 The paymasters were Edmund de la Beche, Keeper of the Wardrobe (E101/388/5) and Walter de Weston (E101/20/25): Prince, 'The strength of English armies', pp. 358–60. Tout used Beche but not Weston (*Chapters*, iv, p. 100–1); J.E. Morris used Weston but not Beche (Morris, 'Mounted infantry in medieval warfare', pp. 93–94).

29 See Appendix 2.

30 Mostly enrolled on the Treaty Rolls: C76/17; C76/18.

obtained had not remained unaltered since their introduction as a recruiting device in the 1290s.[31] Initially, pay *was* provided for those serving for a royal pardon and this was still the case in the early to mid 1330s;[32] but by the early 1340s the terms of service were rather different. The privy seal warrants and captains' certificates of service for the Breton campaign in 1342–43 make it clear that the grant of a charter of pardon was normally dependent upon a year's service in the king's armies, and that a man served 'a ses custages propres'.[33] The crown was willing to make concessions. Men who had served with the earl of Northampton from the summer of 1342 until the following January were awarded pardons with no strings attached.[34] For a man who had only joined the campaign in the autumn, however, the grant of a pardon was conditional upon further service: 'il serra prest de perfourmir le remenant dun an en notre service a ses custages propres ou et quant nous lui voudrons assigner'.[35] Mainpernors, whose names appear with the enrolled pardons,[36] stood surety for the performance of this service. For the campaigns of 1345–47, there was some variety in the terms on offer to criminals seeking rehabilitation through military service. Many pardons stipulate that a year's service had been (or would be) required, though sometimes we find this condition being withdrawn upon payment of a modest sum, perhaps as little as a mark.[37] Although the stipulation of service at the pardon recipient's own expense is only occasionally encountered in the enrolled records,[38] this is hardly surprising given that many of the pardons were being awarded for completed service. Whatever the precise nature of their obligations, those who served at their own cost for a royal pardon would not be included in the

---

[31] For a discussion of the early history of 'service pardons', see N.D. Hurnard, *The king's pardon for homicide before A.D. 1307* (Oxford, 1969), pp. 247–49, 311–26. For a far less precise commentary on mid-fourteenth-century practice, see Hewitt, *The organisation of war under Edward III*, pp. 29–30.

[32] 'A plea roll of Edward I's army in Scotland, 1296', ed. Neville, pp. 25–26; Nicholson, *Edward III and the Scots*, p. 174 (Roxburgh campaign, 1334–35).

[33] For example: C81, file 287, which includes many privy seal warrants; SC1/39, nos. 144–8 (certificates for a quarter of a year's service, issued by the earl of Northampton).

[34] For example: C81/287, nos. 15177, 15186, 15192–93, 15196–97.

[35] This is a standard formula: e.g. C81/287, nos. 15178–85. These terms for earning a 'service pardon' had applied at least to the previous campaign: a warrant dated 17 September 1342, describes how Thomas Mankel *chapellain*, who 'par certeine meinprise' was required to serve on the king's next expedition (i.e. to Brittany) at his own cost, was released from this undertaking at the request of the earl of Suffolk and in return for a promise 'de chaunter pour les almes de noz aun, cestres': C81/286, no. 15008. The same terms can also be seen to have applied to garrison service at Berwick in 1342–43 (SC1/39, no. 154) and on the Isle of Wight a year or two earlier (*CPR, 1338–40*, p. 457).

[36] For an insight into the process of finding sureties in Chancery or in the county court, see C237 (Bails on Special Pardons); file 6 concerns the period of the Breton campaign of 1342–43.

[37] *CPR, 1345–48*, pp. 225, 246, 289.

[38] E.g. pardons issued before or during Derby's Gascon expedition, 1345–46: *CPR, 1345–48*, pp. 44–45, 57.

manpower totals in an army's pay accounts.[39] It will rarely, if ever, be possible to determine their exact numbers because the enrolled lists of pardon recipients are unlikely to be complete. Any adjustments to the figures given in *vadia guerre* accounts, to make allowance for unpaid troops serving in return for pardons, must therefore necessarily be tentative; but in those cases where service for pardons can be seen to have been unpaid, we should perhaps be prepared to add about 5%–10% to the paid strength of an army.

Any attempt to determine the effective strength of an army is further complicated by the fact that some of the troops receiving the king's pay might not actually be on active service. The pay-roll for the Sluys-Tournai campaign is unusual in that, for many retinues, the first day of paid service was the day of the battle in the Zwin estuary.[40] Usually, the start of a spell of paid service began on the day of arrival at the port of embarkation; but what may not be clear from the pay-rolls is that whilst, on a particular day, some retinues were actually on the march in France, others had not yet left England. The Breton campaign of 1342–43, once again, provides a good example. The *vadia guerre* accounts for the expedition give no hint that part of Edward III's army was still at the ports of embarkation in Devon several weeks after the king's fleet had arrived in Brittany. Moreover, it is more or less certain that the some of the infantry contingents entered on the pay-roll never reached Brittany at all.[41]

There remains a further interpretative problem associated with pay-rolls, a problem perhaps more pervasive than those considered so far and certainly quite as perplexing. This is that many *vadia guerre* accounts present an impression of unbroken continuity in personnel numbers, thereby concealing the effects of mortality, desertion, authorised withdrawals, late arrivals and promotions on the size and structure of an army and its constituent companies. Admittedly, this is not a problem with all *vadia guerre* accounts. Some *do* reveal the shifting composition of an army's retinues with meticulous precision,[42] though the reasons for the changes in numbers may not be stated explicitly. In this respect, the level of detail offered in the *vadia guerre*

---

[39] Sometimes, indeed, apparent *lacunae* in an army's structure may be explained in terms of the absence of unpaid units from the *vadia guerre* accounts. In 1335, for example, the earl of Cornwall served with 135 paid men-at-arms, but no paid archers (Nicholson, *Edward III and the Scots*, p. 248); yet the Scottish Rolls for this year include the names of fifty-one men receiving pardons *per testimonium* the earl (C71/15, m. 16). The pardon recipients appear to be archers (none of them can be identified as men-at-arms with known links with the earl): if so, they must have formed a special 'felons company' serving at their own cost.

[40] E101/389/8, mm. 11–16.

[41] See Appendix 2.

[42] For example, the earl of Salisbury's retinue in Scotland during the winter-spring campaign of 1337–38 (E101/20/25, m. 3; E101/20/26, m. 2 – the latter being a more detailed version of the account): personnel numbers are given for a series of consecutive time-spans, very roughly monthly periods.

accounts for the War of Saint-Sardos is most unusual.[43] At times, there is inconsistency in the amount of information supplied. For example, of the separate retinue-level accounts surviving from Buckingham's expedition of 1380–81, only that concerning Sir Ralph Basset's company refers specifically to fatalities,[44] yet we might reasonably expect this long, tough campaign to have given rise to a fairly high level of casualties.[45] The commonest method adopted in the accounts to indicate retinue-level shifts in manpower numbers involves giving a single set of figures for the whole campaign, which is then qualified by deductions for 'man-days' lost. Such deductions, or *vacaciones*, are sometimes painstakingly detailed;[46] but rather more often they exhibit a disconcerting air of artificiality.

Vacaciones might provoke doubts; but many pay-rolls present, wholly or in part, an even tidier, more suspicious picture: the numbers of paid personnel remain the same throughout a campaign, with no allowance apparently being made for campaign attrition or the arrival and departure of individuals. For example, according to his *vadia guerre* account, the earl of Derby's retinue appears to have lost not a single man during the course of his remarkable *chevauchées* in Gascony in 1345–46.[47] Meanwhile, Sir Thomas Dagworth's company serving in Brittany apparently remained at full strength throughout 1346, despite much strenuous campaigning.[48] We are even less inclined to believe the incredibly neat pay-rolls for the Reims campaign. The prince of Wales' retinue – numbering seven bannerets, 136 knights, 443 esquires and 900 horse archers – remained the same size for pay purposes throughout the nine months of the expedition. This was a winter campaign which, according to the narrative sources, was certainly not bloodless, and which involved the loss of no fewer than 395 appraised warhorses in the prince's retinue alone.[49] A similar unconvincing neatness is exhibited by the pay-rolls for a number of

---

[43] BL Additional MS 7967, fos 30r–93v. These accounts reveal that eight men-at-arms died (five are named) and many others withdrew during the course of the campaign for reasons ranging from illness, to attendance at *hastiludia*. Two esquires left Sir Fulk Fitz Warin's retinue to go 'versus partes Lumbard', presumably in pursuit of more lucrative campaigning conditions (ibid., fo. 30v).

[44] E101/39/8, m. 2.

[45] See A. Goodman, *The loyal conspiracy* (London, 1971), pp. 124–26. When Thomas, duke of Gloucester founded Pleshey College in the early 1390s, he made provision for annual commemoration of those who had died during the 1380–81 expedition: R. Gough, *The history and antiquities of Pleshey in the county of Essex* (London, 1803), p. 180.

[46] E.g. the earl of Salisbury's retinue serving at sea in 1373: BL Additional MS 37494, fo. 10r.

[47] E101/25/9.

[48] E101/25/17; J. Sumption, *The Hundred Years War: trial by battle* (London, 1990), p. 496.

[49] E101/393/11, fo. 79r. Apart from withdrawals and casualties, one would have expected some allowance to have been made in the prince's account for elevations to knighthood (cf. *Scalacronica*, p. 157; other retinues on the pay-roll do allow for newly created knights: e.g. E101/393/11, fos 83r, 85r).

other major royal expeditions.[50] Some of the entries in the *vadia guerre* accounts for the Breton campaign of 1342–43 do allow for *vacaciones*, but many of the retinues, such as Sir Hugh le Despenser's, remained wholly unscathed, at least for pay purposes, throughout the campaign. Yet Despenser's retinue was involved in the hard-fought battle of Morlaix and at least one of his knights, Edward le Despenser, was killed there.[51]

How can these improbably streamlined and uncomplicated pay accounts be explained? It is difficult to believe that no movements or losses of personnel actually took place, and yet such *vacaciones* and arrivals should have had an effect on the retinue wage-bills. The terms allowed to the earl of Salisbury in his indenture of 1428, whereby there was to be no reduction in wage receipts for soldiers who were ill or had died,[52] do not represent normal fourteenth-century practice.[53] On occasion, it is clear that captains were serving with more men than the crown was willing to pay for. In these circumstances a retinue, sustained by a plentiful supply of replacements, could legitimately maintain its maximum size in the pay-rolls.[54] Replacements were no doubt commonly employed by captains to fill gaps in their companies and any assessment of the numbers of individuals serving in a particular expeditionary force needs to take account of this.[55] Yet unless it was normal practice for captains to maintain a pool of manpower which was not supported by the king's pay, we must doubt whether sufficient numbers of unemployed men would always be on hand to plug gaps as soon as they appeared.[56] There will often, therefore, have been at least short-term fluctuations in retinue numbers.

It is usual to explain the 'tidiness' of fourteenth-century *vadia guerre*

50 For example, the Roxburgh campaign of 1334–35: Nicholson, *Edward III and the Scots*, p. 181 and appendix 3.

51 E36/204, fo. 106r; C61/54, m. 30; *Murimuth*, p. 127; *CIPM*, viii, no. 395.

52 *Letters and papers illustrative of the wars of the English in France during the reign of Henry the Sixth*, ed. J. Stevenson, 3 vols (London, 1861), i, pp. 410–11. For similar evidence from Lancastrian Normandy, see N.H. Nicolas, *History of the battle of Agincourt*, 3rd edn (London, 1833), appendix 11; and R.A. Newhall, *Muster and review* (Cambridge, Mass., 1940), p. 88.

53 The arrangements whereby the wages of those who had been killed or taken prisoner would be paid for the period prior to their death or capture are conveniently articulated in the records for Buckingham's expedition of 1380, which duly make allowance for *vacaciones* and promotions: E101/39/6, E101/39/8.

54 For example, Sir Ralph de Ufford, as Justiciar of Ireland in 1344–46, was allowed pay for a company of forty men-at-arms: see above pp. 116–17.

55 A muster roll of Thomas, earl of Arundel's retinue in 1415 shows that in addition to the earl himself, sixteen men-at-arms left the siege of Harfleur because of illness and that a further two esquires died there. The majority of these men were, however, replaced, and the earl's pay account consequently makes allowance for only five *vacaciones* amongst the retinue's esquires. E101/41/7.

56 Despenser's army in 1383 was accompanied by 'countless persons with neither horses nor weapons', but such camp-followers were more a nuisance than a fruitful source of replacements: *Westminster*, p. 45. Cf. the 'large pool of soldiers' available to garrison commanders in Lancastrian Normandy: A.E. Curry, 'Military organisation in

accounts in terms of the fraudulent practices of profit-seeking captains, who were able to claim pay for 'absentees and even for non-existent soldiers' because the mechanisms of muster and review were insufficiently rigorous.[57] There can be no doubt that, given the opportunity, some captains would indeed inflate their pay claims with 'dead souls'. Cases such as that concerning John, Lord Neville, accused in the Good Parliament of 1376 of pay fraud during a period of service in Brittany in 1372, probably represent the tip of the iceberg.[58] But whether muster and review controls were quite as 'lax' in the fourteenth century as has sometimes been suggested is open to question. Direct evidence, in the form of collections of muster rolls, is admittedly patchy, but as with the horse inventories, the pattern of documentary survival may not accurately reflect the pattern of production. Where bundles of muster rolls have survived for field campaigns, we see a system of *periodic* manpower checks[59] – and not just at the beginning and end of expeditions. Sometimes, as at Cléry on 5 August 1380, new rolls would be compiled for mid-campaign musters.[60] Alternatively, existing rolls could be marked (or 'pointed')[61] and annotated when men arrived, departed or died. Moreover, as we have seen, some *vadia guerre* accounts document changes in personnel numbers with great precision. The pay-rolls for the 1336 Scottish campaign show, for example, that Sir William de Montagu's company of men-at-arms changed size eight times between 14 June and 3 December, as a result of arrivals and departures.[62] Clearly, regular checks had been made on the personnel of this and, indeed, other retinues in the army.[63] During the following summer we see a further glimpse of the mechanism of inspection. On 25 July

Lancastrian Normandy, 1422–50', Ph.D. thesis, Council for National Academic Awards, 1985, p. 207.

[57] McFarlane, *The nobility of later medieval England*, pp. 26–27.

[58] Sherborne, 'Indentured retinues and English expeditions to France, 1369–1380', pp. 726–27; G. Holmes, *The Good Parliament* (Oxford, 1975), pp. 23, 130.

[59] On monthly musters for field forces in Lancastrian Normandy, see Newhall, *Muster and review*, pp. 112 and n. 252, 123. Cf. French practice in the mid fourteenth century: Contamine, *Guerre, état et société*, pp. 86–94. King John II's Ordinance of 1351 ordered the holding of musters at least twice a month: *Society at war*, ed. Allmand, p. 46.

[60] E101/39/7, m. 4; E101/39/9, mm. 3 and 4. In the case of Sir William de Windsor's retinue, a second mid-campaign muster roll has survived: E101/39/7, m. 3. It can be assigned to the period following 10 February 1381 when a number of personnel changes occurred.

[61] E.g. a roll of Sir Walter Hewitt's retinue (dated only '20 July'): E101/35/2, m. 8. On the use of dots ('pointing') and crosses on muster rolls, see Newhall, *Muster and review*, p. 15.

[62] BL Cotton MS, Nero C. VIII, fo. 241r.

[63] John de Houton had been appointed 'to receive and review the men-at-arms and others' in the English army, a task which included the valuation of warhorses: BL Cotton MS, Nero C. VIII, fos 243v, 280v–81v; Prince, 'The payment of army wages in Edward III's reign', p. 139 and n. 12. Muster rolls survive for the retinues of Henry of Lancaster and Sir Ralph de Neville: E101/15/12 and E101/19/36, m. 4.

the marshal of the army was ordered to make regular reviews of men in the king's pay in order to restrict payment those who were actually present.[64]

Garrison personnel presented particular problems to the crown. The English occupation of Normandy under Henry V and Henry VI, based upon several dozen garrisons (2,500–5,000 men),[65] high-lighted this particularly forcefully, but garrisons had always offered fertile soil for the flourishing of fraudulent practices. Long, uneventful terms of duty encouraged absenteeism; men were liable to take off 'a leurs aventures'.[66] Garrison captains could be counted on to maximise their personal profits if left unsupervised, even though, by employing an understrength garrison, they might endanger the security of the stronghold in their charge.[67] So it is no surprise to find plentiful evidence that mid-fourteenth-century garrisons financed by the English crown were, indeed, kept under close scrutiny. For example, a review of the castle garrison at Edinburgh was made on 18 May 1337 by Sir John de Swanland; and the resulting roll[68] forms part of a valuable collection of annotated muster lists and detailed *vadia guerre* accounts for English royal garrisons in Scotland and the borders during the 1330s and 1340s.[69] Similarly, from the other end of the kingdom, there is every indication that the size and composition of the Isle of Wight garrison in 1338–39 was carefully monitored by the paymaster appointed by the crown, John de Windsor. The frequent changes in manpower numbers recorded in his account suggest that regular and fastidious musters were taken.[70] Evidence from English garrisons in

---

[64] *Rot. Scot.*, i, 497a; Lewis, 'The recruitment and organisation of a contract army', p. 4. Muster rolls exist for the retinues of four captains, including two for Sir Henry de Percy: E101/20/17, mm. 2, 4, 5, 6; E101/20/18, m. 2. Cf. Henry V's rigorous mustering for field campaigns: G.L. Harriss, ed., *Henry V* (Oxford, 1985), pp. 40–41.

[65] Curry, 'Military organisation in Lancastrian Normandy', especially appendices 2–6, which builds on the classic work by R.A. Newhall.

[66] Newhall, *Muster and review*, pp. 53–54. On the development of a modern concept of 'desertion' in the first half of the fifteenth century, see C. Allmand, *The Hundred Years War*, pp. 114–15.

[67] As was alleged of Sir Richard Tempest, constable of Roxburgh castle in the early 1360s: *Bain*, iv, no. 64.

[68] E101/19/24, m. 12; partly printed in *Bain*, iii, pp. 362–63.

[69] See below, pp. 167–68. As with field armies, the comings and goings of personnel during an accounting period were usually recorded on a single annotated muster roll. Allowance would be made for personnel movements in accompanying pay-rolls. The records for Edinburgh and Stirling castles for the period 1340–42 furnish pay details of those who served throughout and then a series of sub-sections for individuals or groups who were present for only part of the time. For example, the muster roll for Stirling shows that Sir John de Stricheley was killed on 10 October 1341 and, appropriately, the pay-roll includes a separate section for 'one knight' whose pay ceased on that day: E101/23/1, mm. 3, 5.

[70] E101/21/32. The crown was evidently only too well aware of the danger of pay fraud on the Isle of Wight. In October 1347 an effort was made to establish whether the garrison maintained during the previous six months, by the keepers of the island and of Carisbrooke castle, had been of the proportions required by the terms of their indentures: *CPR, 1345–48*, pp. 459–60.

France in the fourteenth century is admittedly rather patchier. The indenture between Henry, earl of Derby, and the Gascon captains of Bergerac (September 1345) required the garrison to be mustered for review by the earl's deputy every eight days.[71] Bundles of surviving muster rolls testify to the regular scrutiny to which the personnel serving in the fortresses of the Calais region were subjected.[72] But in respect of its *paid* garrison, Calais was somewhat exceptional. There was no prospect of the English crown being able to pay the wages of more than a handful of garrisons in France,[73] and so for the majority of 'English' strongholds, it was impossible to implement a system of muster and review.[74]

If, as the evidence seems to suggest, muster and review was a normal accompaniment to paid military service, whether in the field or in garrison (and whether the army had been recruited by indenture of war or financed and organised by the wardrobe), are we to ascribe the not inconsiderable number of very 'tidy' fourteenth-century pay accounts to lapses in the system? Was it simply that rigorous muster and review mechanisms were applied to some expeditions, but not others? It is certainly true that periods of administrative experiment, often prompted in part by a desire to 'tighten-up', such as that coinciding with the Scottish operations of 1336–38, have sometimes left a legacy of scrupulously detailed records and an impression, for the modern observer, of unusually strict muster and review practices. But to explain the suspicious neatness displayed by some pay accounts in terms of administrative laxness, exploited by profit-seeking captains, would not be wholly convincing. Their extraordinary tidiness would surely have made these pay-rolls appear just as implausible at the time of their presentation as they do now. The army paymaster or Exchequer officials are unlikely to have been deceived. We may be confident that captains, in their own interests, would keep a watchful eye on absenteeism and mortality in their retinues.[75] Royal

71 Fowler, *The king's lieutenant*, pp. 57–58, 232–33. Froissart offers a description of the mustering of the English garrison at La Rochelle in 1372: Contamine, *Guerre, état et société*, p. 89.

72 See, for example, an excellent set of rolls for 1356: E101/27/6.

73 Muster rolls have survived for a few garrisons: e.g. Neufchâtel-en-Bray in 1363 (BL Additional MS 41567, Q); St Sauveur in 1370–1 (E101/30/38 and E101/31/18); and Brest in 1375–77 (Archives départementales de la Loire-Atlantique, Nantes, E 214) and 1378 (E101/37/2).

74 Fowler, *The king's lieutenant*, pp. 165–70. Some of the garrisons which *were* financed from England, such as those at Brest and Cherbourg during the 1380s, were paid for on the basis of the 'flat-rate' system. A captain received an annual fee from which he had to maintain an adequate garrison; but numbers were rarely specified, nor was he required to hold regular musters: see M. Jones, *Ducal Brittany, 1364–1399* (Oxford, 1970), pp. 148, 152. The flat-rate system had frequently been employed for English garrisons in the Scottish Marches, and in particular at Berwick. In the 1420s, it was used for a proportion of the 'least vulnerable' garrisons in Lancastrian Normandy: Curry, 'Military organisation in Lancastrian Normandy', pp. 222–23.

75 On the work of captains' clerks, see Newhall, *Muster and review*, p. 54; for the employ-

administration would be fully aware of this, so that an excessively tidy account could only be interpreted as a blatant attempt at fraud. A good deal of administrative acquiescence would be necessary for the account to pass unchallenged. It must be conceded that such acquiescence is not beyond the bounds of possibility. Administrative complicity in obviously artificial pay claims may have been offered as a kind of *quid pro quo* for tolerance by captains of heavy campaign costs or long delays in receiving pay from the crown.[76] Inflated claims may, thus, have been allowed to include an element of built-in 'interest' to compensate for probable delays in payment. In the later sixteenth century, a captain in Elizabeth's army might be allowed pay for a number of men who were not actually serving, the extra payment being called 'dead pays'.[77] Thus for every ninety men in a company, a captain might receive pay for one hundred, the extra money being intended as a bonus for the captain, and selected members of the company, to cover costs. A 'dead pays' system was in operation in fifteenth-century Italy *(paga morta)*,[78] but there is no evidence for the existence of such a system in fourteenth-century England. *Regard* payments, which begin to be offered for field campaigns during the 1340s, appear to have been intended to perform a similar function.

Some form of system whereby the crown, in certain circumstances, allowed captains legitimately to claim pay for men who were not in service would go some way to explain the extraordinarily neat pay accounts which are such a common feature of the period. However, the most convincing explanation depends upon neither the operation of a hidden 'dead pays' system, nor a combination of deceit and administrative collusion, but rather involves an understanding of the flexible accounting practices of royal clerks. There is plenty of evidence to suggest that 'tidy' pay-rolls were the product not of fraud, but of mundane clerical practices, which involved the manipulation and summarisation of the figures before they appeared in the final *vadia guerre* account. One way in which this was done was to allow departures and arrivals to cancel out. In this way, the personnel figures could be greatly simplified, within the confines of the total wage-bill and the period of service, with the result that the pay-roll would show a retinue with proportions which it never actually possessed during the course of a campaign. For example, Sir Ralph de Neville's retinue serving in Scotland for the period from mid May to early December 1336, as revealed by the final *vadia guerre* account, consisted of thirty-six men-at-arms, but with the qualification that three knights and ten esquires were absent for forty-two days and one esquire for four days.[79] A draft account for this retinue, a valuable rare survival, divides the period into

ment of 'treasurers of war' by magnate captains, see McFarlane, *The nobility of later medieval England*, pp. 25–26.

76 Cf. A.J. Pollard, *John Talbot and the war in France, 1427–1453* (London, 1983), p. 109.

77 C.G. Cruickshank, *Elizabeth's army*, 2nd edn (Oxford, 1966), pp. 154–58.

78 M. Mallett, *Mercenaries and their masters* (London, 1974), pp. 134–35.

79 BL Cotton MS, Nero C. VIII, fo. 240v.

seven sections and brings us closer to reality. The retinue consisted of thirty men-at-arms from mid May to mid June, attained a peak strength of thirty-nine in late August to early September, but dropped to only twenty during an eight week spell in the autumn. At no stage did it consist of thirty-six men.[80] For the purposes of compiling a neat, compact entry in the Wardrobe Book, fluctuations in manpower numbers have been crudely ironed-out. The *vacaciones* which have been allowed for bear no relation to actual periods of absence; they are simply accounting devices. This is by no means an isolated example. The account for Sir William de Windsor's retinue, part of Bucking-ham's army serving in France and Brittany in 1380–81, allows (amongst other things) for the deduction of 1,033 'knight-days' from a base figure of *twelve* knights serving for a period of 308 days.[81] The survival of a series of muster rolls allows us to see, however, that this figure of *twelve* knights is purely arbitrary;[82] and, moreover, that the *vacaciones* total has been arrived at simply in order to square the number of declared personnel with the amount of pay which was due to Windsor for the service of the *twenty* actual knights who, for varying lengths of time, were members of his retinue during this campaign.[83]

The 'man-at-arms' in the pay-rolls begins, therefore, to resemble a conveni-ent unit of accounting. At times, indeed, that was precisely what he was. According to the final *vadia guerre* account for the 1336 Scottish campaign, Sir John de Tibetot's retinue consisted of nineteen men-at-arms and its size remained unchanged through the summer and into the autumn.[84] Once again, a related record reveals how the pay-roll misrepresents the truth. A horse inventory for Tibetot's company includes only fifteen men-at-arms, but on the same membrane are listed the names of twelve mounted archers, which (a note adds) are accounting as four men-at-arms.[85] In the final pay-roll these

---

[80] E101/19/36, m. 4d; another version of this account is to be found on the front of m. 4.

[81] E101/39/7, m. 2.

[82] E101/39/7, mm. 1, 3, 4. For the first two months of the campaign there were ten knights in Windsor's retinue. Five new knights were created on 24 August 1380, but numbers grad-ually declined to a low point of nine in mid to late January 1381, followed by a slight increase to ten, a figure which was sustained until the end of the campaign at the start of May. For only one short spell, a little over a week in early January 1381, were there actually twelve knights in Windsor's retinue.

[83] The method of calculating the *vacaciones* total of 1033 days involved a partial matching of late arrivals with early departures: 193 days between the departure of three knights and the arrival of three new recruits; 386 days following the withdrawal of four further knights, without subsequent replacement; 454 days before the late arrival of two knights. No account is taken in this calculation of the five newly created knights, nor of the fact that three of them withdrew from service in the early weeks of 1381.

[84] BL Cotton MS, Nero C. VIII, fo. 241r.

[85] E101/19/36, m. 5d. Each archer was being paid fourpence per day and so three of them cost the equivalent of a single man-at-arms. Cf. the Isle of Wight garrison in 1339, where eight hobelars were serving in the place of four men-at-arms from 16 April to 10 November: E101/21/32, m. 4.

twelve archers have actually *become* four of the nineteen men-at-arms in Tibetot's retinue and were it not for the survival of the horse inventory, we would be wholly unaware that these four 'men' are no more than convenient units of account.

As far as the royal clerks were concerned the all-important thing about the final account was that it should record the correct pay total and period of service for each retinue. The numbers of men need bear only approximate resemblance to those who actually served. There was certainly no need to include all the fine detail; indeed, to do so was positively undesirable. In the case of campaigns financed by the wardrobe, the *vadia guerre* records had to fit comfortably into a book of accounts. Summarisation was essential. So, a wholly understandable desire to present the less essential, and in draft documents extremely bulky, information in concise form was felt to justify a process of abidgement which must often have involved a degree of distortion.[86] The historian must accept that there is, what McFarlane aptly called, an 'element of trouble-saving fiction'[87] running through many classes of record, and that the *vadia guerre* accounts are no exception. As we have seen, by no means all pay-rolls appear to be afflicted by this problem; but it is difficult to know when and to what extent the clerical scalpel has been at work. Comparatively few really useful muster rolls and draft pay accounts have survived from the fourteenth century, so we are often left wondering what might lie beneath the surface of comparatively innocent looking pay-rolls, such as those for the Breton campaign of 1342–43. In this particular case, of the twenty-seven retinues shown as fielding at least ten men-at-arms, only eight make allowance for *vacaciones* among the men-at-arms.[88] Where losses *are* allowed for, the numbers involved are very modest and the periods of absence rarely extend for longer than a few weeks. It is difficult to square this impression of limited casualties with what we know of the campaign, marked as it was by much hard fighting – including a pitched battle at Morlaix, a series of assaults on fortified towns and several sieges – and ending with a tempestuous passage back to England, in which several ship-loads of men were lost. According to the pay-roll, of the 200 men-at-arms in the earl of Northampton's retinue (which served in all for 203 days), one knight and two esquires were absent for thirty days and one esquire for forty-seven days.[89] There is a strong odour of accounting invention here. Whatever the real

---

86 Sometimes this was difficult: the earl of Salisbury's retinue in 1336 grew from six to fifty-eight men and such dramatic changes in retinue size could not easily be summarised: BL Cotton MS, Nero C. VIII, fo. 241r.

87 McFarlane, *The nobility of later medieval England*, p. 16.

88 *Vacaciones* amongst the archers in these retinues are rather more numerous: in seventeen of these twenty-seven retinues.

89 E36/204, fo. 106r. The 'absence' of forty-seven days is rather longer than usual; but even so, if the account is taken at face value it suggests that the retinue suffered no losses during the early weeks of the campaign, and in particular during the assault on Morlaix or the battle immediately afterwards.

extent of manpower fluctuations in Northampton's retinue, all have been concealed by a cloak of clerical summarisation. The pay which would be due to a retinue of the strength presented in the account very nearly matches the pay that was actually due to the earl at the end of this arduous campaign, and the difference, a surplus of £6 7s, was easily accounted for by inventing some very modest *vacaciones*.

'Medieval official documents', it has been observed, 'are not always strictly factual statements of what they purport to record'.[90] The historian of late medieval English armies would be wise to take heed of these words and to approach the *vadia guerre* records with caution. A pay-roll is, of course, a highly enticing document. It will usually be clearly laid-out, offering an impression of overall army structure, combined with much informative detail, and it may give no obvious hint of incompleteness. It may well provide insights into the structural changes which armies invariably experienced during the course of campaigns. A good example of this is to be found in William de Farley's *vadia guerre* account for the Reims campaign. The death of the earl of March at the end of February 1360 was followed by the partial break-up of his retinue and the establishment of a number of independent companies led by men who formerly had been members of March's retinue.[91] The *vadia guerre* accounts appear, then, to be an historian's dream, but usually they cannot be taken at face value. There will probably be a sprinkling of transcription errors and, possibly, idiosyncracies of other kinds; Farley's pay-roll for 1359–60 can certainly offer a number of examples of such flaws.[92] But, as we have seen, the primary weakness of *vadia guerre* accounts – the likelihood that the process of clerical summarisation has left us with a distorted impression of personnel numbers – is altogether more serious. Even if the representation of numbers at the start of a campaign is of the correct order of magnitude, the continuous turnover of personnel – late arrivals, early departures, fatalities and deserters – is all too often concealed from view. Thus, as a source for the numbers of men engaged in military service during a particular campaign, such records may offer a less than wholly reliable guide: a consideration which must be borne in mind when attempting to use them as a means of measuring the size and proportions of the military community as a whole.

---

90 E.M. Carus-Wilson and O. Coleman, *England's export trade, 1275–1547* (Oxford, 1963), pp. 19–20.

91 E101/393/11, fo. 79v. A company headed by Sir William Heron entered the king's pay on 7 March 1360 (E101/393/11, fo. 85v; cf. similar 'new' companies on fo. 86r); he had secured letters of protection, dated 24 September 1359, for service in March's retinue: C76/38, m. 10.

92 For example, two consecutive retinue entries with *identical* details (E101/393/11, fo. 86r) and apparent inconsistencies in the operation of the terms of service.

LETTERS OF PROTECTION, CHARTERS OF PARDON AND MUSTER ROLLS

A calculation of the numbers of men employed in expeditionary forces or garrisons in various theatres of war is but a first step to forming an understanding of the military community. An assessment of the size, social composition and changing membership of the military community depends fundamentally upon the identification of the men involved – upon the uncovering of their names and, where possible, the separation of those with the same or similar names into distinct career profiles. It is, indeed, the identification of individuals and the reconstruction of their careers that presents the most intractable problem for the historian of fourteenth-century military service. Although it will often be possible to establish a fairly accurate estimate of the numbers of men-at-arms serving in an army, it will usually only be a minority of them who can be known by name – and a smaller number still who can be identified with absolute confidence as men who served in other campaigns.

What are the principal source materials for the names of serving men-at-arms in the fourteenth century? The records of royal administration predominate to such a degree that it seems hardly necessary to assess the relative contribution of 'record' and 'narrative' sources. Yet we should consider briefly whether the chronicles have anything substantial or distinctive to offer. The nominal references in narrative sources are essentially of two kinds. First, we will often be given the names of the most prominent captains, sometimes presented in the form of a simple list. Such material is not to be scorned. On occasion, the list is quite long, such as that included at the start of the Crécy campaign in the *Acta Bellicosa*;[93] and sometimes a chronicler notes the presence of a captain who is not mentioned in the conventional record sources.[94] The second type of named individual in narrative sources has done something notable: perhaps a chivalrous exploit, such as Sir Robert Benhale's single combat before the battle of Halidon Hill,[95] or Sir Richard Fitz Simon's rescue of the Black Prince at Crécy.[96] Often a man is named because he has been killed or badly wounded.[97] Whether the context is prosaic or colourful, the nominal evidence offered by narrative sources is, however, almost invariably decidedly 'aristocratic' (an archer's exploit, like that

93 *The life and campaigns of the Black Prince*, ed. Barber, p. 29: the fullest and most reliable list of captains for this campaign from a narrative source (cf. *Le Baker*, p. 79; *Murimuth*, p. 199); note, however, that it does not differentiate retinue commanders from prominent bannerets serving in other retinues.

94 Sherborne, 'Indentured retinues and English expeditions to France, 1369–80', p. 719 and n. 2.

95 Le Baker, p. 51.

96 *Froissart*, ed. Lettenhove, v, pp. 476–77.

97 E.g. Sir Thomas Roscelyn, killed as he was coming ashore near Dunnottar in 1336: *Scalacronica*, p. 101.

of John de Doncaster, is rarely recorded);[98] and it is usually insubstantial. Moreover, some chroniclers are treacherous guides, offering the unsuspecting reader corrupt name forms, mistakes and, occasionally, what appears to be pure invention.[99]

Turning to the 'record' sources for fourteenth-century military service, the most consistently available are the lists of letters of judicial protection enrolled on the Chancery rolls.[100] Protections, together with enrolled appointments of attornies, are very much the staple diet of the student of Edwardian armies: a single roll will often yield hundreds of named protection recipients, with many of the names grouped, in a rough and ready way, into retinues.[101] For a good many armies, letters of protection provide the only numerically significant nominal record source,[102] but they must be handled with care. In the first place, the enrolment of a letter of protection is not an absolutely reliable guide to military service. They are statements of intent, rather than firm evidence of performance; and their essential purpose, to provide the recipient with a measure of security from a range of legal actions during a period of military service,[103] was open to abuse. A propertied man intending

---

98 *Le Baker*, pp. 116–18, 284–86; *Avesbury*, p. 414.

99 E.g. Lettenhove, ed., *Froissart*, iv, pp. 377, 380–81 (Crécy campaign).

100 They appear, depending on the theatre of war in which their recipients are to serve, on the Gascon, Patent, Scottish or Treaty Rolls. Compared with the huge number of enrolled protections, very few of the original letters patent have survived. A very rare example, with remains of the Great Seal still attached, is that issued to Henry de Pipe for service in the duke of Lancaster's retinue in 1359: E313/4/16.

101 See, for example, the calendar of protections on the Scottish Rolls (1290s onwards): *Calendar of documents relating to Scotland*, ed. G.G. Simpson and J.D. Galbraith, vol. V (Edinburgh, 1986), part II, pp. 395–579. By comparison with such voluminous evidence, essoin rolls yield only tantilising fragments. The imprecision of Roger Lestraunge of Knokyn's essoin ('in servicio domini regis': Chester 23/3, m. 6d) is typical, but in this instance a protection warrant supplies additional detail: *BPReg*, i, p. 115. (On essoins in Chester county court, see Morgan, *War and society in medieval Cheshire*, p. 114.) Robert de Sussex's essoin in Kings's Bench during the Michaelmas term, 1342 (KB121/7, m. 26d), was probably necessitated by his service in Brittany; he does not have an enrolled protection for this expedition.

102 For an assessment of the importance of letters of protection see Saul, *Knights and esquires*, p. 48. The evidence of protections was used to good effect by J.E. Morris in his pioneering work on Edwardian armies: see, for example, *The Welsh wars of Edward I*, pp. 245–46, 260–62, 290–91 and 'Mounted infantry in medieval warfare', p. 85 n. 2. Cf. also Prestwich, *War, politics and finance under Edward I*, pp. 62–65, 237; Fowler, *The king's lieutenant*, p. 227. For an excellent discussion of the use of protections by crusaders in the thirteenth century, see S. Lloyd, *English society and the crusade, 1216–1307* (Oxford, 1988), pp. 165–69.

103 In 1345, for example, proceedings in King's Bench involving Thomas de Bernardeston were postponed *sine die* following his production of a letter of protection (enrolled: C76/20, m. 22), showing him to be about to depart for Brittany in the retinue of the earl of Oxford: *Public works in medieval law*, ed. C. Flower, 2 vols, Selden Soc., xxxii (1915), pp. 309–10. Cf. cases cited in Morgan, *War and society in medieval Cheshire*, p. 152. Some legal actions, such as assizes of *novel disseisin*, were excepted from standard

to join the king's army would be well advised to acquire a protection before leaving, in order to guard against legal skulduggery in his absence. A man who failed to take this precaution might well find himself discomforted 'par malice de ses adversers'.[104] But there were many who sought protections simply as a means of delaying the legal process or evading it altogether. If most men did duly perform the promised military service, there were nevertheless some who, having been issued with a protection, failed to appear at muster. John de Lambron defaulted in this way. According to an anonymous captain, he had received a protection, but 'est demorrez en pais & ne vint pas ovesque moi en dit voiage [as parties Descoce]'.[105] It is difficult to assess the extent of protection fraud in quantitative terms. The bulk of the evidence, consisting of either letters from captains requesting that an absentee's protection should be revoked or formal orders of revocation enrolled on the Chancery rolls, appears to date from the later fourteenth century, and a good deal of it concerns garrison service.[106] This may suggest a worsening problem, but is more likely to reflect tighter administrative controls: it may be that

judicial protections (Prince, 'The indenture system under Edward III', p. 296; D.W. Sutherland, *The assize of novel disseisin* (Oxford, 1973), pp. 54–55), so that it was often necessary for men to seek, and the crown to allow, broader based legal immunity. In November 1336 Edward III ordered that assizes of *novel disseisin* should be delayed in the case of men in the king's service: *CCR, 1333–37*, pp. 725–26. Cf. similar orders prior to the Crécy campaign: *CCR, 1346–49*, p. 83. For a good example of a man faced by two assises of *novel disseisin* whilst serving overseas and seeking 'remedie solonc les ordinances', see SC1/39, no. 135. Cf. C81/287, nos. 15139, 15141, 15158, 15170 for men seeking delays in assizes of *novel disseisin* during the Breton campaign of 1342–43; each of them had, in addition, secured a standard letter of protection, with clause *volumus*. For a fuller discussion of the 'several methods by which the law took account of royal service' in the fourteenth century, see J.S. Critchley, 'The early history of the writ of judicial protection', *BIHR*, xlv (1972), pp. 196–99. The *Year Books, Edward III* (15 vols, Rolls Ser.) provide insights into the day to day treatment of protections in the courts.

104 SC1/39, no. 135.

105 SC1/41, no. 147. Occasionally we find complaints from aggrieved parties in legal cases: see, for example, the assertion by the abbot of York that one of the abbey's debtors, Nicholas de Portington, was living at home and not on active service (SC1/39, no. 100). Cf. *Rot. Parl.*, i, p. 162a for a similar petition.

106 There are comparatively few enrolled revocations for the period prior to Brétigny; but see, for example: C76/23, m. 8d and *CPR, 1345–48*, p. 190 (1346); C76/30, m. 6 (1352); C76/37, m. 21 (1359). This evidence can be supplemented by records of investigations into individual cases of fraud. In 1360 the sheriffs of London found that Nicholas Mate, who should have been in France with the earl of Warwick, had remained 'in domo sua in warda de Crepulgate London': C258 (*Certiorari – corpus cum causa*), file 13, no. 2; cf. similar cases in files 11–13. A torrent of revocations appear in the 1370s and '80s. On 4 August 1370, for example, twenty-three of the men who should have served in Aquitaine with Sir Walter Hewitt had their protections revoked: C61/83, mm. 1, 2, 5, 7 (protections), *CPR, 1367–70*, pp. 457–58 (revocations). From the 1380s, in addition to the evidence on the Patent Rolls, there are a number of surviving letters requesting revocation of protections: e.g. by the bishop of Norwich (C81/1735, nos. 33–36), by Thomas de Percy, captain of Brest (SC1/41, no. 79), and Hugh de Calveley, keeper of the Channel Islands

more rigorous muster and review methods were obliging captains to notify the authorities when men failed to appear, when previously it would have been easier for them to keep quiet and pocket the absent men's pay.[107]

Confirmation of the performance of military service is possible with only a minority of protection recipients, but we would probably be wrong to assume that defaulting was widespread. An altogether more significant deficiency of the protection lists is their incompleteness. Of the men-at-arms serving in an army, only a proportion would have enrolled protections: rarely would a captain secure protections 'pour lui & toutes ses gens qui irront en sa compaignie'.[108] So, whilst the combined total of men-at-arms for the three expeditions to Brittany in 1342–43, as presented in the pay-rolls, was about 1,900, there are enrolled protections for only 722 individuals.[109] Given that the pay-rolls underestimate the number of men-at-arms serving in this army and that a few protection recipients were non-combatants, it is clear that no more than a third of the men-at-arms involved in this campaign had acquired legal protection for their absence from England. The proportion of men-at-arms who were protection recipients varied from retinue to retinue: Sir Bartholomew de Burgherssh senior had secured protections for two-thirds of his knights and esquires, whilst the earl of Salisbury had done this for less than a fifth of his. The proportion of protection recipients might also fluctuate considerably from one campaign to the next. There are indications that the intended theatre of operations played a part in determining numbers. There is, for example, a clear tendency for a larger percentage of men-at-arms to have protections for overseas expeditions than for campaigns in Scotland.[110] As a consequence of this (and given the overwhelming importance of letters of protection as a source for military service), we are likely to know rather more about the continental dimension of men's careers than about their service against the Scots – a distorting factor which must always

---

(SC1/43, no. 52; cf. *CPR, 1385–89*, p. 267). Such requests are rather scarce for the early decades of Edward III's reign; but see SC1/41, no. 147 and *Bain*, v, no. 733.

[107] A closer control on protection fraud from the 1350s seems to coincide with the 'interposition of the privy seal into the chain of warrants': the privy seal office's increasing control over the issue of protections, as a natural adjunct to its handling of military indentures. See A.L. Brown, 'The authorisation of letters under the great seal', *BIHR*, xxxvii (1964), pp. 130–31.

[108] As envisaged by Sir John Chandos' indenture of war, dated 20 September 1362: E101/68/4, no. 83.

[109] For the manpower totals, see Appendix 2. The great majority of letters of protection for this campaign are to be found on the Treaty Rolls (C76/17; C76/18), with those for Sir Hugh le Despenser's retinue on the Gascon Roll (C61/54), since Aquitaine had been his original destination.

[110] Whereas perhaps as many as two-thirds of the men-at-arms in Edward III's army in the Low Countries in 1338–39 had enrolled protections, the corresponding figure for the Roxburgh campaign (1334–35) and for the great expedition of the following summer was about 20%: C71/14; C71/15.

be borne in mind when considering the composition and service horizons of the mid-fourteenth-century military community.

Why is it that only a proportion (usually a minority) of serving men-at-arms can be found in the lists of enrolled letters of protection? Could it be that a large number of protections were being requested but not collected, or issued but not enrolled? The survival of captains' *fiat* warrants for protections[111] might provide a clue, as it is often possible to correlate warrant and enrolment. In 1327 Sir Henry de Percy requested the issue of protections for no fewer than forty-two men, including twenty-three knights; but of these, only seven appear with enrolled protections on the corresponding Scottish Roll.[112] There are many similar cases of imbalance between the number of protections requested and the number enrolled. On occasion, a marginal cross indicates those names listed in the warrant which do not appear in the corresponding enrolment.[113] Whilst this may represent issue without enrolment,[114] it is far more probable that it marks men who did not collect their protections from Chancery. Some may have withdrawn from the expedition; some may have felt that they could do without a letter of protection or were

---

[111] Most of these authorising bills from captains relate to campaigns of the early to mid fourteenth century. The main series, organised alphabetically by captain, is to be found in Chancery Warrants (C81), files 1719–56; but there are many more in files 1675–1718 and in the volumes of Ancient Correspondence (SC1). A few examples have found their way into the files of Ancient Petitions (SC8). The Black Prince's Register includes orders for the issue of protections under the seal of the exchequer of Chester: e.g. *BPReg*, i, pp. 13, 115 (1346–47). Increasingly from the 1350s captains sent protection request bills to the privy seal office rather than directly to the Chancellor. The bulk of these 'captains bills' were destroyed by fire in 1619, but the records which represent the next stage in the administrative process, privy seal bills authorising the issue of protections, are to be found in large numbers in a long chronological series of Chancery Warrants (C81) files. For example, file 932, containing bills of privy seal for the period 20 June to 30 June 1370, includes many protection warrants for Sir Robert Knolles' retinue. On protection warrants see: Brown, 'The authorisation of letters under the great seal', pp. 130–31; H.C. Maxwell-Lyte, *Historical notes on the use of the great seal of England* (London, 1926), pp. 210–11.

[112] C81/1736, no. 75; C71/11, m. 5. The ratio of knights to esquires suggests that Percy was not seeking protections for all of his men (no pay-roll survives for this campaign). An undated warrant from an unnamed captain states explicitly that 'les autres de ma compaignye nount pas demande protectioun': C81/1752, no. 64.

[113] For example, a warrant for Sir John de Norwich's retinue bound for Gascony in 1337: twelve of the forty-one names do not appear on the Gascon Roll (C81/1750, no. 33; C61/49, m.17). The one enrolled name which does not figure in the warrant, Bartholomew de Estone, appears to have been an afterthought. In a separate letter, John de Norwich asked for a protection for this one remaining man, 'auxi come vous avez fait a mes aultres gentz q[ui] irront en ma dite compaignie & la dite protection vous pleise liverer au portour de cestes': C81/1735, no. 41.

[114] Brown, 'The authorisation of letters under the great seal', p. 129. On the enrolment of Chancery records, see R.F. Hunnisett, 'English Chancery records: rolls and files', *Journal of the Society of Archivists*, v (1974–77), pp. 158–68: an absorbing discussion.

unable to make arrangements for its collection; but others, it seems, resented having to pay two shillings for the privilege. The earl of Northampton surely expressed the feelings of many when he wrote to the Chancellor, Master John de Offord, to complain about the clerk of the hanaper's refusal to issue protections without being paid 'pour le seal'. The earl's men, it seems, would not pay because 'il lour semble dur pour ceo qils mettent en aventure vie et membre'.[115]

Being the product of an earlier stage in the process of retinue recruitment, warrants for protections probably contain a larger proportion of men who ultimately did not serve on campaign than their enrolled equivalents. The numbers of 'drop-outs' are not, however, likely to be large; and against the occasional error from this source should be set the considerable numbers of additional names which the protection warrants supply. They throw light on shadowy or otherwise completely unknown members of the military community. Sometimes they illuminate the early career of a man who later was to become a prominent soldier. Take, for example, Sir Thomas Dagworth. If we confine ourselves to enrolled letters of protection, this most celebrated English knight appears quite suddenly on the military scene as one of the earl of Northampton's principal lieutenants during the Breton campaign of 1345;[116] yet his military apprenticeship with the earl is revealed by his inclusion in protection warrants for two earlier campaigns. Dagworth is at the bottom of the list of the earl's knights in one warrant, whilst if we push back a little further we find him amongst the *armigeri*.[117]

Not only do the *fiat* warrants frequently yield more abundant nominal data than their enrolled equivalents; they are, in fact, superior in several further ways. They are usually clearer about a man's military rank. Often we find the names in a warrant presented as separate lists of 'knights' and 'esquires'. A warrant might also reveal the company structure of a retinue[118] – an aspect of military organisation which is rarely illuminated by enrolled protection lists. There are, however, problems in using the *fiat* warrants. They are less accessible than enrolled protections and it is likely that only a small proportion of them have survived. They are fragmentary records:[119] a warrant might

---

[115] C81/1734, no. 60; cf. N.D. Hurnard, *The king's pardon for homicide before A.D. 1307* (Oxford, 1969), pp. 55–58, on the payment of fees for the issue of charters of pardon.

[116] C76/20, m. 21; the corresponding warrant would seem to be C81/1735, no. 21, which places him top of the list of Northampton's retinue. He had been a member of this earl's retinue for a diplomatic mission in the autumn of 1337: *CPR, 1334–38*, p. 531. By January 1347, he had been appointed king's lieutenant in Brittany: Prince, 'The strength of English armies', pp. 364–65. M. Jones, 'Sir Thomas Dagworth et la guerre civile en Bretagne au XIVe siècle: quelques documents inédits', *Annales de Bretagne*, lxxxvii (1980), pp. 621–39, offers the most complete survey of Dagworth's career.

[117] C81/1735, no. 22; C81/1734, no. 40.

[118] For example, an undated warrant from the earl of Derby indicates the numbers of men-at-arms brought by the more important knights in his retinue: C81/1724, no. 49.

[119] The protections for a single retinue might be requested by means of a whole series of

contain one name or a hundred. Moreover, they are rarely fully dated and often not at all. All this means that correlation with the enrolled lists or, indeed, any kind of chronological sorting would involve considerable labour. When, however, they take the form of long lists of names, neatly grouped according to rank – and when they *can* be precisely dated – the *fiat* warrants provide a most valuable source for military service and for the composition of magnate retinues.[120]

Yet a captain would rarely seek a protection for each and every man-at-arms in his retinue. A *fiat* warrant is very likely to be a partial source, with the bannerets and knights in the retinue more heavily represented than the lesser men.[121] The preponderance of knights is easily explained: letters of protection were sought primarily by men with landed interests. Although a *fiat* warrant may well include a sprinkling of servants and clerks, or individuals intent on gaining relief from creditors,[122] the majority of those seeking protections and ensuring their enrolment were doing so in order to gain legal security for their property for the duration of their absence in the king's service. The availability of protections (along with enfeoffment to use) gave the landholding class some measure of freedom to perform their traditional military responsibilities. We must, therefore, recognise that the most consistently available source for the study of fourteenth-century military personnel is heavily biased towards the propertied. For the most part excluded are sons awaiting their inheritances, landless younger brothers and men of obscure origins making a career of soldiering. This is a most serious deficiency because such men, whether serving as ordinary men-at-arms or as mounted archers,[123] without the strong commitments to county society which could restrict heads of gentry families to serving only occasionally,[124] provided the back-bone of the king's armies, as well as a very useful source of recruits for mercenary companies and crusading expeditions. Occasionally, the curtain of obscurity is raised by chance references in other records. Sir Roger de Beauchamp's will, dating from 1379, mentions that one of his sons, Philip,

---

warrants, but rarely have a complete set survived. Such fragmentation can provide an useful insight into the processes of retinue formation. For example, the earl of Pembroke, whilst awaiting embarkation at Lymington, issued warrants for protections on 1, 3, 12, 15, 17, 19 and 23 June 1347: C81/1736, nos. 10, 11, 13, 14, 55, 57, 61.

120 See, for example, Saul, *Knights and esquires*, chapter 3. Retinue composition is frequently far less clear in the enrolled lists of protections: disorderly arrangement and excessive abbreviation often leads to ambiguity which can only be resolved if the corresponding warrant survives.

121 An extreme example lists thirty-five knights, followed by thirteen esquires (C81/1734, no. 24); a more typical ratio would be thirty-three to thirty-five (C81/1735, no. 15).

122 E.g. *CPR, 1370–74*, p. 295; P.E. Russell, *The English intervention in Spain and Portugal in the time of Edward III and Richard II* (Oxford, 1955), pp. 371–72.

123 Enrolled letters of protection for men explicitly styled archers (e.g. Thomas de Shirburn, for service in the Calais garrison in 1372: C76/55, m. 42) are rare prior to the later fourteenth century.

124 See Saul, *Knights and esquires*, pp. 52–59.

was 'tenuz en un somme dargent' to a knight in Lombardy by name of Sir John Thornbury and adds that another man, John St Martin, was with him.[125] Many of the deponents before the Court of Chivalry were men of this kind: veterans of numerous campaigns – either in the king's service, as merce-naries or crusaders – though often remaining esquires throughout their careers. A good example is William de Thweyt of Heton, a younger son of a lesser gentry family from Norfolk, who though serving on at least nine ex-peditions, obtained a protection at Chancery for only one of them.[126]

The bias towards the propertied members of the military community which colours the evidence of letters of protection is not evident in the case of another important class of fourteenth-century military records: charters of pardon. This does not mean that pardons, whether in the form of authorising warrants or as enrolled lists, are entirely free of their own interpretative difficulties.[127] They offer, of course, only partial coverage of fighting person-nel: fifty-seven of the 400 men in John of Gaunt's *comitiva* in 1359–60 have enrolled pardons, for example.[128] As with letters of protection, the number of enrolled service pardons varies considerably from one campaign to the next. In part, this arises from the vagaries of documentary survival. Not all par-dons were enrolled and the collection of surviving warrants is inevitably incomplete; and some of the pardon rolls have either disappeared altogether or survive only in a fragmentary state.[129] Naomi Hurnard's conclusion, that

---

[125] 'The Bedfordshire wills and administrations proved at Lambeth Palace and in the arch-deaconry of Huntingdon', ed. F.A. Page-Turner, *Bedfordshire Historical Record Society Publications*, ii (1914), p. 8.

[126] For Thweyt's career, see Andrew Ayton, 'William de Thweyt, esquire: deputy constable of Corfe Castle in the 1340s', *Somerset and Dorset Notes and Queries*, xxxii (1989), pp. 731–38. Six of the nine campaigns are mentioned in Thweyt's Court of Chivalry deposi-tion in 1386 (C47/6/1, no. 92); he does not mention the one period of service for which he secured a letter of protection (Gascony in 1337–39, as a member of Sir John de Norwich's retinue: C61/49, m. 17; C81/1750, no. 33).

[127] The pardons are enrolled on the main series of Gascon, Patent, Scottish and Treaty Rolls and on special supplementary rolls (e.g. the Norman and Calais Rolls for the Crécy-Calais campaign). The enrolments should be used in conjunction with the privy seal warrants (C81) which have authorised the issue of pardons. In addition, a scatter of certificates of service, written by captains on behalf of men in their retinues, provide invaluable insights; these are to be found in Ancient Correspondence (SC1) and amongst the files of protection warrants (C81/1719–56). Original charters of pardon have sur-vived in local collections (see, for example, W.G.D. Fletcher, 'Sir Richard de Sandford, knight, 1306–1347', *Transactions of the Shropshire Archaeological and Natural History Society*, 3rd ser., vi (1906), p. 162: Shropshire Record Office, Sandford collection, 2/63); but see also Chancery Files, Cancelled Letters Patent, C266, file 5, for original service pardons from Edward I's reign, which were never collected by recipients or proxies.

[128] Walker, *The Lancastrian affinity*, p. 77.

[129] Hurnard, *The king's pardon for homicide before A.D. 1307*, p. 316. For the Breton campaign in 1342–43, a fragment of a separate pardon roll (C67/28A) strongly suggests that only a proportion of the pardons awarded for service during this campaign were enrolled on the Treaty Rolls (C76/17; C76/18).

'the total of service pardons was undoubtedly higher than the numbers which can now be traced', is surely well-founded, but more worrying to the historian than incomplete survival is the fact that these materials may not always be offering a reliable guide to military service. Take, for example, the 1330s. Details of a great many pardons arising from the Halidon Hill campaign are to be found packed on the Scottish Roll, but they must be treated with scepticism, for it is likely that amongst the criminals serving in return for royal pardons, are many who did not take-up arms at all.[130] That the crown was well aware of the extent of fraud in 1333 is made abundantly clear by a series of tightening-up measures. Justices were not to accept the validity of pardons without corroborative proof of the performance of military service.[131] For the next campaign, during the winter of 1334–35, the numbers and organisation of serving felons was strictly regulated.[132] For the great expedition into Scotland during the following summer, the number of pardons increased significantly once more,[133] but now their issue appears to be based upon the authorisation (*per testimonium*) of retinue captains, a system which continued to operate during the French war. The notes of authorisation, which are usually included on the pardon roll, not only ensure that these records become an altogether more reliable guide to military service,[134] but also facilitate the reconstitution of individual retinues. Most of the major expeditions during the period up to the Treaty of Brétigny gave rise to the issue of several hundred charters of pardon,[135] but the peak was reached for service during the Crécy-Calais campaign, for which several thousand were awarded.[136]

If enrolled letters of protection show us, for the most part, the wealthier

---

130 C71/13; Nicholson, *Edward III and the Scots*, p. 130. J.E. Morris took the evidence at face value: 'Mounted infantry in medieval warfare', p. 93.

131 *CCR, 1333–37*, p. 158. The courts had become vigilant in this respect: for examples, see Hurnard, *The king's pardon for homicide before A.D. 1307*, p. 325 n. 2 and W.R. Jones, 'Keeping the peace: English society, local government and the commissions of 1341–44', *American Journal of Legal History*, xviii (1974), p. 317 n. 41.

132 They amounted to only two hundred men serving in two separate companies: Nicholson, *Edward III and the Scots*, pp. 130, 174.

133 C71/15: large numbers on mm. 10–16, with a scatter on other parts of the roll. By contrast, there are very few on the roll for 1336: C71/16, mm. 29, 36.

134 Hewitt, *The organisation of war under Edward III*, p. 30; Hewitt, *The Black Prince's expedition*, pp. 163–64. For a case of pardon fraud arising from the Breton campaign of 1342–43, see *CPR, 1343–45*, pp. 88–89.

135 E.g. Reims campaign: *CPR, 1358–61*, especially pp. 375–402.

136 *CPR, 1345–48*, pp. 476ff. Service pardons for homicide numbered about 1,700 during Edward I's reign; if all felonies are considered, 'the grand total must have been well over 2,000' (Hurnard, *The king's pardon for homicide before A.D.1307*, p. 316–17). Service pardons continued to be offered, though more selectively, under Henry V: E. Powell, *Kingship, law and society: criminal justice in the reign of Henry V* (Oxford, 1989), pp. 229–40.

men-at-arms in an army, a pardon roll provides a rather different sample of personnel. Whether it is a balanced sample may not be easy to determine, since one of the weaknesses of pardon rolls is their reticence on matters of military status. Whilst the geographical origins of pardon recipients are sometimes specifically stated, and that of their mainpernors very often,[137] it is usually far more difficult to assign an individual to a particular branch of the army, to distinguish between men-at-arms and archers. Sir Hugh de Hastings' request for 'chartres general de tout manere de trespas' for two of his archers is unusually specific about military status.[138] For most campaigns of the Edwardian period, we can probably safely assume that the great majority of pardon recipients were occupants of the lower levels of the military hierarchy. Some were clearly drawn from the dregs of society: 'diverses gentz de religione eschapez et apostates et ensement plusours larounes et robbers de diverses gaioles'.[139] In the absence of a major collection of army muster rolls for the fourteenth century, pardon rolls yield more data on the common, non-aristocratic soldier in English armies than any other source.[140] But the pardon rolls will also include some men of gentle birth. Indeed, given that war service might be offered to the habitual aristocratic criminal as a route to rehabilitation, or at least as a means of channelling aggressive energies into the war effort, the knightly element in the pardon rolls is likely to be both distinctive and interesting. If anything, 'the practice of allowing wilfully violent and litigious landowners to make a new start in France was brought to a fine art by Henry V'.[141] Indeed, Edward Powell has argued that, as far as the aristocracy are concerned, 'a clear correlation . . . exists between criminal prosecution and subsequent military service during Henry V's reign'.[142] Something similar is perceptible under Edward III, with the recruitment of notorious gentry criminals like the Folvilles being merely the tip of a substantial iceberg.[143] A happy consequence of this for the historian of aristocratic military service is the additional nominal evidence which pardon rolls can provide. For example, of the handful of service pardon recipients in 1335 who

---

[137] See, for example, the enrolled pardons for service during the War of Saint-Sardos: C61/37.

[138] SC1/41, no. 43.

[139] As recruited by Sir Robert Knolles in 1370: *Anonimalle*, p. 63.

[140] Cf. the distinctive evidence of 'A plea roll of Edward I's army in Scotland, 1296', ed. Neville.

[141] C. Carpenter, *Locality and polity. A study of Warwickshire landed society, 1401–1499* (Cambridge, 1992), pp. 370, 372.

[142] Powell, *Kingship, law and society*, p. 236.

[143] E.L.G. Stones, 'The Folvilles of Ashby-Folville, Leicestershire, and their associates in crime, 1326–1347', *TRHS*, 5th ser., vii (1957), pp. 128–29; J. Bellamy, *Crime and public order in England in the later Middle Ages* (London, 1973), pp. 86–87; J. Aberth is altogether more sceptical about the wisdom of this policy: 'Crime and justice under Edward III: the case of Thomas de Lisle', *EHR*, cvii (1992), p. 297.

were specifically designated 'knights', four were also in receipt of letters of protection, but three were not.[144]

The combined use of letters of protection and charters of pardon yields an impressive body of data on the personnel of Edwardian armies; but it will be clear from the foregoing discussion that the coverage is both incomplete and riddled with interpretative difficulties. If muster rolls had survived in abundance, as they have for the Lancastrian occupation of Normandy,[145] protections and pardons would be relegated to no more than a supportive role. As it is, the survival of fourteenth-century muster rolls is very patchy, especially for the period before the Treaty of Brétigny. Given their bulk and essentially transitory importance, it is likely that most of the muster rolls were destroyed – along with the draft versions of the final, much-condensed *vadia guerre* accounts – once all the documentation had passed audit. Those muster rolls which have survived serve only to demonstrate the magnitude of our loss. As far as field campaigns of the early to mid fourteenth century are concerned, there are but a handful of surviving muster records. Single retinues in an army are fully illuminated, whilst the remainder of the host lies in shadow. This is the case, for example, with the Weardale campaign of 1327. Muster rolls are available for only two of this army's retinues, those of John de Bedford[146] and John de Hotham, bishop of Ely,[147] and the latter does not, in fact, provide complete coverage. The bishop's company consisted of two bannerets, thirty-five knights (including four who were dubbed at Stanhope) and 133 esquires; but whilst all the bannerets and knights are listed on the muster roll, only fifty-five of the esquires are named. Despite the shortfall, the muster roll still reveals a great deal more about the bishop's men than the corresponding list of protections enrolled on the Scottish Roll. Thirty-nine men have protections, but as usual, a high proportion of these are bannerets or knights; only one of the esquires named on the muster roll also appears in the protection list.[148]

Muster rolls, though few in number and imperfect in their coverage, enable the historian to escape to some extent from the restricted view of the military community which dependence on letters of protection tends to impose. Admittedly, as far as mid-fourteeth-century field campaigns in France are

---

[144] The three with pardons, but without protections, were Sir Hugh de Morizby, Sir Thomas Morieux and Sir John de Lortie: C71/15, mm. 10, 12, 13.

[145] About 3,500 musters and *contrerolles*, 'perhaps half the original number produced, are still extant': A. Curry, 'The nationality of men-at-arms serving in English armies in Normandy and the *pays de conquête*, 1415–1450: a preliminary survey', *Reading Medieval Studies*, xviii (1992), pp. 136.

[146] A company of Londoners: E101/35/2, m. 1; the pay account is E101/18/7. See V.B. Redstone, 'Some mercenaries of Henry of Lancaster, 1327–30', *TRHS*, 3rd ser., vii (1913), pp. 151–66; and Andrew Ayton, 'John Chaucer and the Weardale campaign, 1327', *Notes and Queries*, new ser., xxxvi (1989), pp. 9–10.

[147] E101/18/6.

[148] C71/11, m. 6. Of the twenty men who appear on both muster roll and protection list, all except one were bannerets or knights.

concerned, our glimpses of rank and file men-at-arms are little more than fleeting. Muster rolls have survived for some of the expeditionary forces led by the king's lieutenants and raised by written indentures of war.[149] But there are none at all for the armies led by the king in person and administered by the wardrobe. These fleeting glimpses might enable us to establish geographical and tenurial patterns of recruitment for certain retinues, but for analysis of continuity of service it is necessary to have a *series* of such detailed records. For example, although we have a full muster roll for Henry of Lancaster's retinue in 1336,[150] only thirty-six out of the ninety-five men listed can be seen to have served with this captain on a later occasion.[151] That so many of the men named on this roll seem to have had only a temporary association with Lancaster is almost certainly a false impression, as the bulk of our evidence for subsequent campaigns is drawn from letters of protection and the only other full retinue roll dates from the expedition to Gascony in 1345–46. It is therefore not surprising that whilst only a third of knights and bannerets listed on the 1336 muster roll have no further known military contact with Lancaster, the comparable figure for the esquires is two-thirds.

An aspect of Edwardian military activity which *is* illuminated to some degree by series of muster rolls is garrison service. Individual rolls have survived for a variety of royal garrisons during this period,[152] but the most useful series derive from English-held fortresses in Scotland and the borders during the 1330s and '40s. Muster rolls survive for Berwick in 1338–41, Edinburgh in 1335–37 and 1339–42, Perth in 1338, Roxburgh in 1336 and 1340–42, and Stirling in 1336–37 and 1339–42.[153] When combined with the

---

[149] E.g. Henry, earl of Derby, in Gascony, 1345–46 (E101/25/9); Sir Thomas Dagworth in Brittany, 1346 (E101/25/18); Sir James Audley in Gascony, 1345 (E101/24/20). On the last of these retinues, see Morgan, *War and society in medieval Cheshire*, pp. 75–76. Muster rolls are rather more plentiful for field armies, now invariably raised by indenture, after the resumption of the French war in 1369 (e.g. for the 1380–81 expedition: E101/39/6, 7, 8, 9). Cf. Scotland: the earl of Northumberland's muster rolls for expeditions in 1384 and 1385: E101/40/5; BL Cotton Roll, XIII, 8.

[150] E101/15/12. This document consists, in fact, of two muster rolls of Lancaster's men-at-arms (the first for the period 1 May to 8 September, the second, only a fragment, for the period 9 September to 12 November) and a *restauro equorum* list.

[151] For information on Lancaster's military retinue, see K.A. Fowler, 'Henry of Grosmont, first duke of Lancaster, 1310–1361', Ph.D. thesis, University of Leeds, 1961, appendix C: 9.

[152] E.g. Windsor castle, 1338–39 (E101/21/22); Isle of Wight, 1338–40 (E101/21/32); Dover Castle, 1344–49 (E101/531/21); Jersey, early 1340s (E101/23/28), printed in 'Documents relatifs aux attaques sur les îles de la Manche, 1338–45', ed. M.H. Marett Godfray, *La société Jersiaise pour l'étude de l'histoire. Bulletin*, iii (1877), pp. 39–46.

[153] E101/19/21: Edinburgh, 1335–36. E101/19/24: Edinburgh, 1336–37 (see *Bain*, iii, pp. 360–63). E101/19/27: Roxburgh, 1336. E101/19/40: Stirling, 1336–37. E101/21/16, 17: Perth, 1338. BL Cotton MS, Vespasian F. VII, no. 10: Berwick, 1338–39. E101/22/9: Berwick, 1339. E101/22/20: Edinburgh and Stirling, 1339–40. E101/22/21: Berwick, 1339–41. E101/22/40: Roxburgh, 1340–42. E101/23/1: Edinburgh and Stirling, 1340–42.

evidence from other sources – principally letters of protection, pardons and horse inventories, but also a few muster rolls for individual retinues serving in the Scottish March[154] – these garrison rolls allow us to investigate a most distinctive section of the military community of northern England: that which regarded the manning of royal fortresses as a semi-permanent career.[155] They also cast light on the military retinues of a number of English captains. Take, for example, the men who served under the command of Sir Richard Talbot.[156] He was in command of the Berwick garrison in the late 1330s and early 1340s, a period for which two garrison rolls have survived;[157] and in addition, there is a retinue roll of Talbot's men in the Scottish March during the summer and autumn of 1337,[158] and another of his *comitiva* whilst he was keeper of the town of Southampton in 1340.[159] These four rolls reveal a certain degree of continuity, and versatility, of military service. Fourteen of the men-at-arms who had served with Talbot in 1337 are also to be found in his retinue in the garrison of Berwick. Rather more striking, however, is the appearance of two of these Scottish border veterans, John Buktot and Richard de Tynemuth, in the small Southampton garrison in the spring of 1340. They are present on all four retinue rolls as men-at-arms, which would suggest either a close attachment with Talbot or that they were professional soldiers. Two other men appear in Talbot's retinue in both Scotland and Southampton: Richard Colingbourn and William Hanys. They are particularly interesting because, having served as archers on the south coast in 1340, they appear as hobelars in the Berwick garrison in 1341. Shifts in military status of this kind may have been commonplace in the mid-fourteenth-century military community, but they will rarely be detected unless a run of muster rolls is available.[160]

Muster records, such as those considered here, offer highly detailed, if fleeting, images of the military community in action. In their absence we must be content with a far more restricted view of army composition. Of the 150 or so men listed on Talbot's four retinue rolls, only three have enrolled letters

154 For example, the retinues of Sir John de Lisle in 1338 (E101/20/24), Sir John de Segrave in 1340 (E101/612/2) and Sir Thomas Wake de Lydel in 1342 (E101/23/25).

155 Cf. the Cheshiremen engaged in the defence of principality of Aquitaine in the second half of the fourteenth century (Morgan, *War and society in medieval Cheshire*, pp. 121–84).

156 For a summary of Talbot's career, see *GEC*, xii, part 1, pp. 612–14.

157 E101/22/9: roll of sixty-four men-at-arms (including four knights), thirty-one hobelars and forty-two archers serving in 1339–40. E101/22/21: includes a roll of forty men-at-arms, twenty-four hobelars and thirty-five archers serving in 1341. There is also a pay account, but lacking a muster roll, for Talbot's garrison in 1338–39: E101/21/30.

158 E101/20/18: roll of forty-two men-at-arms (including six knights) and forty horse archers.

159 E101/22/34: roll of thirteen men-at-arms (including one knight) and nine archers.

160 Cf. Pollard, *John Talbot and the war in France, 1427–1453*, p. 90; and A. Curry, 'The nationality of men-at-arms serving in English armies in Normandy and the *pays de conquête*, 1415–1450', p. 135.

of protection during this period.[161] Fortunately it is not always necessary to rely completely upon letters of protection and in this particular case there are two further documents which reveal a little more about Talbot's military companions at this time: a horse inventory drawn-up at the end of 1337 or early in 1338, and a *restauro equorum* account detailing losses during the spring of 1338.[162] The section of the inventory covering Talbot's retinue is rather unusual. Talbot is allowed three horses for 'son corps' (not including one for 'son baner') and of the remaining eighteen horses on the list, nine are not allocated to a named man-at-arms. Nevertheless, the two documents combined provide eleven names,[163] only one of which can be seen amongst the enrolled protections for this time.[164]

THE HORSE INVENTORIES

How does the view of military personnel provided by horse inventories compare with that offered by conventional muster rolls? In one respect the inventories must be regarded as an inferior source. Since the only horses to be valued were those of the 'armoured' military class, the inventories allow us to see the men-at-arms in an army, but not the mounted archers nor even the hobelars.[165] As a consequence, although a chronological series of inventories might enable us to trace patterns of mobility *within* the community of men-at-arms, such records cannot by themselves allow us to detect the ascent into that community by men from lower levels of the military hierarchy – as we sometimes can with collections of muster rolls. Nor could it be argued that the horse inventories (or related sources, such as *restauro equorum* accounts) offer anything approaching a comprehensive view even of the 'armoured' military class. Inventories were compiled at the start of only a proportion of campaigns during the Edwardian period. When they were drawn up, they would include all men-at-arms in receipt of royal pay, from the loftiest of magnates to the least substantial of esquires; and some armies, such as that involved in the War of Saint-Sardos, *are* blessed with unusually rich

---

161 Sir Adam de Shareshull (C71/17, m. 11; C71/18, m. 13); Philip de Buktot (C71/18, m. 13); Alexander de Chesewyk (C71/18, m. 3).

162 E101/35/3, m. 2; E101/388/5, m. 20. The latter shows that Talbot's retinue lost five horses from March to May 1338, with a total value of £51 13s 4d. Apart from Talbot himself, two men appear in both records. Whilst William de Eylesford's £10 horse can be seen to have been appraised and then lost shortly afterwards, Philip de Buktot had a £20 horse at muster but claims for the loss of a mount worth only 10 marks.

163 Eight of whom are familiar from Talbot's other Scottish muster rolls. The three extra names are John de Stanworth (full inventory), Sir Adam Banastre and John de Eylesford (*restauro equorum* account).

164 Philip de Buktot: the protection is dated 24 June 1338, i.e. after he lost his horse (C71/18, m. 13).

165 The inclusion of a list of horse archers at the end of Sir John de Tibetot's inventory in 1336 is highly unusual: E101/19/36, m. 5d.

collections of surviving appraisal records. But no royal army is illuminated by a complete set; and for a number of important expeditions, none of the original inventories have survived, leaving us (if we are fortunate) with nothing more than *restauro equorum* accounts.

The inventories which have survived from the Edwardian period are something of a mixed bag.[166] Some provide no more than a snap-shot image of a retinue at a particular moment: they have not been altered by subsequent annotations or additions and so do not reflect those changes in army structure and composition which were a feature of even short campaigns. A good example is the inventory of the earl of Cornwall's retinue, drawn up at Perth on 8 September 1336.[167] This is a most valuable document – for all too little is known about the personal following of the enigmatic younger brother of Edward III – but it is also a problematic one. It was compiled over five weeks after the retinue had entered the king's pay and the list does not tally exactly with the number of men-at-arms for whom pay was being provided during this period.[168] What is more, the inventory had a very short practical life, for the earl died on 13 September and his retinue appears to have withdrawn from active service as a result.[169] An unannotated inventory such as this takes us no further than the initial muster: it records those who intended to serve and there were always a few men who withdrew from service after their horses had been appraised. Such withdrawals can sometimes be seen in those inventories which have been annotated. For example, several names have been erased from Aymer de Valence's horse inventory of 1315 'quia non venit'.[170] Eustace de Hardreshull intended to join the expedition sailing for Gascony during the summer of 1324 and secured a protection for the period of his absence; but at the last minute he decided not to go and on the annotated version of the inventory, which was drawn up at the port of embarkation, his name has been crossed out and that of William de Hardreshull substituted.[171]

Most inventories acquired annotations and amendments during the weeks

---

166 For a sensibly sceptical approach to one set of inventories, see N.B. Lewis, 'The English forces in Flanders, August–November 1297', *Studies in medieval history presented to F.M. Powicke*, ed. R.W. Hunt, W.A. Pantin and R.W. Southern (Oxford, 1948), pp. 310–11.

167 E101/19/36, m. 1; the earl, one banneret, eleven knights and forty-nine esquires are listed.

168 The retinue (the earl, two bannerets, fourteen knights and sixty-eight esquires) were paid from 28 July. Sixteen of these men were absent for ten unspecified days during this period, but even allowing for this, there should have been more names in the inventory. BL Cotton MS, Nero C. VIII, fo. 240r.

169 Fourteen esquires seem to have left Perth during the course of the autumn, but the majority remained there with the earl's body until 8 December. It is no surprise to find that all of the retinue's appraised horses came through the campaign unscathed.

170 E101/15/6; cf. E101/20/17, m. 8, for similar erasures in Sir Ralph de Neville's retinue for 1337.

171 *CPR, 1321–24*, p. 429; E101/13/35, m. 2. Eustace did in fact go to Gascony in 1325: E101/16/39, m. 1d.

following their compilation and therefore offer evidence of fluctuating military fortunes and changing personnel. Such records are not free of interpretative problems. Take, for example, the other surviving inventories for the English forces in Scotland in 1336. They note when and where individual horses have been killed or 'redditi ad elemosinam', sometimes providing intriguing detail in the process; but they offer only a partial impression of the comings and goings of individual men-at-arms. In the case of Sir Ralph de Neville's retinue, the incomplete coverage of the horse inventory can be seen particularly clearly as a consequence of the chance survival of a range of associated records. The inventory certainly appears to list fewer men than it should: fifty-one men-at-arms have appraised horses, whilst the main *vadia guerre* account for this period allows pay for fifty-six.[172] However, a muster roll and a quite separate pay account, both now bundled with the horse inventories for this campaign, present a rather clearer picture.[173] They show that the composition of the retinue changed every few weeks as men joined and left the king's service. The peak strength of fifty-nine men-at-arms (thirty-nine in Neville's retinue and a detached unit of twenty, forming part of Henry de Percy's company)[174] was reached in late August and early September, but the muster roll shows that sixty-eight different men-at-arms (including Neville) served in the retinue during this period.[175] Of these, seventeen are not listed in the inventory: excluded are all those who joined the retinue on 14 June, plus four of the original company (who presumably left early or had inadequate horseflesh), one of the men who arrived in August and all four of those who appeared in November. Thus, it can be seen how the inventory came to be in its present form. All those who were members of the retinue on 13 to 14 May – a time when Neville himself was about to take a detachment to join Percy's retinue, but just after a new contingent had joined – are listed; and the only other addition was made when Sir Henry le Scrope arrived with a small company of five men-at-arms on 25 August, though for some reason one of his men, Thomas de Boulton, was not included.

It is not clear whether the seventeen men-at-arms who were not included in Neville's inventory in 1336 served without appraised horses and thus without any prospect of gaining compensation for any they might lose, or whether they were included in a different inventory, which has since been lost. The latter is a possibility, but the fact that all of the thirteen horses in Neville's section of the *restauro equorum* account for this campaign can be seen in the full inventory would seem to suggest otherwise.[176] In fact there is firm

---

172 E101/19/36, m. 3d; BL Cotton MS, Nero C. VIII, fo. 240v.

173 E101/19/36, mm. 4 and 4d; there are two versions of the pay account.

174 An indenture of retinue required Neville to serve under Percy with twenty men-at-arms: Bean, *From lord to patron*, p. 57.

175 Thirty-seven men began the campaign on 18 April; thirteen joined on 13 May, a further eight on 14 June, six on 25 August and four on 1 November.

176 BL Cotton MS, Nero C. VIII, fo. 281v.

evidence that some men were serving in 1336 without appraised warhorses. Sir William de Montagu received £100 in compensation for horses which had been lost, but had not been valued.[177] On the other hand, it is not unknown for a retinue's horses to be recorded on several inventories. For example, the surviving inventory roll for English forces in Scotland in 1338 includes only a part of Sir Henry de Percy's retinue. During the early months of 1338, Percy's retinue consisted of eighty-four men-at-arms,[178] but of these, only five knights and fifteen esquires had their horses appraised outside the walls of Dunbar castle on 2 February 1338.[179] Eighteen of Percy's men are included in a *restauro equorum* account for this campaign, but there is no repetition of the horses listed in the inventory,[180] so it can safely be assumed that an additional inventory must at one time have existed for all or part of Percy's retinue. Indeed, given that a *restauro equorum* account can bring together horses lost on many different occasions over a fairly lengthy space of time, it may well be that we have lost not one inventory for Percy's retinue, but a whole cluster.

In common with the other types of record which supply the names of military personnel, the horse inventories are not free of interpretative problems which to some extent affect the quality of the evidence supplied. An inventory may provide comprehensive coverage for a particular moment in time, but give no impression of subsequent changes in personnel. Alternatively, it may include some, but not all, changes in composition or it may embrace only part of a retinue, but without making this partial coverage apparent. Bundles of related documents often include a selection of these different 'types' of inventory. When both inventories and *vadia guerre* accounts are available, there will be, as often as not, an inexact match between the data they supply. But such problems should not be allowed to weigh too heavily in the balance, for as far as the study of the Edwardian military community is concerned, a bundle of horse inventories represents a source of unrivalled richness. To consider a practical example of this, let us examine more closely the collection of inventories compiled at the time of the Scottish expeditions of the later 1330s.

The military operations conducted against the Scots during the years 1336–38 are well served by surviving documentary materials. There are horse inventories and *restauro equorum* accounts for each of these three years[181] and,

177 Ibid., fo. 282r.

178 E.101/388/5, m. 14: Percy, one further banneret, sixteen knights and sixty-six esquires.

179 E.101/35/3, m. 2; these may have been new arrivals, although there is no indication of this in the *vadia guerre* account.

180 E.101/388/5, m. 19. The horses were lost during the relief of Edinburgh castle, at the siege of Dunbar and elsewhere in March, April and May 1338. The only man to appear in both inventory and *restauro equorum* account is John de Umfraville, but he has a different horse in each.

181 Horse inventories: E.101/19/36 (1336); E.101/20/17 (1337); E.101/35/3 (1337–38). Although no more precisely dated by the PRO (*List and Index No. xxxv*, p. 39) than *temp.* Edward III, the last of these can by internal evidence be assigned to the English operations in

in addition, a range of other records including a complete run of *vadia guerre* accounts. By comparing the evidence of the inventories with that of the pay-rolls, it is possible to calculate the proportion of serving men-at-arms who are known by name as a result of the valuation of their warhorses. Let us begin with the records for 1336.[182] Inventories exist for all of the retinues occupying the first two folios of the *vadia guerre* account and two of those on the third. Apart from the small company of John de Houton, who had been appointed to 'receive and review'[183] the English troops and who supervised horse appraisal, none of the retinues listed on the remaining six folios of the account appear in the extant inventory rolls. The coverage is therefore partial, but it is by no means modest, nor is it random. Most of the larger retinues are covered and these comprise a quite distinct section of the English forces serving in Scotland in 1336. Whilst no part of the small army brought by the king himself in June is included in the surviving inventories[184] (and with the exception of the earl of Cornwall's retinue, nor are any of the troops who arrived in Scotland later in the summer and during the autumn), the army which commenced service in May under the command of Henry of Lancaster is represented almost in its entirety.[185] Of the 520 or so men-at-arms serving with Lancaster, all except about forty are listed in the surviving inventories. Records are missing for two of the smaller retinues, accounting for twenty-two names, and only four-fifths of Lancaster's personal retinue are listed. But against these slight blemishes in the evidence must be set the remarkable parity, for the great majority of retinues, between the numbers of men-at-arms receiving pay and the numbers who appear with their horses in the inventories. When the match is not exact there is usually a straightforward explanation.[186] The apparent disparity between Sir John de Tibetot's inventory, which lists fifteen men-at-arms and his *vadia guerre* account, which allows pay for nineteen, is explained by the inventory itself: twelve mounted archers are shown to be providing the service equivalent to four men-at-arms. The inventories for Lancaster's army have not entirely escaped physical damage. Part of the membrane containing the retinues led by Lancaster and Warwick has been torn away, with the result that many of the names have

Scotland during the winter of 1337–38. *Restauro equorum* accounts are to be found among the Wardrobe and Exchequer accounts: BL Cotton MS, Nero C. VIII, fos 280v–82r, 284v–85r (1336 and spring-early summer 1337); E101/20/25 and E101/388/5, mm. 18–20 (for autumn 1337–38).

182 On the military operations during this year, see Prince, 'The army and navy', p. 335; Fowler, *The king's lieutenant*, p. 32; Morgan, *War and society in medieval Cheshire*, pp. 41–42.

183 BL Cotton MS, Nero C. VIII, fo. 243v.

184 For a discussion of the reason for this, see above pp. 106–8.

185 Lancaster was 'capitaneo et duci exercitus domini regis', consisting of about 500 men-at-arms and 1,000 mounted archers. See Appendix 1.

186 The unusual intermingling of the Neville and Percy retinues and the composite nature of Neville's inventory have been discussed above.

been partially or wholly lost.[187] Fortunately, the survival of related records serves to minimise the loss. A muster roll for Lancaster's retinue for the period 1 May to 8 September lists the names of two bannerets, sixteen knights and seventy-seven esquires: in total, ninety-five of the hundred men-at-arms for whom Lancaster received pay.[188] Twenty-one of Lancaster's men are also listed in the *restauro equorum* account for this year; but this record is of far greater value where Warwick's retinue is concerned, for it supplies the names of thirty men, of whom twenty-three relate to the part of the inventory which has been damaged.[189] All except three of the retinues with inventories in 1336 have corresponding entries in the *restauro equorum* account. Of these three, the earl of Cornwall's inventory (as we have seen) had a very short practical life, whilst that of Sir Robert de Tong consisted of only two names. Sir Thomas de Ughtred's inventory shows that one of his men did in fact lose a horse, a loss which has been omitted for some reason from the compensation account.[190]

There is only one retinue in the *restauro equorum* account for which there is no corresponding inventory: a small company commanded by Sir Geoffrey de Mortimer, which served from mid August until November. During this period two of Mortimer's men-at-arms lost their appraised horses.[191] Thus, of the 105 men-at-arms listed in the *restauro equorum* account, 103 appear in the surviving inventories. What should we conclude from this? Assuming that the *restauro equorum* account is a complete record of warhorse losses, it seems clear that horse appraisal was offered to only a proportion of English forces serving in Scotland in 1336. Lancaster's army came before the appraisers in the late spring, and a handful of other retinues later in the year. Montagu's retinue, as we have seen, did not, and he was awarded a gift of £100 to cover the cost of unappraised horses which had been lost. The lack of any reference to horse appraisal in the *vadia guerre* accounts for retinues outside Lancaster's command,[192] suggests that Montagu's predicament was not unique; but few were in as good a position to extract royal favours as the

---

187 Membrane 7: none of the horse valuations have been lost. Damage to m. 5 has affected the earl of Angus' retinue to a limited extent.

188 E101/15/12. The number of personnel appears in fact to have been 101: Henry de Rammeheye, was serving 'avec deux [unnamed] compaignons', whilst Sir Robert de Roos had four *wadletz* who are not separately listed.

189 BL Cotton MS, Nero C. VIII, fos 280v, 281r.

190 Robert de Longvill lost a 'hobby' worth 10 marks at Perth on 6 September. On the other hand, the *restauro equorum* account includes a number of equestrian fatalities which are not mentioned in the inventories (for example, in Lancaster's retinue). There are many minor discrepancies between these two records, particularly concerning horse descriptions.

191 BL Cotton MS, Nero C. VIII, fos 243r, 282r. These two lost horses are also listed on a separate *restauro equorum* fragment (E101/101/14, m. 4), together with two further *equi*, belonging to Sir John de Leukenore and his esquire, which do not appear in any other known record.

192 The association of the commencement of pay with the appraisal of horses, so common a

architect of the Nottingham castle coup. In fact, as we saw in Chapter 4, there are good reasons for thinking that horse appraisal was *not* at this time extended to armies fighting in Scotland under the direct leadership of the king. In this case, then, the pattern of documentary survival is very similar to the pattern of production, but this should be regarded as an exception rather than the rule. A glance at the records for 1337–38, for example, offers a different picture. Admittedly the correspondence between the inventories and the *restauro equorum* accounts for the early summer of 1337 is as close as it is for 1336; but, by contrast, it is clear from the compensation records spanning the period from the autumn of 1337 through to the spring of 1338 that the surviving inventories (which all date apparently from December 1337 or early 1338) represent only a selection of the original series.[193] In particular, none of those which must have been drawn up during the late summer of 1337 has survived.[194]

The dates given on many of the surviving inventories from 1336 show that for most retinues horse valuation coincided with the commencement of royal pay. This bundle of horse rolls offers, therefore, a remarkably complete record of the composition of a small English army at the very start of a period of service. There are admittedly few indications of subsequent changes in composition. Apart from the inventory for Neville's retinue, which gives some (albeit incomplete) indication of arrivals after the first muster,[195] the only notes in the inventories confirming that particular individuals continued in service at a certain date are comments on horse mortality. The annotations usually reveal the date and place of loss. From these scraps of information we can see that many in Lancaster's army took part in Edward III's dramatic ride into the Highlands in July.[196]

Although not as subtle and informative as we would like, the 1336 horse inventories provide as complete a view of the heavy cavalry of a small

feature of the accounts for Edward II's reign, is explicitly made in the case of the retinues of Lancaster himself, Warwick, Oxford, Angus, Buchan, Percy, Badlesmere and Bohun.

[193] E101/20/17 and BL Cotton MS, Nero C. VIII, fos 284v–85r; E101/35/3, E101/20/25 and E101/388/5, mm. 18–20. Seven retinues are included in the *restauro equorum* accounts, but not the inventories, for 1337–38. The earl of Gloucester's retinue appears in an inventory dated December 1337 (E101/35/3, m. 1) and in two quite separate *restauro equorum* accounts: the horses listed in the inventory match with those in one of these (E101/20/25, m. 3), but not with those in the other (E101/388/5, m. 19). The second of the accounts, itemising horses killed in February to April 1338, must be based on a later, lost inventory.

[194] Including, for example, that for the retinue of the earl of Warwick: four of his esquires lost horses during September and October 1337 (E101/388/5, m. 19).

[195] It may be significant that Neville, as Seneschal of the royal household, was directly involved in the process of horse appraisal. Awards of compensation for horse losses were made *per testimonium* Neville and John de Houton: BL Cotton MS, Nero C. VIII, fos 280v ff.

[196] For example, Ralph de Conyngsby's horse, valued at £10, was killed 'in montibus' on 20 July: E101/19/36, m. 3d.

mid-fourteenth-century English field army as could realistically be hoped for. The contrast with the larger, but less comprehensively documented, royal armies of the earlier 1330s is indeed striking. The materials for 1336 form, moreover, the most valuable part of an impressive block of inventory evidence which extends into 1338. Whilst the inventories for 1336 list the names of rather more than 500 men-at-arms,[197] the combined total for the following two years is about 700. The appraisal records for the army commanded by the earl of Warwick during early summer of 1337 supply the names of 341 men-at-arms, or perhaps about three-quarters of those in pay in early to mid June.[198] The comparable records for the period from autumn 1337 to spring 1338 – the campaign which petered out in the fruitless siege of Dunbar – offer the names of about 350 men-at-arms, or a little less than half of those receiving pay in the English field army at the start of the new year.[199] This is clearly the least well documented of the Scottish campaigns of the later 1330s, but the figure of 350 men-at-arms is also not strictly comparable with those of the preceding years, as the surviving retinue inventories supply no more than 275 of the names,[200] with the rest appearing only in the *restauro equorum* accounts for this campaign.[201] Yet to know the names of approaching half of the men-at-arms involved in an English expedition to Scotland represents, from the standpoint of many campaigns, a position of relative documentary abundance. Taken as a collection, the horse inventories, *restauro*

---

[197] This excludes the names lost from Warwick's inventory, but includes the extra evidence supplied by Lancaster's muster roll. As regards *horse values* for 1336, the total is nearer to 550.

[198] This is something of an estimate, as the evidence of the inventories cannot be matched to that of the pay-rolls quite as easily as in 1336. Some of the horse lists are not dated and there was a great deal of fluctuation in retinue size during the summer of 1337. Of the eleven retinues with more than twenty men-at-arms, seven (including the largest) appear amongst the inventories: E101/20/17; BL Cotton MS, Nero C. VIII, fos 245r–47r. For an illuminating discussion of Warwick's army in 1337, see N.B. Lewis, 'The recruitment and organisation of a contract army, May to November 1337'.

[199] For the size of the English forces 'during the first fortnight of the year 1338', see Prince, 'The strength of English armies', pp. 359–60.

[200] Inventories have survived for only a handful of the major retinues involved in the siege of Dunbar; and in sharp contrast with the inventories for 1336, those for the Dunbar campaign appear to be incomplete: others drawn up earlier or later have been lost. For example, the earl of Salisbury's inventory, compiled on 1 January, lists 86 men, but the *vadia guerre* account shows 130–140 men-at-arms in his company at this time: E101/35/3, m. 2d; E101/20/25, m. 3.

[201] There are, in fact, 296 entries in the horse inventories, but ten were extra horses for retinue captains or their (unnamed) banner bearers, and eleven other entries lack names. A number of the men-at-arms' names in the earl of Salisbury's retinue are only partially legible. Seventy-one names (20%) are unique to the *restauro equorum* accounts; a further thirty-nine appear both there and in corresponding inventories (E101/35/3; E101/20/25 and E101/388/5, mm. 18–20). Horse compensation records make little contribution to the 1337 total: all told, they provide only fifteen names and all of these are to be found in surviving inventories (E101/20/17; BL Cotton MS, Nero C. VIII, fos 284v–285r).

equorum accounts and other related records[202] place the English armies of 1336–38 amongst the best documented of the fourteenth century. They show, at an unusual level of detail, the English military community in action at a most important stage in Edward III's reign, when the principal focus of royal ambition was in the process of switching from Scotland to France.

The extent to which the horse inventories allow us to establish the names of knights and esquires serving in Scotland in 1336–38 is thrown into sharper relief when we consider the nominal data yielded by other sources. Had it been necessary to rely upon letters of protection, the nominal roll would have been shorter, less reliable and packed with members of knightly families. Whilst the horse inventories and associated documents for 1336 offer the names of over 500 men-at-arms, the Scottish Roll for this year lists fewer than 250 letters of protection.[203] The combined total for the years 1337–38 is even more striking: 300 enrolled protections,[204] as compared with the names of nearly 700 men-at-arms in the horse inventories and *restauro equorum* accounts. The global figures are actually rather misleading. On the one hand, the retinues which are fully illuminated by inventories are covered very much more thinly by protections than these figures might suggest; on the other, the enrolled protections do provide useful evidence of military service about which the inventories reveal nothing. Thus, whilst all except one of the 1336 inventories were compiled in May or early June, the great majority of the protections enrolled in 1336 have dates which fall during the second half of the year. Of the 520 men-at-arms serving in Lancaster's army during the early summer, no more than a handful have letters of protection;[205] but thirty-nine were issued in mid-August to Sir Anthony de Lucy's garrison at Berwick and twenty-one in late October to Sir Ralph de Stafford and his men.[206] The pattern of evidence for 1337–38 is broadly similar. There are lists of protections of respectable length for two retinues which lack inventories,[207] and very few of the men-at-arms whose horses were valued in May or June 1337 can be found to have had enrolled protections. For example, of the sixty men in Sir

---

202 Including, in 1337, the muster rolls for the retinues of Sir John de Mowbray, Sir Henry de Percy and Sir Ralph de Neville, which have been bundled-up with the horse inventories: E101/20/17, mm. 2, 4, 5, 6.

203 C71/16.

204 C71/17; C71/18.

205 There are no enrolled protections for Lancaster's own retinue (100 men-at-arms); but nine of the earl of Oxford's twenty men have them. More typical are the eight protections for the earl of Warwick's retinue, which consisted, in all, of seventy-four men-at-arms.

206 C71/16, mm. 6, 16. If the fifteen protections which had been issued in January are added, the Berwick garrison can be seen to have accounted for no fewer than 20% of the protections enrolled on the Scottish Roll in 1336: C71/15, mm. 3, 4.

207 Sir Ralph de Stafford's retinue has twenty protections (most with dates in April) and Thomas de Brotherton, earl of Norfolk's has thirty-four (mostly September): C71/17.

Ralph de Neville's retinue who are listed in the inventory drawn-up at Tweedmouth on 2 June, only two have protections on the Scottish Roll.[208]

In fact, there are even fewer protection recipients amongst the men listed in these inventories than there appear to be at first glance. Some of the men receiving a protection for service with a specified captain simply cannot be found in the inventory for that retinue. They may have arrived after, or left before, horse valuation had been completed. But some protection recipients did not actually serve, whilst others were not fighting men at all: servants and other non-combatants, along with a sprinkling of defaulters, mingle with real men-at-arms in enrolled lists of protections. Take, for example, Sir Thomas Wake's retinue in the summer of 1337. Although fourteen protections were enrolled for Sir Thomas and his men – apparently a very respectable proportion of the twenty-five whose horses were valued on 6 June – three are duplicates and four were issued to men who do not appear in Wake's inventory. Two of these unlisted men may have arrived several months after the original muster;[209] one of the others was probably a non-combatant. Thus, between a quarter and a third of the men-at-arms in Wake's retinue can be seen to have had enrolled protections.[210] If the majority of retinues in 1337–38 had a rather smaller proportion of protection recipients than this, there was at least one in which the percentage was substantially larger. Sir Giles de Badlesmere's company, paid from 6 December 1337, consisted of twenty-four men-at-arms and, appropriately enough, that is the number (plus the captain's banner-bearer) listed in his inventory.[211] Of these men, as many as sixteen had enrolled protections, dated 4 December, on the Scottish Roll. But there were four protection recipients who, though apparently members of Badlesmere's retinue, were clearly not serving in a military capacity.[212] This is an unusual case, in that a captain can be seen receiving protections for two-thirds of his combatant retainers (a third, or fewer, was more usual for Scottish campaigns); but it may be more typical in its suggestion of a 20% non-combatant or defaulting element amongst protection recipients. Indeed, on occasion, the non-participatory group amongst protection recipients was rather larger. Twenty-eight men have enrolled letters of protection for service in the earl of

---

208 Sir Ralph de Neville himself and one of his esquires, William de Crathorne: C71/17, m. 18.

209 Sir Gerard Salvayn has a protection, dated 30 May, for Wake's retinue, but does not appear in the inventory; his name has been crossed off Neville's inventory, with the words 'non venit'. A further protection, dated 24 July, may suggest that he did eventually join Wake's company. C71/17, mm. 19, 21; E101/20/17, mm. 8, 8d.

210 It should be noted that Wake's inventory may not have been complete. According to the *vadia guerre* account, the retinue consisted of forty men-at-arms from 7 May (BL Cotton MS, Nero C. VIII, fo. 245r); but it is unlikely that the four missing men are all to be found amongst these fifteen extra men-at-arms.

211 E101/20/25, m. 4; E101/35/3, mm. 1–2.

212 C71/17, m. 3. One of these four men was Robert Flemyng, parson of the church of *Berughby*.

Salisbury's retinue during the winter of 1337–38, but only ten of them are listed in the earl's horse inventory for this campaign (dated 1 January). Nearly eighty of the men on the horse list were serving without the security of an enrolled protection.[213] Some of the eighteen protection recipients who cannot be traced in Salisbury's inventory may nevertheless have been serving in a military capacity, for we know that about forty men-at-arms were excluded for some reason from the process of horse valuation.[214] But even allowing for this, and for a few late arrivals, it is clear that a significant proportion of the protection recipients were not members of the earl's fighting *comitiva*.

There is no denying the value of enrolled letters of protection: they are the most consistently available fourteenth-century military record, frequently offering data on both field armies and garrisons. For some campaigns, they are the only significant nominal source available. But we must not be blind to their weaknesses and, in particular, to the skewed impression of the military community which they provide. Most or all of a retinue's knights will appear in a list of protections, but only a selection of its esquires. To return to a previous example, all of the five knights in Giles de Badlesmere's retinue in 1337–38 have protections; but for the names of the eight esquires who do not, it is necessary to turn to the horse inventory, a source which, in addition, supplies the ranks of all who are named and the internal company structure of the retinue. The horse inventories, then, take us to the very heart of the military community, allowing us to see the shadowy, heterogeneous group of men who comprised the majority of men-at-arms. Much the same can be said of the *restauro equorum* accounts, although at first glance these appear a decidedly inferior form of military record. Since only a proportion of an army's appraised horses would be lost during the course of a campaign, the *restauro equorum* accounts will usually provide fewer names than are to be found in the enrolled lists of protection recipients. But even if comparatively modest, equestrian losses would usually be spread throughout the levels of the military hierarchy, thus ensuring that the resulting *restauro equorum* account offers a representative sub-set of all serving men-at-arms. If protections could be said to present a restricted view of a non-random selection of the military community, and full horse inventories a comprehensive view of that part of the community covered by surviving records, then we may well find that a *restauro equorum* account can provide a *random* sample: a sample which, rather than being weighted in favour of a particular section of the military community, is determined by the fickle fortunes of war.

Some *restauro equorum* accounts perform no more than a useful supporting role, filling gaps in the inventory evidence;[215] but if none of the original

---

213 C71/17, mm. 5, 11; C71/18, mm. 22, 23; E101/35/3, mm. 1d. and 2d.

214 The inventory lists eighty-six men-at-arms for 1 January, whilst there were 130 receiving pay at this time (and 140 soon after): E101/20/25, m. 3.

215 This is the case with the Scottish campaigns of 1336–38 and the War of Saint-Sardos (BL Additional MS 7967, fos 104r–106v).

inventories have survived, a *restor* account may well make a more important contribution. Much will depend upon the number of horses lost. The compensation records for the Scottish campaign of 1322 list only thirty-four appraised horses.[216] Far more substantial are the *restauro equorum* accounts for the Cambrésis-Thiérache campaign of 1338–39 and the Breton campaign of 1342–43. The Cambrésis-Thiérache records contain details of 540 lost horses, of which 450 were appraised mounts.[217] If attention is confined to *English* men-at-arms, the *restauro equorum* account yields about 330 different names, or in the region of 20% of those who were serving in the Low Countries in the autumn of 1339.[218] This global figure conceals significant variations at the retinue level. Some retinues, such as that led by Sir Walter de Mauny, are completely missing from the *restauro equorum* account,[219] whilst sixty (about half) of the earl of Salisbury's men are listed with lost horses.[220] The norm for several of the larger retinues is about 25%.[221] This is certainly not a large proportion. Enrolled letters of protection yield considerably more nominal data: perhaps as many as two-thirds of this army's men-at-arms appear with protections on the Treaty Rolls.[222] At times, indeed, the proportion of protection recipients was even larger. For example, whilst the pay-roll gives a figure of ninety men-at-arms for the earl of Northampton's *comitiva*, as many as eighty-eight men with enrolled protections can be assigned to the earl's retinue. Even allowing for the inclusion of non-combatants and some turnover of personnel, this suggests a remarkably high level of protection receipt. It is hardly surprising that the *restauro equorum* account furnishes the names of only three men who are not also to be found amongst the

---

[216] BL Stowe MS 553, fos 70r–71r. The rest of the *restauro equorum* section is devoted to the unvalued horses of men attached to the royal household, for the loss of which their owners were awarded a fixed sum: 40s

[217] *Norwell*, pp. xciii–xcv; 309–25. Over seventy of these horses were lost by foreign companies and a further handful of continental men-at-arms lost horses whilst serving in the retinues of English captains.

[218] Over 1,600 men-at-arms were in pay in 'English' retinues during the period 23 October to 16 November 1339: Prince, 'The strength of English armies', p. 361.

[219] Mauny had a retinue with a maximum strength of ten knights and thirty-three esquires: *Norwell*, p. 331.

[220] Salisbury's retinue (which consisted of just over 120 men-at-arms) lost sixty-five horses, but five of these were the earl's and one of his men (Sir Robert de Burton) lost two: *Norwell*, pp. 312, 327–28. The following discussion assumes that the pay-rolls offer an essentially accurate picture of manpower numbers; this, as we have seen, may be an unwise assumption to make.

[221] Twenty-one members of the earl of Northampton's retinue (total: ninety men-at-arms) lost horses; and twenty-four of the earl of Derby's (maximum ninety-four men-at-arms). *Norwell*, pp. 309–10, 312–13, 326–27.

[222] About 1,700 letters of protection and attorney appointments are to be found on the Treaty Rolls for 1338–39; allowing for a significant amount of duplication and renewal, about 1,000–1,100 separate individuals appear to be involved (*Treaty Rolls, 1337–39*; C76/14).

protection recipients in Northampton's retinue.[223] Turning to the earl of Salisbury's retinue, however, we find a different situation. Less than a third of his men-at-arms have enrolled protections (or attorney appointments) and yet because half of his military retainers lost a warhorse during the course of the campaign, we still know the names of nearly three-quarters of his retinue. More than half of those who are known by name – thirty-nine out of seventy-seven – appear *only* in the *restauro equorum* account. This retinue is as unrepresentative as Northampton's,[224] and yet it serves to underline a point which has emerged before: that horse inventories and, it seems, horse compensation accounts can do much to correct the skewed impression of aristocratic military service which dependence on protections tends to create. For whilst only half of Salisbury's men who appear in both protection and *restauro equorum* lists are esquires, of those whose names are to be found *only* as a result of losing a horse, three-quarters are men-at-arms who have not assumed the status of knight. Although offering far fewer names than the enrolled lists of protections, the *restauro equorum* account for the Low Countries expedition of 1338–39 appears to be providing something approaching a genuinely random sample of that section of the aristocracy which participated in this campaign. The earl of Salisbury's retinue shows this particularly well. Of the total paid men-at-arms serving under him at the end of the campaign, two-thirds were esquires; and of the sixty men listed in his *restauro equorum* account, two-thirds can be seen to have been esquires.

These conclusions apply equally well to the *restauro equorum* account for the Breton campaign of 1342–43.[225] At first glance, this seems a less promising record. Only 226 men are listed,[226] a figure which may represent about 12% of the total number of men-at-arms serving for pay during this campaign.[227] The proportion of men with lost horses is sometimes higher at the retinue level: the figure is 18.5% for the earl of Northampton's *comitiva* (with 200 men-at-arms, the largest in the army) and over 50% for Sir Thomas de Bradeston's. These higher retinue-level percentages are counter-balanced by the absence from the *restauro equorum* account of several large retinues (those led by the earls of Gloucester, Pembroke and Oxford, and Ralph, Lord Stafford), as well as the great majority of small companies. The coverage, then, is uneven;

---

[223] Sir Adam de Shirburn, Hugh de Neville and Nicholas de Meynill.

[224] The earl of Derby's retinue appears more representative for this campaign. Sixty-two (two-thirds) of his men have enrolled protections or attorney appointments, yet nine additional names are to be found in the *restauro equorum* account.

[225] E36/204, fos 86v–88r; see Appendix 2.

[226] The *restauro equorum* account includes 228 appraised horses, but the earls of Northampton and Devon each have two listed for their personal use.

[227] A reasonably accurate combined figure for the series of expeditions to Brittany in 1342 might be 1,900 men-at-arms. Some individuals will be included twice in this total (e.g. those who served under Mauny in the spring and then returned with the king in the autumn), but they would have had a separately appraised horse for the second period of service.

and since this *restauro equorum* account is a good deal shorter than that for the Cambrésis-Thiérache campaign, can we be confident that it still offers a random sample of men-at-arms? Whilst one in four of all men-at-arms involved in the Breton expeditions were bannerets or knights, the *restauro equorum* account appears to include a slightly smaller proportion of knights: forty-four men, or nearly 20% of those listed with lost warhorses.[228] But allowing for a sprinkling of undetected knights, the sample provided by the *restauro equorum* account would seem, as far as rank-structure is concerned, to be as near a representative sub-set of the whole army as is realistically likely to occur. Indeed, a slight bias in favour of the esquires would not be unwelcome, for as compared with the 226 names supplied by the *restauro equorum* account, 722 separate individuals (rather more than a third of all men-at-arms) have enrolled letters of protection for this campaign.[229] As we have seen, the majority of protection recipients were men concerned to achieve a degree of legal security for their property. Some would go a stage further and appoint attornies to ensure that 'seignorial administration continued unhindered' in their absence.[230] In 1342, 234 men did this before leaving for Brittany. Of these wealthy men, only eighteen had not also secured enrolment of a letter of protection.[231] These, then, represent the top stratum of the militarily-active aristocracy; for a view of the lower layers it is necessary to look elsewhere. First, it would be worth examining the *vadia guerre* accounts.[232] These supply as many as 255 different named individuals, including 158 who were not protection recipients and well over a hundred whose involvement in this campaign could not be ascertained from any other source.

---

[228] Only thirty-four men in the *restauro equorum* account are actually designated 'knights', but such records tend to be a less reliable guide to military rank than the full inventories from which their information has been drawn. Only two of the earl of Derby's men are termed 'knights', yet enrolled letters of protection indicate that at least a further three of the remaining sixteen men-at-arms were also of this status: Sir Adam de Everingham, Sir Richard de la Vache and Sir William de Silithwait (C76/17, mm. 24, 27, 39). With most retinues it is simply a matter of making very slight adjustments: eleven of the thirty-five men listed for Northampton's retinue are presented as knights and we would only wish to add a twelfth – Sir John de Hothum of Bonby (C76/17, m. 36).

[229] C76/17; C76/18; C61/54. It is difficult to be precise about this. Firstly, there will be a number (probably small) of non-combatants included amongst the protection recipients. Secondly, some sections of the army, notably the companies of Robert d'Artois and William de Kildesby, do not appear in the *vadia guerre* accounts and are, therefore, not included in the manpower total; but their letters of protection (including those for fourteen of Artois' men, and nine of Kildesby's) were enrolled with all the others on the Treaty Rolls.

[230] G.A. Holmes, *The estates of the higher nobility in fourteenth-century England* (Cambridge, 1957), p. 75. For an original letter of attorney issued by the earl of Northampton in July 1342, see DL25/1898 (printed in ibid., pp. 123–24). On the work of attornies, see Lloyd, *English society and the crusade, 1216–1307*, pp. 167–69.

[231] Amongst these eighteen were some very prominent men, including an earl and three bannerets.

[232] E36/204, fos 105v–10v.

The men mentioned in the pay accounts are, however, a very mixed bag. An interesting group are the leaders of small companies who were serving without the benefit of enrolled protections.[233] Such men could not rely upon a prominent captain to secure their letters of protection; perhaps, as ordinary knights, they lacked the authority or the experience to do so for themselves.[234] It is also useful to be able to identify the leaders of the archer companies. Men like John Ward, *ductor* of a company of eighty mounted archers from Cheshire, form an interesting section of the military community.[235] The great majority of the extra names supplied by the *vadia guerre* accounts belong, however, to members of the royal household and although a number of these were esquires, doubtless with good sword-arms,[236] many of them were servants and clerks who were not engaged in a military capacity.[237] If such men received *dona pro restauro equorum* they would usually consist of flat-rate payments of 40s for unappraised animals which had not been employed in war.

Although apparently offering many fewer names than the enrolled lists of protections, and somewhat fewer than are supplied by either appointments of attornies or the pay-rolls, the *restauro equorum* account for 1342–43 provides a much more rewarding view of the lower levels of the English military aristocracy than these other sources. About a third of the army's men-at-arms had protections and, appropriately enough for a source supplying a random sample, exactly a third (seventy-six) of the men listed in the *restauro equorum* account were protection recipients. The 150 men who do *not* have protections, and the slightly smaller subset of 139 men whose participation in the Breton campaign is known *only* as a consequence of their loss of a horse, are more important than their numbers might suggest, for they are representatives of those elements of the active military community which are otherwise too rarely visible to historians. The great majority of them are English

---

[233] These include Sir Thomas Beaumont, Sir Robert Fitz Elys, Sir Nicholas Langford, Sir Thomas Swinnerton and Alan, Otes and Thomas Holand. Most retinue commanders are also to be seen in the Issue Rolls, receiving part or all of their wage-arrears at the Exchequer. For example, the three Holand brothers had not yet been fully paid off in February 1346: E403/336, m. 31. The Issue Rolls supply a few names which do not appear in the *vadia guerre* accounts: for example, Thomas Forcer and eight other (unnamed) archers were still receiving arrears for the Breton campaign in October 1345 (E403/336, m. 7).

[234] Cf. in 1355: the Black Prince's administration can be seen actually supplying parchment to the royal Chancery, apparently to expedite the issue of protections for the prince's men: Tout, *Chapters*, v, p. 342 n. 6.

[235] E36/204, fo. 109v. For Ward's career, see Morgan, *War and society in medieval Cheshire*, pp. 43–49.

[236] For example, Edward atte Wode and Guy Brian, who both lost horses during the course of the campaign. Edward atte Wode was to meet a violent death during the Crécy campaign: *The life and campaigns of the Black Prince*, ed. Barber, p. 35; *CIPM*, ix, no. 35.

[237] See, in particular, the lists of names on fos 108r and 108v of the *vadia guerre* account.

esquires;[238] but they also include a few foreign mercenaries, both of knightly rank and ordinary men-at-arms – men like Sir Walter de Landesbergen, a veteran of the Cambrésis-Thiérache campaign.[239] The retinue-level distribution of these shadowy figures is interesting. In some companies they constitute exactly, or very nearly, two-thirds of the men listed in the *restauro equorum* account,[240] but in others, they form a significantly larger proportion. Of the twenty-four men in Sir Walter de Mauny's retinue who lost warhorses, only four had enrolled protections. In fact, fewer than than 10% of the men who served with Mauny during either the spring or autumn campaigns in 1342 appear to have secured protections. It may be that a captain of foreign extraction without long-established tenurial ties in England was more likely to recruit large numbers of landless English 'professionals' and foreign mercenaries.

The men whose involvement in the Breton expeditions of 1342–43 is known to us only through their appearance in the *restauro equorum* account represent little more than 7% of the total number of men-at-arms receiving pay. With only three of the larger retinues do such men amount to significantly more than 10% of men-at-arms.[241] Yet the equestrian compensation account allows us, more fully than any other source, to see the men who occupied the lower levels of the aristocratic military community. There are other sources, certainly, but their contribution to the nominal roll of men-at-arms will either be very slight or unreliable. For example, only a handful of deponents before the Court of Chivalry in the 1380s claimed involvement in the Breton campaign of 1342–43,[242] whilst the evidence yielded by charters of pardon, although impressive in bulk,[243] is less useful than it might be because it is usually insufficiently explicit about the military status of pardon recipients. Knights are often distinguished,[244] but it will normally be difficult to separate ordinary men-at-arms from archers. The same will apply to many

---

238 Although comprising two-thirds of the men in the *restauro equorum* account, they include only ten of the forty-two knights listed there.

239 *Norwell*, pp. 318, 339.

240 For example, the retinues of the earls of Northampton and Derby: twenty-two out of thirty-seven and twelve out of eighteen respectively.

241 The retinues of Sir Hugh le Despenser, Sir John Darcy *senior* and Sir Walter de Mauny.

242 E.g. Thomas Rose esquire., who had served with Sir Robert de Morley 'en le viage del Counte de Norhampton a le rescuse de Brest' and Sir Robert de Marennys who had been at the siege of Vannes: C47/6/1, nos. 20, 27. Neither of these men had enrolled protections for this campaign.

243 Enrolled pardons are primarily to be found on the Treaty Rolls (C76/17, C76/18), but there is also a fragment of a separate pardon roll for this campaign (C67/28A). Not all pardons were enrolled, however, so for completeness it would be necessary to use the authorising warrants included in the privy seal files (C81/287 onwards), together with the few surviving original captains' warrants (e.g. SC1/39, nos. 144–48, from the earl of Northampton).

244 For example, Sir John de Rotse: C81/289, no. 15321.

casual references to military service which are to be found elsewhere in the records. It is not usual for a source to be as informative as that recording Henry de Percy of Wiltshire's receipt of a pardon for not assuming knighthood in response to the distraint order of 1341. The Patent Roll entry adds that he had become a knight on 29 August 1342, whilst serving with Robert de Artois at the siege of Morlaix.[245]

Many of the men-at-arms serving in Edwardian armies, particularly for expeditions in Scotland, saw no necessity for a letter of protection. These included men who, although born into the lesser gentry, had (as yet) little or no landed property of their own; men of rather more obscure origins seeking to make a living, and perhaps gain social advancement, through regular campaigning; and men from abroad, placing their swords at the disposal of the English crown. With such men as these, our knowledge of an individual's career will often rest soley, or very largely, on his appearance in a series of inventories. The Scottish campaigns of 1336–38 are particularly well-documented and it is not surprising that there are a number of men-at-arms who can be seen serving during these years, but at no other time. Most were employed consistently in the retinues of either Sir Henry de Percy or Sir Ralph de Neville[246] and, as members of the military community of the north, they were perhaps unlikely to participate in the early campaigns of the French war. But away from the retinues of the northern magnates are to be found fighting men of a more cosmopolitan frame of mind. That we know anything of the career of William Carless in the later 1330s arises from his inclusion in three separate inventories for the retinue of the earl of Warwick; he is next seen serving in Brittany in 1342–43.[247] The inventories cast occasional shafts of light on a number of other men whose careers straddle the opening campaigns of the French war. Some, like Carless, were loyal to a single lord;[248] others were free-agents, offering their services to a series of captains for expeditions in both Scotland and France. Robert de Longvill served under three different captains in Scotland, but remained with the last of them for the campaign in the Low Countries in 1338–39.[249] Edmund de Roos, who fought in at least two different retinues in Scotland in the later 1330s, appears

---

245 *CPR, 1343–45*, p. 33.
246 For example, Gilbert de Ergom and William Walram (Neville) and Walter de Wessington and Richard de Horsleye (Percy). In each case these men appear in the full inventories for 1336 and 1337 and in the *restauro equorum* account for 1338.
247 BL Cotton MS, Nero C. VIII, fo. 281r; E101/20/17, m. 7d; E101/388/5, m. 19. Carless lost a horse in Brittany (E36/204, fo. 88r), but he also had a protection for this campaign (C76/17, m. 39).
248 For example, Nicholas de Gernon, who served with Henry of Lancaster in 1336 (E101/15/12), 1342 (E36/204, fo. 86v) and 1349–50 in Gascony (E403/355, m. 19; E404/508, no. 78).
249 E101/19/36, m. 2d; E101/20/17, m. 10; E101/35/3, m. 2; *Norwell*, p. 316.

to have moved from one company to another during the course of the first campaign of the French war.[250]

The bare-bones of Edmund de Roos' early career in arms have been uncovered by a fortunate combination of horse inventory and *restauro equorum* entries, but many others are likely to have been less well served by the uneven survival of evidence. Take, for example, three of Roos' companions in Giles de Badlesmere's retinue in 1337–38, the esquires Henry Banaster, Martin Durward and Simon Peverel. None of them appears to have served again in the king's armies; but this may be a false impression arising from the fickleness of the records. It is quite likely that they never acquired the necessary position in either landholding society or the military community to justify letters of protection on a regular basis.[251] Others, however, did manage to achieve this status. For some, the Scottish campaigns of 1336–38 marked the early stages of careers which were to be recorded regularly in the military records during the following decades. Another of the esquires listed in Badlesmere's inventory in 1337–38, Eymer de Rokesle, was to serve repeatedly in the campaigns of the French war until his death at Crécy, but on only one occasion must we rely upon a horse inventory in order to see him.[252] Richard de Totesham, who was a loyal campaigner with the earl of Northampton in the early campaigns of the continental war and who became a middle-ranking captain in Brittany in the mid 1340s,[253] is listed amongst the ordinary esquires of William de Bohun's inventory in 1336.[254] Some of the men who appear on the military scene for the first time in the 1336–38 horse inventories were to become celebrated figures in the French war. For example, amongst the esquires in the earl of Salisbury's retinue who had their horses valued at

---

[250] E101/19/36, m. 2d; E101/35/3, m. 1. During the Cambrésis-Thiérache campaign, Roos is listed with a lost warhorse in two different retinues: *Norwell*, pp. 311, 314. This may well be the 'Esmond de Rose esquire' who, at the age of sixty-nine 'et outre' gave (rather limited) evidence to the Court of Chivalry in the Lovell-Morley case (C47/6/1, no. 91) and the Edmund Rose who was constable of Gorey castle, Jersey, 1372–77: J. Le Patourel, *The medieval administration of the Channel Islands, 1199–1399* (London, 1937), pp. 64, 129.

[251] Martin Durward does have an enrolled protection for the winter of 1337–38, but the proportion of Giles de Badlesmere's retinue who had protections for this campaign is unusually high: C71/17, m. 3.

[252] Rokesle lost a horse during the first major campaign of the French war (*Norwell*, p. 311); he then served overseas in 1340, 1344 and 1346–47 (C76/15, m. 23; C76/19, m. 23; *Crecy and Calais*, pp. 97, 184–85). His death is mentioned in *Eulogium historiarum sive temporis*, ed. F.S. Haydon, 3 vols, Rolls Ser. (London, 1858–63), iii, p. 211.

[253] Protections in 1338–39 (*Treaty Rolls, 1337–39*, nos. 291, 653), 1340 (C76/15, m. 20) and 1342–43 (C76/17, m. 36). In early 1344 Totesham was the leader of the largest retinue (thirty men-at-arms and sixty mounted archers) in a small expeditionary force sent to Brittany: E403/331, m. 29. He is well known as the keeper of the besieged town and castle of Roche Derrien at the time of Dagworth's dramatic rescue in 1347: *Avesbury*, p. 389; Sumption, *The Hundred Years War*, pp. 473, 495, 573–75.

[254] E101/19/36, m. 5.

Mepath on 1 January 1338 are to be found Walter de Bentley and Nigel de Loring.[255]

In addition to illuminating the military careers of the lower strata of the English aristocracy, the horse inventories also allow us glimpses of foreign men-at-arms in the pay of the English crown.[256] The role of non-native contingents in Edwardian armies can be traced to some extent in the *vadia guerre* accounts, but it is the horse inventories and *restauro equorum* accounts which bring the historian a little closer to the members of these mercenary companies.[257] In addition, foreign mercenaries form a small but interesting component of retinues led by English captains in all theatres of war. For example, an inventory for the earl of Oxford's retinue, drawn-up at Tweedmouth on 12 May 1336, includes a John de Ispaynea;[258] and a certain Theodoric de Allemannia lost a horse whilst serving in Sir Reginald de Cobham's retinue in 1338–39.[259] Some of the alien men-at-arms were more exotic. Sir Ralph de Neville's retinue in 1337 included a man who was called, interchangeably, *Henry Sarasyn* or *Sarasyn Henry*.[260]

Since we lack muster rolls for the great majority of Edwardian field armies, the horse inventories stand out as the most important source for the names of the militarily-active section of the aristocracy, and particularly for the names of men occupying the middle and lower levels of the chivalrous class. No other source allows us such a clear view of the rank and file men-at-arms who constituted the greater part of the 'heavy cavalry' element in an Edwardian army. Other classes of record do have a part to play in the reconstruction of this most important section of the military community, and yet consideration of the particular merits of these sources serves only to emphasise the weight and distinctiveness of the evidence supplied by the horse inventories.

Ordinary men-at-arms figure prominently in the surviving records of armorial disputes heard before the Court of Chivalry.[261] There can be no clearer

---

[255] E101/35/3, m. 1d. Cf. Loring's appearance in the pay-rolls for this campaign (E101/20/25, m. 5), a reference noticed long ago by J.E. Morris (*Welsh wars of Edward I*, p. 52). A 'Walter Betle' is listed amongst Sir Richard Talbot's garrison at Berwick in 1339 (E101/22/9, m. 1), but the future renowned soldier of the war in Brittany was surely serving in the Low Countries at this time: *Norwell*, pp. 318, 321.

[256] This includes Scotsmen: e.g. Patrick de Dunbar, who is mentioned in inventories in both 1337 and 1338 (E101/20/17, m. 7; E101/35/3, m. 2) and had acted as a guide for English forces advancing 'versus partes de Selkirk' in 1335 (BL Cotton MS, Nero C. VIII, fo. 274r).

[257] The records of the Cambrésis-Thiérache campaign offer good examples: *Norwell*, pp. 315–16, 321, 324. Cf. K.H. Schäfer, *Deutsche Ritter und Edelknechte in Italien während des 14. Jahrhunderts* (Paderborn, 1911), a study drawing on similar records.

[258] E101/19/36, m. 6; with a 10 mark horse which died at Perth on 26 June.

[259] *Norwell*, p. 314: a £14 horse.

[260] E101/20/17, mm. 6, 8; he had a horse valued at £8.

[261] On the Court of Chivalry, see M. Keen, 'The jurisdiction and origins of the Constable's court', *War and government in the Middle Ages*, ed. J. Gillingham and J.C. Holt (Woodbridge, 1984), pp. 159–69.

indication of their standing in the military community, that their knowledge and experience of war and its usages carried great weight, than the fact that of the deponents in one of the Court's armorial cases in 1380s, between the Lovell and Morley families, esquires and 'gentlemen'[262] outnumbered knights by two to one. In providing their evidence, the deponents often reveal a good deal about their own military careers, with the beginning and end points clearly signposted and specific, sometimes colourful, details on campaigns in which they had played a part.[263] In many cases a window is opened on a career about which the conventional record sources reveal little or nothing. Many of the deponents would remain beyond normal visibility for the greater part of their careers, whether as regular participants in the king's great expeditions, specialists in garrison service[264] or naval operations,[265] or in their ventures into *hethenesse*.[266] Some, like John Raven, would be wholly unknown, were it not for their depositions.[267] It is instructive to see veterans of the Scottish wars following their king's ambitions as they were redirected towards France; and particularly revealing, even with deponents who are well-known to history, to hear men speak about their earliest experiences of war.[268] For many, these

---

[262] E.g. Giles Albert *gentil homme*: C47/6/1, no. 78; cf. nos. 168, 170, 175 and 177. Other deponents claimed to be of 'gentil sanc'.

[263] The most recent discussion of this evidence, focusing on a case heard in 1408–10, is M. Keen, 'English military experience and the Court of Chivalry: the case of Grey v. Hastings', *Guerre et société en France, en Angleterre et en Bourgogne, XIVe–XVe siècle*, ed. P. Contamine, C. Giry-Deloison and M. Keen (Lille, 1992), pp. 123–42.

[264] Sir Hugh Browe of Tushingham testified that his twenty years in arms had been spent 'in the garrisons and companies in France, and never on the great expeditions': *Scrope-Grosvenor*, i, p. 82.

[265] Most of Thomas Rose's deposition (C47/6/1, no. 20) relates to naval activities: he served with Sir Robert de Morley during the earl of Northampton's passage to Brittany in 1342 and also when Morley 'fist arder v villes des costes de Normandie'; and he was at the battles of Sluys and Winchelsea.

[266] In the Scrope-Grosvenor case, 'at least fourteen individual crusaders either testified or were mentioned, their exploits of the previous twenty-five years stretching from Egypt to Lithuania': C. Tyerman, *England and the crusades, 1095–1588* (Chicago and London, 1988), p. 259. For an earlier discussion of crusading activity as revealed by Court of Chivalry evidence, see M. Keen, 'Chaucer's knight, the English aristocracy and the crusade', *English court culture in the later Middle Ages*, ed. V.J. Scattergood and J.W. Sherborne (London, 1983), pp. 45–61.

[267] John Raven told the Court of Chivalry of his service at Sluys, the siege of Tournai, Crécy and Calais, the sea-battle off Winchelsea and the Reims campaign: C47/6/1, no. 6. Perhaps he is to be identified with the John Raven (d. 1395) who is commemorated by a neat little brass in the parish church at Berkhampstead: J.E. Cussans, *History of Hertfordshire*, 3 vols (London, 1870–81), iii, p. 69.

[268] For example, Sir Guy de Brian stated that he had been first armed at Stanhope Park (1327): *Scrope-Grosvenor*, i, p. 76. Five of the thirty-two deponents from the 1380s who claimed to have been involved in the Crécy campaign, emphasised that this had been their first experience of war.

[269] Keen, 'English military experience and the Court of Chivalry: the case of Grey v. Hastings', p. 131.

had been acquired at the age of fourteen or fifteen.[269] Those deponents who mentioned the names of the captains with whom they had served, as many did in the Lovell-Morley case, were laying down evidence of particular value, enabling us to distinguish the restless professional soldier from the man with more permanent ties of allegiance. Beyond the details of particular spells of service can be seen the networks of social relationship within the late-fourteenth-century aristocracy. Competing family claims to particular armorial bearings were supported by groups of knights and esquires bound by common interests. For example, in the Scrope v. Grosvenor case we find the mobilisation of a local military community behind one of the claimants and the weighty support of a magnate's extended military affinity for the other.[270]

For all the useful detail on individual military careers, the vivid tales of deeds of arms and the informed comment on heraldic matters – all of which allow us some insight into the mental world of a military class, it is important to recognise the limitations of the Court of Chivalry evidence. The deposition records as we have them are terse and to the point; these are not potted military memoirs.[271] Indeed, many depositions are very slight: of the five hundred or so which survive from the 1380s,[272] many reveal comparatively little, either because of the youth of the deponents, or because their comments are insufficiently precise to be very helpful. Often it is clear that a deponent is not telling the whole story about his former military life. William de Thweyt, for example, furnishes an impressive list of six expeditions in which he claims to have played a part; but he fails to mention his service in Gascony in 1337–39, Brittany in 1342–43 and Ireland in 1344–46.[273] Many men, it seems, mentioned only what they felt to be strictly relevant to the case in hand, whilst one or two of the older deponents admitted to having defective memories.[274] It is possible, moreover, that the records as we have them do not represent complete transcripts of the proceedings. As far as the compilation of nominal rolls for individual armies is concerned, for most campaigns (except the most recent) the Court of Chivalry depositions can do no more

---

[270] Many of the supporters of Sir Robert Grosvenor's claim to 'azure a bend or' in 1386–7 were militarily experienced Cheshiremen (Morgan, *War and society in medieval Cheshire*, pp. 128–30; Bennett, *Community, class and careerism*, p. 166), whilst many of Sir Richard Scrope's deponents were members of John of Gaunt's affinity. See also M. Keen, 'Chivalrous culture in fourteenth-century England', *Historical Studies*, x (1976), pp. 14–22 and B. Vale, 'The Scropes of Bolton and Masham, c. 1300–1450', D.Phil. thesis, University of York, 1987, pp. 95–105.

[271] Cf. John Carington's early fifteenth-century memoir, which includes details of service : W.A. Copinger, ed., *History and records of the Smith-Carington family* (London, 1907), pp. 72–76.

[272] This excludes the 'civilian' depositions, although these can occasionally be useful in an indirect way.

[273] C47/6/1, no. 92; C61/49, m. 17; C76/18, m. 9; C260/57, m. 28.

[274] For example, Sir Nicholas de Goushill: C47/6/1, no. 29.

than fill some of the gaps left by the more conventional military records. It is certainly useful to have a few extra names, for example, for Edward III's army at Halidon Hill,[275] and perhaps a few dozen for the Reims campaign roll; but the real strength of this category of evidence is less quantitative than qualitative. The depositions present a picture of the military community in action which, in highlighting the roles of both the knights and esquires in Edwardian armies, is far more balanced than that presented by the evidence of letters of protection, and which, therefore, serves to supplement and reinforce the evidence offered by the horse inventories and other full muster records.

To supplement the mainstream records for fourteenth-century armies, there are several further types of documentary source which can occasionally cast shafts of light on otherwise undocumented military service. First, there are the records generated by the operation of various forms of military obligation. Particularly useful are the proffer rolls which have survived for some of the early fourteenth-century armies for which feudal service was required. The roll for the Scottish campaign of 1322 lists the names of over five hundred proffered men-at-arms, the great majority of whom were ordinary esquires.[276] Also useful as a source of military service data are the records arising from the implementation of a short-lived military assessment based on landed income, introduced in the mid-1340s. Hundreds of enrolled writs of exoneration record the fulfilment of landowners' military obligations by named men-at-arms, hobelars and archers, principally in the Crécy-Calais campaign, but also in other parts of France and in Ireland – and occasionally in the 'maritime land' and garrisons in England.[277] Valuable as these military assessment records are, not only for the names of combatants, but also for such matters as the composition of retinues, campaign mortality and the shifting company structures of a royal army long in the field, they are unique to the busy campaigning years of the mid 1340s.

It is quite common to find an unusual and distinctive source supplementing the standard military records. For example, nominal data for several royal armies can be found in heraldic manuscripts. The 'Song of Caerlaverock' mentions by name eighty-seven bannerets serving in Edward I's army in

---

[275] The Lovell-Morley roll offers four men who claim to have been present at Halidon Hill (Henry de Hoo, Sir Nicholas de Goushill, William de Thweyt, and Sir Alan de Heton: C47/6/1, nos. 10, 29, 92 and 97), whilst the Scrope-Grosvenor depositions provide a number of additional names (e.g. William Hesilrigge and Sir Adam de Everingham: *Scrope-Grosvenor*, i, pp. 126, 240–41). The prior of Marton revealed that his church possessed an embroidered coat of arms worn by Sir Alexander de Neville at this battle (ibid., i, pp. 139–40). None of these men have enrolled protections on the Scottish Roll for 1333.

[276] C47/5/10. On the patchy coverage of the nominal records for the army of 1322, see Powicke, *Military obligation in medieval England*, pp. 163–64.

[277] Wrottesley has calendared many examples in *Crecy and Calais*; for a discussion of these sources, see Ayton, 'The English army and the Normandy campaign of 1346'.

1300.[278] The Carlisle Roll of Arms lists 277 knightly participants in Edward III's great Scottish expedition of 1335.[279] Needless to say, a good deal can be gleaned from financial records which are not *exclusively* concerned with military expenditure. Of non-royal records, a particularly good example is the *Journal* of the Black Prince's treasurer John Henxteworth, which is an invaluable source for the names of ordinary participants in the prince of Wales' expedition of 1355–57.[280] On the whole, however, army service data appear only irregularly and in an anecdotal fashion in records which are not first and foremost military records. Whilst we certainly welcome such vivid glimpses of the battlefield as we sometimes find in the records of pleas of knighthood before the Exchequer,[281] records such as these contribute no more than a tiny proportion of the names in a typical reconstructed army roll. What they do is fill out an individual's known career, whilst adding something to our understanding of the aristocracy's role in war.

This is certainly the case with memorial inscriptions. These rarely consist of anything more than a simple reference to the circumstances and place of death, as with Sir Roger de Felbrigg's brass in Felbrigg church, Norfolk, which tells us that he died in Prussia and was buried there. It is certainly most unusual to find a potted biography, as we have with the inscription commemorating Sampson Meverell's career in Lancastrian Normandy, which was made famous in a classic article by K.B. McFarlane.[282] Surely the gem is the inscription which John Leland took down from Sir Matthew de Gourney's tomb in Stoke-sub-Hambdon church, Somerset:[283]

> Icy gist le noble et vaillant Chivaler Maheu de Gurney iadys seneschal de Landes et capitain du Chastel Daques pro nostre seignor le roy en la duche de Guyene, que en sa vie fu a la batail de Beuamazin, et ala a apres a la siege Dalgezire sur le Sarazines, et auxi a les baitailles de Le scluse, de Cressy, de Yngenesse, de Peiteres, de Nazara, Dozrey, et a plusours aultres batailles et asseges en les quex il gaina noblement graund los et honour per le space de xcvi ans, et morust le xxvi jour de Septembre lan nostre seignor Jesu Christ mccccvi que de salme dieux eit mercy, amen.

278 *The siege of Carlaverock*, ed. N.H. Nicolas (London, 1828); Prestwich, *War, politics and finance under Edward I*, pp. 69–70.

279 Cambridge, Fitzwilliam Museum MS 324; see Denholm-Young, *The country gentry in the fourteenth century*, pp. 101–5; cf. *Catalogue of English medieval rolls of arms*, ed. A.R. Wagner, Soc. of Antiquaries, *Aspilogia*, i (London, 1950), pp. 54–56. The last few folios contain the names of several dozen 'German' mercenaries.

280 Morgan, *War and society in medieval Cheshire*, pp. 109–10; Hewitt, *The Black Prince's expedition*, appendix C, pp. 195–216.

281 For example, John de Colby, who claimed to have taken-up knighthood at Crécy: E159/121, m. 228. See also, Powicke, *Military obligation in medieval England*, pp. 176–77; Saul, *Knights and esquires*, p. 42.

282 K.B. McFarlane, 'Bastard feudalism', *BIHR*, xx (1945), pp. 171–72.

283 *The itinerary of John Leland in or about the years 1535–1543*, ed. L.T. Smith, 5 vols, repr. (London, 1964), i, p. 159.

Here we have a summary of an individual's career in arms, somewhat similar to the evidence supplied in Court of Chivalry depositions; and like that evidence, there are both gaps in Gourney's career profile (in this case allowed for by the phrase 'other battles and sieges')[284] and facts which cannot be corroborated. In Gourney's case, there is no real reason to doubt the veracity of the inscription; but we may safely dismiss the suggestion on Peter Legh's brass in Macclesfield church (installed a century after his death), that he had been 'at the batell of Cressie'.[285]

For every man who emerges temporarily into the light as a combatant member of the chivalrous class through a chance documentary reference, or who sketches the outline a fuller martial personality in a Court of Chivalry deposition, there are many more who acquire something of a military identity by virtue of being recorded with an appraised horse in a particular captain's inventory. The association with a captain, whether based upon a short-term contract or a more permanent retaining tie, allows us to find a place for the man-at-arms within the network of relationships which bound together the military community. Few sources can contribute as much as the horse inventories to our knowledge of the composition of military affinities in the Edwardian period. The benefit is perhaps greatest with the retinues of lesser captains, which are often poorly illuminated by other records. That only one of Sir John de Stryvelyn's twenty men-at-arms in Brittany in 1342–43 has an enrolled letter of protection is a common enough problem with retinues of this size.[286] A return to the bundle of inventories for the 1336 Scottish campaign, which include several companies comprising ten to twenty men-at-arms, illustrates how records with comprehensive coverage can transform the study of military relationships. The inventory for Sir John de Segrave's company, for example, lists three knights and fourteen esquires, only four of whom have enrolled letters of protection.[287] Admittedly a single roll offers no more than a glimpse of a captain's recruitment policy. It cannot demonstrate the permanence, or otherwise, of personal ties between the captain and members of his *comitiva*; but a series of rolls might begin to do this. In the case of Sir John de Segrave, we find that only two of the eighteen men in his retinue in 1336 were also serving under his banner in the Scottish March during the

---

284 For example, Gourney participated in the Reims campaign (C76/38, m. 11); and sailed with the earl of Cambridge to Portugal in 1381 (C47/2/49, no. 2).

285 Morgan, *War and society in medieval Cheshire*, p. 139.

286 Walter de Heslerton: C76/17, m. 27. For the brief Scottish campaign during the previous winter, Stryvelyn had served with twenty-three men-at-arms, none of whom had an enrolled letter of protection: E36/204, fos 102r, 106v; C71/21. Cf. the muster roll of Stryvelyn's garrison at Edinburgh castle on 18 May 1337: E101/19/24, m. 12; partly printed in *Bain*, iii, pp. 362–63.

287 E101/19/36, m. 5d; C71/16, mm. 27, 14. Two of the protection recipients were knights; a third, John Waleys, served with Segrave in the Low Countries in 1338–39 (*Norwell*, p. 315).

summer of 1340.[288] Over a shorter period we might expect greater stability of retinue composition, particularly when a captain has a regional power-base and can count upon the support of its military community. For example, the retinues of Henry, Lord Percy (d.1352) drew consistently upon the gentry of Yorkshire: the great majority of his men-at-arms in 1336 (forty out of fifty-five) were also in his *comitiva* for the campaign during the following year.[289]

If some of their strengths are shared by conventional muster rolls, the inventories possess one fundamentally important feature which sets them apart from other forms of muster record: the warhorse valuations. In an inventory, an individual's place in the chivalrous community, his military status, is indicated not only his association with a particular captain, but also by the value of his warhorse. Considerations of precedence and seniority are, of course, built into all types of military record. In the case of Sir Richard Talbot's muster rolls, examined earlier in this chapter, Philip de Buktot's name appears high in the list of *homini ad arma* on the three rolls in which he is included, and it is no surprise to find that he has become a knight by the mid 1340s.[290] But the horse inventories offer more than this: military status is given a numerical value. Having such a convenient means of assessing a man's position in the military community is particularly useful for those who are unlikely to appear often in the military records. Of the men who are listed in either the inventory or the *restauro equorum* account for Sir Richard Talbot's retinue in 1337–38, few have enrolled protections for the campaigns which immediately precede and follow;[291] but rather more information is provided by the appearance of four of them on other horse inventories.[292] These lesser men-at-arms may be shadowy, faceless figures, whose lives are largely hidden from us; but if we know the value of their warhorses, then at least we have a measure of their position in the military hierarchy. If we have several consecutive values at our disposal, then perhaps we have the means of detecting changes in both military status and attitudes of mind.

288 Stephen de Segrave and John de Wetwang, two of thirty-nine men-at-arms serving with Segrave in 1340: E101/612/2.

289 E101/19/36, m. 3; E101/20/17, mm. 4, 5, 9.

290 *Crecy and Calais*, p. 172.

291 Only Sir Adam de Banastre, 1339 (C76/14, m. 4); and Richard le Hunter, 1344 (C71/24, m. 4: Berwick garrison).

292 Richard le Hunter and Geoffery de Wytrington in 1336 (E101/19/36, mm. 5d, 3); Philip de Buktot and John de Eynesford (*alias* Eylesford) in 1342 (E36/204, fos 87r, 88r).

6

The Warhorses of the Edwardian Aristocracy

Only a comparatively small proportion of the horse inventories that are known to have been compiled during the Edwardian period have survived the passage of the centuries, yet careful scrutiny of those that have been preserved can yield information about thousands of warhorses taken to war and appraised during the reigns of the three Edwardian kings. Admittedly there is much about these animals that we would dearly like to know, but about which the inventories and *restauro equorum* accounts reveal nothing. It is certainly to be regretted that neither the height nor the age of the appraised horses were recorded. Despite these limitations, the inventories offer an unrivalled source of information about the warhorses of the Edwardian chivalrous class, particularly if the data, and especially the valuations, are viewed in bulk as well as in detail, and if analysis embraces both the horses and their owners. Such analysis, moreover, can tell us much about the character of the aristocracy itself, for by examining their warhorses, it is possible to assess the social, economic and military status of men-at-arms serving in Edwardian armies; and also, perhaps, to perceive something of their varied responses to the changing nature of warfare during a period in which the English military machine was radically transformed.

CHRONOLOGICAL OVERVIEW

It would be appropriate to begin by attempting a broad overview of the evidence. Table 6.1 shows the mean values of warhorses for English royal armies from the 1280s to the 1360s, the full period for which inventories are available.

Presented in this form, the horse valuation data exhibit a number of striking features. The level of values in the 1360s appears to have been broadly similar to that prevalent at the time of Edward I's second Welsh war in 1282,[1]

---

[1] There had been an increase in warhorse prices since the time of the Norman Conquest. A respectable warhorse would cost about £2 in c. 1100 and, a hundred years later, perhaps 10 marks: F. Barlow, *William Rufus* (London, 1983), p. 284 n. 92; A.L. Poole, *Obligations of society in the twelfth and thirteenth centuries* (Oxford, 1946), p. 52. Matthew Paris' estimate of the value of an ordinary man-at-arms' horse in 1257 (four to ten marks) accords well with the evidence of the earliest inventories from Edward I's reign: H. Chew, *The English ecclesiastical tenants-in-chief and knight service* (Oxford, 1932), p. 93. Although the increase in warhorse prices is usually seen as an indication of qualitative

Table 6.1: Mean warhorse values, 1282–1364

Date and Place of service		Mean Value (£)	No. of horses
1282	Wales	8.5	635
1297	Flanders	11.2	907
1298	Scotland	10.2	1356
1311–15	Scotland	11.9	1267
1324–25	Gascony	11.6	689
1336	Scotland	8.5	542
1337	Scotland	7.6	341
1337–38	Scotland	10.6	367
1338–39	Cambrésis-Thiérache	16.4	376
1342–43	Brittany	14.3	228
1350s	Gascony	12.3	90
1359–60	France	9.0	1160
1361–64	Ireland	7.8	135

Sources: Wales, 1282: C47/2/7. Flanders, 1297: E101/6/28; E101/6/37. Scotland, 1298: *Gough*, pp. 160–237. Scotland, 1311–15: *Bain*, iii, pp. 413–32 (1311–12); E101/15/6 (1315). Gascony, 1324–25: E101/35/2, m. 7; E101/16/38; E101/17/2; E101/13/35; E101/16/39; E101/17/31; BL Additional MS 7967, fos 104r–6v. Scotland, 1336: E101/19/36. Scotland, 1337: E101/20/17. Scotland, 1337–38: E101/35/3. Cambrésis-Thiérache, 1338–39: *Norwell*, pp. 309–25. Brittany, 1342–43: E36/204, fos 86v–88r. Gascony, 1350s: E101/172/4; E101/170/20, fos 75r–76r; E403/355, m. 19. France, 1359–60: E101/393/11, fos 79r–116v. Ireland, 1361–64: E101/28/11; E101/29/5.

but there had been significant fluctuations during the intervening period. The tabulated data suggest an increase in the general level of warhorse values during the reign of Edward I,[2] a levelling-off under Edward II, and a slight fall during the first decade of Edward III's rule. Far more marked is the contrast between the average values for the Scottish campaigns of the later 1330s and those for the early campaigns of the Hundred Years War, but the peak achieved by English warhorse values during the Cambrésis-Thiérache campaign was not sustained. The warhorses taken to Brittany in 1342–43 appear,

---

improvement, prompted by heavier armour and equipment, it does seem broadly in line with general price movements for livestock: H.E. Hallam, ed., *The agrarian history of England and Wales, II, 1042–1350* (Cambridge, 1988), pp. 745–55, especially table 7.4: 'Livestock prices by decades, 1160–1356'.

2   The sharpness of the increase between 1282 and 1297 is to some extent disguised by the mean value for the Flanders expedition, which is held down by some very low valuations (e.g. the appraised mounts of a group of Welsh constables; they include a rouncey valued at 12s: E101/6/28, m. 3). Cf. Table 6.2.

on average, to have been rather less highly priced than those involved in the first campaign of the war, and the values for the 1350s and 1360s show a far more marked decline. Thus, the mean value of the warhorses appraised at the start of the Reims campaign of 1359–60 was only a little over half the peak-level of twenty years earlier, and with the Irish expeditions of the 1360s we find a return to the low level of the early 1280s.

Presenting the valuation data as a chronological series of calculated means reveals the general trend in warhorse values during the Edwardian period, but it also conceals a great deal. In particular, it gives no impression of the spread of individual values lying 'behind' the mean value for each expedition. Table 6.2, a grouped frequency distribution, summarises the spread of values found in each separate collection of inventories.[3]

Table 6.2: Spread of warhorse values, 1282–1364

Date and Place of service		Under £10	£10–£19.9	£20 and over
1282	Wales	66%	27%	7%
1297	Flanders	49%	40%	11%
1298	Scotland	59%	30%	11%
1311–15	Scotland	50%	31%	19%
1324–25	Gascony	51%	33%	16%
1336	Scotland	61%	35%	4%
1337	Scotland	71%	27%	2%
1337–38	Scotland	61%	28%	11%
1338–39	Cambrésis-Thiérache	34%	37%	29%
1342–43	Brittany	47%	30%	23%
1350s	Gascony	50%	34%	16%
1359–60	France	71%	27%	2%
1361–64	Ireland	78%	18%	4%

The proportions of low-value (under £10) and high-value (£20 and over) warhorses can be seen to have fluctuated a great deal, whilst the middle-value range was more stable, accounting for between 25% and 35% of all warhorses for most sections of the data series. The surviving inventories for the Scottish campaigns of the later 1330s are dominated by low-value horseflesh.

[3] Cf. M. Vale, 'Warfare and the life of the French and Burgundian nobility in the late Middle Ages', table 2: a frequency distribution of 'Valuations of horses in English Gascony' based on three inventories listing Gascon nobles and their horses: E101/14/4 (1294–97); E101/13/30 (1297); E101/17/38 (1323).

The rolls for 1337 in particular have only a handful of high-value horses,[4] whilst the higher mean for the winter 1337–38 expedition can be seen to have been achieved through an expansion of the high-value group, combined with a commensurate reduction in the numbers of low-value horses.[5] The peak in the series of mean values, the first campaign of the Hundred Years War, is seen in Table 6.2 to have resulted from a very significant shrinkage in the numbers of low-value horses, with a corresponding growth in the high-value category.[6] The slight dip in the overall level of values for the Breton campaign was the consequence of increased numbers of low-value horses, whilst still holding a high proportion, nearly one in four, of high-value mounts.[7] Although it must be interpreted with a certain amount of caution, the data suggesting a decline in warhorse values after the 1340s are particularly interesting. The spread of values for service in Gascony in the 1350s is practically identical to that for the War of Saint-Sardos of the mid 1320s; but, as we saw in Table 6.1, the data for the Reims campaign indicate a sharp fall in the level of warhorse values in England and the trend downwards appears to be continued with the Irish expeditions of the 1360s. Table 6.2 shows this development to have been the result of a dramatic collapse in the numbers of high-value horses,[8] and a massive consolidation in the low-value range: about three out of four warhorses were appraised at less than £10. This compares with two out of three in the early 1280s, but by the later fourteenth century, the low-value range had become narrower, for it no longer included horses valued at under 100s as it had earlier in the century.[9] One hundred shillings was now the minimum acceptable value and a great many horses were

---

4   Seven with valuations of £20 and one appraised at £40.

5   Forty-one horses valued at £20 or more, with twelve of these having valuations of £40 or above.

6   About 9% of warhorses had values of £40 or above, an extraordinarily large proportion of highly priced animals. For the Falkirk inventories, for example, the equivalent figure is 2%.

7   6% had values of £40 or above.

8   The data for the Reims campaign may be a little misleading. Because the information appears in aggregated form in the original source, only a very small subset is available for analysis in Table 6.2: there is disaggregated information for only sixty-six individual horses. Although the mean value of this subset (£8.3) is only a little less than that for the whole group of 1,160 horses, it probably includes a rather smaller proportion of high-value horses than would be truly representative. Of the 135 warhorses appearing in the Irish expedition inventories of the 1360s, only five fall into the high-value category; four were valued at £20, the fifth was the earl of Stafford's 80 mark destrier.

9   The Welsh and Scottish campaigns of the late thirteenth and earlier fourteenth century show a declining presence of low-value horses: those appraised at less than £5 represent 21% of the total in 1282, 15% in 1298 and about 10% of those in the inventories of the later 1330s. For overseas expeditions from the time of the War of Saint-Sardos, the minimum valuation appears to have been £5. In fact, most horses valued at less than £10 for continental campaigns were registered at either 100s, 10 marks or £8.

assessed at exactly this amount.[10] The imposition of a minimum valuation may well have served to keep the overall level of values a little higher than would otherwise have been the case.

Before proceeding any further, it would be prudent to assess the quality of the sources which lie behind the summary statistics presented in Tables 6.1 and 6.2. A relatively abundant collection of horse inventories has survived from the reigns of Edward I and Edward II (particularly the former), and it would have been unrealistic, and perhaps unnecessary, to attempt to utilise them all. The first five entries in the tables summarise the valuation data contained in a representative selection of these documents. For the period after the accession of Edward III rather fewer records of this kind are available and the tables make use of the data from practically all significant horse inventories and related sources to have survived from the remainder of the fourteenth century. Even so, suitable data are available for only a minority of years and a striving for completeness has necessitated the use of a varied collection of records including not only full inventories, but also *restauro equorum* lists and summary accounts. Thus the data series is very incomplete, inconsistent in provenance and contains parts which may not be strictly compatible.[11] But does it still offer an essentially reliable body of information on the warhorses of the Edwardian military community?

It would be perfectly natural to assume that the most reliable parts of the data series would be those which are based entirely upon complete inventories. This is certainly the case when the inventories are lengthy and embrace all, or at least a very significant proportion, of an army's contingent of men-at-arms. In the event, not a single major military operation is illuminated by a *complete* set of inventories, and few are blessed with more than very partial coverage. Conclusions are always more securely based upon a substantial body of evidence, but the main problem arising from the incompleteness of the surviving inventories is not simply lack of bulk; it is that the available data may not constitute a representative sample of the now admittedly unobtainable whole. Some attention will be devoted in due course to the relationship between levels of warhorse values and the standing of retinue commanders, but suffice to say at this stage that a collection of inventories that embraces only a selection of an army's retinues may well be offering a distorted impression of the level of warhorse values for the army as a whole.

---

[10] For the Irish expeditions of the 1360s as many as 35% of appraised warhorses on the surviving inventories are given values of 100s. The pattern is not consistent at the retinue level: 50% of Sir Eustace d'Auberchicourt's men had 100s horses, but only 14% of the earl of Stafford's.

[11] For this reason, the data have been left in the form of annual mean values, and the more sophisticated forms of presentation appropriate for prices data have not been attempted.

Armies are themselves 'samples', each with an individual character. An army included only a proportion of the active military community and the make-up of its personnel, together with the quality of the warhorses which each man-at-arms chose to bring on campaign, was very much determined by the circumstances and locality of service. To establish with confidence the individual character of armies, it is necessary to be sure that due allowance has been made for the 'distortion factor' introduced by incomplete collections of inventories.

Many of the gaps in the inventory evidence arise quite simply from the hazards of time, but there is an additional cause of incompleteness, particularly prevalent during the reigns of the first two Edwards, which is that inventories were only compiled for those sections of armies which were receiving royal pay.[12] The horses of feudal contingents, and of those serving voluntarily but without pay, were not recorded. In the main, it is unlikely that their mounts would differ significantly in quality from the appraised warhorses of paid troops. Nevertheless, the problems arising from the incompleteness of the evidence need always to be borne in mind, even when dealing with the most ample collections of inventories. In the case of Edward I's reign, there are several such collections for important royal armies and the data provided by three of these, for the second Welsh war of 1282, the Flanders expedition of 1297 and the Falkirk campaign of 1298, have been included in Tables 6.1 and 6.2.[13]

After the turn of the century, evidence on this scale for major expeditions is less frequently available. Horse inventories are lacking for all of the royal expeditions to Scotland during Edward II's reign.[14] What we have instead are horse lists for smaller forces: a miscellany of retinue-level inventories which form a weighty, exceedingly varied but essentially unfocused collection. Perhaps the most substantial single set concerns a group of English garrisons in Scotland in 1311–12.[15] There are 773 appraised horses listed in these inventories with a mean value of £9.5, a low figure which reflects the nature of the

---

12 Moreover, as we have seen, the valuation of warhorses was no longer an automatic accompaniment to paid military service under Edward III.

13 On the inventories for the second Welsh war and the Falkirk campaign, see Prestwich, *War, politics and finance under Edward I*, pp. 50–51, 68–69. The inventories for 1298 list over 1,300 men and may provide an essentially complete record of paid men-at-arms, yet 'there were probably two or three times as many unpaid cavalry in the English army' (Prestwich, *Edward I*, p. 481). On the two major inventory rolls for the Flanders expedition, see N.B. Lewis, 'The English forces in Flanders, August-November 1297', *Studies in medieval history presented to F.M. Powicke*, ed. R.W. Hunt, W.A. Pantin and R.W. Southern (Oxford, 1948), pp. 310–11.

14 Evidence for the warhorses involved in the Bannockburn campaign is restricted to a small collection of Wardrobe debentures concerned with *restauro equorum* payments: E404/482, files 31, 32. A *restauro equorum* account exists for the 1322 campaign, but it is surprisingly brief (thirty-four appraised horses), given the hardships which the English army is said to have endured: BL Stowe MS 553, fos 69v–71r.

15 BL Cotton MS, Vespasian C. XVI, fo. 12r–19v; printed in *Bain*, iii, pp. 413–32.

service involved and the fact that the garrison rolls include very few knights.[16] The men of these garrisons do not constitute a typical sample of the chivalrous class of the 1310s. If we might expect to see a balanced cross-section of the military community in the composition of a major royal army, then in garrison personnel will surely be found a very distinctive sub-set of that community. The smaller collections of inventories from Edward II's reign are a very mixed bag. On the one hand, there are the retinues of veteran captains of the border country, like Sir Andrew de Harcla. The majority of those who served with Harcla were local men. They had low-value warhorses (75% were valued at less than £10), presumably suited to the rough campaigning terrain, and so the mean value for Harcla's retinue was never high: from £6 to £9.[17] On the other hand, there is the earl of Pembroke's small army which served in the Scottish March in the summer and autumn of 1315. A total of 293 warhorses have an average value of £18.4, with one of the four retinues in Pembroke's command having a mean as high as £22.[18] Here are to be seen the flower of the English military community, with a most impressive array of horseflesh:[19] men like Robert, Lord Mohaut, who was able to afford an £80 horse for himself and to provide an 80 mark mount for his retainer, Sir John de Bracebridge.[20] On the evidence of this inventory, J.E. Morris suggested that there had been an increase in horse values since Edward I's reign.[21] But the level of values prevalent in Pembroke's force is, as much as those of the English garrisons and Harcla's borderers, unlikely to be typical of the broader chivalrous community at this time.[22] The earl of Pembroke was one of the foremost political and military figures of his day and his retinue included a high proportion of knights and bannerets (over 25%), which would tend to

---

[16] Fewer than 5% of the men-at-arms listed are knights. The pay-rolls for these garrisons (*Bain*, iii, pp. 393–412) show that the small number of knights listed in the inventories is not the consequence of scribal imprecision.

[17] £9 in January 1313; £6.8 in July 1314; £6 in November 1314. In each case, Harcla's company numbered a little over thirty men; in the second and third cases, nearly half of his men had horses valued at less than £5. E.101/14/15, mm. 2, 4, 5.

[18] E.101/15/6. Retinue-level means: the earl of Pembroke (£19.3), Bartholomew de Badlesmere (£18.5), Robert de Mohaut (£22.2) and Richard de Grey (£13.7). For Pembroke's operations, see J.R.S. Phillips, *Aymer de Valence, earl of Pembroke, 1307–1324* (Oxford, 1972), pp. 88–91.

[19] Of the men in Pembroke's army, 75% had warhorses valued at £10 or more; 35% at £20 or higher. By comparison, of the garrison troops discussed above, 40% had horses appraised at £10 or above and only 10% at £20 or higher.

[20] E.101/15/6, m. 2; for Mohaut's provision of Bracebridge's horses, see M. Jones, 'An indenture between Robert, Lord Mohaut and Sir John de Bracebridge for life service in peace and war, 1310', *Journal of the Society of Archivists*, iv (1972), pp. 384–94; Bean, *From lord to patron*, pp. 53–54.

[21] Morris, 'Mounted infantry in medieval warfare', p. 85 n. 2.

[22] The same may be said of the twenty-two destriers and coursers, with a mean value of £32, listed in a Wardrobe Book, dated 4 Edward II (Bodleian Library, Tanner MS 197, fo. 42r): see J.S. Hamilton, 'Piers Gaveston and the royal treasure', *Albion*, xxiii (1991), p. 204 n. 15.

inflate the number of high-value warhorses in the inventory. The norm, which might be expected for a major field army composed of a more balanced selection of personnel, probably lay somewhere between the extremes which have been considered.[23] Accordingly, in Table 6.1, the evidence of the Scottish garrisons and Pembroke's army has been combined in a single figure: £11.9. The resulting mean value is offered only very tentatively, but it is probably not altogether misleading.

That the mean value for the early 1310s is, indeed, of the right order of magnitude is suggested by the data for the English expeditionary forces in Gascony in 1324–25. The army involved in the War of Saint-Sardos is one of the most fully documented of the later Middle Ages. An excellent set of pay-rolls offers a minutely detailed view of the shifting size and composition of the army's many small component companies.[24] As for the names of those who served in the army, our main source is a collection of horse inventories.[25] Although not a complete set, they do offer a very impressive body of evidence, listing 329 men and warhorses from the earl of Kent's retinue and the fleet which arrived in the autumn of 1324, and 360 from the second fleet, which reached Gascony in May 1325.[26] It is unlikely that the loss of a proportion of the original inventories has introduced a serious element of distortion into the evidence.[27] The picture presented is, indeed, a very consistent one. The mean for the first fleet (217 values) is £10.7, whilst that for the second (234 values) is £10.3. Although the corresponding figure for the warhorses in

---

[23] For example, Sir Henry de Percy's retinue, serving from Carlisle in 1306, had a mean value of £14: E101/612/15, m. 1.

[24] The *vadia guerre* sections of Nicholas Huggate's account book: BL Additional MS 7967, fos 30r–75r. This can be supplemented by a number of further accounts: E101/17/5; BL Additional MSS 17,363 and 26,891, fos 1r–49v; BL Cotton MS, Julius C. IV, section 16 (Latin and French versions of parts of the pay-roll). For the course of events, see *The War of Saint-Sardos*, ed. P. Chaplais, *(1323–1325)*, Camden Soc., 3rd ser., lxxxvii (1954); cf. N. Fryde, *The tyranny and fall of Edward II, 1321–1326* (Cambridge, 1979), chapter 10 and Vale, *The Angevin legacy and the Hundred Years War, 1250–1340*, pp. 227–44.

[25] The earl of Kent's expeditionary force: E101/35/2, m. 7. The 'first fleet': E101/16/38, E101/17/2, E101/13/35. The 'second fleet': E101/16/39, E101/17/31 (Warenne's retinue). The first, fourth and sixth of these records have not hitherto been identified. In all, the inventories provide the names of nearly 700 men-at-arms, about twice as many as appear in the enrolled lists of protections for this campaign (CPR, 1321–24; CPR, 1324–27; C61/36). There is an additional roll listing over two hundred pardon recipients (C61/37).

[26] Although 689 separate warhorses are listed, a quarter of them (173) lack a valuation, either because omitted from the inventory (as with the whole of Warenne's retinue, and part of Kent's) or because of documentary damage. It is also evident that some of the original inventories have not survived, for the *restauro equorum* section of Huggate's book of accounts (BL Additional MS 7967, fos 104r–106v) lists seventy-six appraised horses, and thirty-five of these cannot be traced in any of the existing inventories.

[27] The mean value of the thirty-five lost horses which do not appear in the inventories is admittedly rather high (£15.7); but, as we shall see, *restauro equorum* accounts quite often include a larger proportion of high-value horses than appear in the original inventories.

Kent's company is much higher (£18.9), this is wholly in keeping with the earl's status and a fair reflection of the calibre of the men in his retinue.[28]

The War of Saint-Sardos is the last major continental expedition for which a substantial collection of original inventories has survived. Thereafter, the only comparable surviving materials are those which were drawn up for the Scottish expeditions of 1336–38. They form an impressive corpus of documents, but their coverage is far from complete. As was seen in Chapter 5, the most comprehensively covered expeditionary force is that led by Henry of Lancaster in the early summer of 1336; and yet, even in this case, Lancaster's troops formed only part of the English forces serving in Scotland during this year. It is also a little unfortunate that these inventories illuminate minor military operations directed by magnates, rather than major expeditions led by the king himself. Similar limitations affect the value of the only other collection of original inventories from Edward III's reign, a small bundle of appraisal records for a selection of the retinues serving with Lionel, duke of Clarence's expeditionary force in Ireland in 1361–64.[29] Table 6.3 summarises the contents of these documents, which yield a little under a hundred valuations.[30]

Table 6.3: Mean warhorse values for retinues
serving in Ireland, 1361–64.[31]

Captain	No. of horses	Mean value
Sir Eustace d'Auberchicourt	20	£6.7
Sir Robert de Ashton	6	£6.1
Sir John de St Lowe	6	£6.7
Sir William de Windsor	7	£7.7
Sir Thomas de Hoggeshawe	5	£6.3
Earl of Stafford	50 (21)	£10.0 (£9.5)

[28] Only 30% of warhorses in Kent's retinue were valued at less than £10, and 45% at £20 or more; the corresponding figures for the first and second fleets are more than 50% and about 10%.

[29] P. Connolly, 'The financing of English expeditions to Ireland, 1361–1376', *England and Ireland in the later Middle Ages*, ed. J. Lydon (Blackrock, Co. Dublin, 1981), p. 105, gives the size of the army as 197 men-at-arms and 670 horse archers, quoting E101/28/21 (the relevant fos are 3v–6v, 7v–9r, 10r–10v). Cf. Prince, 'The strength of English armies', p. 369; J.A. Watt, 'The Anglo-Irish colony under strain, 1327–99', *A new history of Ireland, II: medieval Ireland, 1169–1534*, ed. A. Cosgrove (Oxford, 1987), p. 386.

[30] E101/28/11.

[31] Only the first two-thirds of the roll for the earl of Stafford's retinue can be read with absolute confidence, but the mean value given here is reliable enough; this is supported, indeed, by the corresponding figure for Stafford's lost horses (in brackets in the table): E101/28/21, fo. 14v. Of those included in Table 6.3, only Stafford's retinue served from the autumn of 1361 (his horses were valued in Bristol on 18 August). The retinues of Windsor

The evidence is incomplete on two levels: not all of the retinues in Clarence's army are included,[32] and of those that are there, several are not completely listed.[33] The overall mean of £8.5 has clearly been inflated by the high-value horseflesh of Stafford's retinue.[34] The other retinue-level means are all in the region of £6 to £7; and turning to the sadly faded inventory of Sir William de Windsor's retinue, drawn up in Liverpool on 1 February 1364,[35] we find that the average of the forty or so horse values which can be read with reasonable confidence (the great majority), is £6.2.[36] The figure of £7.8 in Table 6.1 is based upon all of these data. If it is perhaps a little speculative, bearing in mind the incompleteness of the records and their variable legibility, it is unlikely to be too wide of the mark.

If the appraisal data for the Irish expeditions of the early 1360s are derived from a combination of imperfect inventories and an insubstantial *restauro equorum* account, for the French campaigns of the preceding decades we must rely wholly upon records of horse losses. *Restauro equorum* accounts are necessarily only partial in their coverage, for only a proportion of an army's appraised warhorses would be lost during the course of a campaign. For this reason, such records should always be handled with caution. But provided that the number of horses lost is both fairly large and forms a significant proportion of the total number appraised (say, at least 10%), it is likely that the equestrian values listed in the *restauro equorum* account will be broadly representative of those of the original inventories. For example, 19.5% of the horses listed in the surviving inventories for the Scottish campaign of 1336 are to be found in the corresponding *restauro equorum* account; and the mean value of the horses in the full inventory is £8.5, whilst that for those which have been lost is £8.7.[37] The lists of warhorses lost during

and Hoggeshawe were paid from June 1362 (but their horses were valued later), those of d'Auberchicourt, Ashton and St Lowe, from March or April 1363: E101/28/21, fos 5r, 7v, 8r, 10r, 10v (the *vadia guerre* account).

32 Of those serving from the autumn of 1361, most notably the duke's own retinue (five knights, sixty-four esquires and seventy archers), but also Sir John de Carreu's company, do not have horse inventories: E101/28/21, fos 3v, 6v.

33 Only Ashton's and St Lowe's companies are fully covered; about half of d'Auberchicourt's men-at-arms and considerably fewer of Windsor's and Hoggeshawe's are listed. Windsor's inventory is in fact a list of lost horses: it tallies exactly with his entry in the *restauro equorum* account.

34 He was the effective commander of the expedition and his retinue was the largest in the army: one banneret, seventeen knights, seventy-eight esquires and a hundred mounted archers at the outset of the campaign (E101/28/21, fo. 5r). The *restauro equorum* account, listing thirty-five horses with a mean value of £8.9, is also strongly influenced by the horseflesh of Stafford's retinue (E101/28/21, fo. 14v).

35 E101/29/5.

36 As the first three entries, including Windsor's own horse, are missing, we might expect this mean to be a slight under-estimate.

37 In the case of the Scottish expedition of the summer of 1337, only 4.7% of the horses listed in the full inventories were lost. Whilst the mean value of these sixteen horses is

the Cambrésis-Thiérache campaign of 1338–39 and the Breton campaign of 1342–43 are both of respectable length, the former consisting of 450 horses (though fewer than 380 of these were lost by members of 'English' retinues) and the latter of 228. Since these figures represent, respectively, in the region of 20%[38] and about 12%[39] of the total numbers of horses appraised, it would seem probable that the *restauro equorum* accounts are, indeed, offering broadly representative samples. The mean values for these expeditions presented in Table 6.1 are unlikely to be very wide of the mark: they may, perhaps, be a little high,[40] thereby extending slightly the apparent leap in values at the start of the French war. There is certainly the possibility of wayward figures at the retinue level, where horses of unusually low or high value amongst small numbers of lost mounts would give a misleading impression.[41] But such extremes balance out when the data are examined at the level of the whole army. Indeed, the great advantage of a good *restauro equorum* account is that very often it will cover *a whole army*, utilising, and drawing samples from, a very large and varied collection of retinue-level inventories. It has been seen already how such *restor* accounts offer a representative cross-section of personnel, a mix of men drawn from all levels of the military aristocracy; we may be fairly confident that their warhorses will also constitute a balanced sample of those appraised for a particular army.

This is an important conclusion, because records of horse losses, as distinct from horse appraisal, provide the main pillars of evidence for the first phase of the French war. Our knowledge of warhorse values for the Reims campaign of 1359–60 also rests very firmly on *restauro equorum* data, albeit at an even further remove from the original inventories than is usually the case.

£11.3, that for the complete inventories is only £7.6 – a very significant discrepancy. E101/19/36; E101/20/17; BL Cotton MS, Nero C. VIII, fos 280v–82r.

[38] This is a very approximate figure: it includes only those warhorses lost by English retinues and uses as a 'total of appraised horses', the number of men-at-arms in pay in October and November 1339: about 1,600 (Prince, 'The strength of English armies', p. 361). The number of horses appraised during the lengthy period of service in the Low Countries in 1338–40 must, however, have been considerably greater than this (there were a number of men who received compensation for more than one lost horse), and it is against that higher figure that the total of equestrian fatalities should really be compared.

[39] Based upon a total of about 1,900 men-at-arms receiving pay for service in Brittany; for a discussion of the size and structure of this army, see Appendix 2.

[40] This is common with less substantial datasets, as with the horses lost by Aymer de Valence's company in 1315 (E101/15/6). The evidence for these losses takes the form of annotations on the original inventory. The mean value of the 293 horses listed is £18, whilst that of the twenty-seven which were lost (generally rendered 'ad Elemosina') is £21.7.

[41] In the case of the Breton campaign of 1342–43, mean values at the retinue level (taking into account only those which have lost at least ten horses) range from £7.9 to £24.6, but as we shall see, such variation may arise not only from the distorting effects of unrepresentative subsets, but also from the rank structure of individual retinues and the status of captains and men-at-arms.

The evidence involves a very large number of horses (1,160 with a mean value of £9), but it is offered in the form of retinue-level aggregates: numbers of horses lost and their total value.[42] Information about individual horses and their owners is therefore lacking (except where a captain is claiming for only one lost horse),[43] but in every other respect the data should be comparable with conventional *restauro equorum* records, and in particular with those emanating from the early campaigns of the war. The size of the sample is certainly adequate, representing about a third of the total number of warhorses appraised at the start of the campaign.[44] There is, not surprisingly, some diversity of mean values at the retinue level,[45] but the high and the low averages tend to balance out and the majority in any case lie quite close to the overall mean of £9,[46] a figure which, we can be fairly confident, effectively summarises the level of warhorse values for this army.

The evidence for the level of warhorse values for the Reims campaign, though offered only in aggregated form and, therefore, at some distance in administrative terms from the horse inventories compiled at the outset of the expedition, forms an essential component in the data series presented in Table 6.1. It constitutes the main body of evidence indicating a decline in warhorse values during the post-plague period. As a major royal expedition to northern France, the circumstances of the Reims campaign are directly comparable with those of the two well-documented expeditions early in the

---

[42] Included amongst the *vadia guerre* accounts in Farley's Wardrobe Book: E101/393/11, fos 79r–116v. These figures exclude the evidence from two retinues: Sir William de Granson (fo. 86v), who was allowed £600 for an unspecified number of lost horses; and Sir Frank de Hale (ibid.), who received 1000 marks for *restauro equorum*. The latter looks like a lump-sum payment, probably unrelated to the actual value of the horses lost. See Appendix 3, Table A, for retinue-level figures.

[43] There are sixty-six such retinues and this subset of individual horses has a mean value of £8.3: a little less, therefore, than the average for all horse losses in 1359–60.

[44] The army would have included nearly 3,500 men-at-arms in 'English' retinues, but the earl of Arundel's company (135 men-at-arms) appears not to have left England. In addition, about 700 continental men-at-arms took an active part in the campaign, but none of their pay accounts mention the loss of horses and their mounts may not have been appraised. The army consisted of a large number of separately accounting units: of about 550 retinues or companies included in the *vadia guerre* account, nearly 400 were lead by Englishmen. The proportion of appraised horses lost varies a great deal at the retinue level. On the one hand, the prince of Wales claimed £3,355 6s. 8d. for 395 horses, suggesting that two-thirds of his men-at-arms lost a warhorse during the campaign. On the other, Sir Edward Kendale accounted for the loss of a single £6 horse (E101/393/11, fos 79r, 84v). The accounts of about two-thirds of English captains include no mention of lost horses.

[45] Of those retinues which have lost at least ten horses, the highest mean is £20.3, for the earl of Warwick's company, and the lowest £6.3, for the earl of March's. However, Sir Thomas Ughtred's nine horses averaged at £5.9, and Sir John de Beauchamp's eight at £5.4.

[46] E.g. the horses of the prince of Wales and the duke of Lancaster (who combined lost 611) had means of £8.5 and £9.8 respectively.

war. By contrast, the remaining relevant data from the 1340s, '50s and '60s (not all of which is included in Tables 6.1 and 6.2) derive from rather different forms of military endeavour: service, sometimes in garrisons, in Gascony and Ireland in small armies led by magnates. These data are, moreover, far less weighty than those available for the Reims campaign: fragmentary and rather miscellaneous in form, they can do no more than supply supportive evidence. This evidence certainly seems to fit quite neatly into the time series of valuation data, but it is necessary to be aware of its limitations.

First and foremost, it is exceedingly sparse. Of the many inventories and related administrative documents which are known to have been drawn up, very few have survived. References to horse inventories *are* occasionally to be found in the records for this period[47] and they have left their mark in summary *restauro equorum* payments;[48] yet the original rolls have, for the most part, disappeared. The picture for the 1340s, after the Breton campaign of 1342–43, is particularly bleak. Indeed, there is but one reasonably substantial document, a record of horse losses during Sir Ralph de Ufford's term of office as Justiciar of Ireland in the mid 1340s,[49] and this poses a number of interpretative problems which rather diminish its usefulness. It is unlike any other *restauro equorum* account to have survived from the fourteenth century. It consists of two parts. The first comprises ten valued horses, which rather than being assigned to specific men-at-arms, are given names incorporating a recognisable surname or title – like Bayard Derby and Morel Ufford. The second part consists of a more conventional list of thirty-nine men-at-arms with associated valued horses, but it is unusual in that horse descriptions are not provided and, more significantly, in that fifteen of the men are claiming for two horses and one, Sir Adam Percevall, for three.[50] Here, as on a number of other occasions during this period of experiment, normal practice was clearly not being adhered to, and the evidence of the resulting *restauro equorum* account is not, therefore, compatible with that of other records of warhorse losses. Many of the horses in Ufford's list, appearing either separately or in multiples, have very low values,[51] whereas, for other campaigns after the start of the French war, a minimum value of 100s appears to have

---

[47] E.g. the 'cedule contenance aucuns chivaux' of the earl of Pembroke 'prisez avant son aler vers les parties de Gascoigne & illoeqes perduz': E159/123, m. 99d.

[48] E.g. in Henry of Lancaster's account for his service in Gascony in 1345–7: E101/25/9, m. 1.

[49] C260/57, m. 28.

[50] As we have seen, it was customary for only one warhorse per man-at-arms to be appraised at the start of a period of service. Although a replacement horse would be valued, most of Ufford's men who were claiming for more than one horse had sustained their losses on a single occasion. Eight men each lost two or three horses in a sharp skirmish in the Moiry Pass in 1345. Robin Frame, 'The justiciarship of Ralph Ufford: warfare and politics in fourteenth-century Ireland', *Studia Hibernica*, xiii (1973), p. 23, rather understates Ufford's losses.

[51] Of sixty-six horses listed, at least twenty-one have values under 100s; the lowest valuation (20s) was for two horses lost by Thomas Burton.

been the norm. Some of the horses appearing in Ufford's list may not have been 'first string' warhorses at all, but palfreys or hackneys: extra horses of a kind required by all men-at-arms on active service, but not usually qualifying for compensation if lost. Some of them might even be archer mounts.[52] This suspicion is reinforced by the inclusion in the list of seven sumpters and eighteen cart horses.[53] Such animals would certainly not normally be found in a *restauro equorum* account. The list does include, on the other hand, a respectable amount of high quality horseflesh: eleven of the horses (one in six) were valued at £20 or above, with the best, the 'Bayard de Leyston', worth £50. Although calculation of a mean value for Ufford's retinue would serve no useful purpose, the significant proportion of high-value horses in Ufford's inventory is instructive, and provides supportive evidence of a kind for the high level of warhorse values presented in the *restauro equorum* accounts for the Cambrésis-Thiérache and Breton campaigns. Weightier evidence is forthcoming from another quarter. For the loss of forty-three 'destriers, coursers and other horses' during his term of service in Gascony in 1345–47, the earl of Derby claimed the enormous sum of £1,384 13s 4d, which represents a mean value of £32.[54] It may be that warhorse values really were reaching a peak during the mid 1340s, but it is also possible that Derby's men had lost mounts of unusually high quality, the magnificent horseflesh reflecting the large proportion of knights and bannerets in the retinue and the high calibre of personnel which the earl was able to attract into his service. Unfortunately, comparative evidence for the years immediately preceding the Black Death is lacking. The horse inventories drawn up prior to the Crécy-Calais campaign have been lost and the records of *restor* payments for this expedition are unhelpful.[55]

The evidence for the 1350s, prior to the Reims campaign, is as patchy and inconsistent as for the latter part of the previous decade. The only serviceable records, a miscellaneous collection, derive from English operations in Gascony and may not offer a view of the warhorse which is altogether typical of the wider military community at this time. Only one genuine horse inventory has survived and this is no more than a fragment, containing a mere nine horse values.[56] A *restauro equorum* account for the mid–1350s lists fifteen horses owned by English knights and esquires.[57] A file of warrants authorising payment of compensation for lost horses, together with a set of

---

[52] However, service in Ireland, like Scotland, was very different from France. The nature of the terrain would have persuaded many to make use of small, hardy and inexpensive horses.

[53] These horses (not included in the totals quoted in n. 51 above) were also lost in the Moiry Pass; the combined value of all twenty-five was £55.

[54] E101/25/9, m. 1.

[55] The Issue Rolls include *combined* payments for *restauro equorum* and wages: e.g. for Sir John de Strivelyn's retinue (E403/340, m. 34).

[56] E101/172/4, m. 45: part of Sir John de Cheverston's retinue in 1356.

[57] E101/170/20, fos 75r–76r. Similar fragments cast a little light on the horses of Englishmen

corresponding receipts, yields a further twenty-four.[58] At a greater remove from conventional horse inventories are two documents listing horses which had been delivered into the hands of the constable of Bordeaux by Englishmen about to leave the duchy for England. The first, concerning the earl of Lancaster's retinue and dating from 1350, lists twenty-seven men (approximately a third of Lancaster's men-at-arms) who between them received payments for forty-two horses.[59] The sale prices are not ungenerous;[60] but it should be noted that the mean value (£13.7), which is less than half that for the horses lost by Lancaster's men in 1345–47, includes fifteen 'second string' mounts: horses which would not appear in a normal horse inventory. The second list dates from a couple of years later. Unfortunately the prices agreed by the constable of Bordeaux when he received the horses of some of the earl of Stafford's men-at-arms prior to their departure from Gascony towards the end of 1352 have not been recorded. What the list offers are the sums which were secured when twelve of these horses were re-sold.[61] The prices are very low (nearly all are less than £5) and are obviously incompatible with other warhorse value data from the 1350s. There remains, therefore, a total of ninety horses for the entire decade prior to the Reims campaign, with an average value of £12.3. As with the data for the 1310s, this figure conceals diverse elements; but it is also based on rather too few data, some of which are not derived from pre-campaign horse appraisal lists. Lancaster's retinue of 1350 contributes nearly half of the total number of horses, with a mean value which, though relatively high, probably does not adequately reflect the quality of the 'first string' warhorses assembled in the earl's retinue. The

in Gascony in the 1330s (E101/166/11, mm. 36–37 and E101/167/3, m. 32) and the 1350s (E101/170/12, fo. 61r).

[58] E101/172/4, nos. 1–43: warrants and receipts dated from February 1354 to October 1361.

[59] E403/355, m. 19. The debentures for all but one of the men listed on the Issue Roll have survived: E404/508, nos. 51–72, 74, 76–79. Six men-at-arms were selling two horses and three were disposing of three; Sir Stephen de Cusington sold four horses including a destrier valued at 100 marks. The sales took place shortly before Lancaster's departure for England in March 1350, at which time the earl had in his retinue two bannerets, twenty-three knights and fifty-four esquires, as well as eighty-seven mounted archers: Fowler, *The king's lieutenant*, pp. 86 n. 14, 88.

[60] The wording of the debentures suggests that the horse values were determined for the purpose of the sale, rather than being taken from an existing inventory.

[61] In addition to these twelve, there are five others which had been acquired from men serving with Sir John de Cheverston: E101/170/20, fos 19r–21v. The great majority were sold to Gascons; the exception was a horse, previously owned by Hugh Pauffot, which was sold to Thomas de Hampton for £3 4s. The earl of Stafford's retinue left Gascony at the beginning of December, having been in the duchy for less than five months; some, at least, of their horses were taken back to England. For this period of service, Stafford received £686 13s 4d to cover the cost of horses bought for his retinue in Gascony, as well as a *restauro equorum* payment of £500, a suspiciously neat sum (E101/26/25). The latter payment may well include the value of the horses acquired by the constable of Bordeaux: his account (E101/170/20, fos 19r, 20r, 21r) states that they had been delivered to him 'quasi perdit'.

restauro equorum list mentioned above offers a rather higher mean value: £15.2.[62] But a figure of just over £9 would probably be a more representative average for the horses of Englishmen engaged in garrison duty in Gascony,[63] with a rather higher mean value likely in the case of some of the expeditionary forces sent out from England.[64]

The evidence is anything but water-tight, but it seems to point to a decline in warhorse values during the 1350s. By the time of the Reims campaign they had certainly subsided to a level only a little above half that which they had occupied at the start of the French war. The evidence for developments after 1360 is hardly more plentiful.[65] The data from the inventories for Clarence's Irish expedition indicate a further decline in values to a level similar to that prevailing at the time of the second Welsh war of 1282. Given the distinctive demands of campaigning in Ireland, more directly comparable with the evidence for the great expedition of 1359–60 is the award of 1000 marks in compensation for the loss of 100 horses by Sir John Chandos' men during his mission to implement the terms of the Treaty of Calais. He was, therefore, being given a fixed rate of *10 marks* per horse,[66] whereas Sir Thomas Dagworth had been compensated at a fixed rate of *£10* per horse for losses in Brittany fifteen years earlier.[67] Perhaps in this simple comparison we have as clear an indication as any of the general trend in warhorse values in the mid fourteenth century.

THE WARHORSE IN FOURTEENTH-CENTURY ENGLAND: RISE AND DECLINE

The *lacunae* in the inventory evidence after the early 1340s cannot be filled by warhorse prices data of a more conventional kind, for such data are also exceedingly sparse and those which we have may well be quite misleading. Many of the prices data relate to purchases of expensive horses for royal

---

[62] E101/170/20, fos 75r–76r.

[63] Based on the materials contained in E101/172/4. Such garrison troops were a distinctive group within the military community of mid- and late-fourteenth-century England.

[64] As we have seen, no proper evidence for Stafford's expedition has survived. Sadly, the same applies to the prince of Wales' expedition in 1355–57, although it is known that horse inventories were compiled: Hewitt, *The Black Prince's expedition*, p. 33.

[65] For example, the cost of 201 horses lost by John of Gaunt's retinue in Gascony in 1370–71 is buried in a general payment of £32,380: J. Sherborne, 'The cost of English warfare with France in the later fourteenth century', *BIHR*, l (1977), p. 139. It is difficult to draw wholly reliable conclusions from a scatter of *restauro equorum* references in John of Gaunt's register for the early 1370s, but the tendency is for horses to be valued at 100s or 10 marks (e.g. *JGReg, 1371–75*, ii, nos. 896, 939, 1031). By the 1370s, a 25 mark warhorse, such as that lost by Sir John Cresy during the 'last voyage' in Normandy and Picardy, is a mount of above average quality (ibid., no. 908).

[66] E101/28/10. Chandos' retinue had lost twenty-seven warhorses during the Reims campaign at an average value of £12.6: E101/393/11, fo. 82r.

[67] E101/25/17.

use.[68] Such costly animals would hardly be typical of those acquired by the militarily-active sections of the lesser gentry. But is it not possible to confirm the pattern of the statistical series of warhorse values, and in particular the weaker parts of the series, by reference to the general trend of prices during the Edwardian period? After all, it is usually felt that luxury goods, although defying attempts at conventional prices analysis, 'are likely to have joined in the general price trend'.[69] In fact, the match is found to be very imperfect. The pattern of horse values which has been considered in this chapter is not closely related to the trend in ordinary livestock prices in the fourteenth century, and at several points (for example, in the mid 1310s and at the start of the Hundred Years War) it departs significantly from that trend.

Conventional prices data and the evidence of warhorse inventories are, therefore, decidedly uneasy companions; but there should be no surprise in this, for they were the products of different processes. First, account must be taken of the influences affecting the decisions of horse appraisers. Although no doubt intending a high level of accuracy in their valuations, they were restricted by their own experience and knowledge, by the conflicting interests of their royal master and the horse-owners who came before them; and by the fact that they were concerned to reflect *normal* price levels and not short-term fluctuations. Even if the horse values do approximate to normal price levels, there are good reasons for thinking that the inventories do not necessarily offer data which are directly comparable with standard national prices data. The problem arises from the selectivity of the horse inventories: from the circumstances determining the quality of the warhorses appearing in these records. No set of inventories offer a wholly random sample of the warhorses in the kingdom at any given point in time. All were strongly influenced by the particular section of the military community which was being drawn upon, by the status and backgrounds of the personnel concerned, but also by the theatre of war in which they were to operate and the identity of the captain with whom they were to serve. Thus, behind each inventory must be imagined a complex of individual decisions: men choosing what they felt to be suitable mounts from their own stables or from horse-dealers, according to where and with whom they were intending to serve. Since the time series of warhorse values is composed of a sequence of such records, all very much determined by the character of the manpower listed and the nature of the military task in hand, is it any wonder that on occasion the pattern of summary statistics which can be compiled from them diverges sharply from the normal trend of prices data?

What were the determinants of the pattern of warhorse values which have been observed for the late thirteenth and early fourteenth centuries? For the

---

68 E.g. in 1342 Sir Ralph de Stafford sold two destriers with a combined value of £80 to John Brocas, Keeper of the King's Horses (E36/204, fo. 79v), whilst in 1348 Brocas bought a destrier worth £50 from John de Grey de Ruthyn (E403/341, m. 5).

69 Dyer, *Standards of living in the later Middle Ages*, p. 37.

most part, the fluctuations in the data series can be explained in terms of changes in the quality of horseflesh: an improvement in the overall quality of warhorses from the late thirteenth century, but with ups and downs in the level of values in keeping with the character and circumstances of each army; as a consequence, that is, of the multitude of choices made by individual fighting men faced by the prospect of a particular form of service. Thus, when we see sharp shifts in the level of values we should imagine sharp contrasts in warhorse quality, and not horses of uniform quality whose prices have been subjected to inflationary or deflationary pressures. This is not wholly to discount the role of underlying economic trends. At several stages during the period they appear to have reinforced the 'movement' of horse values. But it is one thing to accept the background influence of economic trends and quite another to interpret the fluctuations in inventory valuation levels as responses to short-term economic impulses. 'Naturally', as Philippe Contamine has observed, 'the price of warhorses varied in accordance with the laws of supply and demand';[70] but the prices charged by horse-dealers shortly before a major campaign and the valuations recorded in inventories were not necessarily closely related.

The high level of warhorse values exhibited by the inventory of the earl of Pembroke's heavy cavalry serving in the Scottish Marches in 1315 (mean value: £18.4) has been discussed already.[71] In this inventory, as clearly as any from the early decades of the fourteenth century, can be seen the result of a concerted breeding programme, initiated during the early years of Edward I's reign, aimed specifically at the production of 'great horses'. Such *grandz chivaux* are few in number in an inventory from the second Welsh war of 1282: a mere 7% of the horses have values over £20 and the most costly of over 600 horses listed are two which are valued at £40.[72] By contrast, over a third of the three hundred warhorses on Pembroke's inventory of the mid 1310s have a value of £20 or higher, and over 10% are registered at £40 or more.[73] The production of high-quality steeds was only the most striking aspect of a general improvement in the stock of the kingdom's warhorses and although less spectacular than the emergence of the 'great horse', the shrinkage in the numbers of low-value warhorses employed in the king's armies was a further most significant feature of the period. Pembroke's army in 1315 had no horses valued at less than £5. This may be exceptional, but in the garrison inventories of 1311–12, which we might expect to include a rather larger than usual proportion of cheap warhorses, mounts valued at under £5 constitute

---

[70] Contamine, *War in the Middle Ages*, p. 131. For example, the increase in horse prices in 1445 shortly prior to Charles VII's creation of the *ordonnance* companies: as Olivier de la Marche put it, 'every gentleman thought if he were to appear on a good horse he would be more easily recognised, sought after and received into the companies'.

[71] E101/15/6.

[72] C47/2/7.

[73] There are twelve £40 horses, eleven at £50, six at £65, one at £80 and one at £100.

less than 9% of the horses listed, as compared with nearly a quarter in the corresponding records for 1282. This contrast is particularly striking when it is remembered that fewer than 4% of the garrison personnel were knights or bannerets, whilst about 24% of men-at-arms in the 1282 inventory were of knightly status.

These two aspects of the Edwardian horse-breeding revolution, the production of high-quality steeds and the general improvement in the quality of horseflesh with which rank and file men-at-arms served, combined to bring about a steady increase in the overall level of warhorse values from the 1280s to the 1310s (and indeed beyond, although masked in part by the nature of the data). Allowance should be made for the underlying economic currents of the period, but with due caution. Whilst it is probable that price inflation in the early fourteenth century contributed to some extent to the general increase in the level of warhorse values,[74] we must strongly doubt whether, for example, the high values registered in Pembroke's inventory in 1315 can be explained by reference to supply shortages arising from either the prevailing adverse agrarian conditions, and particularly the livestock murrain, of the 1310s,[75] or the severe equestrian losses which had been suffered at Bannockburn. Pembroke had been associated with high equestrian values before the 1310s: in 1307 the mean value of his retinue's horses was an astonishing £28.9;[76] and the explanation is surely quite simply that his men were serving with very fine horseflesh, the product of several decades of specialist breeding.

If, as has been argued, the fluctuations in warhorse values as presented in summarised form in Tables 6.1 and 6.2 are essentially a reflection of contrasts in quality, then how is the most notable quality-contrast, that of the later 1330s, between the level of values for the Scottish campaigns and those of the first royal expedition of the Hundred Years War, to be explained? The English warhorse, it seems, reached its apogee at the start of the French war and this in spite of general economic stagnation and a steady fall in prices during the 1320s, '30s and '40s. The idea of a peak in warhorse quality needs, however, to be amplified and qualified. The level of values achieved in 1338–39 is impressive because it embraces the equestrian resources of a major royal army. There had been (and would continue to be) assemblies of troops on a smaller scale with higher levels of warhorse values, but the mean and spread of horse values for the Cambrésis-Thiérache campaign was for a much larger

---

[74] I. Kershaw, 'The great famine and agrarian crisis in England, 1315–1322', *Peasants, knights and heretics*, ed. R.H. Hilton (Cambridge, 1976), p. 88.

[75] The livestock farming catastrophes of 1315–17 were 'largely though not wholly confined to sheep' and there is no direct evidence of murrain affecting warhorses (Kershaw, 'The great famine and agrarian crisis in England, 1315–1322', pp. 103–11). Although horse murrain is reported on individual studs at various times, there is no sign of a significant, widespread outbreak in the fourteenth century. On the evidence for murrain, see Davis, *The medieval warhorse*, p. 93.

[76] *Bain*, v, no. 655.

and more varied body of manpower and seems, therefore, to demonstrate the widespread availability of high-quality warhorses amongst the Edwardian military community at this time. A stock of great horses could not have been assembled over-night; it was the result of a long process of specialist breeding. But the focus on Scotland prior to the late 1330s had ensured that it was not fully revealed by earlier expeditions. Thus, the suddenness of the peak in the time series at the start of the French war, together with the depth of the preceding trough, may be more apparent than real.

Conditions at the time of horse appraisal could affect equestrian valuation levels.[77] Yet there can be no doubt that men were employing warhorses of relatively modest quality for the Scottish theatre of war and considerably more expensive ones for campaigns in France. About 64% of horses appraised for the three Scottish expeditions of the later 1330s had values of less than £10 and only 5% were registered at £20 or above, whilst the corresponding figures for the first campaign of the French war were 34% and 29%, with about 9% valued at over £40. A number of explanations can be offered. To some extent we are seeing in these figures the warhorses of different sections of the military community. A number of northern magnates, along with many knights and esquires from this region, exercised a strong influence on the character of royal armies and garrison forces in Scotland and the Marches, but played little or no part in the early campaigns of the continental war. On the other hand, the fact that a major section of the aristocracy, a powerful group of magnates and king's bannerets, contributed retinues to expeditions in both Scotland and France ensured that many members of the military community *were* faced by the prospect of serving in two sharply contrasted theatres of war.

Practical considerations no doubt played a prominent role in decisions about horseflesh. It is clear that Scotland's rough, inhospitable terrain, combined with the minimal opportunities for chivalrous encounters in the north, caused many men to leave their best warhorses at home; there was no point in exposing them to unnecessary hazards. It is difficult to see how the 'great horse' could be an asset during a Scottish campaign, but it took some time for the English aristocracy as a whole to appreciate this (particularly while there remained the possibility of a major setpiece equestrian battle, as at Falkirk

---

[77] The question of demand will be considered in connection with the Reims campaign. Suffice to say here, the English army of 1338–39 was not one of the larger ones of the period. It is possible, but not on balance likely, that the horse appraisers had been instructed to be more generous than usual in their assessments: the crown was, it will be remembered, offering double the customary pay rates for this expedition. It is also unlikely that the operation of a minimum valuation of £5 for overseas expeditions, but not for those in Scotland, has introduced a serious element of incompatibility. If all the under £5 horses in the inventories for 1336 (sixty-seven), 1337 (fifty-five) and 1337–38 (eight) are treated as though valued at £5, the effect on the mean value for each expedition is scarcely detectable; if they are removed altogether the mean for each expedition increases by less than £1 (i.e. to £9.2, £8.4 and £10.8 respectively).

and Bannockburn), even though it had long been recognised by the military community of the northern borders. The contrast, as we have seen, between the horseflesh of Sir Andrew de Harcla's men and those employed by the earl of Pembroke's command in the mid 1310s is striking indeed. But in 1327 an eminently sensible royal proclamation emphasised that men-at-arms should bring 'runcinos veloces fortes et asperos' for service against the Scots and that they should not postpone their departure 'pro defectum equorum dextrariorum'.[78] There are, as we have seen, very few highly priced steeds on the 'Scottish' horse rolls of 1336–38 and only a tiny minority (thirteen horses, 1% of the total) are described as destriers, the true *equis magnis*. An alternative to the destrier, of high quality but more suited to the campaigning conditions of the north, appears to have been found in the courser, perhaps best described as a heavy hunter. Fifty-three coursers, representing over 4% of the horses listed, are to be seen in the Scottish inventories of the later 1330s. This is a rather larger proportion, indeed, than are to be found in the *restauro equorum* records for the Cambrésis-Thiérache campaign.[79]

The first major expedition of the French war brought the prospect of very different campaigning conditions: terrain suitable for heavy cavalry and the expectation of worthy, chivalrous opponents. Is it entirely fanciful to see, in the peaking of horse values for this expedition, the desire of the English military class to cut a dashing chivalrous figure on the continental stage; a spontaneous re-assertion of their traditional identity, after years of unrewarding and uncomfortable campaigning in the inhospitable north? They would be allied with, and pitted against, the flower of European chivalry. Faced by this challenge, men-at-arms at all levels of the military hierarchy can be imagined selecting the finest warhorses from their stables and from the stocks of horse dealers. The consequence was a leap in the level of horse valuations and a return of the destrier – eighteen of them, comprising nearly 5% of the total number of horses in the *restauro equorum* account.

There is a certain amount of speculation in this interpretation of the valuation data for the 1330s; it is always difficult to ascertain the motives lying behind the actions – and choices – of such shadowy figures in the past. Yet, in this particular case, it is at least possible to demonstrate what those choices were, for behind the fluctuations in the summary statistics for warhorse values lie the decisions of hundreds of individual men, and some at least are recoverable. Of about seventy men who appear in the horse appraisal records for both the Scottish and the French expeditions of the later 1330s, three-quarters served with a more expensive warhorse in France.[80] This can

---

78 *Rot. Scot.*, i, p. 208.

79 Cf. 6% of the warhorses in the *restauro equorum* account for the Breton campaign, where they would be suited to the terrain. They were also the favoured type of 'prestige' horse for service in Ireland.

80 A further eleven served with horses of similar value in both theatres of war. Walter de Rossington, for example, had a 10 mark warhorse in 1336, a £10 one in 1337 and, for the

be seen to have occurred at all levels of the military hierarchy and in the case of half of the men concerned, the value of their mount had at least doubled.[81] In part this may be attributable to normal career development: the broadening of military experience, the assumption of knighthood, elevation to the status of retinue commander, or transference into the service of a captain of higher standing. Sir Robert de Rouclif's £20 warhorse for the Cambrésis-Thiérache expedition was a very considerable improvement on the 100s mount with which he is listed for the 1337–38 winter campaign in Scotland; but he does seem to have assumed the order of knighthood during the intervening period.[82] In 1336 Roger de Beauchamp had been an esquire in the earl of Cornwall's retinue with a £10 warhorse, but in the records of the first campaign of the French war we see him, now one of the king's household knights, with a magnificent £27 steed.[83] Advancement would usually find embodiment in higher quality horseflesh; and yet it is clear that elevation in the military community did no more than provide *extra* impetus for an improvement in equestrian quality which was stimulated in large part by the contrasting nature of military service in Scotland and France.

With the Breton expedition of 1342–43, the next of Edward III's military enterprises to be illuminated by a *restauro equorum* account, the general level of warhorse values was still high, but as the summary statistics in Tables 6.1 and 6.2 show, the heights which had been reached in 1338–39 were not maintained. The overall mean value was £14.3 as compared with £16.4, the fall being the consequence of a significant growth in the numbers of moderately-priced mounts (£5–£9.9), at the expense, fairly evenly, of both middle- and high-value horses.[84] Once again, examining the evidence at the level of individual men-at-arms reveals the multitude of decisions which lie behind the summary statistics; and again, the pattern of individual experience tends to confirm the overall trend of values. Men going to Brittany continued to

---

continental campaign, a £10 mount in 1338–39. The majority of the cases of decline involve only marginal shifts in value: for example, Roger de Dallingridge, from 10 marks (1336) to £5 (1338–9). On Dallingridge's career, see Nigel Saul, *Scenes from provincial life* (Oxford, 1986), pp. 38, 67–8.

[81] In some exceptional cases the increase had been four- or five-fold: for example, Sir Nicholas de Cantilupe (£20 in 1336; an £80 destrier in 1338–9). Sir William de Bohun had been a retinue captain during the summer of 1336 with a £20 destrier, whilst during his first major continental expedition as an earl, he lost a destrier of the highest calibre, appraised at £100.

[82] Rouclif had served with a £10 horse in 1336. A considerably less dramatic increase following knighthood can be seen in the case of Sir Robert de Longvill: a rise from 10 marks to £10. Rouclif and Longvill served in Sir John de Beaumont's retinue in both Scotland and the Low Countries.

[83] *Norwell*, pp. 301, 325, 346, 389. Sir Nigel Loring's career mirrored Beauchamp's quite closely: he had an £8 horse during the winter of 1337–38 and a steed valued at £26 6s 8d in 1338–39.

[84] The numbers of high-value warhorses remained very respectable, however: fifty-four (23%) appraised at £20 or more, with fourteen of these at £40 or higher value.

select warhorses of a higher quality than they had employed in Scotland during the previous decade,[85] yet many who had served in the Low Countries in 1338–39 appear in the records with less expensive warhorses in 1342.[86] The experience of Sir Otes de Grandison reflects the overall trend precisely: he had warhorses appraised at £20, £40 and £30 for service in Scotland, the Low Countries and Brittany respectively.[87] The pattern of individual behaviour is by no means uniform, which is only to be expected given the comparatively small difference between the mean values of 1338–39 and 1342–43, and the fact that the choice of less expensive horseflesh in 1342 would go against the forward momentum of many individual careers.[88] There are, nevertheless, numerous cases broadly in line with the overall trend of mean values; and some, indeed, which display an extraordinary fall in value between 1338 and 1342. For example, Sir Richard de la Vache's warhorse in 1342 was only a third of the value of his mount in 1338–39, a fall from £30 to £10, and Theobald Trussell's horse for Brittany shows a similar sharp change in quality, from £20 to 10 marks. If for most men the downward shift in value was rather less marked,[89] then there were, nevertheless, a group of veteran men-at-arms whose warhorses for the Breton campaign had, in quality, slipped right back to the level of the Scottish campaigns of the previous decade. Both Sir Thomas de Morieux and Sir John de Neville had served with 20 mark horses in 1337–38 and 1342–43, but with a £20 steed in the Cambrésis in 1339. In some cases, indeed, the warhorse which a man selected for Brittany was given a lower value than that which he had employed in an earlier Scottish expedition.[90]

85 Of nearly thirty men listed in the horse appraisal records for both Scotland in the later 1330s and Brittany in 1342–43, two-thirds employed a more expensive warhorse for the overseas expedition and in only five cases do we see an actual decline in value. At all levels of horseflesh quality major leaps in value can be perceived. Roger de Wodeham had served twice in Scotland (1336, 1337–38) with a 100s horse, but joined the earl of North-ampton's retinue in Brittany with a £10 steed. Sir Walter de Selby (on whose unfortunate demise in 1346, see *Anonimalle*, pp. 23–24) had a 20 mark horse in 1336 and a 40 mark courser in 1342. But for most men the upward curve of advancement was rather less steep. Nicholas Gernon, for example, had a 10 mark horse in 1336 and a £8 mount in 1342; in Ireland in the mid-1340s he lost two horses with a combined value of £10 (C260/57, m. 28); and in Gascony in 1350 he sold a horse valued at 20 marks (E403/355, m. 19; E404/508, no. 78).

86 58% of the thirty-six men for whom a comparison is possible.

87 In addition, his 40 mark horse for the War of Saint-Sardos fits very well into this sequence: E101/35/2, m. 7. On Grandison, see *GEC*, vi, pp. 65–66.

88 For example, Sir Michael de Poynings as a knight bachelor in 1338–39 had a £20 horse, and as a banneret in 1342–43 had a £40 steed.

89 E.g. Sir Philip le Despenser, who had a 40 mark horse in 1342, as compared with a £30 mount in 1338–39. This represented a very considerable improvement on the £10 horse with which he had served in 1336. Sir Robert de Malteby is recorded with a 40 mark horse in both the Low Countries and Brittany.

90 This is the case, for example, with Roger Darcy and William de Lacy.

Why did men take less valuable horses to Brittany? It is probably that practical considerations were uppermost in their minds. The voyage to Brittany's western and southern ports was longer and more hazardous than the quick cross-channel hop to the Low Countries, and it would be understandable for men to feel disinclined to expose warhorses of the highest quality to such a disorientating, debilitating and potentially disastrous experience. Although the loss of an appraised horse during the voyage would be compensated by the crown, a man-at-arms would travel with several horses and he would have to meet the cost of replacing his unappraised mounts himself. Such considerations would apply as much, if not more, to service in Gascony and may well explain the depressed level of values exhibited in most of the inventories drawn up prior to the War of Saint-Sardos.[91] By the mid 1340s it was normal for men who were engaged for service in Gascony to be given the option of acquiring horses upon arrival in Bordeaux,[92] and they sometimes sold them before returning to England. This may indeed help to explain the high level of warhorse values indicated in the earl of Derby's *restauro equorum* claim for his expedition of 1345–47. But in the case of the Breton campaign of 1342–43, we know that the English army's horses were transported from England and that during the stormy return voyage several ship-loads were lost, thus no doubt confirming many men's worst fears.[93]

The reduced level of warhorse values in 1342 may also have been a response to developments in the English conduct of war. An Edwardian campaign in France might involve fast-moving raids, a protracted siege or a defensive battle in which the whole army fought on foot. The implications of this for the aristocratic warrior and particularly for his 'great horse' may well have been fully appreciated by the English military community by the early 1340s; for if all these aspects of warfare were indeed to play a part during the course of a few months campaigning in Brittany, they had already been displayed in earlier expeditions. It is impossible to be sure of the psychological effects of the long and fruitless investment of Tournai, or to determine how quickly men recognised the implications of the tactical dispositions at Halidon Hill and Buironfosse; or, indeed, whether they appreciated that the

---

[91] The mean for the greater part of the evidence for 1324–25 is about £10.5, but the figure for the expedition as a whole is forced up by the assembly of high-quality horses in the earl of Kent's retinue, which has a mean of £18.9.

[92] For example, according to the indenture, dated 13 March 1345, between Edward III and the earl of Derby, those of the earl's men who 'ne se voillent monter des chivaux decea la meer, mes faire le pourveance par delea' could have their horses appraised in Bordeaux rather than before leaving England (Fowler, *The king's lieutenant*, appendix 4, no. 1).

[93] *Murimuth*, p. 135. It is uncertain how many horses fell victim to the storm. One narrative source states that two hundred horses were lost, together with three hundred men: *Melsa*, iii, pp. 51–52. The *restauro equorum* accounts for 1342–43 list 228 horses for which compensation was due, but neither explain the circumstances of these losses, nor give any indication of casualties amongst unappraised horses.

terrain in parts of the Armorican peninsula was very like that which they had come to know only too well in Scotland. But such considerations, combined with a certain justifiable anxiety about taking much-prized steeds on a sea-journey 'round the dangerous headlands of Finistère',[94] will probably have contributed to some at least of the decisions over horseflesh in 1342.

The response of individuals to the prospect of the Breton expedition, as reflected in the quality of their warhorses, was by no means uniform. Traditional attitudes concerning the role of the knightly class, and the equipment demanded by that role, would not disappear overnight; it was to be a few years before the full force of the Edwardian military revolution would be reflected in a significant decline in the quality of the English warhorse. By the 1360s this had taken place. Over 75% of the horses listed in the surviving inventories from the Irish expedition of the early 1360s have values of less than £10; the mean value is under £8. The contrast with the early campaigns of the Hundred Years War requires no emphasis.[95] Yet should not a depressed level of warhorse values be expected for service in a theatre of war which in some respects resembled conditions in Scotland? Gerald of Wales had made the point that 'in France [war] is carried on in a champaign country, here [in Ireland] it is rough and mountainous; there you have open plains, here you find dense woods'.[96] Should we not, therefore, be a little wary of basing general conclusions about the English warhorse of the 1360s upon the Irish evidence? This would not be because the personnel in the inventories were unrepresentative of the military community as a whole: operations in Ireland in the 1360s, as they had been in the mid 1340s, attracted large numbers of veterans from the French and Scottish wars.[97] But English men-at-arms proposing to serve in Ireland would surely choose horses of modest

---

[94] Jones, *Ducal Brittany, 1364–1399*, p. 9.

[95] It is difficult to illustrate this contrast by reference to the lives of individual men-at-arms. Few careers were sufficiently long and well documented, and the consequences of natural career development would, in any case, tend to work against the general downward trend of values. Sir Nicholas de Goushill lost a £10 horse during the Cambrésis-Thiérache campaign of 1338–39, whilst the courser with which he served in Ireland from November 1362 was valued at £8 (*Norwell*, p. 311; E101/28/11, m. 2).

[96] Quoted in K. Simms, 'Warfare in the medieval Gaelic lordships', *Irish Sword*, xii (1975), pp. 98–99.

[97] The captains and ordinary men-at-arms were predominently *English* and many had experience of several theatres of war. Thomas de Hoggeshawe, for example, had a naval command in 1355 and served during the Reims campaign: E101/26/34; E101/393/11, fo. 86r. Another of the captains in Ireland, Sir John de Carreu, was a veteran retinue commander from the early days of the French war: Cambrésis-Thiérache, 1338–39 (*Norwell*, pp. 338); Brittany, 1342–43 (E36/204, fos 107r, 109r); Normandy and Calais, 1346–47 (*Crecy and Calais*, p. 201). But he also saw service in Scotland in 1341–42 (E36/204, fo. 102v) and was a prominent member of Sir Ralph Ufford's powerful retinue in Ireland in the mid 1340s (receiving a 40 mark per annum fee: C260/57, m. 28). Of the fifty or so of Ufford's men for whom some record of other military service has been found, at least two-thirds also took part in continental expeditions before or after they went to Ireland

stature and value, which were suited to the rough terrain, in the same way as they had become accustomed to doing for service in Scotland. In the later 1330s, as we have seen, the contrast in quality between the horses chosen for Scottish campaigns and those selected for expeditions to France was often very great. For that period the evidence of the summary statistics is under-lined very forcefully by the experience of scores of individuals. Such detail is not available for the late 1350s and early 1360s, yet there is no reason to doubt the reliability of the summarised evidence. The mean value of over a thou-sand warhorses lost during the Reims campaign is £9, whilst that calculated from the surviving inventories for Clarence's Irish expedition is £7.8. By 1360, therefore, the difference in the quality of horseflesh employed in contrasting theatres of war was less clear-cut than it had been twenty years earlier. Whilst the evidence from Clarence's Irish expedition is wholly consistent with simi-lar military activity earlier in the century, the level of values for the continen-tal theatre of war had fallen sharply during the two decades since the start of the French war.

In the data for the Reims campaign there is unequivocal evidence of a major decline in warhorse quality, not simply for one section of the military community or for the prosecution of one dimension of the Edwardian war effort, but for the English chivalrous class as a whole. These are not, admit-tedly, disaggregated data: it is not possible to see individual men-at-arms and their steeds. Yet the pattern of mean values at retinue level conveys an unam-biguous message. Of nearly 118 retinue-level means for the Reims campaign, only thirty-three (28%) are of £10 or more.[98] Of those seventeen retinues which lost at least ten warhorses, all except three have a mean under £10. The earl of Warwick's very high mean is exceptional, but more arresting is the string of modest figures for the other great English captains of the Edwardian age.[99] The earl of Northampton's very low mean of £7.8 stands in striking contrast with the equivalent figure (£17.9) for the Breton campaign. The earl of Derby's mean for over 200 lost horses, £9.8, is less than a third of the figure for his losses in Gascony in the mid 1340s. The evidence for the decline of the English warhorse would appear to be incontrovertible: a decline in values which runs contrary to the price-trend in continental Europe.[100]

It has been argued that the decline in the English warhorse was essentially a consequence of the transformation in the conduct of war in the mid fourteenth century, a by-product of the Edwardian military revolution. The

and about half had seen service in Scotland. The incompleteness of the evidence almost certainly prevents an even larger proportion being detected.

[98] By comparison, for the 1342–43 Breton campaign, of thirty retinue-level means, all except eight (73%) reach or exceed £10. For the Reims campaign, see Appendix 3; for the Breton campaign, see Appendix 2.

[99] The earl of Stafford's mean for forty-six lost horses, £9.4, is actually lower than that for his retinue's horses in Ireland in 1361 (£10): E101/393/11, fo. 80r; E101/28/11.

[100] Vale, *War and chivalry*, pp. 125–26; idem, 'Warfare and the life of the French and Burgundian nobility in the late Middle Ages', p. 178.

traditional role of the 'great horse' had largely disappeared. Great barded horses, of the kind which had been spurred-on towards the Scottish schiltroms at Falkirk and Bannockburn, were no longer at the centre of English tactical thinking. The rigours of a *chevauchée* called for different virtues, mobility and stamina rather than weight and stature. These altered military priorities could be satisfied by less expensive horses. A few destriers continued to be taken on active service – the costly prestige symbols of great men;[101] but coursers were more suited to hard campaigning conditions[102] and they became popular amongst the wealthier section of the knightly community.[103] In general, and at all levels of the military community, men had become content to serve with cheaper horseflesh. The result was a compression of warhorse values into a comparatively narrow band (see Table 6.2): the great majority of appraised horses now fell within the range from £5 to 20 marks.[104] The prospect of spending less on warhorses would have been welcomed at a time when men-at-arms would have needed to spend more on personal body armour. It has been estimated that a full outfit during the later fourteenth century might cost from £10 to £15.[105] The crown's abandonment of horse appraisal and *restauro equorum* in the early 1370s can only have served to reinforce the trend towards cheaper horses as men sought to ensure that the new terms of military service worked to their advantage.

But is this a wholly satisfactory explanation of the decline in English warhorse values? To what extent did the prevailing economic conditions during the years following the Black Death contribute to the downward trend? It would be natural to assume that the falling-away of warhorse prices during the 1350s was at least in part the consequence of a significant drop in demand, following the removal at a stroke of perhaps 25% of the aristocracy,

---

101 For example, the only destrier listed in the inventories of the Irish expedition of the early 1360s was an 80 mark horse belonging to the earl of Stafford. He also had a £20 *trotter* for more practical use: E101/28/11, m. 3. Destriers and other *grantz chivaux* retained an important role in the ceremonial activities of great men, including their funerals.

102 The detailed household accounts of the earl of Derby's expeditions to Prussia in the early 1390s mention coursers, but not destriers: *Expeditions to Prussia and the Holy Land made by Henry, earl of Derby*, ed. L.T. Smith, Camden Soc., new ser., lii (1894). 'Great horses' would have been wholly unsuited to the forests and bogs of eastern Europe: for graphic descriptions of the conditions, see E. Christiansen, *The northern crusades* (London, 1980), pp. 160–66; and F.R.H. Du Boulay, 'Henry of Derby's expeditions to Prussia, 1390–1 and 1392', *The reign of Richard II*, ed. F.R.H. Du Boulay and C. Barron (London, 1971), pp. 160–61.

103 Coursers need not be expensive, however. All five of the appraised horses in Sir Thomas de Hoggeshawe's retinue in 1362 are described as coursers and their values range from 100s to £8: E101/28/11, m. 2.

104 E.g. only five of the 135 horses in the inventories for Clarence's Irish expedition have values above 20 marks.

105 L. James, 'The cost and distribution of armour in the fourteenth century', *Transactions of the Monumental Brass Society*, x, 4 (1967 for 1966), pp. 226–31.

the traditional military class.[106] Yet the decline in warhorse values is not mirrored by a decline in market prices in the 1350s.[107] Initially, the sudden drop in demand did cause prices to plummet; as Knighton observed, 'a man could buy for half a mark a horse which formerly had been worth forty shillings'[108] and the chronicler's words are borne out by the prices data for livestock.[109] But after 1350 prices quickly recovered and 'rose to levels higher than in the decade or so before the Black Death',[110] largely as a consequence of coinage debasement, combined with an increased *per capita* supply of money.[111]

Monetary factors, then, had the effect of holding the general level of prices at a relatively high level, despite the shrinkage in demand. Yet in the case of the warhorse, it might reasonably be doubted whether there had been a fall in demand during the 1350s. The evidence suggests that the landholding class was less seriously affected than the rest of the population by the first visitation of the plague and that the *pestis secunda* of 1361 caused a rather higher level of mortality.[112] Moreover, there is every indication that the numbers of active combatants in the 1350s remained high. In addition to the garrisons paid for by the English crown, men from England 'had established themselves on their own account in many places throughout the realm of France'.[113] There were major royal expeditions in the mid–1350s and the Reims campaign of 1359–60 saw the assembly of one of the greatest armies of the fourteenth century, in which well over 3,000 English men-at-arms served.[114] The years following the battle of Crécy had witnessed an expansion of the active military community, partly set in motion by royal pressure (a short-lived military assessment based upon landed wealth), but prompted primarily

[106] An estimate based upon J.C. Russell's analysis of inquisitions *post mortem*: *British medieval population* (Albuquerque, 1948), pp. 215–18.

[107] In the absence of systematic data for the sale of warhorses, we must rely on general prices data and in particular that for livestock.

[108] *Knighton*, ii, p. 62.

[109] H.E. Hallam, ed., *The agrarian history of England and Wales, II, 1042–1350* (Cambridge, 1988), p. 721.

[110] Ibid; E. Miller, ed., *The agrarian history of England and Wales, III, 1348–1500* (Cambridge, 1991), pp. 433ff.

[111] Hallam, ed., *The agrarian history of England and Wales, II, 1042–1350*, pp. 721, 725; Miller, ed., *The agrarian history of England and Wales, III, 1348–1500*, pp. 440–41; J.L. Bolton, *The medieval English economy, 1150–1500* (London, 1980), p. 78. It was only from the later 1370s that prices began to fall.

[112] McFarlane, *The nobility of later medieval England*, pp. 168–71; A.E. Nash, 'The mortality pattern of the Wiltshire lords of the manor, 1242–1377', *Southern History*, ii (1980), pp. 31–43.

[113] *Scalacronica*, p. 134.

[114] A. Ayton, 'English armies in the fourteenth century', *Arms, armies and fortifications in the Hundred Years War*, ed. A. Curry and M. Hughes (Woodbridge, 1994). By comparison, there may have been as many as 4,000 English men-at-arms in the army before Calais in 1347.

by campaigning successes and the opportunities offered by the war in France. This expansion had two dimensions. Firstly, there was an increase in the level of commitment, a temporary 're-militarisation', of the traditional chivalrous class: a new-found enthusiasm for continental campaigning which contrasts sharply with the lukewarm attitude displayed in previous reigns. Combined with this was a broadening of the military community at its lowest levels – the levels embracing both men-at-arms and archers, whose numbers were swelled, as Sir Thomas Gray put it, by 'young fellows who hitherto had been of but small account', some of whom 'became exceedingly rich and skilful in this war . . . many of them beginning as archers and then becoming knights, and some captains'.[115] There will have been professionals of low birth among the 3,000 and more English men-at-arms who set out with Edward III on the march to Reims; but the great majority of the *homini ad arma* had been drawn from England's 9,000 to 10,000 noble and gentry families. Contemporary observers were evidently impressed by the massive turnout of the English aristocracy in 1359. As Jean le Bel observed,[116]

> chascun s'apresta de partir, si ne demoura ne chevalier, n'escuier, ne homme d'onneur entre xx et xl ans en Angleterre, ou qui ne fust honteux de demourer, quant ilz virent que le noble [roy] leur sire retournoit en France si poissaument, siques tous princes, barons, chevaliers, escuiers et gens de toute sorte vinrent aprez le roy a Douvres, le mielx habilliez que poeurent.

It is hardly surprising that, according to a report from commissioners of array, 'touz les plus' of the secular landholders in Leicestershire in 1359–60 'sount en le service le Roi'.[117] Here, if anything, were conditions likely to stimulate an *increase* in warhorse prices through pressure of demand. How does this affect the interpretation of the level of values as revealed by the *restauro equorum* accounts for the Reims campaign? Could they actually be inflated by the weight of unusually heavy demand?

Warhorse prices might be expected to rise shortly before a major expedition,[118] but we cannot be sure of the magnitude of such increases, or how far this would vary regionally. There is evidence that horse-dealers were only too keen to take advantage of conditions of increased demand.[119] But how many men, unable to supply all their mounts from their own stables, were forced to seek suitable horseflesh at the last minute? The prince of Wales cannot have been alone in needing to visit the horse-dealers at Smithfield. Yet his purchase

[115] *Scalacronica*, pp. 131, 134.
[116] *Jean le Bel*, ii, p. 298.
[117] SC1/41, no. 23.
[118] Cf. France in 1302: 'the announcement of the expedition against the Flemings . . . caused [horse] prices to rise': Contamine, *War in the Middle Ages*, p. 96.
[119] E.g. the complaint in parliament in 1369 about the 'trop excessive pris' charged by horse-dealers and armourers: *Rot. Parl.*, ii, 300a. Cf. Russell, *The English intervention in Spain and Portugal in the time of Edward III and Richard II*, p. 304 n. 2.

of a destrier costing £50 from 'Little Watte of Smethefeld' in October 1359,[120] or Thomas, Lord Morley's acquisition of two coursers, costing £8 and 8 marks, in 1416,[121] are rare glimpses of what must have been commonplace, pre-embarkation transactions. Whatever men were obliged to pay in these circumstances, temporary price increases arising from short-term surges in demand are unlikely to have had an effect on inventory valuations. The horse appraisers at the ports of embarkation would base their judgements on the *normal* level of warhorse prices. As agents of the crown, they would record the lowest reasonable valuation for a horse, not an inflated figure which the king might in due course be required to pay. Moreover, despite the pressure of demand throughout the 1350s, there are no signs of major supply shortages which could have had an effect on *long-term* price levels. It would be unwise to read too much into the regular royal proclamations prohibiting the export of horses[122] (or indeed into the trade restrictions which were periodically imposed upon England).[123] Nor should widespread epidemics be perceived in isolated outbreaks of horse murrain, such as that which caused the deaths of twenty-seven of the king's horses in the care of William de Fremelesworth between October 1357 and September 1358.[124] None of these phenomena in themselves suggest that there was a crisis in warhorse supply. If direct evidence of warhorse breeding for the mid fourteenth century is decidedly patchy,[125] such as there is tends to suggest that steady demand for warhorses from the 1330s had served to stimulate the necessary breeding programmes in England.[126] Horse-breeding by the crown is illuminated by an impressive series of *equitia* accounts. As R.H.C. Davis has shown, the onset

---

[120] *BPReg*, iv, p. 326. London was, no doubt, an expensive place to buy horses: cf. *BPReg*, i, pp. 79, 88.

[121] Staffordshire Record Office, D641/3/R/1/2. I am grateful to Dr Philip Morgan for supplying me with a transcript of this MS.

[122] For example, *CCR, 1354–60*, p. 111; cf. E101/508/19 (Cinque Ports). *CCR, 1364–68*, p. 370; cf. E199/25/57 (London). Such measures are to be seen throughout the period.

[123] C. Gaier, *L'industrie et le commerce des armes dans les anciennes principautés belges du XIIIe siècle à la fin du XVe siècle* (Paris, 1973), p. 70 n. 29; W. Childs, *Anglo-Castilian trade in the later Middle Ages* (Manchester, 1978), pp. 121–22.

[124] E101/105/12.

[125] As indeed it is for France: V. Chomel, 'Chevaux de bataille et roncins en Dauphiné au XIVe siècle', *Cahiers d'Histoire*, vii (1962), p. 5; but cf. R.-H. and A.-M. Bautier, 'Contribution à l'histoire du cheval au Moyen Age', *Bulletin philologique et historique du comité des travaux historiques et scientifiques*, 1978, pp. 9–75.

[126] As happened during the sixteenth century: for a most illuminating discussion, see J. Thirsk, *Horses in early modern England: for service, for pleasure, for power*, Stenton lecture, University of Reading, 1977 (Reading, 1978). See also G. Parker, *The military revolution* (Cambridge, 1988), p. 70. At times of intense military activity in the later thirteenth and earlier fourteenth centuries, France imported large numbers of warhorses from Italy: as many as 2,500 in 1296–97, for example (R.-H. and A.-M. Bautier, 'Contribution à l'histoire du cheval au Moyen Age', pp. 63–68).

of the war with France provoked a resurgence of activity on the royal studs which reached a peak in the early and mid 1340s. Although affected to some extent by the Black Death, breeding activity held up well until the period immediately after the Treaty of Brétigny.[127] It is probable that the enthusiastic breeding of warhorses by the king had been mirrored by similar vigour on the estates of the nobility and gentry,[128] with the result that the English army in 1359–60, though undoubtedly making use of some imported beasts,[129] was able to rely to a considerable extent upon domestic supplies.[130]

KNIGHTS AND ESQUIRES

If the major mobilisation of the English aristocracy on the eve of the Reims campaign gave rise to unusually heavy demand for warhorses, then in the main that demand was for substantially less valuable horses than had been required for the Cambrésis-Thiérache campaign at the start of the French war. The passage of twenty years, which had witnessed the full development of the Edwardian military revolution, had irreversibly changed the needs and the attitudes of the community of militarily active knights and esquires in England. But when a member of that community selected a warhorse for active service, his choice was influenced not only by the tactical developments of the period or by the expected conditions of a particular theatre of war; it was influenced, indeed conditioned, by his personal circumstances – by his rank and wealth – and by the military status of the captain with whom he was to serve.

That there was a relationship of some kind between military rank and warhorse quality is only to be expected, and it can be observed readily enough in any inventory. But for the essential patterns of that relationship to be thrown into sharp relief, it is necessary to analyse the data in bulk. Table 6.4

---

127 Davis admits that his conclusions on royal horse-breeding are based upon a count of stud accounts, rather than a count of horses and personnel contained in those accounts: Davis, *The medieval warhorse*, pp. 86–91.

128 This can be seen where records exist: for the prince of Wales' horses and stud farms in the 1350s, see *BPReg*, iv, pp. 15, 28, 330.

129 For royal purchases from a Lombard merchant in 1359, see Davis, *The medieval warhorse*, p. 91. For evidence of the high regard in which Italian horseflesh was held in English aristocratic circles in the late fourteenth century, one need look no further than the words placed by Chaucer in the mouth of his Squire (*Canterbury Tales*, p. 130). Good warhorses could also be obtained from Germany at this time: in 1372 John of Gaunt spent £224 on horses from this source (*JGReg, 1371–75*, ii, no. 896).

130 The 'passage' figures supplied in Farley's accounts for the Reims campaign appear to suggest that Edward III's army arrived in France with a serious shortage of horses. But this information should not be taken at face value, for it is revealing not so much the difficulties of obtaining suitable horseflesh in England, as the problems involved in assembling a large transport fleet. For a discussion of this subject, see Appendix 3.

shows the mean values of warhorses employed by knights and esquires for a selection of the better documented expeditions of the Edwardian period.[131]

Table 6.4: Mean warhorse values (£ sterling) and military rank[132]

		Esquires	Knights
1282	Wales	7	15
1297	Flanders	9	24
1298	Scotland	8	20
1311–15	Scotland	10	33
1324–25	Gascony	8	21
1336–38	Scotland	7	14
1338–39	Low Countries	12	30
1342–43	Brittany	10	29

Throughout the period a sharp contrast can be seen between the quality of warhorses employed by knights and those taken on campaign by esquires: a knight's horse was typically twice as valuable as an esquire's. In Edward I's reign, moreover, it was usual for a knight's steed to be an *equus* and for esquires to ride rouncies.[133] If the data for men of knightly status are examined a little more closely, a qualitative difference of similar proportions can be detected between the warhorses of knights bachelor and those of knights banneret. For the Scottish expeditions of the later 1330s, the mean value of bannerets' horses was £22, whilst that for the mounts of ordinary knights was £13. The equivalent figures for the Cambrésis-Thiérache campaign were £52 for bannerets and £27 for knights.[134] Some of the most expensive war-

---

131 For Edward I's reign, cf. Morris, *The Welsh wars of Edward I*, p. 82 and N.B. Lewis, 'An early indenture of military service, 27 July 1287', *BIHR*, xiii (1935), pp. 87–88.

132 Sources: as for Table 6.1. Knights banneret and knights bachelor are not consistently distinguished in the inventories and *restauro equorum* accounts; as a consequence, the 'knights' category in Table 6.4 includes men of both levels of knighthood. The data for Scotland in the 1310s include the garrison rolls for 1311–12 (mean values: esquires, £9; knights, £25) and the inventory for the earl of Pembroke's army in 1315 (mean values: esquires, £12; knights, £36). The *restauro equorum* accounts for the Cambrésis-Thiérache and Breton campaigns do not always distinguish between knights and esquires and this may affect the mean values for these expeditions in Table 6.4; but the margin of error is unlikely to be significant. The data for campaigns after 1342–43 are either not suitable or insufficiently numerous to allow reliable means for knights and esquires to be calculated.

133 In an inventory for the Welsh war of 1282 (C47/2/7), the rouncies have a mean value of £6.7, whilst the corresponding figure for *equi* is £13.3. All except eighteen of the 452 rouncies were in the possession of esquires, whilst the great majority of *equi* were listed alongside the names of knights.

134 Thirty-seven bannerets and 214 knights can be identified in the inventories for the Scottish expeditions of the later 1330s. The mean values for the Cambrésis-Thiérache are based upon data for nine bannerets and seventy-four knights.

horses associated with earls and bannerets were destriers, the true 'great warhorses' of the Edwardian era. These prized possessions were typically valued at over £50.[135] Coursers were usually less expensive and during the early campaigns of the Hundred Years War the majority of them are listed alongside the names of prominent knights bachelor;[136] but for service in the less hospitable war zones, like Scotland and Ireland, coursers replaced destriers as the preferred warhorse of the leaders of the chivalrous class.

Behind the mean values presented in Table 6.4 lies some diversity of experience. Sir Adam de Ashurst's £8 warhorse – and, indeed, Sir Thomas de Fallesleye's, valued at a mere 8 marks – were considerably less valuable than many steeds appraised for *esquires* at the start of the 1342 Breton campaign.[137] Such examples are not difficult to find, for poor knights and wealthy esquires were not uncommon in the English military community. Naturally enough, retinue commanders would often serve with warhorses of a quality higher than that normally expected of men of their rank. In the 1342–43 *restauro equorum* accounts, Sir Reginald de Cobham and Sir Walter de Mauny, both bannerets and captains of retinues, are named alongside magnificent steeds valued at 100 marks and £100 respectively. But the warhorses of Edward III's most trusted lieutenants were exceptional beasts. Neither they, nor indeed the low-value mounts listed against the names of less wealthy knights, should be permitted to divert attention from the essential thrust of the evidence: that there was a general tendency for men to serve with warhorses of a quality appropriate to their rank, or in other words, a framework of horse value 'differentials' based on rank (and reflecting the differentials in the pay scale),[138] which persisted throughout the Edwardian period, irrespective of shifts in the general level of values during that time. Hints of these differentials are sometimes to be found in indentures of retinue. Retainers may be required to serve 'bien et covenablement mountez, armez et arraiez . . . come a soun estat partent',[139] or they may be given a warhorse 'come affiert por un Baneret'.[140] But awareness of the scale of differentials can most

---

135 In the *restauro equorum* accounts for the Cambrésis-Thiérache campaign, eighteen destriers have a mean value of £53; in 1342–43, eleven destriers have an average value of £57.

136 Mean values for coursers: Cambrésis-Thiérache, £29; 1342–43, £27.

137 E36/204, fos 87r, 87v.

138 The intervals in the scale of daily pay rates for esquires, knights and bannerets (1s, 2s, 4s) are reproduced quite accurately in the warhorse value 'differentials': e.g. the means for 1336–38 were £7 for esquires, £13 for knights bachelor and £22 for bannerets. P. Contamine has detected a similar pattern of rank differentials in the values of *chevaux d'armes* recorded in fourteenth-century French inventories: *Guerre, état et société*, pp. 20, 655–56 (Annexe XII, A).

139 *JGlndRet*, nos. 10–14.

140 Indenture between Thomas, earl of Lancaster and William Latimer, 15 May 1319: printed in G.A. Holmes, *The estates of the higher nobility in fourteenth-century England* (Cambridge, 1957), pp. 122–23.

readily be demonstrated by tracing the careers of individuals in the horse inventories: when a man's assumption of knighthood, or his exchange of the knightly pennon for a banner, can be seen to have been accompanied by a commensurate increase in the value of his warhorses.[141] Thus, as an esquire, Roger de Beauchamp served in 1336 with a £10 horse, but two years later, now a knight, he is listed with a mount valued at £27. Similarly, Sir Hugh le Despenser's rise from knight bachelor to banneret during the course of the Scottish campaigns of the later 1330s, reinforced by his assumption of the role of retinue captain, was accompanied by an increase in horse value from 20 marks to £40.

To what extent does an examination of the relationship between military rank and warhorse quality contribute to our understanding of the general trends in English warhorse values during the fourteenth century? Clearly the overall quality of an army's warhorses would be influenced to a degree by the size of the contingent of bannerets and knights among its men-at-arms. The fact that a very high proportion (40%) of the men-at-arms in the earl of Derby's expeditionary force bound for Gascony in 1345 were men of knightly status – either bannerets or knights – probably goes some way to explain the exceptionally high mean value of the forty-three warhorses for which Derby claimed compensation: £32.[142] On the other hand, it is clear that the very low mean for Sir Andrew de Harcla's retinues serving in the Scottish border country in the 1310s (£7.3) is partly the result of the small proportion of knights (less than 8%) serving in these companies.[143] Might not the downward trend in English warhorse values during the second half of the fourteenth century be due, in part at least, to a fall in the numbers of knights serving in royal armies? Did the period which saw a decline in average warhorse values from over £16 for the Cambrésis-Thiérache campaign to £9 for the Reims campaign, also witness a sharp reduction in the numbers of serving knights? Half a century ago, Noel Denholm-Young perceived 'a steady decline in the number of knights from the eleventh century to the end of the Middle Ages, interrupted only by a sudden and temporary rise begun by Edward I';[144] and, more recently, several historians have argued that distraint

---

[141] Enhancement of equipment, including horseflesh, was a necessary accompaniment to the assumption of knighthood. Newly created knights and bannerets would often receive grants from the crown or a great lord to allow them to make the initial capital outlay and to sustain a more expensive life-style. John de Ipres, for example, received an annuity of £20 from John of Gaunt after being knighted on the field of Nájera, 'por le mielz meintenir lordre de chivaler': *JGIndRet*, no. 1.

[142] E101/25/9, m. 1.

[143] The mean value for the warhorses of Harcla's knights was £14.4, whilst for his esquires it was as low as £6.7: E101/14/15, mm. 2, 4, 5.

[144] 'Feudal society in the thirteenth century: the knights', *Collected papers of N. Denholm-Young*, (Cardiff, 1969), p. 84. J. Quick, 'The number and distribution of knights in thirteenth-century England: the evidence of the Grand Assize lists', *Thirteenth-century England I*, ed. P.R. Coss and S.D. Lloyd (Woodbridge, 1986), pp. 114–23 does not differ

of knighthood was employed by the English crown from 1224 until at least the 1340s primarily as a means of increasing the numbers of knights available for military service.[145] Despite the full flourishing of what has been termed 'chivalric knighthood' during the Edwardian period,[146] the fourteenth and early fifteenth centuries witnessed a general decline in the numbers of knights in society: from about 1,250 to 1,500 in 1300, to no more than a few hundred by the 1430s.[147] Yet the detailed pay accounts available for many Edwardian expeditions suggest no really significant decline in the *proportion* of knights in major royal armies until the 1370s. Over 15% of the men-at-arms serving with Edward I in Flanders in 1297 were knights,[148] and a slightly higher proportion of those listed in the Falkirk campaign inventories were of knightly status; but for several armies of the late thirteenth and early fourteenth centuries the proportion can be seen to have been significantly higher: about one in four.[149] In the small army which saw service in Scotland under the earl of Pembroke's command in 1315, over 26% of its men-at-arms were knights or bannerets and the mean value of its warhorses was £18.4. The early continental expeditions of Edward III's reign could boast an equally high proportion of knightly combatants: over 25% in the Low Countries in 1338–39 and over 26% in Brittany in 1342–43.[150] For the Reims campaign, however, we find that for every knightly combatant, there were now four, rather than three, esquires. When it is further recognised that amongst the reduced numbers of knights were a smaller proportion of bannerets, it is possible to see how shrinkage in the numbers of participating knights *could* have contributed to some extent to the lower level of warhorse values

---

significantly from Denholm-Young's estimates of knightly numbers for the late twelfth century. See also P.R. Coss, *Lordship, knighthood and locality. A study in English society c.1180–c.1280* (Cambridge, 1991), chapter 7; idem, *The knight in medieval England, 1000–1400* (Stroud, 1993), pp. 70–71.

145 S.L. Waugh, 'Reluctant knights and jurors: respites, exemptions and public obligations in the reign of Henry III', *Speculum*, lviii (1983), pp. 937–86; Powicke, *Military obligation in medieval England*; Saul, *Knights and esquires*, pp. 38–47. David Crouch stresses the 'administrative . . . problems posed by lack of knights . . . The shortage of dubbed knights on the battlefield was not necessarily a great worry': *The image of aristocracy in Britain, 1000–1300* (London, 1992), p. 146.

146 Coss, *The knight in medieval England, 1000–1400*, chapter 5.

147 Given-Wilson, *The English nobility in the late Middle Ages*, pp. 69–71; S. Thrupp, *The merchant class of medieval London, 1300–1500*, paperback edn (Michigan, 1962), p. 276. The 1430s figure is based on H.L. Gray, 'Incomes from land in England in 1436', *EHR*, xliv (1934), pp. 607–39. The extent to which men with sufficient wealth were successfully evading knighthood is shown by the fact that there were as many as 1,000 landholders in 1436 enjoying an annual income of £40 or more.

148 Lewis, 'The English forces in Flanders, August-November 1297', pp. 312–13.

149 The proportion of bannerets and knights in the inventories for both the Welsh war of 1282 and the War of Saint-Sardos is nearly 24%.

150 1338–39: Prince, 'The strength of English armies', p. 361; 1342–43: E36/204, fos 105v–110v.

recorded in the financial accounts for the army of 1359–60. It may well be instructive to find that whilst 20% the earl of Northampton's men-at-arms were knights and the mean value of this retinue's forty lost horses was £7.8, one in three of the earl of Warwick's men-at-arms were knights, and the mean value of his lost horses, twenty of them, was as high as £20.3.[151] But it would be unwise to argue the point too vigorously. In simple numerical terms, the turnout of bannerets and knights for the Reims campaign, over 700 men, was very impressive; and even as a proportion of all participating men-at-arms, the knightly element in this army was larger than that achieved for some campaigns earlier in the century.[152] The decline in the numbers of knights was, therefore, a contributory rather than primary factor, serving to reinforce the downward trend in warhorse values stimulated first and foremost by developments in English fighting methods.[153] It was only in the 1370s, when significantly fewer knightly personnel were recruited for English expeditionary forces,[154] that diminishing numbers of *militi strenui* could have played a leading part in the decline of the English warhorse.

CAPTAINS AND RETINUES

The quality of a captain's warhorse was usually a fairly accurate measure of his position in the military hierarchy. His horse would generally be more valuable than those of his retainers and often of higher quality than those employed by others of comparable military rank.[155] The warhorses of the leading captains – those of comital rank and the foremost bannerets – were animals of the finest quality. A great man's warhorse had to be in harmony with, and reflect, his *dignitas*.[156] Thus, the five earls whose retinues are included in the inventories for the 1336 Scottish campaign each have horses valued at £40,[157] whilst none of the other captains on the list have a horse

---

151 E101/393/11, fo. 79v.

152 For example, the corresponding figure for the great army raised during the summer of 1335 was a little over 18% (Prince, 'The strength of English armies', p. 357) and for the army serving in Scotland during the winter of 1341–42, 19% (E36/204, fos 102r–104r).

153 In this connection, it is worth noting that the mean warhorse value for the Scottish expeditions of 1336–38 was low, less than £9, despite the fact that nearly 24% of the men-at-arms listed in the inventories were knights.

154 Only about 13% of the men-at-arms in John of Gaunt's army in 1373 were knights and the proportion fell further to about 5–6% for the expeditions of 1375 and 1380. See Sherborne, 'Indentured retinues and English expeditions to France, 1369–1380', pp. 729, 730, 732; and 744–5 (on the difficulties of recruiting sufficient numbers of knights during this period).

155 Cf. France: Contamine, *Guerre, état et société*, p. 80.

156 A.S. Cook argued that 'white horses were in favour with the great': 'The historical background of Chaucer's Knight', *Transactions of the Connecticut Academy of Arts and Sciences*, xx (1916), p. 167 n. 11; but this is not borne out by the evidence of the horse inventories.

157 The earls of Angus, Buchan, Cornwall, Oxford and Warwick: E101/19/36.

worth over £20. One of the seven bannerets leading a retinue in 1336, William de Bohun, was soon to be raised to an earldom. Following his elevation, he had horses valued at £100 in both the Cambrésis-Thiérache and Breton campaigns.[158] But great warhorses were not the sole preserve of those captains who were members of the titled nobility. Loyal service could enable men of modest gentry stock to acquire wealth and high military standing. In this respect, few careers were as meteoric as that of John Molyns and it is fortunate that a good deal of information about this man's warhorses survives in the records, providing apt illustration of his acquisition of great personal fortune.[159] The *restauro equorum* account for the Scottish campaign of 1337 shows Molyns claiming for the loss of four coursers, worth, in all, £76 13s 4d.[160] Multiple claims of this kind were unusual. Indeed, the account notes that it was satisfied 'by the king's special order', such privileged treatment being available to those who had been with Edward III on that fateful October night in Nottingham in 1330. Molyns' claims for losses in Scotland seem modest, however, when compared with those which he submitted as a retinue commander after the Cambrésis-Thiérache campaign. Although only a banneret, Molyns had served with a destrier valued at £100,[161] a magnificent animal matched by only three others of comparable value in the *restauro equorum* account for this army.[162] Molyns had risen to dizzy heights indeed (his former patron, the earl of Salisbury,[163] had to make do with a destrier valued at £60); but it was a privileged status which was not to last.[164]

A captain's military standing found expression not only in the value of his own warhorses; it is also often to be seen in the quality of his retinue's horseflesh. A typical army embraced retinues of various sizes, under the leadership of a range of major and minor captains, and horse appraisal records will usually reveal a correspondingly wide spectrum of retinue-level

---

158 *Norwell*, p. 309; E36/204, fo. 86v.

159 On this fascinating, if wholly disreputable man, see: Tout, *Chapters*, iii, p. 89; N. Fryde, 'A medieval robber-baron: Sir John Molyns of Stoke Poges, Buckinghamshire', *Medieval legal records, edited in memory of C.A.F. Meekings* (London, 1978), pp. 198–221; G.R. Elvey, 'The first fall of Sir John Molyns', *Records of Buckinghamshire*, xix (1972), pp. 194–98; *GEC*, ix, pp. 36–39.

160 BL Cotton MS, Nero C. VIII, fo. 185r. They were worth £12, £18, £20 and £26. 13s. 4d. Early in the following year, Molyns lost a courser worth £20 in the Scottish Marches: E101/388/5, m. 20. He had clearly built up a good stable, for in 1337 he was able to ingratiate himself with the king still further by presenting a destrier to his royal master: BL Cotton MS, Nero C. VIII, fo. 283r.

161 *Norwell*, p. 314.

162 Owned by the earl of Northampton, Sir John de Montgomery and Sir Peter de la Mare: ibid., pp. 309, 312, 317. There were probably other destriers of this quality which came through the campaign unscathed.

163 Molyns is described as Salisbury's *scutifer* in 1332: BL Cotton MS, Galba E. III, fo. 186r.

164 For his fall, late in 1340, and the great wealth which was confiscated by the king, see Fryde, 'A medieval robber-baron: Sir John Molyns of Stoke Poges, Buckinghamshire', pp. 201–2; Elvey, 'The first fall of Sir John Molyns'.

mean values. As might be expected, the retinues of the highest ranking, militarily-active members of the nobility were frequently those with high quality horseflesh. The mean value of all appraised warhorses killed during the Cambrésis-Thiérache campaign was over £16, but for two of the captains of comital rank, the earls of Northampton and Derby, their retinue-means far exceeded this figure: £24 and £29 respectively.[165] Yet there were others, who were not members of the titled nobility, whose retinues also lost an array of expensive warhorses during this campaign. One of these was Sir John Molyns. The mean value of his company's horses, over £31, was the highest of any in the army. Another was John Charnels, king's clerk and Deputy Treasurer of the Exchequer, but holding the rank of banneret.[166] Indeed, turning to the evidence for the Breton campaign of 1342–43, it is the untitled captains who lead the way. With the mean warhorse value for this army at just over £14, the captains with the highest retinue-level figures were Sir Reginald de Cobham and Sir Walter de Mauny: bannerets who like Moleyns had amassed wealth and influence through their closeness to the king, but unlike him avoided overstepping the mark.[167]

These examples, captains and retinues serving in the early campaigns of the French war, are all dependent upon the evidence of *restauro equorum* accounts: records which, because listing only equestrian losses, may convey a misleading impression of warhorse quality at the retinue level, particularly if the sample is small. This may explain why the earl of Warwick's lost horses during the Reims campaign had a mean value of £20, as compared with the figure of £9 for the army as a whole. The high mean for Warwick's retinue stands out because the corresponding figures for the great majority of the army's larger retinues occupy a narrow range of values close to the overall mean.[168] Given the lack of detail on individual horses and their owners in the records for this campaign, we cannot tell whether the retinue-level means are reliable. At least with conventional *restauro equorum* accounts, which list each equestrian casualty individually, it is easier to assess whether the mean

---

[165] The earl of Salisbury, who had lost more horses than any other captain (sixty-five), was rather further behind, with a mean value of £19: *Norwell*, pp. 309–12.

[166] *Norwell*, pp. 314, 317. Charnels' retinue-mean was over £23. Only those captains with retinues losing at least ten horses have been taken into account.

[167] For Cobham, see *GEC*, iii, p. 353. For Mauny, see *GEC*, viii, pp. 571–76 and G.A. Snead, 'The careers of four fourteenth-century military commanders serving Edward III and Richard II in the Hundred Years War', MA thesis, University of Kent, 1968, pp. 11–36. Mauny had, of course, led the first expeditionary force sent to Brittany in 1342. Both Cobham and Mauny were royal household bannerets: E36/204, fo. 89r.

[168] For a summary of the *restauro equorum* data for the Reims campaign, see Appendix 3. Warwick's men lost twenty horses, 17% of those appraised for the retinue. The mean value for Sir Frank de Hale's retinue is also quite high (£15.5; 43 horses), but the amount which he received for his men's equestrian losses, 1,000 marks, looks suspiciously like a lump sum.

values are likely to be based upon representative samples of horseflesh.[169] On occasion, it would seem that they are not. During the Breton campaign of 1342–43 the retinue of Sir Thomas de Bradeston lost eleven horses with a mean value of less than £8;[170] but Bradeston's own horse is not included in the *restauro equorum* account, nor it seems are those of any of his knights.[171] By contrast, the horses lost by Sir Reginald de Cobham's company include the captain's own splendid destrier, valued at 100 marks, and the horse of Sir John de Gise, worth 40 marks.[172] Had Bradeston's company lost a slightly different selection of horses, the retinue mean may well have been considerably higher,[173] and rather more in keeping with this captain's status, for like Cobham and Mauny, Bradeston was one of the rising stars of Edward III's regime.[174]

Although in some respects flawed, the horse appraisal and *restauro equorum* data nevertheless yield plentiful evidence demonstrating the existence of a relationship between the status of captains and the equestrian resources of their retinues. How was it that the quality of a particular retinue's warhorses could be influenced by the identity of its captain? Did the captain himself provide the horses for the personnel of his retinue? Some historians have

---

[169] It is possible to measure how representative the sample of lost horses is when both full inventory and *restauro equorum* account are available. With the materials for the 1336 Scottish campaign, the mean value of the horses listed in the surviving inventories is £8.5, as compared with £8.7 for those which were lost. Greater disparity can be seen at the level of individual retinues, but this is not surprising as the number of horses involved is often very small. In the case of Sir Henry de Percy's retinue, the mean value of twelve lost horses (£8.4) is a very accurate reflection of the figure for the whole retinue (£8.5), and the same applies to the retinues of several other captains, most notably the earl of Warwick. For other captains the difference between the sub-set and the whole is rather greater, but (except where very few horses are involved) not so great as to have a seriously distorting effect. The mean value of Henry of Lancaster's twenty-one lost horses was, for example, £1 less than that for his retinue as a whole. It would be prudent to allow for a margin of error of this magnitude when using *restauro equorum* materials which cannot be verified by consultation of the original inventories.

[170] E36/204, fo. 88r.

[171] Apart from himself, Bradeston received pay for *three* knights, fifteen esquires and seventeen mounted archers (E36/204, fos 106v, 109r). None of those who lost horses are given the title of knight, nor do they include any of the knights receiving letters of protection for service in Bradeston's retinue, of whom there were *four* (C76/17, m. 24).

[172] E36/204, fo. 87r. There are also four £20 warhorses listed.

[173] During the Cambrésis-Thiérache campaign, Bradeston received compensation for only two horses, but at 40 marks and £20 they were more valuable than any of the warhorses lost by his men in 1342 (*Norwell*, p. 315). Indeed, the owner of the £20 horse, John de Apprele, is also to be found in Bradeston's *restauro equorum* account in 1342, but this time with an animal worth only 20 marks. Here, once again, is seen the effect of the theatre of war on the quality of warhorse employed.

[174] For Bradeston, see *The Berkeley MSS by John Smyth of Nibley*, ed. Sir John Maclean, 3 vols (Gloucester, 1883), i, pp. 282–86; *GEC*, ii, p. 273; and Saul, *Knights and esquires*, pp 76–78. Like Molyns, Bradeston's career may have benefited from involvement in the Nottingham Castle *coup*.

assumed that this was so,[175] but whilst gifts of warhorses from lord to retainer are often mentioned in the terms of indentures (as well as in the
narrative sources of the period),[176] it is evident that comparatively few men
benefited from this kind of largesse. A favoured retainer[177] or a military
subcontractor[178] might be supplied with a warhorse by lord or captain, but in
such cases the superior contracting party would rarely be responsible for the
horseflesh of the accompanying company of men-at-arms. In this way a
leading captain could ensure that his principal followers and lieutenants were
horsed at a level commensurate to his and their status; but to provide warhorses for all the members of a retinue would have entailed a prohibitive
financial outlay. It seems clear, then, that most men-at-arms supplied their
own horseflesh.[179] Indeed, this responsibility is stated explicitly in many subcontracts and indentures of retinue, along with the assurance that the cost of
equestrian losses would be met by the captain.[180] It would seem, therefore,
that a captain's influence on the quality of his retinue's warhorses arose, in
the main, from his control over recruitment.

Only the core of a magnate's military retinue would consist of permanent,
indentured retainers, but the importance of these men was greater than their
numbers might suggest, for they could be depended upon and some would
bring with them their own companies of fighting men.[181] Most men-at-arms

---

[175] Prince, 'The indenture system under Edward III', p. 294; cf. Bean, *From lord to patron*,
pp. 238–44.

[176] See, for example, Froissart's account of the careers of the German mercenaries, Bacon
and Crokart: *Society at war*, ed. C.T. Allmand (Edinburgh, 1973), p. 89.

[177] For example, Sir John Sully, retained by the Black Prince (1353): *BPReg*, ii, p. 45–46;
discussed in Bean, *From lord to patron*, pp. 58–59. Provisions of this kind are to be found
in many indentures of retinue: see ibid., pp. 45, 46, 49, 51, 53, 54, 57, 62, 63, 64.

[178] For example, Sir Hugh Fitz Simon, who contracted to serve with a company of twelve
men-at-arms in Ralph, Lord Stafford's retinue for one year (16 March 1347): *Crecy and
Calais*, p. 192. Similarly, in an indenture drawn up a couple of weeks later, Sir Thomas
Ughtred, who was to serve in the king's army with a company of twenty men-at-arms
and twenty archers, was allowed 'covenable mounture pour son corps demesne sicome
appertient a son estat': E101/25/33. Cf. Sir Maurice de Berkeley's contract with the crown
(18 April, 1315) for the defence of Berwick: Berkeley was to receive four 'chevaux darmes
. . . du doun le Roy', but his company of twenty men-at-arms were to be 'bien montez &
apperaillez a sa troveure' (E101/68/2, no. 35).

[179] For examples of men being equipped by relatives, see A. Goodman, 'Responses to
requests in Yorkshire for military service under Henry V', *Northern History*, xvii (1981),
p. 248.

[180] The terms of Geoffrey Walsh's agreement with the earl of Salisbury, drawn up in July
1347, specified that Geoffrey 'serra a se mounture propre & son chival darmes sera preise
& encas qil sera perdutz en le service le dit counte, le dit Geffrei avera restitucioun':
E101/68/3, no. 68. Indentures continued to stipulate that sub-contractors would be 'a son
monture propre' after the abandonment of *restauro equorum* in the early 1370s:
E101/68/5, no. 107; Walker, 'Profit and loss in the Hundred Years War', p. 102; Goodman, 'The military subcontracts of Sir Hugh Hastings', p. 115.

[181] For examples, see note 177 above. K.B. McFarlane's pioneering work ('Bastard feudal-

served on the basis of temporary contracts intended to last no longer than the duration of a single campaign.[182] These men might be military 'professionals', like Jankyn Nowell, whom Sir Hugh Hastings recruited for service in France in 1380. Such an approach to recruitment had drawbacks. As Anthony Goodman has noted, 'the contractor . . . might end up with a group unused to working together or containing men prone to indiscipline and desertion'.[183] Consequently, many captains sought, where possible, to raise their military retinues among neighbours and tenants, relatives and friends: regular service under the same banner need not be based upon a permanent retaining bond. A commander of high standing would be responsible for recruiting retinues numbering hundreds, perhaps thousands, of men; but he may well have a well-stocked pool of knights and esquires to choose from. Landed interests in several parts of the realm would bring him naturally into contact with a variety of regional military communities. If a member of the royal household or a trusted counsellor of the king, he would have ready access to an even wider selection of the active military class; and during the course of previous campaigns he would have become acquainted with the pick of English free-lance 'professionals' and foreign mercenaries.

Being able to offer his men the prospect of honour and the chance of great rewards, it was possible for a leading captain to build an impressive *comitiva*, incorporating men of wealth and military reputation: men who would serve with high-class horseflesh. There is no better example of this than the fine array of knightly personnel accompanying the earl of Derby to Gascony in 1345 (eight bannerets and eighty-seven knights out of a total of 250 men-at-arms), and the very high level of warhorse values suggested by Derby's *restauro equorum* claim is entirely in keeping with the standing of this most glittering assembly of (mainly) English chivalry.[184] However, even the greatest of captains would also need to recruit heavily among men of sub-knightly status. This was inevitable, given the numerical preponderance of esquires in the military community. There was, of course, never any shortage of ambitious young men – those 'younger sons' so beloved of historians[185] – seeking

ism', *BIHR*, xx (1945), pp. 165–66; *The nobility of later medieval England*, pp. 102–4) has been developed by later workers in the field of magnate retinues: e.g. G.A. Holmes, *The estates of the higher nobility in fourteenth-century England* (Cambridge, 1957), pp. 79–80; Fowler, *The king's lieutenant*, pp. 181–86; Goodman, *John of Gaunt*, chapter 10.

182 On subcontracts, see Sherborne, 'Indentured retinues and English expeditions to France, 1369–1380', pp. 742–44; Goodman, 'The military subcontracts of Sir Hugh Hastings'; Walker, 'Profit and loss in the Hundred Years War'.

183 Goodman, *John of Gaunt*, p. 212.

184 E101/25/9. Note that only fifteen of the ninety-five bannerets and knights had a perma-nent connection with Lancaster, involving the grant of land or annuities: Fowler, *The king's lieutenant*, p. 183.

185 See, for example, G. Duby, 'Youth in aristocratic society', *The chivalrous society* (Lon-don, 1977), pp. 112–22; R. Bartlett, *The making of Europe. Conquest, colonisation and cultural change, 950–1350* (London, 1993), chapter 2.

to join the retinue of a renowned captain: men for whom a quiet life in England had little appeal and who recognised that military service offered perhaps the only prospect of achieving social advancement. Gaining admittance, albeit temporarily, into a great man's following brought an esquire close to a source of patronage in circumstances in which he might hope to make a good impression with the sword and thereby forge a lasting association. Ordinary men-at-arms most often found their way into a magnate's *comitiva* as members of subcontracted companies; they can be readily enough detected, their warhorses providing an indication of their modest means. Some never quite achieved the break-through they were seeking; but a few, like Walter Bentley, were ultimately very successful. Bentley, a Yorkshireman of rather obscure origins, first comes to our attention whilst serving in Scotland in 1338 under the earl of Salisbury. He entered the earl's service, with a horse valued at a mere £5, as a consequence of being the *valet* of Sir William de la Zouche.[186] In the same retinue was another young esquire destined for great things, but as yet listed with a warhorse of unremarkable quality: Nigel Loring.[187] Such men as Bentley and Loring emerged from a crowd of ordinary esquires who as a group were far from homogeneous. Alongside the young hopefuls were men occupying various points in the spectrum of military commitment. At one extreme were unambitious 'occasional' soldiers; at the other were hardened veterans, the steely core of the military community, men much sought after by captains, their skills and experience invaluable but not necessarily detectable in the appraised value of their mounts. Some of these regular campaigners avoided knighthood, together with the public responsibilities and expense which the accolade entailed; and they have usually remained obscure figures as a result.[188] Of those veterans who did assume the knightly estate during the course of long careers, many became respected, though hardly leading, figures in the

---

186 E101/35/3. For Bentley's career, see M. Jones, 'Edward III's captain's in Brittany', p. 100 and the anonymously published, *A brief note upon the battles of Saintes and Mauron, 1351 and 1352* (Guildford, 1918), which contains rather more than its title suggests. The inventories illuminate the early careers of several other men who, like Bentley, were to become captain-lieutenants in Brittany: Sir John de Hardreshull, Sir John de Avenel and Sir Robert de Herle.

187 Loring's horse was worth £8, but within a year he was serving in the Low Countries as a member of the king's household with a horse valued at £26 6s 8d: *Norwell*, p. 325.

188 William de Thweyt is a good example: A. Ayton, 'William de Thweyt, esquire: deputy constable of Corfe Castle in the 1340s', *Somerset and Dorset Notes and Queries*, xxxii (1989), pp. 731–38. Although only an esquire, he was appointed marshal of Sir Ralph Ufford's army, numbering over 2,000 paid troops, raised for the suppression of the earl of Desmond's rebellion in Ireland in the summer of 1345. The very modest fee (a bonus payment to supplement standard wages) which he received for this period of service (100s for a year, when knights were in receipt of at least two or three times as much) is a reflection of his social standing rather than his military worth. In this sense, Ufford's fee roll (C260/57, m. 28) presents a view of the military community very similar to that offered by horse inventories.

chivalrous community. Sir Nicholas de Goushill is a good example. In 1362 we see him in Ireland with a warhorse valued at a mere £8.[189] However much the selection of this modest steed was a response to expected campaigning conditions in Ireland (and, indeed, was in line with the general trend of warhorse values), it disguises the presence of a distinguished war veteran, a man who had first borne arms at Halidon Hill some thirty years before and who had been a participant in many of the great military events of his age;[190] a man, moreover, who as an esquire had served with a £10 warhorse in the first campaign of the French war.[191]

It is not always easy, then, to detect the men of true military worth in the horse inventories. The experience and skills of many reliable veterans, like Goushill, are scarcely conveyed by the quality of their warhorses and it is only by piecing together their careers from a range of sources that their important role in the Edwardian military community can be gauged. It is rather the men of wealth, the top stratum of the aristocracy, who stand out in the inventories: the senior members of county gentry families and the men of established military reputation who had capitalised on their campaigning experience. Good examples of such men are Sir Nicholas de la Beche, Sir William de Greystoke, Sir Reginald de Mohun and Sir Richard Talbot: all were principal members of magnate retinues in the Breton campaign of 1342–43 and all served with destriers or coursers assigned a value of at least £30.[192] The heavy concentrations of wealthy knights in the retinues of the foremost captains of the period certainly contributed to the high level of horse values which are so often to be found in the appraisal records of those

---

189 Goushill's mount was a courser, but the next man on the list, an esquire, had a warhorse valued at £9: E101/28/11, m. 2.

190 Goushill's career, which included the sieges of Tournai and Vannes, the Gascon expeditions of Henry of Lancaster and the Black Prince, and John of Gaunt's *chevauchée* of 1369, is illuminated by a deposition before the Court of Chivalry (Lovell-Morley case, 1386: C47/6/1, no. 29). He also served in the Low Countries in 1338–39, in the Scottish Marches during the summer of 1340 (E101/612/2) and in Brittany in 1360 (C76/40, m. 10; CPR, *1358–61*, p. 542). He had become a knight by 1345: E101/25/9.

191 *Norwell*, p. 311. Goushill's campaigning life had not been blessed by lucky windfalls, but for him (as indeed for many of his colleagues in arms) the main cause of frustration and impoverishment lay in his domestic circumstances, and in particular the extraordinary longevity of his parents, Thomas and Agnes. Nicholas entered into part of his inheritance in 1370, shortly after returning from what was to be his last campaign in France, and the rest followed four years later: *CIPM*, xiv, no. 30 (Thomas de Goushill, Nicholas' father), cf. *CIPM*, vi, no. 750 (Walter de Goushill, Nicholas' grandfather). Nicholas died in 1393. Robert Thoroton, *The antiquities of Nottinghamshire, with additions by John Throsby*, 3 vols (London, 1797), iii, pp. 61–64; J.G. Bellamy, 'The parliamentary representation of Nottinghamshire, Derbyshire and Staffordshire in the reign of Richard II', MA thesis, University of Nottingham, 1961, pp. 281–86. On the predicament of the man awaiting his inheritance, cf. Walker, 'Profit and loss in the Hundred Years War', pp. 101–2.

192 Beche (£60) and Greystoke (£50) served with the earl of Northampton; Mohun (£30) with the earl of Derby; Talbot (£40) with Hugh, Lord Despenser: E36/204, fos 86v, 87r.

retinues. Yet high retinue-level mean values cannot always be so easily explained: the precise nature of the relationship between the captain and the quality of his retinue's horseflesh is sometimes difficult to establish. Take, for example, the case of Sir John Molyns' retinue during the Cambrésis-Thiérache campaign of 1338–39. Molyns' life is a catalogue of extreme behaviour, fired it would seem by a tireless ambition to augment his personal wealth and enhance his standing in the political community. His retinue during the Cambrésis-Thiérache campaign, twenty-seven men-at-arms and twenty-four archers, was not large; perhaps about right for a prominent banneret.[193] It was not in terms of numbers of men that Molyns sought to rival his social superiors, but rather through the splendour of his company's appearance. This included the quality of his men's warhorses, which we know about because Molyns claimed compensation for the loss of thirteen of them:

Table 6.5: The appraised warhorses lost by Sir John Molyns' retinue, 1338–39[194]

Sir John Molyns	1 destrier	£100
Philip de Lymbury	1 courser	£40
John de Strechele	1 courser	£30
William Cifrewast	1 courser	£25
Alan de Holland	1 courser	£50
Simon de Norton	1 courser	£30
Edmund Rose	1 equus	£12
Robert de Sussex	1 equus	£12 13s 4d
Peterkin de Colonia	1 equus	£10
Richard Biroun	1 equus	20 marks
John Peche	1 equus	£24
Sir Corondus de Stene	1 equus	£50
Richard Courzon	1 equus	£14

Molyns claimed, therefore, £411 for thirteen horses, including his own destrier and five coursers.[195] The mean value of these warhorses, £31.6, was the highest for any single retinue and nearly twice that for the army as whole. The abnormally high level of horse values cannot be explained by reference to the social standing of Molyns' men, for the retinue included no more than three knights and only one of these appears on the *restauro equorum* list.[196] Indeed, particularly notable are the consistently high values of the horses

---

[193] *Norwell*, pp. 332, 357. Molyns' retinue during the summer of 1340 was of very similar size: twenty-four men-at-arms and twenty-four archers (E101/22/35).

[194] *Norwell*, pp. 314–15; Cifrewast appears, incorrectly, as Cisrewast in the printed text.

[195] It is worth noting that of 376 horses included in the *restauro equorum* account for this army, only thirteen were coursers.

[196] The *restauro equorum* list may be a little misleading: Corondus de Stene is clearly a knight, and John de Strechele was certainly a knight by the summer of 1340 (E101/22/35), but he may have been one of the four new creations of October 1339, noted

listed alongside men who were not apparently knights. It would seem, therefore, that Molyns himself was responsible. The effect of his 'influence' on
warhorse quality can be seen most clearly in the case of two of his men-at-
arms, who can be traced on earlier horse inventories. Both Philip de Lymbury
and Simon de Norton had been members of the earl of Cornwall's retinue in
Scotland in 1336: the former with a very cheap 5 mark horse, the latter with
one valued at £8.[197] Lymbury is also known to have served in the north in
1337–38, this time with a horse appraised at £8.[198] In his case, therefore, the
horse which he lost during the Cambrésis-Thiérache campaign was worth
five times the value of his previous mount; in Norton's, the increase was
four-fold. Even allowing for the usual inclination to take more expensive
horses to France than to Scotland, the values of these men's horses in 1338–39
were exceptional.

It is possible that some captains stipulated a minimum acceptable standard
of warhorse at the time of recruitment: the price, as it were, of admission
into a great retinue. The captain had, after all, his reputation and standing in
the military community to consider.[199] The normal rivalry between members
of the chivalrous class would contribute to the same end. An individual
man-at-arms was as much concerned with his own reputation as with that of
his master, and the quality of his warhorse could enhance, or detract from,
that reputation. Arriving at muster with the necessary standard of horseflesh
would not present a problem for a wealthy knight. But we must doubt
whether Philip de Lymbury or Simon de Norton had the means of acquiring
the kind of horses listed in Molyns' *restauro equorum* account; and, in any
case, if a high standard of horseflesh was expected, not all of Moleyns' men
responded. Amongst the esquires with more moderately priced horses, the
veteran campaigner Robert de Sussex served in the Low Countries and
Scotland with mounts of very similar value.[200] It appears very likely, therefore, that Molyns himself supplied some of the horses listed in the *restauro*

---

by the *vadia guerre* account (*Norwell*, p. 332). Alan de Holand had become a knight by
1342–43 (E36/204, fo. 107r) and Philip de Lymbury by 1345 (E101/25/9, m. 3).

[197] E101/19/36, m. 1.

[198] E101/35/3.

[199] On the noble household as 'an aristocratic trapping', see D. Crouch, *The image of
aristocracy in Britain, 1000–1300*, chapter 9.

[200] Robert de Sussex was a man of modest personal fortune, having only a little property in
Market Overton, Rutland, acquired on lease in 1332: *CFR, 1327–37*, p. 295; *CIPM*, xii,
no. 165. Nevertheless he served in Scotland in 1338 with a horse valued at £12, rather
above the average for an esquire and showing a marked improvement upon his 10 marks
mount of two years earlier: E101/19/36, m. 7d; E101/35/3. By the outbreak of the French
war, Sussex was a seasoned veteran, having campaigned in Scotland with near professional regularity throughout the 1330s under Henry de Percy (1333 and early 1334:
C71/13, m. 31; C71/14, m. 26) and then Giles de Badlesmere (1334, 1336, 1337, 1338:
C71/14, m. 13; C71/16, m. 28; C71/17, m. 3). The connection with Badlesmere was a
logical one, for he was lord of the manor of Market Overton; whilst Sussex's military
association with Molyns in 1338 (following Badlesmere's death), probably arose from

equorum account, perhaps as a means of attracting sought-after men-at-arms into his service,[201] or possibly in fulfilment of contracts with indentured retainers. There is little hard evidence concerning Molyns' retaining ties. Of the twelve men listed in the *restauro equorum* account, two (John de Strechele and Simon de Norton) were to continue in Molyns' service in the summer of 1340.[202] Norton, at least, appears to have been closely tied to Molyns,[203] and may have received his splendid £30 courser in 1338 as reward for services promised or already performed. But although his retinue's warhorses certainly do reflect the extent of his newly acquired power and status, there is another possible interpretation of the evidence: that Molyns' *restauro equorum* claim was a fraudulent one, or rather that he induced the appraising officers at the port of embarkation to record inflated valuations for ordinary horses. Such behaviour would have been entirely in character.

Few retinue-level horse appraisal records present such intriguing, if intractable, interpretative difficulties as does Molyns' compensation claim for the 1338–39 campaign. But there are few which pose no problems at all. Take, for example, Sir Walter de Mauny's section of the *restauro equorum* account resulting from the Breton campaign of 1342–43. Mauny, who arrived in England with Philippa of Hainault in 1327, carved out for himself a most distinguished place in the Edwardian regime, largely through loyal and effective service in the king's war in France. We would expect him to have assembled a distinguished company of men and horseflesh for the Breton campaign. In the event, the high level of warhorse values for his retinue (a mean of £24.58) was well above those for the other large companies of this particular English army: a full £5 above the nearest rival (Sir Reginald de Cobham's retinue) and £10 above the figure for the whole army.[204] Mauny's compensation account (see Table 6.6) contains an unusually high proportion of

Molyns' acquisition of the rent of Sussex's leasehold property: *The Victoria history of the counties of England: Rutland*, 2 vols (London, 1908–35), ii, pp. 141–42, 143.

[201] At least two of Molyns' men were German mercenaries: Peterkin de Colonia and Corondus de Stene, the latter with a very valuable horse.

[202] C76/15, m. 21; E101/22/35. Both Norton and Strechele continued their military careers into the 1340s, after Molyns' fall, under the banners of different captains. Two other men served in Molyns' retinue in both 1338–39 and 1340: John Fitz Bernard and Roger de Puttenham (*Treaty Rolls 1337–39*, no. 331; C76/14, m. 13; E101/22/35). Philip de Lymbury fought under various captains (1340: C76/15, m. 22; 1342: C76/17, m. 25) before settling into the service of Henry of Lancaster in the mid 1340s (1344: C76/19, m. 19; 1345–47: E101/25/9, m. 3). In November 1347 he was about to go on pilgrimage overseas: *CPR, 1345–48*, p. 422. For his later career, see Fowler, *The king's lieutenant*, p. 183 and n. 89.

[203] He is described as Molyns' valet in an application for letters of protection (C81/1733, no. 18) and, elsewhere, is seen carrying a letter from Molyns to Chancery (C81/1773, no. 24). Norton's association with Molyns may not have been a long-standing one, however, for in 1336 he had appeared in a protection warrant as Sir Andrew de Sakeville's *valet*: C81/1723, no. 16.

[204] See Appendix 2, Table A for retinue-level figures.

Table 6.6: The appraised warhorses lost by Sir Walter de Mauny's retinue, 1342–43

Sir Walter de Mauny	1 destrier	£100
Sir Baldwin de Freville	1 destrier	£52
Thomas de Belhous	1 courser	£40
Walter de Laundesbergh	1 equus	50 marks
Robert de Wylughby	1 equus	50 marks
Almaric de Newhall	1 equus	50 marks
Herman de Burgoign	1 equus	50 marks
John de Eston	1 equus	50 marks
Walter de Byntre	1 equus	40 marks
Henry de Romeseye	1 equus	40 marks
John de Corkele	1 equus	40 marks
Robert de Skardeburgh	1 equus	40 marks
Thomas Buset	1 equus	£20
Richard de Derby	1 equus	£20
John de Ellerton	1 equus	£20
Richard de Stapelton	1 equus	£10
John de Seint More	1 equus	£10
Robert de Catfeld	1 equus	£10
John Darras	1 equus	£8
John de Belhous	1 equus	10 marks
Robert de Newers	1 equus	100s
John de Kirkeby	1 equus	100s
John de Overton	1 equus	100s
Henry de Ardern	1 equus	100s

expensive warhorses. About two-thirds of them are valued at £20 or more, as compared with less than a quarter for the army as whole. This is admittedly a *restauro equorum* account,[205] but there is no reason to suspect that the sample of lost warhorses is unrepresentative of the whole retinue, that a disproportionately large number of horses were lost by the higher ranking members of Mauny's company. In fact, the very opposite appears to have been the case. Mauny's two retinues in 1342–43 both fielded significantly smaller proportions of knights than the army as a whole. Even so, only one of the men named in the *restauro equorum* account is recorded as a knight[206] and the majority were not recipients of letters of protection, the latter being a useful (though admittedly imperfect) guide to social standing and wealth.[207] The

205 There is also some complication arising from the fact that Mauny commanded the spring 1342 expedition and also served in the main expeditionary force in the autumn. It is not clear whether the *restauro equorum* account covers losses sustained by both of Mauny's two separate retinues, or only one of them.

206 The *restauro equorum* account is not a consistently reliable guide to military rank, but only two others among those named in Mauny's list can be shown to have been knights in 1342: Richard de Stapelton (C76/17, m. 17) and Walter de Landesbergen (*Norwell*, pp. 318, 339).

207 Of the twenty-four men who lost horses, only Mauny himself, Sir Baldwin de Freville, Sir Richard de Stapelton and John de Eston have enrolled protections.

evidence would seem to suggest that whilst Mauny had attracted few prominent members of the English knightly class into his retinue, many of those who did serve under him had rather better warhorses than would normally be expected of men of their status. Indeed, several of Mauny's men experienced a dramatic leap in horse quality. Sir Baldwin de Freville's £52 destrier represents a very marked improvement upon the £10 horse with which he is listed in the *restauro equorum* account for the Cambrésis-Thiérache campaign.[208]

With Mauny's retinue in 1342–43, as with Molyns' in 1338–39, one is left wondering how it was that such impressive horseflesh came to be recorded alongside the names of men of comparatively modest standing. It may well be that both Mauny and Molyns had felt the need to draw on their own resources, to supply warhorses from their own stables to some, at least, of their military retainers.[209] It would have been useful at this point to compare these *restauro equorum* data with similar records for other expeditions in which Mauny and Molyns were involved. Unfortunately no comparable material for either Molyns or Mauny appears to have survived. Such comparison is possible for a number of other captains (see Tables 6.7 and 6.8) and in these cases the relationship between individual commanders and the equestrian resources of their retinues can be examined over a sequence of campaigns in different theatres of war.

Table 6.7: Mean warhorse values (£): a selection of captains, 1336–60[210]

Name	Scotland 1336–38		Flanders 1338–39		Brittany 1342–43		France 1359–60	
earl of:								
Lancaster	8.3	(79)	29.1	(27)	11.1	(18)	9.8	(216)
Northampton	8.4	(56)	24.1	(24)	17.9	(38)	7.8	(40)
Salisbury	12.6	(89)	19.1	(65)	14.0	(10)	–	
Warwick	8.0	(145)	–		10.5	(12)	20.3	(20)
John de Beaumont	6.8	(12)	13.7	(15)	–		–	
Regd. de Cobham	–		9.4	(9)	19.4	(11)	7.8	(18)
John Darcy, snr.	9.3	(24)	12.2	(14)	9.8	(14)	–	
Hugh le Despenser	11.4	(17)	–		12.7	(16)	–	
All warhorses	8.9		16.4		14.3		9.0	

208 The increase for the German mercenary, Walter de Landesbergen, was from £9 15s (*Norwell*, p. 318) to 50 marks. John de Eston appears with a £4 horse in the retinue of William de Bohun in 1336 (E101/19/36, m. 5d); he may be the man who served with a 50 mark warhorse under Mauny in 1342–43.

209 Little is known of Mauny's retaining ties, but several of those listed in his *restauro equorum* account for 1342–43 are known to have served under him in earlier expeditions: John de Belhous, Walter de Bintre, John de Eston, Richard de Stapleton and Robert de Wylughby.

210 The bracketed figures are the numbers of warhorses included in the calculated means;

The data in Table 6.7 highlight very clearly the spread of retinue-level figures lying behind the overall mean value for each expedition. In some cases, the pattern of values for individual captains departs significantly from the general trend of values for the period. Admittedly, with some captains there is broad agreement with the general trend; and, where the evidence is available, the sequence of mean values usually shows a sharp increase at the start of the Hundred Years War, followed by a decline. But within this very simple schema there is much variation. The circumstances of individual career development were obviously important in this. In general, few untitled captains scaled the heights reached by the retinues of Edward III's inner circle of earls. The mean values for the companies of those captains who were not in the front rank frequently fell short of the value for the army as a whole. Sir John Darcy's retinue is a good example of this.[211] For both of the early campaigns of the French war, his retinue's mean was at least £4 less than that for the whole army. The figures for the earl of Northampton's retinue are appropriate for a captain of his standing. The scale of the improvement in warhorse quality in the late 1330s was no doubt a consequence of Bohun's elevation to an earldom,[212] while his mean values for 1342–43 and 1359–60 are very much in line with the period's general downward movement in values. Nevertheless, the degree of contrast between the figures for 1338–39 and those for the Reims campaign is indeed striking. A fuller sequence of data is available for Henry of Lancaster, for in addition to the figures in Table 6.7, there is a little material arising from his spells of service in Gascony in 1345 and 1350. Lancaster was the greatest magnate outside the immediate royal family and perhaps the most talented English captain of the Edwardian age. The peaks in the sequence of mean warhorse values for his retinue amply reflect his pre-eminence. The figure for the Cambrésis-Thiérache campaign is nearly twice that for the English army as a whole, and the mean value of the forty-three horses lost by his men during his *chevauchées* in Gascony in 1345–47 was

---

sources, as for Table 6.1. For a captain to be included in Table 6.7, information had to be available for at least ten warhorses for two or more theatres of war. The 'Scotland 1336–38' figures may be based upon the data from one or more campaigns; for a breakdown of these figures see Table 6.8. The data from the inventories for the Irish expeditions of 1361–64 have been excluded because earlier comparative evidence is available for only one captain, the earl of Stafford. His retinue mean was £9.4 for the Reims campaign and £10 for service in Ireland in the early 1360s.

211 Sir John Darcy was a prominent figure in Edward III's court: he was successively Steward of the royal household (1337–40) and King's Chamberlain (1341–46): Tout, *Chapters*, iii, p. 89 and n. 1; vi, pp. 43, 46. His 'Scottish' mean, which refers to the army of 1337, needs to be seen in the context of an inventory which includes a high proportion of retinues with depressed horse values.

212 Elevation to the earldom of Derby appears to have had a similar effect on Lancaster's retinue. Salisbury's high 'Scottish' mean, £12.6, refers to his retinue in 1337–38 – that is, after he had secured his earldom.

even higher: £32.[213] Given this, the corresponding figure for 1350, £13.7, is surprisingly low; but the source lying behind it, a record of horse *sales*, may not be strictly compatible with the evidence of the inventories.[214] Altogether more reliable is the duke's low mean value for the 1359–60 campaign; and it is entirely consistent with the figures for the great majority of the army's major retinues. For this campaign Lancaster headed a retinue of well over a thousand fighting men, including nearly 600 men-at-arms:[215] a small army in itself, rivalling in size and splendour the company of the prince of Wales. Yet the average value of the horses lost by the duke's men-at-arms was no more than a third of the level recorded for his retinue at the start of the continental war. By the late 1350s, then, Lancaster's men-at-arms, in common with the English aristocracy in general, were going on active service with markedly less costly warhorses than had previously been the case.

Some of the figures presented in Table 6.7 diverge sharply from the normal pattern. Sir Reginald de Cobham's mean value for the 1338–39 campaign is lower than we might expect, whilst the corresponding figure for the Breton expedition represents an increase of over 100%: a reversal, therefore, of the usual trend. The low figure is actually not difficult to explain. Norwell's *restauro equorum* account lists the names of nine men with their lost horses: Cobham himself is not amongst them and none are designated knights. Since the retinue included a small proportion of knights (four, including Cobham, out of thirty-seven men-at-arms), it would seem that it is the unusual preponderance of esquires which explains the low mean for this expedition.[216] Cobham's retinue in 1342–43 had a *slightly* more impressive array of knights: seven out of forty-nine. Perhaps the general level of values for the retinue really was higher than in 1338–39; but equally we are drawn to the conclusion that the sample of horses lost in Brittany included a large proportion of the retinue's more expensive mounts. Among them were Cobham's own magnificent 100 marks warhorse and five others valued at £20 or more. At first glance, the opposite appears to have been the case with Henry of Lancaster's equestrian losses in 1342, for the trough in this captain's sequence of mean values seems to be the consequence of a disproportionately heavy

---

213 E101/25/9. As we have seen, Lancaster assembled a very distinguished body of men-at-arms for this expedition, 40% of whom were of knightly status.
214 E403/355, m. 19; for a discussion of this source, see above, p. 208. The individual horse values ranged from 100 marks to 100s. It is worth noting that nearly a third of Lancaster's men-at-arms were of knightly estate and more than half of those listed in the sales list are recorded as knights. The overall level of values may, however, have been affected by the fact that fifteen of the horses were 'second-string' mounts.
215 E101/393/11, fo. 79v.
216 *Norwell*, pp. 313, 330. Other factors should not be discounted, however. Only one of Cobham's men in the *restauro equorum* list can be traced in earlier inventories and he, John de Lulleford with a 10 mark horse, can be detected serving with a slightly more valuable (11 mark) warhorse in the preceding Scottish expedition: E101/35/3, m. 1.

representation of *esquires* in his *restauro equorum* account.[217] These records are not, however, a consistently reliable guide to rank. Moreover, the presence of several men who had served with considerably more valuable horses in the Cambrésis[218] may suggest that Lancaster's list of lost horses from the 1342–43 campaign does indeed accurately reflect the level of values for the whole retinue: a retinue whose horseflesh had been more depressed than most by the prospect of a campaign in Brittany.[219]

It may be possible, then, to offer an explanation when a retinue's equestrian resources appear not to reflect its captain's position in the military hierarchy, or are sharply at variance with the horse valuation levels for the rest of the army. On the one hand, a captain could have recruited an unusually large – or small – number of knights; or he might have deviated from normal practice and supplied warhorses to some or all of his men-at-arms. On the other hand, the horse appraisal or compensation records could be offering misleading evidence. The values recorded in the inventories were inevitably affected by the outlook and level of expertise of the team of appraisers at the point of muster. A *restauro equorum* account may present a sample of a retinue's horseflesh which is anything but random. Such factors as these – though precisely which may not always be clear – will account for many of the inconsistencies in warhorse values at the retinue level, whether isolated cases of retinues with improbably high values (such as the cases of Molyns and Mauny considered earlier) or sequences of eccentric mean values, such as that for the earl of Warwick's *comitiva* from the 1330s to the Reims campaign.[220]

---

217 Of eighteen warhorses lost by members of Lancaster's retinue, only two are assigned to knights and only three were valued at £20 or more. Of Lancaster's men-at-arms, 22% were knights, a respectable proportion.

218 The drop in value for John de Dyngeley was from 40 marks to 20 marks; for Richard de la Vache, from £30 to £10; for Theobald Trussell, from £20 to 10 marks. There were a few slight increases (e.g. Reginald de Mohun: £30 in 1342, 40 marks in 1338–39), but the circumstances of men like Nicholas Gernon (a 10 marks horse for Scotland, 1336; £8 for Brittany, six years later) tend to confirm the impression that the level of values for Lancaster's retinue were unusually depressed in 1342–43.

219 The 1342–43 mean for the earl of Warwick's retinue was also unusually low and, once again, this may reflect a disproportionate representation of esquires amongst those losing horses (ten out of twelve) or a preponderance of low value horses in the retinue as a whole (nine out of the twelve lost horses were valued at 10 marks or less) or a combination of these factors. Two of Warwick's esquires (William Carless and Thomas Foliot) had horses which were cheaper than those with which they had served in Scotland. Against this, Sir Robert Herle's £24 warhorse represented an improvement, though not especially marked, on his mounts of the later 1330s – valued at 20 marks and £20.

220 His retinue's mean value in 1342–43 was even lower than Henry of Lancaster's, whilst the figure for the Reims campaign was over double that for the army as a whole. The sequence of his three retinue means for the Scottish campaigns, 1336–38, runs contrary to the general trend (see Table 6.8).

Table 6.8: Scottish expeditions, 1336–38 – mean warhorse values (£) for selected captains[221]

Name	1336	1337	1337–38
earl of:			
Angus	6.3 (30)	–	–
Arundel	–	–	11.8 (41)
Buchan[222]	9.3 (36)	–	–
Cornwall	8.7 (62)	–	–
Gloucester	–	–	11.7 (62)
Lancaster	8.3 (79)	–	–
Northampton	8.4 (56)	–	–
Oxford	10.3 (20)	–	–
Salisbury	–	–	12.6 (89)
Warwick	7.3 (74)	8.6 (67)	8.5 (4)
Giles de Badlesmere	9.0 (20)	–	8.9 (25)
John de Beaumont	–	–	6.8 (12)
Ralph Dacre	–	7.6 (21)	–
John Darcy, senior	–	9.3 (24)	–
Hugh le Despenser	–	–	11.4 (17)
John de Mowbray	–	7.0 (38)	11.7 (5)
Ralph de Neville	9.5 (51)	7.3 (62)	14.0 (7)
Henry de Percy	8.5 (56)	6.7 (90)	7.2 (38)
John de Segrave	9.3 (18)	–	–
John de Tibetot	9.5 (15)	–	–
Richard Talbot	–	–	9.1 (28)
Thomas de Ughtred	9.3 (14)	–	7.7 (5)
Thomas Wake	–	8.7 (25)	–
All warhorses	8.5	7.6	10.6

Though in some cases inconsistent, a captain's influence on the quality of his retinue's horseflesh was shaped by his authority during the recruitment process and, more generally, by the place he occupied in the military community. Earls and knights were members of different divisions of the chivalrous league, of course, but a captain's 'place' in the military community was determined not merely by his rank. There was always room for individuality, such as that which enabled Molyns and Mauny to rise to a height beyond that attained by most bannerets. There was room, too, for the existence of identifiably separate groups within the military community; indeed, fourteenth-century England was a patchwork of local or regional military communities, some of which had distinctive and sharply focused martial preoccupations. Of the community of the Welsh March, R.R. Davies has noted that, until 1300 at least, 'military vigilance was a precondition of lordship . . . war was

221 Sources: as for Table 6.1.
222 Henry de Beaumont.

less a pastime and more a way of life'.[223] Under the Black Prince's lordship, the energies of the military community of Cheshire were directed principally into the war in Aquitaine.[224]

Edward III's captains were not, then, a homogeneous group. Admittedly there were many whose careers were far from narrowly focused, men who fought in several theatres of war. In the 1330s, for example, Edward III's friends among the nobility, together with the military resources of the royal household, campaigned with him first in Scotland and then in France. But the armies which served in the interest of the English crown in the Scottish wars were somewhat different in composition from those raised for continental campaigns. There was a section of the aristocracy whose attention was primarily turned towards Scotland and the borders: a group of magnates and a broad constituency of knights and esquires whose interests lay in northern England. Captains like Sir Henry de Percy (d.1352) and Sir Ralph de Neville (d.1367), leading retinues drawn from the gentry of the northern shires,[225] made important contributions to major royal expeditions to Scotland; but more significantly, they bore the brunt of border defence, both routine garrison work and the altogether more strenuous efforts required to oppose a major Scottish invasion, as in October 1346. The northern military community embraced not only the border counties, but also areas at some remove from the March, since regularly serving captains would naturally seek to recruit in their landholding heartlands. The Percies, although having growing territorial interests in Northumberland, relied heavily on friends, neighbours and tenants, as well as retainers, from their traditional centres of power in Yorkshire.[226] During the 1330s and 1340s, the northerners were on active

---

[223] R.R. Davies, *Lordship and society in the March of Wales, 1282–1400* (Oxford, 1978), pp. 67–68.

[224] Morgan, *War and society in medieval Cheshire*; Bennett, *Community, class and careerism*, chapter 9.

[225] These retinues can sometimes be studied in detail. For example, the basic proportions of Percy's *comitiva* for much of his active campaigning life can readily be ascertained from pay records (1322–23: BL Stowe MS 553, fo. 57r; 1327: E372/173, m. 10; 1334–37: BL Cotton MS, Nero C. VIII, fos 233r, 236v, 240v, 245r; 1337–38: E101/388/5, m. 13; *Norwell*, pp. 346, 362; 1341–42: E36/204, fos 102r, 103v; 1347: E101/25/10, mm. 5, 11). The names of the men-at-arms serving under his banner are known in large numbers for only some of these expeditions – those which are illuminated by horse inventories and muster rolls (1336: E101/19/36, m. 3; 1337: E101/20/17, mm. 4, 5, 9; winter 1337–38: E101/35/3, m. 2). But lists of enrolled protections offer evidence which is by no means negligible: e.g. seven protections for the Weardale campaign, sixteen for the siege of Berwick and sixteen for the Roxburgh campaign (C71/11, m. 5; C71/13, mm. 28, 31; C71/14, mm. 2, 10, 11, 14, 15).

[226] A. Goodman, 'Introduction', *War and border societies in the Middle Ages*, ed. A. Goodman and A. Tuck (London and New York, 1992), pp. 11; and A. Tuck, 'The Percies and the community of Northumberland in the later fourteenth century', ibid., pp. 178–95. Yorkshire had, of course, been subjected to Scottish raids during the reign of Edward II. Note also, in the later fourteenth century, a 'reluctance on the part of the crown to

service as often as any group in the English military community, yet they took comparatively little part in continental expeditions during the early years of the war.[227]

The military outlook of the northern captains and the regular members of their retinues, hardened by the experience of decades of intermittent fighting in the border country, was well attuned to the conditions of the Scottish March. How far can this be seen in the quality of their warhorses as recorded in the horse inventories? The records from the later 1330s offer an excellent opportunity to consider this question. At first glance, there does seem to be a difference between the quality of horseflesh employed by northern retinues and that which is to be seen in the inventories of captains who had recruited in other parts of England. Confining our attention to the figures based upon respectable amounts of data, Table 6.8 shows that the highest mean values are associated with the retinues of captains whose centres of power did not lie in the north of England; and, indeed, that some of the lowest means are recorded for the retinues of northern magnates. The essential thrust of this evidence would *appear* to be that, either through inclination or because of limited personal resources, the northern gentry served in the rough terrain of the borders and Scotland with less expensive warhorses than were normally employed by men from further afield. It is certainly true that some of the northern retinues did include an unusually large proportion of low-value warhorses. While 12% of all warhorses in the inventories of the 1330s were valued at less than £5, 20% of Henry de Percy's men had low-value warhorses

permit the engagement of local men' for garrison service in the immediate border area (A. Tuck, 'War and society in the medieval north', *Northern History*, xxi (1985), p. 45); and the mobilisation of the counties north of the Trent in times of military emergency.

[227] For example, a number of the captains serving with Edward III in Scotland in 1341–42 did not accompany him to Brittany in the following autumn: Gilbert Umfraville (earl of Angus), Henry de Percy, Thomas and Anthony de Lucy, Robert Clifford, Ralph de Neville (E36/204, fos 102r–4r, 105v–10v). After the start of the French war, the defence of northern England was largely left to the military community of the counties north of the Trent: J. Campbell, 'England, Scotland and the Hundred Years War in the fourteenth century', *Europe in the late Middle Ages*, ed. J. Hale, R. Highfield and B. Smalley (London, 1965), pp. 192–93. Men from this area were generally not encouraged to join continental armies, though a not insignificant number, particularly from counties not actually bordering Scotland, did pursue careers in France during the early years of the war. Examples from the East Riding include Walter de Heslerton (C76/14, m. 4; C76/17, m. 27) and Sir John de Hothum: *Norwell*, p. 314 (40 marks horse); E36/204, fo. 86v (£20). The bishop of Durham's involvement in the 1346 campaign ensured that there were northerners at Crécy. Later in the fourteenth century periods of truce allowed greater participation in the French war. The experienced border fighter, Sir Thomas Gray, has left us an eyewitness account of the Reims campaign. Sir Henry de Percy took the opportunity of serving in France during the Anglo-Scottish truce from 1385 to 1388: Goodman, 'Introduction', *War and border societies in the Middle Ages*, ed. Goodman and Tuck, p. 13.

and as many as 50% of the earl of Angus' company in 1336.[228] By contrast, none of the earl of Salisbury's military retainers in 1337–38 had warhorses worth less than £5; and 17% of them are listed alongside mounts worth £20 or more (as compared with only 5% of all those appearing in the inventories of the period). The contrast should not be overstated, however. Nearly all of the higher mean values – those in excess of £20 – are associated with the inventories for the 1337–38 campaign. Clearly it was the involvement of the earls of Salisbury, Arundel and Gloucester that was largely responsible for bringing the mean value for this army up to £10.6;[229] but few 'northern' captains are included in the full inventory for this expedition, so a proper comparison is not really possible. The figure for the Percy retinue is certainly low, despite including a respectable proportion of knights (11 out of 38), but it seems that only part of his retinue is listed in the inventory and the *restauro equorum* account; and it is, in any case, only reasonable to expect the highest quality of horseflesh to be found in the companies of earls. The impression conveyed by the inventories from 1336 is, moreover, very different. The retinues of captains from outside northern England figure prominently in the horse lists, but on this occasion there is no difference between the retinue-level means of, for example, the earl of Cornwall, Henry of Lancaster and William de Bohun and that of Henry de Percy. The highest mean, for the earl of Oxford's retinue, is only a little above that for Ralph de Neville's.

The bundle of inventories for the 1337 expedition exhibit a low overall level of values: somewhat lower than for the previous year and decidedly below that displayed in the 1337–38 inventory. At first glance this appears to be the result of a preponderance of northern captains in the horse rolls for 1337. There are few leaders who are not from the community north of the Trent and these are not high value retinues.[230] Yet there are reasons for believing that the mean values for the northern magnates in these records, and for Percy and Neville in particular, are artificially low. Although the mean for Warwick's retinue in 1337 was higher than it had been in 1336, both Percy and Neville experienced a sharp fall of about £2 from their 1336 levels. The decline in values appears not to have been a consequence of changing retinue composition, but rather a matter of the same men-at-arms serving with less expensive horses. Thus, of the 152 men-at-arms listed in the retinue inventories of Neville and Percy in 1337, seventy had served in the previous year. Of these, thirty-eight (54%) brought less expensive warhorses in 1337 and

---

[228] It is significant that only four of the thirty men-at-arms in Angus' retinue were of knightly status; but such a deficiency of knights is not evident in, for example, Percy's retinue.

[229] Their high means are partly attributable to the fact that each of them had more than one valuable warhorse appraised for their own use: Salisbury (100 marks, £50, £40, 40 marks); Arundel (100 marks, £30, 40 marks, 20 marks); Gloucester (80 marks, 80 marks).

[230] On the composition of this army, see Lewis, 'The recruitment and organisation of a contract army, May to November 1337', pp. 9 and n. 6, 10.

nineteen (27%) had mounts of identical value.[231] Sir William de Aton, a prominent member of Percy's retinue and a veteran fighter against the Scots, was amongst those who registered a decline in warhorse value in 1337 (from 20 marks to £10). When he returned to Scotland the following winter, Aton's warhorse was assigned a higher value, £12. An improvement of this kind was shared by two-thirds of the men who were named on all three of the major inventories from the later 1330s.[232] In the case of Sir Ingram de Umfraville, the recovery brought the value exactly back to the level of 1336 (£12, £8, £12). It is easier to draw attention to this short-lived dip in horse values than to account for it. Perhaps the men entrusted with the task of horse appraisal in 1337 were less generous than their counterparts in 1336 or 1337–38. Indeed, given the short time-span, it is even possible that some individual warhorses appear on more than one of these inventories, but were assigned different values on each occasion.

Clearly, the records prepared by the appraisers in 1337 need to be handled with caution. Nevertheless, taking the collection of inventories from the later 1330s as a whole, it is evident that there was no significant difference between the level of warhorse values normally prevailing in northern magnate retinues and that for those companies originating from other parts of the realm, provided always that the captains were of comparable military status. There were admittedly few high-value warhorses registered against the names of members of the northern military community. Only seven out of the 304 horses appearing in the Percy and Neville inventories had values of £15 or more. A rather larger proportion of the knightly class from the rest of England had high quality horseflesh, but the number is still not large. Salisbury's retinue in 1338 is exceptional: a quarter of the eighty-nine men listed in his inventory have horses valued at £15 or over. But Salisbury was in the best position to attract the flower of the aristocracy into his service, and to demand high standards of horseflesh from them. Men of the calibre of Sir Edward de Montagu, Sir Thomas de Berkeley, Sir John de Beauchamp, Sir Ralph de Ufford and Sir John de Sully, with horses valued at between 40 and 50 marks, were members of Salisbury's retinue in 1338. By contrast, none in Percy's retinue for this campaign had a horse valued at over £20, the highest values being registered for men from his own family or the Yorkshire gentry.[233] To a degree, then, contrasts in levels of warhorse values are to be explained in terms of different patterns of recruitment. But Salisbury's 1338

---

[231] In many cases, the decline was fairly modest: e.g. Sir Robert Bertram, 20 marks (1336) and £12 (1337); Sir Edmund de Clavering, 20 marks and £10. But for some it amounted to a 50% or more fall: William Fitz Henry, £10 and £5; William de Foxholes, £8 and 4 marks.

[232] Fourteen of the twenty-one men who figure in all three inventories show an increase in 1337–38, following a decline (or no change in value) in 1337.

[233] For example, Sir William and Sir John de Percy (£20, £16), Sir William de Aton (£12), an unspecified knight of the Heslarton family (20 marks) and Sir Robert Bertram (£10).

retinue is an extreme case. The earl of Warwick's three horse lists from the later 1330s display very different characteristics. His recruiting net was cast quite widely. In 1337 it took in Sir John de Beauchamp and Sir Hugh le Despenser, as well as lesser men from various parts of the realm. Yet only four out of 145 warhorses listed in his inventories had values of £15 or more; nearly three-quarters of them were worth less than £10 and one in ten, less than £5.

The majority of the most valuable horses in the inventories of the later 1330s were associated with men from outside the northern military community. But most of the ordinary knights and esquires listed in these rolls have more moderately valued mounts and within this much larger group of personnel it is less easy to see any relationship between geographical origins and quality of horseflesh. Typical men-at-arms, of equivalent status, from north and south would serve with horses of similar quality. For the northerner, born into a tradition of border fighting, the choice of a warhorse was not a matter for lengthy deliberation; and by the 1330s, it was clear to the active military community throughout England what was demanded by conditions in Scotland. In this respect, there had certainly been a change since Edward II's reign. During the 1310s the contrast between the warhorses brought by the men in the earl of Pembroke's army and those employed by Andrew de Harcla's northern borderers was very marked, the latter's inexpensive, but hardy, mounts being much better suited to the terrain, but also in many cases all that could have been afforded. The experience of an individual, Sir John de Hardreshull, illustrates the change in outlook very well. He served in Scotland with a 40 marks warhorse in 1315, but in 1336 opted for a mount valued at only 20 marks.[234] By the 1330s, then, northerner and southerner appear to make essentially similar responses to the prospect of service against the Scots, but these were similar responses from very different stand-points. The differences, in character and outlook, between the northern military community and that from other parts of England are, thus, very largely concealed within a single 'Scottish' inventory. They are, however, clearly enough revealed when a broader view, which embraces the whole corpus of extant horse rolls, is taken. Sir Alexander de Hilton served under Sir Ralph de Neville throughout the 1330s[235] and John Tempest was as consistent in his military support of Sir Henry de Percy. Both appear in three consecutive horse inventories, their warhorses varying little in value from one roll to the next,[236] but neither Hilton nor Tempest, nor indeed their captains, appear to have ventured further afield. Their military horizons stretched no further than the northern theatre of war. This cannot be said of many in the English military community in the mid fourteenth century. When Laurence Basset and John de Goldesburgh followed their captain, the earl of Salisbury, from

234 E.101/15/6, m. 1; E101/19/36, m. 1.
235 Hilton was with Neville at Halidon Hill: C71/13, m. 20.
236 Hilton: all three horses valued at 20 marks. Tempest: £8, £5, £6.

the siege of Dunbar to the Low Countries in 1338, they (along with the great majority of those who travelled from Scotland to the continent) acquired more expensive horseflesh on the way to the port of embarkation.[237] They were choosing warhorses suitable for the expected circumstances of the campaign in the same way as they had prior to going to Scotland. A change in retinue or a rise in military status could have the effect of magnifying the increase in value. When Sir John de Avenel joined Salisbury's retinue for the continental campaign, he brought a warhorse which, at £50, was worth five times the value of his mount for the recent Scottish campaign.[238] The fourfold increase in the value of Robert de Rouclif's horseflesh appears to have been an accompaniment to his assumption of knighthood during the months separating service in Scotland and departure for the continent.[239]

CONCLUSION

No animal is more noble than the horse, since it is by horses that princes, magnates and knights are separated from lesser people.

Jordanus Ruffus[240]

The potent symbolism of the great horse, as an expression of the status and function of the knightly class, was a commonplace feature of the art and literature of medieval England. By their direct association of the knights and esquires in the military community with carefully described and valued horseflesh, the inventories and *restauro equorum* accounts add substantial documentary weight to this imagery. But they go a good deal further than this, for through these equestrian descriptions and valuations the inventories provide a means of assessing the position of individuals within the knightly class. Assessment of a man's status through the quality of his warhorses depends, of course, upon knowledge of the general patterns in the horse valuation data. It is necessary to be aware of the relationship between military rank, the standing of individual captains and warhorse quality; and of the movements in the general level of values through the period, as well as short-term fluctuations related to the conditions of particular theatres of war. Against an understanding of these background patterns, it is possible to place the circumstances of thousands of individuals into proper perspective. A man's warhorse can be compared with both the mean value and the spread of values for a particular campaign and, indeed, with the norms for his rank and for the retinue in which he served. The value of his warhorse, combined with its

---

237 Valuation increases: Basset, £10 to £20; Goldesburgh, £5 to £12.

238 This man, or perhaps more probably an esquire of the same name serving with a 10 mark horse in Scotland in 1338 (E101/35/3, mm. 1, 2), may be he who later became captain-lieutenant of Brittany.

239 Rouclif had a £5 horse in Scotland and a £20 mount in Flanders, on both occasions serving under John de Beaumont.

240 Quoted in Davis, *The medieval warhorse*, pp. 107–8.

other attributes, has thus become an index of his standing within the military community. Social and military status has acquired a numerical value.

Learning something about individual men-at-arms through the quality of their warhorses is especially useful for those whose lives are poorly illuminated by readily accessible information of other kinds: the thousands of faceless men about whom scarcely more than their names are known. There are admittedly limitations to using the horse valuation data in this way. It must be remembered that horse values were determined by teams of appraisers and that consistency of judgement, from team to team and from one campaign to the next, cannot always be relied upon. Quite apart from distortions introduced by the subjectivity of the appraisal process, it is not always certain that men were listed with warhorses of their own choosing. Whilst most fighting men would serve with their own horses, there would always be a proportion of them whose mounts were supplied by their captains; and occasionally a man can be seen taking over someone else's horse during the course of a campaign.[241] Then again, we need to be clear about what a warhorse is likely to reveal about its owner. Weight of military experience was not necessarily reflected in horseflesh. It was only likely to be so if accumulated experience was accompanied by personal enrichment and social elevation. Similarly, if in Edward II's reign it is sometimes possible to associate a certain type and standard of warhorse with a particular regional military community, by the 1330s such patterns are far less readily evident in the horse valuation data.

Although important, these limitations should be kept in proper perspective. They do not seriously dent the usefulness of the horse valuations as a guide to a man's social standing and economic resources. The horse valuation is undoubtedly a very simple measure of wealth, but we would be unwise to underestimate its potential merely because of its simplicity. There are, after all, several good reasons for taking it seriously. Firstly, the existence of a relationship between a man's disposable income and the standard of his military equipment, including his horseflesh, is only to be expected; and, indeed, such a relationship forms the basis of many of the English crown's experiments in military assessment in the fourteenth century.[242] Secondly, though not in any sense a sophisticated source, the lack of complexity of the horse valuation data is in fact a positive advantage. The uncomplicated evidence of the inventories can be combined without difficulty with that offered by other military records (such as letters of protection and muster rolls), which can offer less precise indications of personal wealth and military precedence. Thirdly, the inventory evidence has a very wide coverage. A simple guide to wealth is offered for a very large number of men over a period of

---

241 E.g. on 15 December 1324 Edmund de Duddeden took over the appraised warhorse of Sir Nicholas de Latimer, who had died on the previous day: BL Additional MS 7967, fo. 31v.

242 For examples from the early 1320s and mid 1340s, see Powicke, *Military obligation in medieval England*, pp. 149, 196.

three reigns: a body of evidence which stands in striking contrast with that supplied by more conventional sources. The availability of manorial account rolls and rentals for the property of the lay aristocracy is at best patchy, and for some parts of England these records are very scarce.[243] Inquisitions *post mortem*, although more plentiful, are a less reliable guide to landed income.[244] Their coverage, moreover, is largely confined to the property of tenants in chief.[245] Like rolls of arms,[246] then, inquisitions *post mortem* cast light on only a section of the lay landholding community. Potentially of greater value are the records associated with the short-lived military assessment of the mid 1340s, by which specific manpower demands were made of individual landowners on the basis of their income (for example, a landowner with property worth £25 *per annum* was to provide an equipped man-at-arms).[247] Various types of records were generated by this recruiting experiment.[248] The original returns take the form of county-level lists of landowners, with

[243] For example, Gloucestershire: Saul, *Knights and esquires*, pp. 205–6. Several small collections of accounts have received detailed attention: see, for example, Saul, *Scenes from provincial life*, chapter 4 (east Sussex); R.H. Britnell, 'Production for the market on a small fourteenth-century estate', *EcHR*, 2nd ser., xix (1966), pp. 380–87 (Essex).

[244] C.D. Ross and T.B. Pugh, 'Materials for the study of baronial incomes in fifteenth-century England', *EcHR*, 2nd ser., vi (1953–4), pp. 186–89; Saul, *Knights and esquires*, pp. 206–7. But for a more positive view of the value of inquisitions *post mortem*, particularly as a source for 'the physical composition of the demesne and the annual value of its constituent parts', see B.M.S. Campbell, J.A. Galloway and M. Murphy, 'Rural land-use in the metropolitan hinterland, 1270–1339: the evidence of the inquisitions *post mortem*', *Agricultural History Review*, xl (1992), pp. 1–22. Somewhat similar, but much less familiar, are the records generated during distraint of knighthood proceedings in the Exchequer. These supply two views of an individual's property: the testimony of the landholder himself and the judgement of a local jury (for a discussion of procedure, see Powicke, *Military obligation in medieval England*, pp. 177–78). The enrolled depositions and inquisitions are to be found in the Memoranda Rolls of the King's Remembrancer (E159), *Recorda*. Original files have survived for a few cases: e.g. E198/4/1 (Robert de Vere, 1357); E199/34/14 (Robert de Sallowe, 1344–47). Although useful as a guide to the property of prosperous esquires, this is not an abundant source: for example, about 150 names are included in the original sheriffs returns for the 1333 distraint (E198/3/18; C47/1/19), but only in a minority of cases did individuals claim insufficiency of property and therefore necessitate the gathering of detailed information on their sources of income.

[245] Not all are major landholders: R.H. Hilton, 'The content and sources of English agrarian history before 1500', *Agricultural History Review*, iii (1955), p. 14.

[246] N. Denholm-Young drew attention to a group of rolls of arms dating from the 1330s, suggesting that they represented 'a Who's Who for 1334–5, or a Peerage, Baronage, and Knightage of England on the eve of the Hundred Years War': *The country gentry in the fourteenth century* (Oxford, 1969), p. 96. Although a valuable source, they reveal nothing of men below the rank of knight.

[247] Powicke, *Military obligation in medieval England*, pp. 195–99; G. Harriss, *King, parliament and public finance in medieval England to 1369* (Oxford, 1975), pp. 392–95.

[248] For a discussion of these records, see Ayton, 'The English army and the Normandy campaign of 1346'.

estimated annual property values against each name expressed as round sums, from 100s to £1,000. These returns cast much light on the lower levels of the lay landholding community, the 'lesser gentry'. Had they survived in anything like complete form, they would have provided a rare opportunity to reconstruct the basic patterns of lay landholding throughout the kingdom. But the uneven survival and illegibility of these lists, and the fragmented nature of related records, frustrates anything more than local studies.[249] There are no sources of comparable form and scope until the income tax records of the fifteenth century, of which the most often discussed corpus of documents is that of 1436[250] and the earliest significant collection dates from 1412.[251] By comparison, the lay subsidy and poll-tax records of the fourteenth century are of limited value as a guide to knightly wealth.[252]

By comparison with the conventional sources for the study of aristocratic wealth and status, the horse inventories offer simple, but plentiful evidence, wholly free from in-built bias towards particular sections of the lay landholding community. They illuminate all levels of the aristocracy, from earls to the humblest of esquires, and by virtue of the relative precision of the horse valuations the subtle contours of the military community are brought into view. Of the knights, the wealthier can be readily distinguished from the less affluent. Esquires who were apparently possessed of resources sufficient to support knighthood stand out starkly amongst men of more modest wealth.[253] Precedence within families is also reflected in horse values. In 1336 Henry de Cresswell *senior* had an £8 horse and his son, Henry, a mount valued at 10 marks.[254] At a rather higher level of the military community, Sir Thomas de Poynings served with a £20 warhorse, whilst his son, Sir Michael, had a 20 mark steed.[255]

---

[249] For analysis of the largely legible Gloucestershire returns, see Saul, *Knights and esquires*, pp. 33–34.

[250] H.L. Gray, 'Incomes from land in England in 1436', *EHR*, xliv (1934), pp. 607–39 was the pioneering article; for subsequent discussions, see T.B. Pugh and C.D. Ross, 'The English baronage and the income tax of 1436', *BIHR*, xxvi (1953), pp. 1–28; T.B. Pugh, 'The magnates, knights and gentry', *Fifteenth-century England, 1399–1509*, ed. S.B. Chrimes, C.D. Ross and R.A. Griffiths (Manchester, 1972), pp. 97–101. Cf. C. Carpenter, *Locality and polity. A study of Warwickshire landed society, 1401–1499* (Cambridge, 1992), pp. 50–79.

[251] S. Payling, *Political society in Lancastrian England. The greater gentry of Nottinghamshire* (Oxford, 1991), chapter 1 and appendix 1; J.M.W. Bean, 'Landlords', *The agrarian history of England and Wales, III, 1348–1500*, ed. E. Miller (Cambridge, 1991), pp. 526–42.

[252] Saul, *Knights and esquires*, pp. 207–8.

[253] Cf. the lesser Gascon nobility in the 1290s and 1320s: Vale, *The Angevin legacy and the Hundred Years War, 1250–1340* , pp. 110–11.

[254] E101/19/36, m. 7; BL Cotton MS, Nero C. VIII, fo. 280v.

[255] The inventory (E101/19/36, m. 1) refers to both men as Thomas, but this is clearly a mistake (cf. a protection request bill: C81/1723, no. 17). In the War of Saint-Sardos, Thomas and Michael de Poynings had served with warhorses separated in value by only

The usefulness of horse valuations as a guide to the status and wealth of individual men-at-arms is perhaps most evident when it is possible to perceive changes over time, when a man's campaigning life is illuminated by a sequence of warhorse values. By setting an individual within the context of the collective experience of the military community, it is possible to assess whether his career in arms has developed in a conventional way. Significant changes in status and/or wealth usually found expression in appropriate choices of horseflesh. Most obviously this occurred when men became knights or bannerets: Richard Blundell's exchange of a 10 marks *equus* for a £20 courser as an accompaniment to the receipt of knighthood is but one of many examples of this.[256] And, as we have seen, it could sometimes occur when men entered the service of a prominent captain. The valuation data can act, therefore, as a barometer for the measurement of shifts in status; but they are also a means of observing the responses of individuals to changes in campaigning conditions. For large numbers of men, it is possible to see how horseflesh quality was influenced by the prospect of service in different theatres of war or by the general developments in fighting methods which formed part of the Edwardian military revolution. For many military enterprises, fairly consistent patterns of behaviour can be detected; most men responded in an essentially similar way to the prospect of a particular campaign. Yet there were always some who appear to be swimming against the current. Whilst there are dangers in focusing too much attention on this minority group (it would be all too easy to obscure the main thrust of the evidence), it is with such men as these that the horse valuations really come into their own as a guide to a man's fortunes. It might be the force of individual career development which has served to override the normal trend of the period. Whilst the general level of horse values for the 1342–43 campaign was rather lower than had prevailed in 1338–39, the value of Sir Michael de Poynings' warhorse in Brittany was double that of his previous steed (£20 to £40); but this was only fitting for a man who had become a banneret, a leader of a company in the king's army and the head of an important Sussex gentry family.[257] Then there are those whose warhorse values remained stable, or even dropped a little, at the start of the Hundred Years War, instead of following the normal trend of significant increase.[258] Sometimes the explanation may lie in a temporary cash-flow crisis or a more

---

a few shillings (E101/13/35). The size of the differential between father and son was usually greater than this. In the winter of 1337–38, Maurice de Berkeley's £10 mount was much less valuable than either that ridden by his father (Sir Thomas de Berkeley, 40 marks) or that supplied to his father's banner bearer (24 marks): E101/35/3, m. 2d.

[256] E101/35/3, m. 3 (1337–38); E36/204, fo. 87r (1342–43).

[257] Saul, *Scenes from provincial life*, p. 37.

[258] For example, William de Lacy and Roger Darcy both served in Scotland and the Low Countries with horses of similar value, but took a cheaper mount to Brittany in 1342. Roger Dallingridge had a 10 mark mount in 1336, but one valued at only £5 for the continental campaign of 1338–39.

permanent contraction of disposable resources, for such were familiar problems for the medieval gentry.[259] For some men, the cost of previous periods of military service, including the cost of replacing warhorses for which compensation was either not due or very slow in coming, will have restricted their purchasing power. Indeed, given these costs, it is hardly surprising that war veterans are often to be found with horseflesh of moderate quality. But then, men with campaigning experience were also the most likely to perceive at an early stage the full implications of current developments in fighting methods: developments which by the time of the Treaty of Brétigny had contributed so decisively to a general decline in the quality of warhorses employed by English armies.

Perhaps Richard de Totesham was influenced by such considerations when he selected an unexceptional 10 mark warhorse for the Breton campaign of 1342–43, a horse of identical value to that with which he had served in Scotland in 1336.[260] Unfortunately we shall never know. Rarely, indeed, are we able to uncover with absolute certainty the circumstances lying behind a particular sequence of valuations. But by examining an individual's warhorses over a number of campaigns it may be possible to catch a glimpse of the life of an otherwise faceless man, to see something of his predicament and perhaps gain a fleeting insight into his attitudes to military service. Little or nothing may be known from other sources of his status in the military community – and certainly nothing of his views concerning the military developments of the time – but through the careful description and valuing of his warhorses he acquires a few distinctive characteristics which help to make him an individual amidst the crowd of men-at-arms serving in Edwardian armies.

---

259 Saul, *Scenes from provincial life*, pp. 181–84; idem, 'A "rising" lord and a "declining" esquire: Sir Thomas de Berkeley III and Geoffrey Gascelyn of Sheldon', *Historical Research*, lxi (1988), pp. 345–56.

260 E36/204, fo. 86v; E101/19/36, m. 5. Totesham had already done a good deal of campaigning by 1342. He was to become one of Edward III's most dependable middle-ranking captains and later fought a duel by judgement of the *parlement* of Paris: *Mémoires pour servir de preuves à l'histoire ecclésiastique et civile de Bretagne*, ed. Dom P.H. Morice, 3 vols (Paris, 1742–6), i, col. 1578.

Appendix 1
The Scottish Campaign, 1336

Captain	Pay[1] commenced	No. of[1] men-at-arms	Date of[2] inventory	No. of m/a[2] listed	Horses[3] lost
Henry of Lancaster	1 May	100	1 May	79	21
Earl of Warwick	1 May	74	1 May	74	30
Earl of Oxford	13 May	20	12 May	20	3
Earl of Angus	14 May	30	14 May	30	2
Earl of Buchan	17 May	36	17 May	36	7
Sir Henry de Percy, bnt	14 May	54	14 May	56	12
Sir Ralph de Neville, bnt	14 May	50	? May	51	13
Sir Giles de Badlesmere, bnt	4 May	20	4 May	20	2
Sir John de Segrave, bnt	14 May	18	14 May	18	1
Sir Thomas de Ughtred, bnt	9/17 May	12/15	17 May	14	0
Sir Ranulph de Dacre, bnt	21 May	15		no inventory	
Sir Bartholomew de Favacourt, knt	1 May	7		no inventory	
Sir John de Tibetot, bnt	5 May	19	4 June	15	1
Sir William de Bohun, bnt	1 May	56	?	56	5
John de Houton	9 April	6	13 May	7	6
Robert Tong	?	?	?	2	–
Earl of Cornwall	28 July	85	8 Sept	62	–
Sir Geoffrey de Mortimer, bnt	16 Aug	7	restauro equorum only		2

[1] Based on *vadia guerre* accounts (BL Cotton MS, Nero C. VIII, fos 240r–44r), except in the case of the retinues of Percy and Neville, which draw on the more detailed pay accounts included in E101/19/36, mm. 3, 4d. Neville's fifty men-at-arms include a company of twenty which were about to leave to join Percy's retinue (under the terms of an indenture of retinue: see Bean, *From lord to patron*, p. 57). Robert Tong's company cannot be traced in the pay-roll, yet he appears under a separate heading in the bundle of inventories.

[2] Based on the bundle of inventories: E101/19/36. Most of the retinue inventories are separately dated. Neville's inventory contains a number of mid-campaign additions; Tibetot's lists only fifteen men-at-arms, but also the names of twelve horse archers providing the service of four men-at-arms.

[3] Figures based upon inventory annotations and the *restauro equorum* account: BL Cotton MS, Nero C. VIII, fos 280v–82r.

Appendix 2
The Breton Campaign, 1342–43

What was the size of the English army in Brittany in 1342–43? With an apparently complete and detailed *vadia guerre* account available for this campaign,[1] establishing the basic proportions of Edward III's army ought perhaps to be a straightforward task. Unfortunately this pay-roll, like many, presents a number of obstacles to the historian. First, the separate expeditions to leave England in 1342 need to be disentangled, a task which cannot be achieved soley by reference to the periods of paid service assigned to individual retinues in the pay-rolls. Sir Walter de Mauny's force, serving from mid-March until early July 1342, stands out clearly enough in the pay-roll: it consisted of about 340 men – 133 men-at-arms[2] and 210 horse archers. Identifying the constituent retinues of the earl of Northampton's small army, in pay from late July but only arriving in Brittany on 18 August, is complicated not only by the fact that they do not form a single block in the pay account, but also because one of the retinues entering the king's pay in July, that led by Sir Hugh le Despenser, did not form part of Northampton's expeditionary force. Originally intended for Gascony, Despenser's men (seventy-three men-at-arms and twenty-six horse archers) stopped en route on the south-west coast of Finistère and were diverted to Brest to bolster the Countess of Montfort's garrison.[3] Later, they joined Northampton's army;[4] but at the time of disembarkation, that earl, accompanied by the earl of Devon and Ralph, Lord Stafford, had with him about 640 men (320 men-at-arms, 310 horse archers,[5]

---

1 In the book of accounts of William Edington, Keeper of the Wardrobe: E36/204, fos 105v–10v. Several historians have used these *vadia guerre* accounts to estimate the size of the English forces in Brittany in 1342–43. According A.E. Prince there were 1,820 men-at-arms, 1,890 horse archers and 1,150 foot archers serving from September 1342 ('The strength of English armies', p. 363). Michael Prestwich estimated that there were 2,000 men-at-arms, 1,780 horse archers, 1,750 infantry 'in Brittany in the autumn of 1342' ('English armies in the early stages of the Hundred Years War: a scheme in 1341', p. 109), whilst Michael Jones calculated that 'Edward arrived with some 2,000 men-at-arms, 1,780 horse archers and 1,650 infantry in late October' ('Edward III's captains in Brittany' p. 107). Sumption, *The Hundred Years War: trial by battle*, pp. 390–408 offers a most useful discussion of the assembly and operations of the English forces in 1342–43.

2 Twenty-eight of these served only from 15 May to 30 June: E36/204, fo. 105v.

3 Sumption, *The Hundred Years War: trial by battle*, p. 399. Pay-roll: E36/204, fo. 106r. Protections for service in Gascony: C61/54, m. 30 *passim*.

4 Hugh le Despenser's retinue was certainly at Morlaix: one of his men, Edward le Despenser (C61/54, mm. 18, 30), was killed in the battle: *Murimuth*, p. 127; *CIPM*, viii, no. 395.

5 Of these, 184 are in fact described as 'hominum armatorum et sagittariorum equitum': E36/204, fo. 108v.

10 foot archers), of whom rather fewer than 550 received pay until the end of the campaign.[6] So much is relatively straightforward, but the army which arrived in Brittany in the autumn poses greater problems. The pay-roll suggests that it consisted of about 4,500 men (1,373 men-at-arms, 1,412 horse archers and 1,714 foot soldiers).[7] These figures are misleading in a number of respects, however. The king's fleet, sailing from Sandwich and Winchelsea, landed in Brittany in late October. A further sizeable force was due to leave Dartmouth and Plymouth in early November, but poor weather and insufficient shipping caused delays. As a result, part of the army, although receiving pay (and therefore included in the manpower totals stated above), did not join the king until much later and some contingents appear not have reached Brittany at all. The earl of Gloucester, who received pay from 8 September for a retinue consisting of 106 men-at-arms and 80 horse archers, can be seen from other records to have still been in Plymouth on 15 November.[8] There is no indication in the pay-roll entry for Gloucester's retinue, nor indeed in that for the earl of Pembroke's men, that over two months of paid service were spent at ports of embarkation in Devon.

Similar doubts surround the service of other sections of Edward III's army. It is clear from the *vadia guerre* accounts that the great majority of the archers and foot soldiers serving in separately recruited companies had left the king's pay by Christmas: about 800 men as early as mid-November (only about three weeks after Edward III left England for Brittany) and nearly 1,000 more in mid-December. At best, then, these men served for only a short period in Brittany and there are good reasons for thinking that a proportion of them did not reach the duchy at all. A company of 600 'Welshmen' under the command of Edmund Hakelut was forced by 'the fury of the sea' to abandon the journey to Brittany and land in the Isles of Scilly.[9] Hakelut himself is not mentioned in Edington's *vadia guerre* account (although he is recorded elsewhere drawing pay in September 1342 for a company of

6 The earl of Devon's retinue (56 men-at-arms and 60 archers) left the king's pay in early November: E36/204, fos 107v, 110v.

7 Plus about 272 paid non-combatants, twenty of whom – Robert Werinton's company of carpenters and engineers – did not begin to receive pay until December. The earl of Oxford's retinue (thirty-five men-at-arms and twenty-four horse archers) left the king's pay on 21 November (ibid., fo. 105v). Geoffrey le Baker states that Oxford was one of Northampton's lieutenants (*Le Baker*, p. 76), but this is not supported by other chroniclers (e.g. *Murimuth*, p. 125). The pay-roll indicates that he did not begin to receive the king's pay until 2 September, and letters of protection were still being issued to members of his retinue as late as mid-October (C76/17, m. 19).

8 E36/204, fos 106r, 108v. Gloucester was party to two indentures dated Plymouth, 8 and 15 November (indentures attached to a set of accounts: E101/23/22). An expenses account for the men sent to appraise Gloucester's warhorses at Plymouth shows that they did not complete their task until 12 November (E101/23/36). The fact that Gloucester's retinue does not appear in the *restauro equorum* accounts may suggest that it took little or no part in the campaign.

9 CPR, 1343–45, p. 494.

Welshmen intended for Brittany),[10] but a company of 400 Welshmen, led by Kenric Duy, which *is* to be found in the account,[11] may have formed part of Hakelut's command. A quite separate pay-roll, that of John de Kermond, includes 350 English and Welsh archers assembled at Plymouth for the voyage to Brittany. Kermond's account covers no more than a short period in November 1342 and it is clear from an indenture attached to it that these archers, like the retinues of the earls of Gloucester and Pembroke, were still in Plymouth as late as the 15 November.[12] Once again it is difficult to identify these men in Edington's *vadia guerre* account. Only two of the company commanders figure in both pay-rolls, Kenric Duy and William de Burton, and in both cases they have been assigned far more men in Edington's account than they have in Kermond's. It would seem likely that, of the troops assembled at the Devon ports of embarkation, only the personal retinues of Gloucester and Pembroke actually arrived in Brittany.[13]

Edington's *vadia guerre* account seems to be a most imperfect guide to the proportions of the army which actually served with Edward III in Brittany. Many of those receiving the king's pay can have spent very little time in the duchy and some did not leave England at all. On the other hand, there appear to have been companies which, although not discernible in Edington's account, certainly did take part in the campaign.[14] The impression of completeness conveyed by Edington's *vadia guerre* account is particularly misleading where the earl of Northampton's expeditionary force is concerned. Two sizeable retinues which are known to have formed part of Northampton's army during the late summer of 1342 are not included in the pay-roll: those of Robert d'Artois, who probably brought about 120 men-at-arms and 120 archers, for whose wages he was granted an assignment of 158 sacks of wool; and William de Kildesby, who was assigned 85 sacks and 3 quarterons of wool for the service of 10 knights, 39 esquires and 100 archers.[15] Taking

---

10 E403/326, m. 30.

11 E36/204, fo. 109v.

12 E101/23/22. The four companies of English archers (comprising a little less than half of the total) were paid for only seven days and appear to have left the king's service on 11 November whilst still at Plymouth. The Welshmen served for a few days beyond 15 November.

13 Sumption, *The Hundred Years War: trial by battle*, p. 406. In late July 1342 the Chamberlain of South Wales was far from confident that the issues of his bailiwick would be sufficient to pay the wages of as many as 1,650 Welsh infantry during their journey to Winchelsea: SC1/41, no. 116. There must be some doubt about how many men actually served.

14 Madoc ap Houell (with sixty-five Welshmen), and Hugh de Woverham (with nineteen other archers) were issued with pay in May 1343 for earlier service in Brittany: E403/328, m. 10.

15 CCR, *1341–43*, pp. 564, 569; CPR, *1340–43*, p. 415. Protections (and appointment of attorneys) for fourteen of Artois' men and nine of Kildesby's are to be found on the Treaty Roll for 16 Edward III: C76/17, mm. 8, 29, 36, 37, 38. Some of Artois' protection requests have survived: C81/1719, nos. 19–25. Kildesby is named by the chroniclers as one of

Artois' and Kildesby's retinues into account, along with Despenser's retinue, Northampton's expeditionary force at the time of the battle of Morlaix may have consisted of about 1,100 Englishmen, with roughly equal numbers of men-at-arms and archers, plus an indeterminate number of Bretons.[16] Computing the size of Edward III's army on, say, Christmas Day 1342 is more problematic. After allowing for the departure (or non arrival) of significant numbers of men in November and December, the balance of evidence suggests that Edward may have had with him as many as 3,600 – 3,700 men (with men-at-arms and archers in just about equal proportions) receiving pay from various sources.[17]

These manpower totals do not attempt to take account of those who were performing service in return for charters of pardon: men who, for this campaign, served 'at their own expense' and who, therefore, should not have been included in the pay-roll personnel numbers.[18] Nor have our manpower

Northampton's lieutenants (*Le Baker*, p. 76; *Murimuth*, p. 125). The absence of both Artois and Kildesby from the *restauro equorum* account in Edington's Wardrobe Book (E36/204, fos 86v–88r) is only to be expected, given their absence from the *vadia guerre* account. It is unlikely that their men's warhorses were appraised. Less easy to explain is the omission from the *restauro equorum* account of several other large retinues which do appear on Edington's pay-roll: those of the earls of Oxford, Pembroke and Gloucester and Sir Ralph Stafford. Stafford accompanied Northampton and served through the campaign; Oxford's pay stopped on 21 November; Gloucester and Pembroke, as we have seen, arrived late.

16 Mauny's small force had left the king's pay prior to Northampton's arrival. For the planned strength of Northampton and Artois' expeditionary force, see M. Jones, ed., 'Some documents relating to the disputed succession to the duchy of Brittany, 1341', *Camden Miscellany, xxiv*, Camden Soc., 4th ser., ix (1972), p. 72. Sumption (*The Hundred Years War: trial by battle*, p. 400) believes that Northampton 'had at his disposal about 2,400 Englishmen and an unknown number of Bretons'. This figure includes Mauny's men 'who had been in Brittany since the spring', but can we be sure of this? Three members of Mauny's first retinue (Sir Richard de Stapleton, Richard Godsalm and John de Eyston) can be seen securing new protections prior to the Hainaulter's return to the duchy in late October: C76/17, mm. 16, 17, 39, 44.

17 Excluded from this figure are all the retinues and archer companies which left the king's pay before Christmas Day. Included in it are the retinues of the earls of Gloucester and Pembroke (who are assumed to have arrived in Brittany by this date), Robert d'Artois and William de Kildesby. The inclusion of Artois' retinue is particularly conjectural, for he died in November (E. Déprez, 'La mort de Robert d'Artois', *Revue Historique*, xciv (1907), pp. 63–66) and we cannot be sure whether his men stayed in the king's service. One of them, the banneret Sir John de Hardreshull (C76/17, mm. 16, 18, 37), certainly did, for he, together with a company of three knights, eight esquires and six horse archers, was taken into the king's pay on 13 November. On 25 January, prior to the king's departure from the duchy, Hardreshull and Eon de la Roche, lord of Lohéac, were appointed joint captain-lieutenants in Brittany. Hardreshull served with a slightly augmented company until his capture at Quimper on 28 April 1344. E372/188, m. 55. For Hardreshull's career, see Jones, 'Edward III's captains in Brittany'. On Edward III's army in December 1342, cf. Sumption, *The Hundred Years War: trial by battle*, p. 406.

18 Several hundred charters of pardon arising from this campaign are enrolled on the Treaty

estimates made any allowance for the effects of campaign casualties, deserters and authorised withdrawals. The *vacaciones* (i.e. numbers of men absent for specified numbers of days) which are included in Edington's *vadia guerre* account have been ignored. They are quite clearly nothing more than accounting devices: a means of ensuring that a retinue's stated number of personnel, itself a product of a certain amount of clerical manipulation, matches the total pay due to its captain. Neither actual losses nor indeed the precise size of retinues at various stages of the campaign can be recovered from the summarised personnel figures offered by the pay-rolls.

The figures presented in the 'Numbers of men-at-arms: Total paid' columns in Table A (p. 263),[19] taken directly from Edington's *vadia guerre* account, need to be viewed in this light. They do not purport to represent retinue-level manpower numbers for any single point in the campaign. But they probably indicate the right order of magnitude for the campaign as a whole and offer, therefore, a reasonable measure of overall numbers of men-at-arms against which can be compared the numbers of protection recipients (acknowledging that some of these were non-combatants) and the numbers of men who lost warhorses during the campaign.

Rolls (C76/17 and C76/18), but there is also a separate, fragmentary pardon roll (C67/28A).

[19] All of the larger retinues are included; also, the smaller companies led by 'fighting' knights (i.e. excluding clerks of knightly rank).

Table A: The Breton campaign, 1342–43.

Captain	NUMBERS OF MEN-AT-ARMS					RETINUE PERSONNEL				
			Total paid			Total	- with	- with	- losing	Mean
	Earls	Bnts.	Knts.	Esqs.	Total	known	protn.	attorn.	horses	horse value
First expedition, spring 1342										
Sir Walter Mauny, bnt[20]	0	1	21	111	133	11	10	4	–	
Second expedition, summer 1342										
Earl of Northampton	1	6	52	141	200	92	69	19	37	17.87
Earl of Devon	1	1	10	44	56	18	15	4	5	17.56
Sir Ralph Stafford, bnt	0	2	21	51	74	28	28	4	0	–
Totals:	2	9	83	236	320	138	112	27	42	
Sir Hugh Despenser, bnt	0	2	13	58	73	32	20	6	16	12.67
Third expedition, autumn 1342										
Earl of Gloucester	1	1	18	86	106	44	43	7	0	–
Earl of Warwick	1	2	20	74	97	44	35	13	12	10.56
Earl of Pembroke	1	2	12	50	65	30	30	8	0	–
Earl of Derby	1	3	37	142	183	75	62	30	18	11.07
Earl of Salisbury	1	2	17	75	95	27	18	9	10	14.03
Earl of Suffolk	1	1	14	40	56	14	9	2	6	19.61
Earl of Oxford	1	1	7	26	35	8	7	3	0	–
Sir Maurice Berkeley, bnt	0	1	4	15	20	8	6	2	2	12.67
Sir Thomas Bradeston, bnt	0	1	3	15	19	17	9	2	11	7.85
Sir Bart. Burgherssh snr., bnt	0	3	14	51	68	49	46	11	11	11.58
Sir Reginald Cobham, bnt	0	1	6	42	49	22	18	2	11	19.39
Sir John Darcy snr., bnt	0	3	12	56	71	47	37	8	14	9.79
Sir Robert Ferars, bnt	0	1	6	31	38	11	9	1	2	14.50
Sir William Fitz Warin, bnt	0	1	1	8	10	6	3	2	3	11.00
Sir Walter Mauny, bnt	0	1	15	90	106	30	10	3	24	24.58
Sir Michael Poynings, bnt	0	1	2	10	13	5	4	1	4	20.50
Sir John Stryvelyn, bnt	0	1	2	18	21	2	1	1	0	–
Sir Ralph Ufford, bnt	0	1	3	12	16	3	1	1	2	12.67
Sir William Edington, bnt[21]	0	0	1	19	20	14	8	4	8	7.96
Sir Thomas Hatfield, bnt[21]	0	0	3	16	19	16	14	9	3	14.89
Sir John Ufford, bnt[21]	0	0	0	20	20	3	3	2	0	–
Sir Phillip Weston, bnt[21]	0	0	2	19	21	11	11	2	0	–
Sir Simon Basset	0	0	1	2	3	1	1	1	0	–
Sir Giles Beauchamp	0	0	1	2	3	1	1	1	0	–
Sir John Beauchamp	0	0	1	3	4	1	1	0	0	–
Sir Roger Beauchamp	0	0	1	2	3	1	1	1	0	–
Sir Thomas Beaumont	0	0	1	4	5	2	0	0	1	5.33

[20] Included in Mauny's retinue numbers are four men-at-arms who served with Sir Walter Wetewang. It is assumed that Mauny's section of the *restauro equorum* account, which lists twenty-four equestrian fatalities, is concerned with losses suffered by his retinue during the winter of 1342–43 following his return to Brittany in the king's expedition. Four of the twenty-four men who lost horses have letters of protections and all were issued in October 1342.

[21] Clerks serving with the rank of banneret.

Captain	Earls	Bnts.	Total paid Knts.	Esqs.	Total	Total known	- with protn.	- with attorn.	- losing horses	Mean horse v
Sir John Brocas	0	0	1	8	9	1	1	1	0	–
Sir Bart. Burgherssh *jnr.*	0	0	1	2	3	1	1	0	0	–
Sir John Carreu	0	0	1	2	3	1	1	1	0	–
Sir Edward Chaundos	0	0	1	2	3	1	1	0	0	–
Sir Gawain Corder	0	0	1	5	6	4	4	1	0	–
Sir Richard Cornwall	0	0	1	1	2	1	1	1	0	–
Sir William Coucy	0	0	1	2	3	1	1	1	0	–
Sir Robert Dalton	0	0	1	4	5	2	2	1	0	–
Sir Richard Damory	0	0	1	2	3	2	2	1	0	–
Sir John Darcy *jnr.*	0	0	1	4	5	2	1	1	1	16.00
Sir Robert Fitz Elys	0	0	1	2	3	1	0	0	1	10.00
Sir Otes Holand	0	0	1	2	3	1	0	0	0	–
Sir Thomas & Sir Alan Holand	0	0	2	3	5	2	0	0	0	–
Sir Nicholas Langford	0	0	1	2	3	1	0	0	0	–
Sir John Lisle	0	0	1	2	3	1	1	1	0	–
Sir Nigel Loring	0	0	1	2	3	3	2	1	0	–
Sir Thomas Pabenham	0	0	1	2	3	1	1	1	0	–
Sir John Shirbourn	0	0	1	2	3	1	1	1	0	–
Sir John Sturmy	0	0	2	2	4	7	7	1	1	12.00
Sir William Stury	0	0	1	5	6	1	1	0	0	–
Sir Thomas Swinnerton	0	0	1	2	3	1	0	0	0	–
Sir Will Trussell de Cublesdon	0	0	2	6	8	2	2	2	0	–
Sir Henry Tyes	0	0	1	2	3	1	0	0	0	–
Sir Ralph Vernon	0	0	1	3	4	1	1	0	0	–
Sir Thos Wake de Blisworth	0	0	1	2	3	1	1	1	0	–
Sir Alan Zouche	0	0	1	2	3	3	1	1	2	11.67
Totals of these retinues:[22]	7	27	233	1,001	1,268	536	421	143	147	

[22] According to the pay-rolls, the overall manpower totals for the third expedition were: seven earls, twenty-seven bannerets, 233 knights and 1,106 esquires – or 1,373 men-at-arms in all. A total of 722 individuals obtained protections for service in Brittany in 1342–43 (note that several men are included twice in this total, having served under Mauny in the spring and again in Edward III's army later in the year); 234 men secured attornies and 226 lost appraised warhorses.

Appendix 3
The Reims Campaign, 1359–60

Table A: Horse losses

Captain	Horses lost	Mean horse value (£)	NO. OF HORSES Passage	Repassage	MS ref.
Edward, prince of Wales	395	8.49	1369	2114	79
Henry, duke of Lancaster	216	9.82		1611	79v
Earl of Richmond	62	7.89	741	792	79
Earl of Stafford	46	9.41	414	486	80
Sir Frank de Hale[1]	43	15.50			86v
Earl of Northampton	40	7.81	336	702	79v
Sir John Chandos	27	12.57	134	108	82
Sir Ralph Basset	20	7.16		135	80v
Earl of Warwick[2]	20	20.34	398	193	79v
Sir Reginald de Cobham	18	7.82	149	157	80v
Earl of Suffolk	18	9.22	134	214	80
Sir Henry de Percy	16	8.31		257	82
Sir Almaric St Amand	15	8.19	43	78	81v
Earl of March	15	6.34			79v
Sir William la Zouche	14	8.07	112	170	81
Earl of Salisbury	13	7.17	90	201	80
Sir John Cherleton	12	7.36	109	162	81
Sir John de Wynwik	10	10.02	36	55	87v
Sir John Cobham	9	8.19		102	81v
Sir William de Farley	9	7.98			87v
Sir Thomas Ughtred	9	5.93		81	81v
Sir Richard de Vache	9	10.00		23	82
Sir John de Beauchamp	8	5.38		126	81v
Sir Guy de Brian	7	10.79	12	198	80v
Sir Edward le Despenser	7	7.60	100	150	80v
Sir Reginald de Grey	6	10.05		107	81
Lionel, earl of Ulster	6	8.36	126	164	79
Edmund Langley	5	6.63		145	79
Sir Michael de Poynings	5	7.17		48	81
Sir Nicholas de Burnell	4	11.46	15	44	81

[1] Hale's *restauro equorum* payment, 1000 marks, has the appearance of a lump sum rather than a true reflection of appraised values; cf. Sir William de Granson, who received exactly £600 for an unspecified number of equestrian casualties: E101/393/11, fo. 86v.

[2] Farley's accounts include a second entry for the earl of Warwick, for service as king's lieutenant in Normandy, May–September 1360: ibid., fo. 87r. During this spell of duty his men lost three horses with a mean value of £15.78. He was paid for the re-passage of 203 horses.

Captain	Horses lost	Mean horse value (£)	NO. OF HORSES		MS ref.
			Passage	Repassage	
Sir Nicholas de Loveigne	4	16.54		20	82v
Thomas de Mussenden	4	11.42		23	113, 113v
Sir Matthew de Asshton	3	12.22		10	90v
Sir Amanieu de Pomers	3	20.22			86
Sir Thomas de Swynnerton	3	8.72		23	82v
Richard de Ask	2	12.92		18	102v
Sir William Baude	2	5.17		10	85v
Sir Thomas de Beauchamp	2	11.00		11	83v
Sir Thomas de Berkeley	2	5.17		10	82v
Master John de Branktre	2	5.00		10	89
Sir William de Clee	2	8.33		11	87v
Sir John de Edyngdon	2	6.67		8	83
Sir John Kyriel	2	7.25	20	56	81v
Helmyng Leget	2	9.00		12	102v
Robert Mahfield	2	5.33		5	113v
Sir Richard de Pembridge	2	16.67		13	82
William Peterouth	2	7.50		8	113v
Sir Henry de Sneith	2	9.00		6	88
Sir Edward de Seern	2	6.33		4	85v
Sir John de Swynle	2	6.33		7	88
Richard Syward	2	5.00	8	7	100
Sir William de Tirington	2	8.33		8	88v
Sir Guy de Warwick	2	8.33	4	18	82v
Robert Alby	1	5.00		2	100
Roger Archer	1	6.67			106v
John Beauchamp de Holt *snr.*	1	6.67			103v
John Beauchamp de Holt *jnr.*	1	6.67		2	106v
Sir Henry de Beaumont	1	15.67		24	83
John Beer	1	6.67		13	113
John Bluet	1	10.00		3	99v
Sir Peter de Breux	1	5.00		12	83v
Sir William Bukbrugg	1	8.00		6	89v
Master Jordan de Canterbury	1	5.00		8	90
Thomas Chamberlein	1	6.00		3	106
John de Chirby	1	7.33		7	101v
Walter de Condon	1	10.00		4	101v
Robert de Corby	1	10.00		7	100, 100v
John Crook	1	8.00		3	105, 105v
John Dalton	1	6.00		3	90v
William Danvers	1	8.00		6	103, 103v
James Dicheford	1	5.00			114
Thomas de Ednestowe	1	10.00		4	102
John Elleford	1	6.67		8	104v
John de Ellerton	1	17.33		3	99
Sir Roger Elmrugg	1	10.00		12	83v
Robert Erhuth	1	12.00		5	101
Thomas de Eton	1	13.33		3	105
Sir Henry de Grey	1	7.33		7	85v
John de Haddon	1	8.00		7	99

			NO. OF HORSES		
Captain	Horses lost	Mean horse value (£)	Passage	Repassage	MS ref.
John de Hamelton	1	5.00		3	105
Roger de Hampton	1	5.33		4	105v
John Herling	1	26.67		7	100v
Sir Adam de Hilton	1	13.33		10	88v
Sir Thomas Hogshawe	1	10.00			86
Sir William de Huntlowe	1	8.67		3	89
Richard Huntyngdon	1	8.00		2	101v
Richard Immeworth	1	5.00		3	99v
William de Iselham	1	5.00			89v
Sir Edward St John	1	8.00		16	84v
Roger Jolif	1	8.00		4	114v
Sir Edward de Kendale	1	6.00		16	84v
Sir John de Kyngeston	1	8.00			84
Sir Thomas de Kyngeston	1	10.00		12	84
William de Leght	1	6.00		3	90
John Lestrange	1	8.00		3	99v
Sir William de Loughtburgh	1	6.67		6	89
Sir Nicholas de Louth	1	6.00		11	88
Edward Lovetoft	1	10.00		3	105v
John Lovetoft	1	10.00		3	105v
Robert del March	1	8.00		3	104
Sir John Marmion	1	5.67		7	85
John Mayn	1	5.33		3	100
Richard Metford	1	6.67		1	89v
Sir Thomas Moigne	1	13.33		11	84
Richard Pace	1	6.00		20	114
Leonard de Perton	1	5.00		2	101
Richard Potenhale	1	5.00		3	101v
Sir John Potenhale	1	18.00		6	84v
William de Redenesse	1	6.67		3	90
William de Risceby	1	10.00		7	100v
Sir John de Saxton	1	5.00			89
Sir Richard de Skidby	1	8.00		8	88
Geoffrey de Styvecle	1	5.00	4	3	105
Sir Wiliam de Sunde	1	5.50		7	88
Richard de Tatton	1	16.67		3	106v
Sir Richard de Thoern	1	6.67		8	88v
Thos. de Thorneton – pavilioner	1	5.00		4	115v
Sir William de Tideswelle	1	5.00		4	89
John Yonge	1	5.00		2	107v

HORSE TRANSPORTATION: PASSAGE AND RE-PASSAGE PAYMENTS

In the *vadia guerre* accounts for the Reims campaign, the entry for a 'model' captain, receiving the full range of service benefits, will include details of the composition of his retinue and the amounts of pay, *regard* and *restauro equorum* due. In addition, sums are allocated for the passage and re-passage of his retinue's horses, and in the process what appear to be exact numbers of horses taken to France in the autumn of 1359 and returning from Calais the following spring are given.[3] In this way, the crown can be seen to have paid for the passage of 4,471 horses and the re-passage of 10,861. Given that the army which left England included well over 3,000 men-at-arms and over 5,000 mounted archers, it is reasonable to assume that it would have required at least four times as many horses as are allowed for in Farley's book of accounts.[4] If we take the shipment figures at face value, then, it is difficult to escape the conclusion that King Edward's army arrived in France seriously deficient in horseflesh.

How is this apparent shortfall to be explained? Was there a shortage of warhorses in England in the autumn of 1359? If so, many men would have had to acquire suitable horses in France, either by purchase[5] or as booty. Even allowing for losses during the campaign (1,203 horses) and the sale of animals before leaving France, a significantly larger number would remain to be brought home, no doubt to the benefit of domestic breeding stock. Attractive as the horse-shortage theory might be, it can provide no more than a partial explanation.[6] In fact, it does not really fit the evidence. A national shortage of warhorses would have given rise to a pattern of figures very different from that recorded in Farley's Wardrobe Book. Of nearly four hundred companies led by English captains, only twenty-five received horse passage payments

---

3   E101/393/11, fos 79r–116v. These horse shipment figures have been quoted before, although only for selected captains: Hewitt, *The organisation of war under Edward III*, p. 88, who takes them to be 'the actual numbers of horses transported'. Cf. Hewitt, *The horse in medieval England*, pp. 73–74.

4   This estimate is based on the normal shipment allowances (see above, p. 58) and assumes only one horse for each mounted archer. We might also allow for pack-horses, since we know that this army was supported by a substantial supply train (see *Jean le Bel*, ii, pp. 312–13). A *pontis*, costing £55 8s, was built near Calais to facilitate disembarkation of the king's great army: E101/174/7, fo. 14r.

5   On buying horses upon arrival in France, see Hewitt, *The Black Prince's expedition*, p. 33. Over a hundred years later John Pympe wrote to his friend Sir John Paston, asking him to find 'the jentyllest hors in Calice that is to be sold': *The Paston letters*, ed. J. Gairdner, new edn (Gloucester, 1983), nos. 906 and 907.

6   The prince of Wales may not have had as many good horses with him as he would have liked. He was buying horses at the very last minute before leaving for France (*BPReg*, iv, p. 326); and he bought a horse costing 80 marks from one of his knights, Sir John de Hide, during the campaign (ibid., p. 355).

from the crown in 1359.[7] If we are to take the accounts at face value, therefore, the vast majority of retinues, including some of the largest, brought no horses at all to France.[8] A great captain would certainly never arrive at a port of embarkation with a wholly unmounted retinue; but, if faced by an insufficient supply of shipping, he might be obliged to leave some or all of his horses in England.

Shortages of horse transports, rather than warhorses, are known to have hindered some English expeditions in the fourteenth century. In 1352, for example, many of the warhorses of the earl of Stafford's retinue were left in England because of insufficient shipping.[9] Given the size of Edward III's army in 1359, it had probably been anticipated that the assembly of a large enough transport fleet was going to be difficult, even though only a short sea crossing was involved.[10] Indeed, Sir Thomas Gray, a member of the prince of Wales' retinue, confirms that the king 'was grievously delayed for want of ships, wherefore he could neither land [his forces] all at once nor at the place he intended'.[11] But the shipping shortage was not as severe as Farley's accounts might lead us to believe; they cannot be taken at face value.[12] In the normal course of events, captains did not receive allowances for the passage of their retinues. This was because the organisation of transport fleets – consisting, in the main, of privately-owned merchant vessels drawn temporarily into the king's service from a multitude of communities around the coast of England – was the responsibility of the crown.[13] Indeed, it was only when the

---

7   Ranging from the prince of Wales, who was paid for the passage of 1,369 horses, to Robert Alein, who accounted for only one: E101/393/11, fos 79r, 111r. See Table B, below.

8   Eight captains each received payment for the re-passage of over a hundred horses, but nothing for the outward journey.

9   Stafford's men had to buy horses upon arrival in Gascony, which cost the crown £686 13s 4d: E101/26/25. A similar shortage affected the next significant overseas operation after Brétigny, the duke of Clarence's expedition to Ireland: A.J. Otway-Ruthven, *A history of medieval Ireland*, 2nd edn (London, 1980), p. 286.

10 In the summer of 1338 a total of 361 ships (crewed by over 12,500 men) were mobilised for the transportation of an English army consisting of perhaps 5,000 men, about a third of whom were foot soldiers (*Norwell*, p. ciii; Prince, 'The strength of English armies', p. 361). By comparison, in 1359 over 10,000 Englishmen (the majority of whom were mounted) travelled to France with Edward III.

11 *Scalacronica*, p. 145.

12 To do so would lead to difficulties. The duke of Lancaster (who was paid re-passage for 1,611 horses) received nothing for the conveyance of his retinue's mounts to Calais: E101/393/11, fo. 79v. Yet within a few days of arriving he had set off on a *chevauchée* through Artois and Picardy: Fowler, *The king's lieutenant*, p. 201. The global passage and re-passage figures suggest the availability of more than twice as many ships for the return journey as were on-hand for the outward trip, which is highly unlikely.

13 On the impressment and re-fitting of the transport fleet in the summer of 1338, see *Norwell*, pp. cii–civ. For broader perspectives, see Hewitt, *The organisation of war under Edward III*, chapter 4; J.W. Sherborne, 'The English navy: shipping and manpower, 1369–1389', *Past and Present*, xxxvii (1967), pp. 163–75; C.F. Richmond, 'The war at sea',

government was unable to organise sufficient shipping that it was necessary for individual retinue commanders to arrange their own transportation; and, for doing this, they received appropriate compensation from the crown. Thus, the passage and re-passage payments in Farley's accounts were intended to cover the transport costs of those horses which had not been carried by the fleet mobilised and paid directly by royal administration.[14] If any of Edward III's captains experienced difficulty getting their retinue's horses to Calais in the late autumn of 1359 it would, therefore, most probably have been those who received 'passage' payments! As it was always difficult to arrange shipping to transport armies back to England – and since, in the spring of 1360, there had already been some mobilisation of vessels for defence purposes[15] – it should be no surprise to find that Farley's accounts allow substantial re-passage payments for most of the English captains in the army.[16] The horse-shipment figures in Farley's accounts provide, therefore, an indication not so much of shortages of warhorses in mid-fourteenth century England as of the severe administrative problems posed by the transport needs of overseas expeditions.

Table B: Horse transportation – passage figures

Captain	NO. OF HORSES		Horses lost	Mean horse value (£)	MS ref.
	Passage	Repassage			
Edward, prince of Wales	1369	2114	395	8.49	79
Earl of Richmond	741	792	62	7.89	79
Earl of Stafford	414	486	46	9.41	80
Earl of Warwick	398	193	20	20.34	79v
Earl of Northampton	336	702	40	7.81	79v
Sir Reginald de Cobham	149	157	18	7.82	80v
Sir John Chandos	134	108	27	12.57	82

The Hundred Years War, ed. K. Fowler (London, 1971), pp. 96–121; T.J. Runyan, 'Ships and mariners in later medieval England', *Journal of British Studies*, xvi (1977), pp. 1–17.

[14] For an incomplete collection of detailed pay-rolls for this transport fleet, see E101/27/22, 23, 24 and 25.

[15] E.g. 'Cog Johan de Gofford', serving at sea with twenty-five armed men and twenty-five archers from mid-January to mid-may 1360: E101/27/21. On the defence mobilisation, see G.L. Harriss, *King, parliament and public finance in medieval England to 1369* (Oxford, 1975), p. 398.

[16] 326 captains received re-passage payments. A useful comparison can be made with the return of Edward III's army at the end of the Cambrésis-Thiérache campaign, in January and February 1340. A section of William de Norwell's Wardrobe Book gives details of the amounts due to individual captains for the transportation of their horses from Sluys back to England (*Norwell*, pp. 386–92). The system employed on this occasion (more rigidly structured than that in 1359–60) is discussed in B. Lyon's 'Introduction' to *Norwell*, pp. civ–cv.

| Captain | NO. OF HORSES | | Horses lost | Mean horse value (£) | MS ref. |
	Passage	Repassage			
Earl of Suffolk	134	214	18	9.22	80
Lionel, earl of Ulster	126	164	6	8.36	79
Sir William la Zouche	112	170	14	8.07	81
Sir John Cherleton	109	162	12	7.36	81
Sir Walter de Mauny	104	112			80v
Sir Edward le Despenser	100	150	7	7.60	80v
Earl of Salisbury	90	201	13	7.17	80
Sir Almaric St Amand	43	78	15	8.19	81v
Sir John de Wynwik	36	55	10	10.02	87v
Sir John Kyriel	20	56	2	7.25	81v
Sir Nicholas de Burnell	15	44	4	11.46	81
Sir Guy de Brian	12	198	7	10.79	80v
Sir John de Cherleton	8	17			83v
Richard Syward	8	7	2	5.00	100
Philip de la Gere	4	3			102v
Geoffrey de Styvecle	4	3	1	5.00	105
Sir Guy de Warwick	4	18	2	8.33	82v
Robert Alein	1	1			111

Bibliography

I. MANUSCRIPT SOURCES

PUBLIC RECORD OFFICE, LONDON

Chancery

C47	Chancery Miscellanea
C61	Gascon Rolls
C67	Patent Rolls (Supplementary)
C71	Scottish Rolls
C76	Treaty Rolls
C81	Chancery Warrants
C237	Chancery Files : Bails on Special Pardons
C258	: *Certiorari (corpus cum causa)*
C260	: *Recorda*
C266	: Cancelled Letters Patent

Duchy of Lancaster

DL25	Deeds, Series L

Exchequer

E36	Treasury of Receipt, Books
E101	King's Remembrancer, Accounts Various
E159	K.R., Memoranda Rolls
E198	K.R., Documents relating to serjeanties, knights' fees, etc
E199	K.R., Sheriff's Accounts
E313	Augmentation Office, Letters Patent (Original)
E372	Lord Treasurer's Remembrancer, Pipe Rolls
E403	Exchequer of Receipt, Issue Rolls
E404	Ex. of R., Warrants for Issues; Wardrobe Debentures

Judicial records

KB121	King's Bench, Essoin Rolls

Palatinate of Chester

Chester 23	Essoin Rolls

Special Collections

SC1	Ancient Correspondence
SC8	Ancient Petitions

BRITISH LIBRARY, LONDON

Additional Manuscripts
Cotton Manuscripts
Stowe Manuscripts

BERKELEY CASTLE

Select Charter 526

BODLEIAN LIBRARY, OXFORD
Ashmole MS 15A   Ashmolean Roll of Arms

FITZWILLIAM MUSEUM, CAMBRIDGE
MS 324   Carlisle Roll of Arms

JOHN RYLANDS LIBRARY, MANCHESTER
Latin MS 240

STAFFORDSHIRE RECORD OFFICE, STAFFORD
D 641   Lord Stafford's MSS

II. PRINTED PRIMARY SOURCES

The Anonimalle Chronicle, 1307–1334, ed. W.R. Childs and J. Taylor, Yorkshire Archaeological Soc., Record Ser., cxlvii (1991 for 1987)

The Anonimalle Chronicle, 1333–1381, ed. V.H. Galbraith (Manchester, 1927)

The alliterative Morte Arthure, ed. V. Krishna (New York, 1976)

'The Bedfordshire wills and administrations proved at Lambeth Palace and in the archdeaconry of Huntingdon', ed. F.A. Page-Turner, *Bedfordshire Historical Record Soc.*, ii (1914), pp. 3–59

The Berkeley MSS by John Smyth of Nibley, ed. Sir John Maclean, 3 vols (Gloucester, 1883)

Calendar of Ancient Correspondence concerning Wales, ed. J.G. Edwards (Cardiff, 1935)

Calendar of Close Rolls

Calendar of documents relating to Scotland, ed. J. Bain, 4 vols (London, 1881–88)

Calendar of documents relating to Scotland, v, ed. G.G. Simpson and J.D. Galbraith (Edinburgh, 1986)

Calendar of Fine Rolls

Calendar of Inquisitions Post Mortem (London, 1906–74)

Calendar of Liberate Rolls, 1226–72, 6 vols (London, 1917–64)

Calendar of Patent Rolls

Calendar of Memoranda Rolls (Exchequer). Michaelmas 1326–Michaelmas 1327 (London, 1968)

Catalogue of English medieval rolls of arms, ed. A.R. Wagner, Soc. of Antiquaries, *Aspilogia*, i (London, 1950)

Catalogue of seals in the Department of Manuscripts in the British Museum, ed. W de G. Birch, 6 vols (London, 1887–1900)

Chronicles of England, France, Spain and the adjoining countries . . . by Sir John Froissart, ed. and trans. T. Johnes, 2 vols (London, 1848)

Chronicles of the revolution, 1397–1400: the reign of Richard II, ed. C. Given-Wilson (Manchester, 1993)

Chronicon Galfridi le Baker de Swynebroke (1303–56), ed. E.M. Thompson (Oxford, 1889)

Chronicon Henrici Knighton, ed. J.R. Lumby, 2 vols, Rolls Ser. (London, 1889–95)

Chronicon Monasterii de Melsa, ed. E.A. Bond, 3 vols, Rolls Ser. (London, 1866–68)

Chronique de Jean le Bel, ed. J. Viard and E. Déprez, 2 vols (Paris, 1904–5)

The complete works of Geoffrey Chaucer, ed. F.N. Robinson, 2nd edn (London, 1957)

Crecy and Calais, ed. G. Wrottesley (London, 1898)

Decreta regni Hungariae, 1301–1457, ed. F. Döry, G. Bónis and V. Bácskai, Publicationes archivi nationalis Hungarici, fontes ii (Budapest, 1976)

Diplomatic documents, i (1101–1272), ed. P. Chaplais (London, 1964)

Documents illustrating the crisis of 1297–98 in England, ed. M. Prestwich, Camden Soc., 4th ser., xxiv (1980)

'Documents relatifs aux attaques sur les îles de la Manche, 1338–45', ed. M.H. Marett Godfray, La société Jersiaise pour l'étude de l'histoire, *Bulletin*, iii (1877), pp. 39–46

'The earliest roll of household accounts in the muniment room at Hunstanton for the 2nd year of Edward III [1328]', ed. G.H. Holley, *Norfolk Archaeology*, xxi (1923), pp. 77–96

English historical documents, iv (1327–1485), ed. A.R. Myers (London, 1969)

Les essais de Michel de Montaigne, ed. P. Villey, 3 vols (Paris, 1922–23)

The essential portions of Nicholas Upton's 'De Re Militari' before 1446, trans. John Blount, ed. F.P. Barnard (Oxford, 1931)

Eulogium Historiarum Sive Temporis, ed. F.S. Haydon, 3 vols, Rolls Ser. (London, 1858–63)

Expeditions to Prussia and the Holy Land made by Henry, earl of Derby in 1390–91 and 1392–93, ed. L.T. Smith, Camden Soc., new ser., lii (1894)

Fernao Lopes: The English in Portugal, ed. D.W. Lomax and R.J. Oakley (Warminster, 1988)

Foedera, conventiones, litterae etc., ed. T. Rymer, revised edn by A. Clarke, F. Holbrooke and J. Coley, 4 vols in 7 parts (Record Comm., 1816–69)

La guerre de cent ans vue à travers les registres du Parlement (1337–1369), ed. P-C. Timbal (Paris, 1961)

Higden, Ranulph, *Polychronicon*, ed. C. Babington and J.R. Lumby, 9 vols, Rolls Ser. (London, 1865–86)

The Holkham Bible Picture Book, ed. W.O. Hassall (London, 1954)

Household accounts from medieval England, part 1: introduction, glossary and diet accounts, ed. C.M. Woolgar, Records of Social and Economic History, new ser., xvii (Oxford, 1992)

'Indentures of retinue with John of Gaunt, duke of Lancaster, enrolled in Chancery, 1367–1399', ed. N.B. Lewis, *Camden Miscellany, xxii*, Camden Soc., 4th ser., i (1964), pp. 77–112

Issue Roll of Thomas de Brantingham, ed. F. Devon (London, 1835)

The itinerary of John Leland in or about the years 1535–1543, ed. L.T. Smith, 5 vols, repr. (London, 1964)

John of Gaunt's Register, 1371–75, ed. S. Armitage-Smith, 2 vols, Camden Soc., 3rd ser., xx–xxi (1911)

John of Gaunt's Register, 1379–83, ed. E.C. Lodge and R. Somerville, 2 vols, Camden Soc., 3rd ser., lvi–lvii (1937)

Letters and papers illustrative of the wars of the English in France during the reign of Henry the sixth, ed. J. Stevenson, 2 vols in 3 parts, Rolls Ser. (London, 1861–64)

Liber Quotidianus Contrarotulatoris Garderobiae, 1299–1300, ed. J. Topham et al. (London, 1787)

The life and campaigns of the Black Prince, ed. R. Barber (Woodbridge, 1986)

Life of the Black Prince by the herald of Sir John Chandos, ed. M.K. Pope and E.C. Lodge (Oxford, 1910)

List of documents relating to the household and wardrobe, John-Edward I (London, 1964)

The Luttrell Psalter, ed. E.G. Millar (London, 1932)

Mémoires pour servir de preuves à l'histoire ecclésiastique et civile de Bretagne, ed. Dom P.H. Morice, 3 vols (Paris, 1742–6)

Middle English metrical romances, ed. W.H. French and C.B. Hale (New York, 1930)

Ministers accounts of the earldom of Cornwall, 1296–1297, ed. L.M. Midgley, 2 vols, Camden Soc., 3rd ser., lxvi and lxviii (1942, 1945)

Monumenta juridica: the Black Book of the Admiralty, ed. Sir T. Twiss, 4 vols, Rolls Ser. (London, 1871–76)

Murimuth, Adam, *Continuatio Chronicarum* and Robert de Avesbury, *De Gestis Mirabilibus Regis Edwardi Tertii*, ed. E.M. Thompson, Rolls Ser. (London, 1889)

Northern petitions, ed. C.M. Fraser, Surtees Soc., cxciv (1981)

Oeuvres de Froissart, ed. K. de Lettenhove, 28 vols (Brussells, 1867–77)

Ordonnances des roys de France de la troisième race, ed. D.F. Secousse et al., 21 vols (Paris, 1723–1849; repr., 1967–68)

Pageant of the birth, life and death of Richard Beauchamp, earl of Warwick, K.G., 1389–1439, ed. Viscount Dillon and W.H. St John Hope (London, 1914)

Parliamentary writs and writs of military summons, ed. F. Palgrave, 2 vols in 4 (London, 1827–34)

The Paston letters, ed. J. Gairdner, new edn (Gloucester, 1983)

'A plea roll of Edward I's army in Scotland, 1296', ed. C.J. Neville, *Miscellany XI*, Scottish History Soc., 5th ser., iii (1990), pp. 7–133

Praestita Roll, 14–18 John, ed. J.C. Holt, Pipe Roll Soc., new ser., xxxvii (1964)

Public works in medieval law, ed. C. Flower, 2 vols, Selden Soc., xxxii (1915); xl (1925)

Records of the wardrobe and household, 1286–1289, ed. B.F. Byerly and C.R. Byerly (London, 1986)

Register of Edward the Black Prince, ed. M.C.B. Dawes, 4 vols (London, 1930–33)

The Registers of Roger Martival, bishop of Salisbury, 1315–30, ed. K. Edwards, C.R. Elrington, S. Reynolds and D.M. Owen, 4 vols, Canterbury and York Soc. (1959–72)

Report of the MSS of Lord Middleton of Wollaton Hall, Nottinghamshire, Historical Manuscripts Commission, lxix (London, 1911)

'Roll of arms of the knights at the tournament at Dunstable, in 7 Edward III', *Collectanea, Topographica et Genealogica*, iv (1837), pp. 389–95

Rolls of arms of the reigns of Henry III and Edward III, ed. N.H. Nicolas (London, 1829)

The Romance of Alexander. A collotype facsimile of MS Bodley 264, ed. M.R. James (Oxford, 1933)

Rotuli Parliamentorum, ed. J. Strachey et al., 6 vols (London, 1767–83)

Rotuli Scotiae, ed. D. Macpherson et al., 2 vols (Record Comm., 1814)

Rymes of Robyn Hood, ed. R.B. Dobson and J. Taylor (London, 1976)

Scalacronica. The reigns of Edward I, Edward II and Edward III as recorded by Sir Thomas Gray, ed. and trans. H. Maxwell (Glasgow, 1907)

Scotland in 1298: documents relating to the campaign of Edward I in that year, ed. H. Gough (London, 1888)

The Scrope and Grosvenor controversy, ed. N.H. Nicolas, 2 vols (London, 1832)

Select charters, ed. W. Stubbs, 9th edn, repr. (Oxford, 1957)

The siege of Carlaverock, ed. N.H. Nicolas (London, 1828)

Sir Christopher Hatton's book of seals, ed. L.C. Loyd and D.M. Stenton (Oxford, 1950)

Sir Gawain and the Green Knight, ed. J.R.R. Tolkien and E.V. Gordon, 2nd edn (Oxford, 1967)

Society at war, ed. C.T. Allmand (Edinburgh, 1973)

'Some documents relating to the disputed succession to the duchy of Brittany, 1341', ed. M. Jones. *Camden Miscellany, xxiv*, Camden Soc., 4th ser., ix (1972), pp. 1–78

Testamenta Eboracensia or the wills registered at York . . . from the year 1300 downwards, part 1, ed. J. Raine, Surtees Soc., ii (1836)

The 1341 royal inquest in Lincolnshire, ed. B.W. McLane, Lincoln Record Soc., lxxviii (1988)

Thuróczy, János, *Chronica Hungarorum, i*, ed. Elisabeth Galántai and Gyula Kristó (Budapest, 1985)

———, *Chronicle of the Hungarians*, ed. F. Mantello and P. Engel (Bloomington, Indiana, 1991)

Treaty Rolls, ii, 1337–39, ed. J. Ferguson (London, 1972)

The Tree of Battles of Honoré Bonet, ed. G.W. Coopland (Liverpool, 1949)

Two memoirs of Renaissance Florence. Diaries of Buonaccorso Pitti and Gregorio Dati, trans. J. Martines, ed. G. Brucker (New York, 1967)

The unconquered knight. A chronicle of the deeds of Don Pero Niño, trans. and ed. J. Evans (London, 1926)

The War of Saint-Sardos, 1323–1325, ed. P. Chaplais, Camden Soc., 3rd ser., lxxxvii (1954)

The Wardrobe Book of William de Norwell, 12 July 1338 to 27 May 1340, ed. M. Lyon, B. Lyon, H.S. Lucas and J. de Sturler (Brussells, 1983)

The Westminster Chronicle, 1381–1394, ed. and trans. L.C. Hector and B.F. Harvey (Oxford, 1982)

Year Books, Edward III, 15 vols, Rolls Ser. (London, 1883–1911)

III. SECONDARY SOURCES

Aberth, J., 'Crime and justice under Edward III: the case of Thomas de Lisle', *EHR*, cvii (1992), pp. 283–301

Alban, J.R., 'English coastal defence: some fourteenth-century modifications within the system', *Patronage, the crown and the provinces in later medieval England*, ed. R.A. Griffiths (Gloucester, 1981), pp. 57–78

Alcock, L., *Economy, society and warfare among the Britons and Saxons* (Cardiff, 1987)

Alexander, J., and P. Binski, eds, *Age of chivalry* (London, 1987)

Allmand, C., *Lancastrian Normandy, 1415–1450* (Oxford, 1983)

———, *The Hundred Years War* (Cambridge, 1988)

Anderson, M.D., *The choir stalls of Lincoln Minster* (Lincoln, 1967)

Anon., *A brief note upon the battles of Saintes and Mauron, 1351 and 1352* (Guildford, 1918)

Armitage-Smith, S., *John of Gaunt* (London, 1904)

Arnold, B., *German knighthood, 1050–1300* (Oxford, 1985)

Arslan, E., 'La statua equestre di Cangrande', *Studie in onore di F.M. Mistrorigo*, ed. A. Dani (Vicenza, 1958)

Astill, G.G., 'An early inventory of a Leicestershire knight', *Midland History*, ii (1973–74), pp. 274–83

——, 'The medieval gentry: a study in Leicestershire society, 1350–1399', Ph.D. thesis, University of Birmingham, 1977

Atiya, A., *The crusade in the later Middle Ages*, repr. (New York, 1970)

Ayton, A., 'William de Thweyt, esquire: deputy constable of Corfe Castle in the 1340s', *Somerset and Dorset Notes and Queries*, xxxii (1989), pp. 731–38

——, 'John Chaucer and the Weardale campaign, 1327', *Notes and Queries*, new ser., xxxvi (1989), pp. 9–10

——, 'The warhorse and military service under Edward III', Ph.D. thesis, University of Hull, 1990

——, 'War and the English gentry under Edward III', *History Today*, xlii, 3 (March 1992), pp. 34–40

——, 'Military service and the development of the Robin Hood legend in the fourteenth century', *Nottingham Medieval Studies*, xxxvi (1992), pp. 126–47

——, 'The English army and the Normandy campaign of 1346', *England and Normandy in the Middle Ages*, ed. D. Bates and A. Curry (London, 1994)

——, 'English armies in the fourteenth century', *Arms, armies and fortifications in the Hundred Years War*, ed. A. Curry and M. Hughes (Woodbridge, 1994)

Bachrach, B.S., 'On the origins of William the Conqueror's horse transports', *Technology and Culture*, xxvi (1985), pp. 505–31

Backhouse, J., *The Luttrell Psalter* (London, 1989)

Barber, R. and J. Barker, *Tournaments. Jousts, chivalry and pageants in the Middle Ages* (Woodbridge, 1989)

Barker, J, *The tournament in England, 1100–1400* (Woodbridge, 1986)

Barlow, F., *William Rufus* (London, 1983)

Barnie, J., *War in medieval society. Social values and the Hundred Years War* (London, 1974)

Bartlett, R., *The making of Europe. Conquest, colonisation and cultural change, 950–1350* (London, 1993)

Bartusis, M.C., *The late Byzantine army. Arms and society, 1204–1453* (Philadelphia, 1992)

Bautier, A-M., and R-H. Bautier, 'Contribution à l'histoire du cheval au Moyen Age', *Bulletin Philologique et Historique du Comité des Travaux Historiques et Scientifiques* (1976), pp. 204–49; (1978), pp. 9–75

Bean, J.M.W., *From lord to patron. Lordship in late-medieval England* (Manchester, 1989)

——, 'Landlords', *The agrarian history of England and Wales, III, 1348–1500*, ed. E. Miller (Cambridge, 1991), pp. 526–86.

Bellamy, J.G., 'The parliamentary representation of Nottinghamshire, Derbyshire and Staffordshire in the reign of Richard II', MA thesis, University of Nottingham, 1961

——, *Crime and public order in England in the later Middle Ages* (London, 1973)

Bennett, Matthew, 'The status of the squire: the northern evidence', *The ideals and practice of medieval knighthood*, vol. I, ed. C. Harper-Bill and R. Harvey (Woodbridge, 1986), pp. 1–11

————, '*La Règle du Temple* as a military manual or how to deliver a cavalry charge', *Studies in medieval history presented to R. Allen Brown*, ed. C. Harper-Bill, C.J. Holdsworth and J.L. Nelson (Woodbridge, 1989), pp. 7–19

Bennett, Michael J., *Community, class and careerism. Cheshire and Lancashire society in the age of Sir Gawain and the Green Knight* (Cambridge, 1983)

Blair, C., *European armour*, 3rd impr. (London, 1979)

Blastenbrei, P., *Die Sforza und ihr Heer* (Heidelberg, 1987)

Bloom, J.H., *English seals* (London, 1906)

Bolton, J.L., *The medieval English economy, 1150–1500* (London, 1980)

Borosy, A., 'The *militia portalis* in Hungary before 1526', *From Hunyadi to Rákóczi. War and society in late medieval and early modern Hungary*, ed. J.M. Bak and B.K. Király (Brooklyn, New York, 1982), pp. 63–80

Bosworth, C.E., 'Recruitment, muster and review in medieval Islamic armies', *War, technology and society in the Middle East*, ed. V.J. Parry and M.E. Yapp (London, 1975), pp. 59–77

Boutruche, R., 'The devastation of rural areas during the Hundred Years War and the agricultural recovery of France', *The recovery of France in the fifteenth century*, ed. P.S. Lewis (London, 1971), pp. 23–59

Brady, R., *A complete history of England* (London, 1700)

Brereton, J.M., *The horse in war* (Newton Abbott and London, 1976)

Britnell, R.H., 'Production for the market on a small fourteenth-century estate', *EcHR*, 2nd ser., xix (1966), pp. 380–87

Brown, A.L., 'The authorisation of letters under the Great Seal', *BIHR*, xxxvii (1964), pp. 16–31

————, 'The English campaign in Scotland in 1400', *British government and administration. Studies presented to S.B. Chrimes*, ed. H. Hearder and H.R. Loyn (Cardiff, 1974), pp. 40–54

————, *The governance of late medieval England, 1272–1461* (London, 1989)

Brown, R.A., 'The status of the Norman knight', *War and government in the Middle Ages*, ed. J. Gillingham and J.C. Holt (Woodbridge, 1984), pp. 18–32

Brown, S.D.B., 'Military service and monetary reward in the eleventh and twelfth centuries', *History*, lxxiv (1989), pp. 20–38

Burke, P., ed., *A new kind of history: from the writings of Febvre* (London, 1973)

Burne, A.H., *The Crecy war* (London, 1955)

Campbell, B.M.S., J.A. Galloway and M. Murphy, 'Rural land-use in the metropolitan hinterland, 1270–1339: the evidence of the inquisitions *post mortem*', *Agricultural History Review*, xl (1992), pp. 1–22

Campbell, J., 'England, Scotland and the Hundred Years War in the fourteenth century', *Europe in the late Middle Ages*, ed. J. Hale, R. Highfield and B. Smalley (London, 1965), pp. 184–216

————, 'Was it infancy in England? Some questions of comparison', *England and her neighbours, 1066–1453*, ed. M. Jones and M. Vale (London, 1989), pp. 1–17

————, 'The sale of land and the economics of power in early England: problems and possibilities', *The Haskins Society Journal*, i (1989), pp. 23–37.

Carpenter, C., *Locality and polity. A study of Warwickshire landed society, 1401–1499* (Cambridge, 1992)

Carr, A.D., *Owen of Wales: the end of the house of Gwynedd* (Cardiff, 1991)

Carus-Wilson, E.M., and O. Coleman, *England's export trade, 1275–1547* (Oxford, 1963)

Catto, J., 'Religion and the English nobility in the later fourteenth century', *History and imagination. Essays in honour of H.R. Trevor-Roper*, ed. H. Lloyd-Jones, V. Pearl and B. Worden (London, 1981), pp. 43–55

Chew, H.M., *The ecclesiastical tenants-in-chief and knight service* (Oxford, 1932)

Childs, W.R., *Anglo-Castilian trade in the later Middle Ages* (Manchester, 1978)

Chomel, V., 'Chevaux de bataille et roncins en Dauphiné au XIVe siècle', *Cahiers d'Histoire*, vii (1962), pp. 5–23

Christiansen, E., *The northern crusades* (London, 1980)

Clutton-Brock, J., *Horse power. A history of the horse and the donkey in human societies* (London, 1992)

Complete peerage, The, ed. G.E. Cokayne, revised by V. Gibbs, H.A. Doubleday and Lord Howard de Walden, 12 vols in 13 (London, 1910–57)

Connolly, P., 'The financing of English expeditions to Ireland, 1361–1376', *England and Ireland in the later Middle Ages*, ed. J. Lydon (Blackrock, Co. Dublin, 1981), pp. 104–21

Contamine, P., *Guerre, état et société à la fin du Moyen Age. Etudes sur les armées des rois de France, 1337–1494* (Paris, 1972)

———, 'Les compaignies d'aventure en France pendant la guerre de cent ans', *Mélanges de l'École Française de Rome*, lxxxvii (1975), pp. 365–96

———, 'Froissart: art militaire, pratique et conception de la guerre', *Froissart: historian*, ed. J.J.N. Palmer (Woodbridge, 1981), pp. 132–44

———, *War in the Middle Ages* (London, 1984)

Cook, A.S., 'The historical background of Chaucer's Knight', *Transactions of the Connecticut Academy of Arts and Sciences*, xx (1916), pp. 161–240

Copinger, W.A., ed., *History and records of the Smith-Carington family* (London, 1907)

Coss, P.R., *Lordship, knighthood and locality. A study in English society c. 1180–c.1280* (Cambridge, 1991)

———, *The knight in medieval England, 1000–1400* (Stroud, 1993)

Critchley, J.S., 'Summonses to military service early in the reign of Henry III', *EHR*, lxxxvi (1971), pp. 79–95

———, 'The early history of the writ of judicial protection', *BIHR*, xlv (1972), pp. 196–213

Crouch, D., *The image of aristocracy in Britain, 1000–1300* (London, 1992)

Cruickshank, C.G., *Elizabeth's army*, 2nd edn (Oxford, 1966)

Curry, A., 'Military organisation in Lancastrian Normandy, 1422–50', Ph.D. thesis, Council for National Academic Awards, 1985

———, 'Sex and the soldier in Lancastrian Normandy, 1415–1450', *Reading Medieval Studies*, xiv (1988), pp. 17–45

———, 'The nationality of men-at-arms serving in English armies in Normandy and the *pays de conquête*, 1415–1450: a preliminary survey', *Reading Medieval Studies*, xviii (1992), pp. 135–63

Cussans, J.E., *History of Hertfordshire*, 3 vols (London, 1870–81)

Davies, R.R., *Lordship and society in the March of Wales, 1282–1400* (Oxford, 1978)

Davis, R.H.C., 'The medieval warhorse', *Horses in European economic history: a preliminary canter*, ed. F.M.L. Thompson (Reading, 1983), pp. 4–20

————, 'The warhorses of the Normans', *Anglo-Norman Studies X. Proceedings of the Battle Conference, 1987*, ed. R.A. Brown (Woodbridge, 1988), pp. 67–82

————, *The medieval warhorse: origin, development and redevelopment* (London, 1989)

Denholm-Young, N., *History and heraldry, 1254–1310* (Oxford, 1965)

————, *The country gentry in the fourteenth century* (Oxford, 1969)

————, 'Feudal society in the thirteenth century: the knights', *Collected papers of N. Denholm-Young* (Cardiff, 1969), pp. 83–94

————, 'The tournament in the thirteenth century', *Collected papers of N. Denholm-Young* (Cardiff, 1969), pp. 95–120

Dennison, L., ' "The Fitzwarin Psalter and its allies": a reappraisal', *England in the fourteenth century*, ed. W.M. Ormrod (Woodbridge, 1986), pp. 42–66

Dent, A.A., 'Chaucer and the horse', *Proceedings of the Leeds Philosophical and Literary Society*, ix (1959–62), pp. 1–12

————, *Horses in Shakespeare's England* (London, 1987)

Déprez, E., 'La mort de Robert d'Artois', *Revue Historique*, xciv (1907), pp. 63–66

Du Boulay, F.R.H., 'Henry of Derby's expeditions to Prussia, 1390–1 and 1392', *The reign of Richard II*, ed. F.R.H. Du Boulay and C. Barron (London, 1971), pp. 153–72

Duby, G., 'Youth in aristocratic society', *The chivalrous society* (London, 1977), pp. 112–22

————, *The legend of Bouvines*, English trans. (Cambridge, 1990)

Dyer, C., *Standards of living in the later Middle Ages* (Cambridge, 1989)

Edwards, P., *The horse trade of Tudor and Stuart England* (Cambridge, 1988)

Elvey, G.R., 'The first fall of Sir John Molyns', *Records of Buckinghamshire*, xix (1972), pp. 194–98

Firth, C.H., *Cromwell's army*, 3rd impr. (London, 1962)

Fletcher, W.G.D., 'Sir Richard de Sandford, knight, 1306–1347', *Transactions of the Shropshire Archaeological and Natural History Society*, 3rd ser., vi (1906)

Forey, A., *The military orders from the twelfth to the early fourteenth centuries* (Basingstoke and London, 1992)

Fowler, G.H., 'A household expense roll, 1328', *EHR*, lv (1940), pp. 630–34

Fowler, K., 'Henry of Grosmont, first duke of Lancaster, 1310–1361', Ph.D. thesis, University of Leeds, 1961

————, 'Les finances et la discipline dans les armées anglaises en France au XIVe siècle', *Les Cahiers Vernonnais*, iv (1964), pp. 55–84

————, *The king's lieutenant. Henry of Grosmont, first duke of Lancaster, 1310–1361* (London, 1969)

————, *The age of Plantagenet and Valois*, repr. (London, 1980)

————, 'L'emploi des mercenaires par les pouvoirs ibériques et l'intervention militaire anglaise en Espagne (vers 1361–vers 1379)', *Realidad e imagenes del poder: España a fines de la Edad Media*, ed. A. Rucquoi (Valladolid, 1988), pp. 23–55

Frame, R., 'The justiciarship of Ralph Ufford: warfare and politics in fourteenth-century Ireland', *Studia Hibernica*, xiii (1973), pp. 7–47

————, *English lordship in Ireland, 1318–1361* (Oxford, 1982)

————, 'Military service in the lordship of Ireland, 1290–1360: institutions and society on the Anglo-Gaelic frontier', *Medieval frontier societies*, ed. R. Bartlett and A. MacKay (Oxford, 1989), pp. 101–26

Frappier, J., 'Les destriers et leur épithètes', *La technique littéraire des chansons de geste* (Paris, 1959), 85–104

Fryde, N., *The tyranny and fall of Edward II, 1321–1326* (Cambridge, 1979)

———, 'A medieval robber baron: Sir John Molyns of Stoke Poges, Buckinghamshire', *Medieval legal records, edited in memory of C.A.F. Meekings* (London, 1978), pp. 198–221

Gaier, C., 'Analysis of military forces in the principality of Liège and the county of Looz from the twelfth to the fifteenth century', *Studies in Medieval and Renaissance History*, ii (1965), pp. 205–61

———, 'La cavalerie lourde en Europe occidentale du XIIe au XVIe siècle', *Revue Internationale d'Histoire Militaire*, xxxi (1971), pp. 385–96

———, *L'industrie et le commerce des armes dans les anciennes principautés belges du XIIIe siècle à la fin du XVe siècle* (Paris, 1973)

Gillingham, J., 'Richard I and the science of war in the Middle Ages', *War and government in the Middle Ages*, ed. J. Gillingham and J.C. Holt (Woodbridge, 1984) pp. 78–91

———, 'William the Bastard at war', *Studies in medieval history presented to R. Allen Brown*, ed. C. Harper-Bill, C.J. Holdsworth and J.L. Nelson (Woodbridge, 1989), pp. 141–58

Giurescu, C.C., 'Les armées Roumaines dans la lutte pour la défense et l'indépendance du pays, du XIVe au XVIe siècle', *Revue Internationale d'Histoire Militaire*, xxxiv (1975), pp. 5–21

Given-Wilson, C., 'The ransom of Olivier du Guesclin', *BIHR*, liv (1981), pp. 17-28

———, *The royal household and the king's affinity: service, politics and finance, 1360–1413* (New Haven and London, 1986)

———, *The English nobility in the late Middle Ages* (London, 1987)

———, 'The king and the gentry in fourteenth-century England', *TRHS*, 5th ser., xxxvii (1987), pp. 87–102

———, 'Wealth and credit, public and private: the earls of Arundel, 1306–1397', *EHR*, cvi (1991), pp. 1–26

Göller, K.H., 'A summary of research', *The alliterative Morte Arthure. A reassessment of the poem*, ed. K.H. Göller (Cambridge, 1981)

Goodman, A.E., *The loyal conspiracy. The lords appellant under Richard II* (London, 1971)

———, 'The military subcontracts of Sir Hugh Hastings, 1380', *EHR*, xcv (1980), pp. 114–20

———, 'Responses to requests in Yorkshire for military service under Henry V', *Northern History*, xvii (1981), pp. 240–52

———, *The Wars of the Roses. Military activity and English society, 1452–97* (London, 1981)

———, 'Introduction', *War and border societies in the Middle Ages*, ed. A. Goodman and A. Tuck (London and New York, 1992), pp. 1–29

———, *John of Gaunt. The exercise of princely power in fourteenth-century Europe* (Harlow, 1992)

Gough, R., *The history and antiquities of Pleshey in the county of Essex* (London, 1803)

Gray, H.L., 'Incomes from land in England in 1436', *EHR*, xliv (1934), pp. 607–39

Green, L., *Castruccio Castracani* (Oxford, 1986)

Guilhiermoz, P., *Essai sur l'origine de la noblesse en France au Moyen Age* (Paris, 1902)

Hallam, H.E., ed., *The agrarian history of England and Wales, II, 1042–1350* (Cambridge, 1988)

Hamilton, J.S., 'Piers Gaveston and the royal treasure', *Albion*, xxiii (1991), 201–207

Harriss, G.L., *King, parliament and public finance in medieval England to 1369* (Oxford, 1975)

———, 'The king and his magnates', *Henry V. The practice of kingship*, ed. G.L. Harriss (Oxford, 1985), pp. 31–51

Harvey, R., *Moriz von Craûn and the chivalric world* (Oxford, 1961)

Harvey, S., 'The knight and the knight's fee in England', *Peasants, knights and heretics*, ed. R.H. Hilton (Cambridge, 1981), pp. 133–73.

Hatcher, J., *Plague, population and the English economy, 1348–1530* (London, 1977)

Hay, D., 'The division of the spoils of war in fourteenth-century England', *TRHS*, 5th ser., iv (1954), pp. 91–109

———, 'Booty in border warfare', *Transactions of the Dumfriesshire and Galloway Natural History and Antiquarian Society*, 3rd ser., xxxi (1952–53), pp. 145–66

Hayes, M.H., *Horses on board ship. A guide to their management* (London, 1902)

Hébert, M., 'L'armée Provençale en 1374', *Annales du Midi*, xci (1979), pp. 5–27

Herben, S.J., 'Arms and armour in Chaucer', *Speculum*, xii (1937), pp. 475–87

Hewitt, H.J., *The Black Prince's expedition of 1355–1357* (Manchester, 1958)

———, *The organisation of war under Edward III* (Manchester, 1966)

———, *The horse in medieval England* (London, 1983)

Hill, M.C., *The king's messengers, 1199–1377* (London, 1961)

Hilton, R.H., 'The content and sources of English agrarian history before 1500', *Agricultural History Review*, iii (1955), pp. 3–19

Hockey, S.F., *Insula vecta. The Isle of Wight in the Middle Ages* (London and Chichester, 1982)

Holmes, G.A., *The estates of the higher nobility in fourteenth-century England* (Cambridge, 1957)

———, *The Good Parliament* (Oxford, 1975)

Hudson, W., 'Norwich militia in the fourteenth century', *Norfolk Archaeology*, xiv (1901), pp. 263–320

Hunnisett, R.F., 'English Chancery records: rolls and files', *Journal of the Society of Archivists*, v (1974–77), pp. 158–68

Hurnard, N.D., *The king's pardon for homicide before A.D.1307* (Oxford, 1969)

Hyland, A., *Equus. The horse in the Roman world* (London, 1990)

James, L., 'The cost and distribution of armour in the fourteenth century', *Transactions of the Monumental Brass Society*, x, 4 (1967 for 1966), pp. 226–31

Jankovich, M., *They rode into Europe. The fruitful exchange in the arts of horsemanship between East and West* (London, 1971)

Janson, H.W., 'The equestrian monument from Cangrande della Scala to Peter the Great', *Aspects of the Renaissance: a symposium*, ed. A.R. Lewis (Austin and London, 1967), pp. 73–85

Jones, M., *Ducal Brittany, 1364–1399* (Oxford, 1970)

———, 'An indenture between Robert, Lord Mohaut and Sir John de Bracebridge for life service in peace and war, 1310', *Journal of the Society of Archivists*, iv (1972), pp. 384–94

————, 'Sir Thomas de Dagworth et la guerre civile en Bretagne au XIVe siècle: quelques documents inédits', *Annales de Bretagne*, lxxxvii (1980), pp. 621–39

————, 'The Breton civil war', *Froissart: historian*, ed. J.J.N. Palmer (Woodbridge, 1981), pp. 64–81

————, 'Edward III's captains in Brittany', *England in the fourteenth century*, ed. W.M. Ormrod (Woodbridge, 1986), pp. 99–118

————, 'Sir John de Hardreshull, king's lieutenant in Brittany, 1343–5', *Nottingham Medieval Studies*, xxxi (1987), pp. 76–97

Jones, T., *Chaucer's Knight. The portrait of a medieval mercenary*, repr. (London, 1982)

Jones, W.R., 'Keeping the peace: English society, local government and the commissions of 1341–44', *American Journal of Legal History*, xviii (1974), pp. 307–20

Keen, M., 'Brotherhood in arms', *History*, xlvii (1962), pp. 1–17

————, *The laws of war in the late Middle Ages* (London, 1965)

————, 'Chivalrous culture in fourteenth-century England', *Historical Studies*, x (1976), pp. 1–24

————, 'Chaucer's knight, the English aristocracy and the crusade', *English court culture in the later Middle Ages*, ed. V.J. Scattergood and J.W. Sherborne (London, 1983), pp. 45–61

————, *Chivalry* (New Haven and London, 1984)

————, 'The jurisdiction and origins of the Constable's court', *War and government in the Middle Ages*, ed. J. Gillingham and J.C. Holt (Woodbridge, 1984), pp. 159–69

————, *The outlaws of medieval legend*, revised paperback edn (London, 1987)

————, *English society in the later Middle Ages, 1348–1500* (Harmondsworth, 1990),

————, 'English military experience and the Court of Chivalry: the case of Grey v. Hastings', *Guerre et société en France, en Angleterre et en Bourgogne, XIVe–XVe siècle*, ed. P. Contamine, C. Giry-Deloison and M. Keen (Lille, 1992), pp. 123–42

Kershaw, I., 'The great famine and agrarian crisis in England, 1315–1322', *Peasants, knights and heretics*, ed. R.H. Hilton (Cambridge, 1976), pp. 85–132

La Borderie, A. de, *Histoire de Bretagne*, 6 vols (Rennes, 1896–1914)

Laking, G., *A record of European armour and arms through seven centuries*, 5 vols (London, 1920–22)

Lander, J.R., 'The Hundred Years War and Edward IV's 1475 campaign in France', *Crown and nobility, 1450–1509* (London, 1976), pp. 220–41 and appendix E

Langdon, J., *Horses, oxen and technological innovation* (Cambridge, 1986)

Larner, J., *The lords of Romagna* (London, 1965)

Lawrence, H., *Heraldry from military monuments before 1350 in England and Wales*, Harleian Soc., xcviii (1946)

Le Patourel, J.H., *The medieval administration of the Channel Islands, 1199–1399* (London, 1937)

Lewis, N.B., 'An early indenture of military service, 27 July 1287', *BIHR*, xiii (1935), pp. 85–89

————, 'An early fourteenth-century contract for military service', *BIHR*, xx (1944), pp. 111–18

————, 'The English forces in Flanders, August-November 1297', *Studies in medieval history presented to F.M. Powicke*, ed. R.W. Hunt, W.A. Pantin and R.W. Southern (Oxford, 1948), pp. 310–18

————, 'The last medieval summons of the English feudal levy, 13 June 1385', *EHR*, lxxiii (1958), pp. 1–26

————, 'The recruitment and organisation of a contract army, May to November 1337', *BIHR*, xxxvii (1964), pp. 1–19

————, 'The summons of the English feudal levy: 5 April 1327', *Essays in medieval history presented to Bertie Wilkinson*, ed. T.A. Sandquist and M.R. Powicke (Toronto, 1969), pp. 236–49

————, 'The feudal summons of 1385', *EHR*, c (1985), pp. 729–43

Lloyd, S., *English society and the crusade, 1216–1307* (Oxford, 1988)

Lucas, H.S., *The Low Countries and the Hundred Years War, 1326–1347* (Ann Arbor, 1929)

Lydon, J.F., 'The hobelar: an Irish contribution to medieval warfare', *The Irish Sword*, II, v (1954), pp. 12–16

Lyon, B., 'The feudal antecedent of the indenture system', *Speculum*, xxix (1954), pp. 503–11

————, *From fief to indenture* (Cambridge, Mass., 1957)

————, 'The role of cavalry in medieval warfare: horses, horses all around and not a one to use', *Mededelingen van de Koninklijke Academie voor Wetenschappen, Letteren en Schone Kunsten van België*, xlix (1987), 75–90

Maddicott, J.R., *Thomas of Lancaster, 1307–1322* (Oxford, 1970)

————, 'Poems of social protest in early-fourteenth-century England', *England in the fourteenth century*, ed. W.M. Ormrod (Woodbridge, 1986), pp. 130–44.

Mallett, M.E., *Mercenaries and their masters. Warfare in Renaissance Italy* (London, 1974)

Mallett, M.E. and Hale, J.R., *The military organisation of a Renaissance state. Venice c. 1400–1617* (Cambridge, 1984)

Marshall, C., *Warfare in the Latin east, 1192–1291* (Cambridge, 1992)

Mason, J., 'Sir Andrew de Harcla, earl of Carlisle', *Transactions of the Cumberland and Westmorland Antiquarian and Archaeological Society*, xxix (1929), pp. 98–137

Maxwell-Lyte, Sir H.C., *A history of Dunster and of the families of Mohun and Luttrell*, 2 vols (London, 1909)

————, *Historical notes on the use of the Great Seal of England* (London, 1926)

McFarlane, K.B., 'Bastard feudalism', *BIHR*, xx (1945), pp. 161–81

————, 'A business-partnership in war and administration, 1421–1445', *EHR*, lxxviii (1963), pp. 290–308

————, 'An indenture of agreement between two English knights for mutual aid and counsel in peace and war, 5 December 1298', *BIHR*, xxxviii (1965), pp. 200–8

————, *The nobility of later medieval England* (Oxford, 1973)

————, *England in the fifteenth century. Collected essays*, ed. G.L. Harriss (London, 1981)

McGlynn, S., 'The myths of medieval warfare', *History Today*, xliv, 1 (January 1994), pp. 28–34

McKisack, M., *The fourteenth century, 1307–1399* (Oxford, 1959)

Ménabréa, L., 'De l'organisation militaire au moyen-âge, d'après des documents inédits', *Mémoires de l'Académie Royale de Savoie*, 2nd ser., i (1851), pp. 179–224

Miller, E., ed., *The agrarian history of England and Wales, III, 1348–1500* (Cambridge, 1991)

Miller, H., *Henry VIII and the English nobility* (Oxford, 1986)

Mitchell, S.K., *Taxation in medieval England* (New Haven, 1951)

Morgan, P., *War and society in medieval Cheshire, 1277–1403* (Manchester, 1987)

Morris, J.E., *The Welsh wars of Edward I* (Oxford, 1901)

———, 'Cumberland and Westmorland military levies in the time of Edward I and Edward II', *Transactions of the Cumberland and Westmorland Antiquarian and Archaeological Society*, iii (1903), pp. 307–27

———, *Bannockburn* (Cambridge, 1914)

———, 'Mounted infantry in medieval warfare', *TRHS*, 3rd ser., viii (1914), pp. 77–102

Nash, A.E., 'The mortality pattern of the Wiltshire lords of the manor, 1242–1377', *Southern History*, ii (1980), pp. 31–43

Neilson, N., 'The king's hunting and his great horses', *The English government at work, 1327–36*, ed. J.F. Willard and W.A. Morris (Cambridge, Mass., 1940), i, pp. 435–44

Newhall, R.A., *The English conquest of Normandy, 1416–1424* (New York, 1924)

———, *Muster and review* (Cambridge, Mass., 1940)

Nicholson, R., *Edward III and the Scots. The formative years of a military career, 1327–1335* (Oxford, 1965)

Nicolas, Sir N.H., *History of the battle of Agincourt*, 3rd edn (London, 1833)

Orme, N., *From childhood to chivalry. The education of the English kings and aristocracy, 1066–1530* (London, 1984)

Ormrod, W.M., *The reign of Edward III. Crown and political society in England, 1327–1377* (New Haven and London, 1990)

Otway-Ruthven, A.J., *A history of medieval Ireland*, 2nd edn (London, 1980)

Palmer, J.J.N., 'The last summons of the feudal army in England (1385)', *EHR*, lxxxiii (1968), pp. 771–75

———, *England, France and Christendom, 1377-99* (London, 1972)

Parker, G., *The military revolution* (Cambridge, 1988)

Payling, S., *Political society in Lancastrian England. The greater gentry of Nottinghamshire* (Oxford, 1991)

Perroy, E., 'L'administration de Calais, 1371–1372', *Revue du Nord*, cxxxii (1951), pp. 218–27

Phillips, J.R.S., *Aymer de Valence, earl of Pembroke 1307–1324. Baronial politics in the reign of Edward II* (Oxford, 1972)

Pollard, A.J., *John Talbot and the war in France, 1427–1453* (London, 1983)

Pollock, Sir F., and F.W. Maitland, *The history of English law before the time of Edward I*, 2 vols, repr. (Cambridge, 1968)

Poole, A.L., *Obligations of society in the twelfth and thirteenth centuries* (Oxford, 1946)

Porter, E., 'Chaucer's Knight, the alliterative *Morte Arthure*, and the medieval laws of war: a reconsideration', *Nottingham Medieval Studies*, xxvii (1983), pp. 56–78

Powell, E., *Kingship, law and society: criminal justice in the reign of Henry V* (Oxford, 1989)

Powell, J.M., *The anatomy of a crusade, 1213–1221* (Philadelphia, 1986)

Powers, J.F., *A society organised for war. The Iberian municipal militias in the central Middle Ages, 1000–1284* (London, 1988)

Powicke, F.M., *The thirteenth century, 1216–1307* (Oxford, 1953)

Powicke, M.R., 'The English commons in Scotland in 1322 and the deposition of Edward II', *Speculum*, xxxv (1960), pp. 556–62

————, *Military obligation in medieval England* (Oxford, 1962)

————, 'Lancastrian captains', *Essays in medieval history presented to Bertie Wilkinson*, ed. T.A. Sandquist and M.R. Powicke (Toronto, 1969), pp. 371–82

Prestwich, J.O., 'War and finance in the Anglo-Norman state', *TRHS*, 5th ser., iv (1954), pp. 19–43

————, 'The military household of the Norman kings', *EHR*, xcvi (1981), pp. 1–35

Prestwich, M., 'Victualling estimates for English garrisons in Scotland during the early fourteenth century', *EHR*, lxxxii (1967), pp. 536–43

————, *War, politics and finance under Edward I* (London, 1972)

————, *The three Edwards. War and state in England, 1272–1377* (London, 1980)

————, 'English armies in the early stages of the Hundred Years War: a scheme of 1341', *BIHR*, lvi (1983), pp. 102–13

————, 'Cavalry service in early fourteenth-century England', *War and government in the Middle Ages*, ed. J. Gillingham and J.C. Holt (Woodbridge, 1984), pp. 147–58

————, *Edward I* (London, 1988)

————, *English politics in the thirteenth century* (Basingstoke and London, 1990)

Prince, A.E., 'The strength of English armies in the reign of Edward III', *EHR*, xlvi (1931), pp. 353–71

————, 'The indenture system under Edward III', *Historical essays in honour of James Tait*, ed. J.G. Edwards, V.H. Galbraith and E.F. Jacob (Manchester, 1933), pp. 283–97

————, 'The importance of the campaign of 1327', *EHR*, l (1935), pp. 299–302

————, 'The army and navy', *The English government at work, 1327–1336*, ed. J.F. Willard and W.A. Morris (Cambridge, Mass., 1940), i, pp. 332–93

————, 'The payment of army wages in Edward III's reign', *Speculum*, xix (1944), pp. 137–60

Prior, J.H., 'Transportation of horses by sea during the era of the crusades: eighth century to 1285 A.D.', *The Mariner's Mirror*, lxviii (1982), pp. 9–30; 103–25

Pugh, T.B., 'The magnates, knights and gentry', *Fifteenth-century England, 1399–1509*, ed. S.B. Chrimes, C.D. Ross and R.A. Griffiths (Manchester, 1972), pp. 86–128

Pugh, T.B., and C.D. Ross, 'The English baronage and the income tax of 1436', *BIHR*, xxvi (1953), pp. 1–28

————, 'Materials for the study of baronial incomes in fifteenth-century England', *EcHR*, 2nd ser., vi (1953–54), pp. 185–94

Quick, J., 'The number and distribution of knights in thirteenth-century England: the evidence of the Grand Assize lists', *Thirteenth-century England I*, ed. P.R. Coss and S.D. Lloyd (Woodbridge, 1986), pp. 114–23

Ramsay, J.H., 'The strength of English armies in the Middle Ages: estimates of chroniclers and modern writers', *EHR*, xxix (1914), pp. 221–27

Redstone, V.B., 'Some mercenaries of Henry of Lancaster, 1327–1330', *TRHS*, 3rd ser., vii (1913), pp. 151–66

Rees, G., 'The longbow's deadly secrets', *New Scientist*, 5 June 1993, pp. 24–25

Reese, M.M., *The royal office of Master of the Horse* (London, 1976)

Richardson, H.G., and G.O. Sayles, *The governance of medieval England* (Edinburgh, 1963)

Richmond, C.F., 'The war at sea', *The Hundred Years War*, ed. K. Fowler (London, 1971), pp. 96–121

Rogers, C.J., 'The military revolutions of the Hundred Years War', *The Journal of Military History*, lvii (1993), 241–78

Rosenthal, J.T., *The purchase of paradise* (London, 1972)

Roskell, J.S., *The Commons in the Parliament of 1422* (Manchester, 1954)

Roskell, J.S., L. Clark and C. Rawcliffe, eds, *The history of Parliament: the House of Commons, 1386–1421*, 4 vols (Stroud, 1993)

Rubin, M., 'Small groups: identity and solidarity in the late Midddle Ages', *Enterprise and individuals in fifteenth-century England*, ed. J. Kermode (Gloucester, 1991), pp. 132–50

Runyan, T.J., 'Ships and mariners in later medieval England', *Journal of British Studies*, xvi (1977), pp. 1–17

Russell, J.C., *British medieval population* (Albuquerque, 1948)

Russell, P.E., *The English intervention in Spain and Portugal in the time of Edward III and Richard II* (Oxford, 1955)

Salzman, L.F., 'The property of the earl of Arundel, 1397', *Sussex Archaeological Collections*, xci (1953), pp. 32–52

Sanders, I.J., *Feudal military service in England* (Oxford, 1956)

Saul, N.E., *Knights and esquires. The Gloucestershire gentry in the fourteenth century* (Oxford, 1981)

———, *Scenes from provincial life. Knightly families in Sussex, 1280–1400* (Oxford, 1986)

———, 'A "rising" lord and a "declining" esquire: Sir Thomas de Berkeley III and Geoffrey Gascelyn of Sheldon', *Historical Research*, lxi (1988), pp. 345–56

Schäfer, K.H., *Deutsche Ritter und Edelknechte in Italien während des 14. Jahrhunderts* (Paderborn, 1911)

Sherborne, J.W., 'Indentured retinues and English expeditions to France, 1369–1380', *EHR*, lxxix (1964), pp. 718–46

———, 'The English navy: shipping and manpower, 1369–89', *Past and Present*, xxxvii (1967), pp. 163–75

———, 'The battle of La Rochelle and the war at sea, 1372–75', *BIHR*, xlii (1969), pp. 17–29

———, 'The cost of English warfare with France in the later fourteenth century', *BIHR*, l (1977), pp. 135–50

———, 'John of Gaunt, Edward III's retinue and the French campaign of 1369', *Kings and nobles in the later Middle Ages*, ed. R.A. Griffiths and J. Sherborne (Gloucester, 1986), pp. 41–61

Simms, K., 'Warfare in the medieval Gaelic lordships', *The Irish Sword*, xii (1975), pp. 98–108

Snead, G.A., 'The careers of four fourteenth-century military commanders serving Edward III and Richard II in the Hundred Years War', MA thesis, University of Kent, 1968

Stanes, R.G.F., 'Sir Guy de Brian, K.G.', *Reports and Transactions of the Devon Association*, xcii (1960), pp. 248–78

Stones, E.L.G., 'The Folvilles of Ashby-Folville, Leicestershire, and their associates in crime, 1326–1347', *TRHS*, 5th ser., vii (1957), pp. 117–36

Storey, R.L., 'The wardens of the marches of England towards Scotland, 1377–1489', *EHR*, lxxii (1957), pp. 593–615

Stretton, G., 'Some aspects of medieval travel, with special reference to the wardrobe accounts of Henry, earl of Derby, 1390–93', *TRHS*, 4th ser., vii (1924), pp. 77–97

Sumption, J., *The Hundred Years War: trial by battle* (London, 1990)

Sutherland, D.W., *The assize of novel disseisin* (Oxford, 1973)

Thirsk, J., *Horses in early modern England: for service, for pleasure, for power,* Stenton lecture, Univerity of Reading, 1977 (Reading, 1978)

Thordeman, B., *Armour from the battle of Visby, 1361,* 2 vols (Stockholm, 1939)

Thorold-Rogers, J.E., *A history of agriculture and prices in England, 1259–1793,* 7 vols (Oxford, 1866–1902)

Thoroton, R., *The antiquities of Nottinghamshire, with additions by John Throsby,* 3 vols (London, 1797)

Thrupp, S., *The merchant class of medieval London, 1300–1500,* paperback edn (Michigan, 1962)

Tolley, T., 'Eleanor of Castile and the "Spanish style" in England', *England in the thirteenth century,* ed. W.M. Ormrod (Stamford, 1991), pp. 167–92

Tout, T.F., 'The tactics of the battles of Boroughbridge and Morlaix', *EHR,* xix (1904), pp. 711–15

———, 'Some neglected fights between Crécy and Poitiers', *EHR,* xx (1905), pp. 726–30

———, *Chapters in the administrative history of medieval England. The wardrobe, the chamber and the small seals,* 6 vols (Manchester, 1920–33)

———, *The place of the reign of Edward II in English history* (Manchester, 1936)

Tuck, A., 'War and society in the medieval north', *Northern History,* xxi (1985), pp. 33–52

———, 'The Percies and the community of Northumberland in the later fourteenth century', *War and border societies in the Middle Ages,* ed. A. Goodman and A. Tuck (London and New York, 1992), pp. 178–95

Tyerman, C., *England and the crusades, 1095–1588* (Chicago, 1988)

Vale, B., 'The Scropes of Bolton and Masham, c. 1300–1450', D.Phil. thesis, University of York, 1987

Vale, J., *Edward III and chivalry* (Woodbridge, 1982)

Vale M., *Piety, charity and literacy among the Yorkshire gentry, 1370–1480,* Borthwick Papers, l (University of York, 1976)

———, *War and chivalry. Warfare and aristocratic culture in England, France and Burgundy at the end of the Middle Ages* (London, 1981)

———, 'Warfare and the life of the French and Burgundian nobility in the late Middle Ages', *Adelige Sachkultur des Spätmittelalters. Internationaler Kongress, Krems an der Donau, 22 bis 25 September 1980* (Vienna, 1982), pp. 169–94

———, 'The Gascon nobility and the Anglo-French war, 1294–98', *War and government in the Middle Ages,* ed. J. Gillingham and J.C. Holt (Woodbridge, 1984), pp. 134–46

———, *The Angevin legacy and the Hundred Years War, 1250–1340* (Oxford, 1990)

———, 'The Anglo-French wars, 1294–1340: allies and alliances', *Guerre et société en France, en Angleterre et en Bourgogne, XIVe–XVe siècle,* ed. P. Contamine, C. Giry-Deloison and M. Keen (Lille, 1992), pp. 15–35

Verbruggen, J.F., *The art of warfare in western Europe during the Middle Ages,* trans. S. Willard and S.C.M. Southern (Amsterdam, 1977)

The Victoria history of the counties of England: Rutland, 2 vols (London, 1908–35)

Waley, D.P., '*Condotte* and *condottieri* in the thirteenth century', *Proceedings of the British Academy,* lxi (1975), pp. 337–71

Walker, R.F., 'The Anglo-Welsh wars, 1217–1267', D.Phil. thesis, University of Oxford, 1954

Walker, S.K., 'Profit and loss in the Hundred Years War: the subcontracts of Sir John Strother, 1374', *BIHR*, lviii (1985), pp. 100–6

———, *The Lancastrian affinity, 1361–1399* (Oxford, 1990)

Wallace-Hadrill, J.M., *Early germanic kingship in England and on the continent* (Oxford, 1971)

Watt, J.A., 'The Anglo-Irish colony under strain, 1327–99', *A new history of Ireland, II: medieval Ireland, 1169–1534*, ed. A. Cosgrove (Oxford, 1987), pp. 352–96

Waugh, S.L., 'Reluctant knights and jurors: respites, exemptions and public obligations in the reign of Henry III', *Speculum*, lviii (1983), pp. 937–86

———, 'Tenure to contract: lordship and clientage in thirteenth-century England', *EHR*, ci (1986), pp. 811–39

Willard, J.F., *Parliamentary taxes on personal property, 1220 to 1334* (Cambridge, Mass., 1934)

Wright, S.M., *The Derbyshire gentry in the fifteenth century*, Derbyshire Record Soc., viii (Chesterfield, 1983)

Index